Beyond Goals

To Anthony Samir, Noah David, and Sophie David, life with you is special beyond any goal that I could have imagined.

—*Susan David*

I would like to dedicate this book to all the groups at Sheffield Hallam University, the Bristol Critical Coaching group and a number of EMCC conferences who said what they had to say and enabled me to find my voice.

—*David Megginson, Sheffield Hallam University, UK*

Few people have given me such opportunities to learn than my son Jonathan, who has Down's Syndrome and is on the autistic spectrum. Jonathan will always need care, and every achievement he makes is a struggle. Observing and encouraging him has taught me as much about goals and goal-setting as all the books and research papers I have read!

—*David Clutterbuck*

P.S. Jon just competed in a Special Olympics ice skating event and came away very proudly with a clutch of medals.

Beyond Goals

Effective Strategies for Coaching and Mentoring

Edited by

SUSAN DAVID,
Harvard University, USA

DAVID CLUTTERBUCK
Clutterbuck Partnership, UK

DAVID MEGGINSON
Sheffield Hallam University, UK

GOWER

Published by
Gower Publishing Limited
Wey Court East
Union Road
Farnham
Surrey, GU9 7PT
England

Ashgate Publishing Company
110 Cherry Street
Suite 3-1
Burlington, VT 05401-3818
USA

www.gowerpublishing.com

British Library Cataloguing in Publication Data
A catalogue record for this book is available from the British Library.

The Library of Congress has cataloged the printed edition as follows:
David, Susan A.
    Beyond goals : effective strategies for coaching and mentoring / by Susan David, David Clutterbuck and David Megginson.
        pages cm
    Includes bibliographical references and index.
    ISBN 978-1-4094-1851-1 (hardback : alk. paper) — ISBN 978-1-4094-1852-8 (ebook) — ISBN 978-1-4724-0167-0 (epub)
    1. Goal (Psychology) 2. Mentoring. 3. Personal coaching. I. Clutterbuck, David. II. Megginson, David, 1943- III. Title.

    BF505.G6D366 2013
    158.3 — dc23
                                                                        2013006116
ISBN 9781409418511 (hbk)
ISBN 9781409418528 (ebk — PDF)
ISBN 9781472401670 (ebk — ePUB)

Printed and bound in Great Britain by
TJ International Ltd, Padstow, Cornwall.

Contents

List of Figures   *vii*

List of Tables   *ix*

About the Editors   *xi*

Notes on Contributors   *xiii*

Foreword   *xxi*

Preface   *xxv*

Acknowledgements   *xxvii*

Reviews of Beyond Goals   *xxix*

List of Abbreviations   *xxxi*

1   Goals: A Long-term View   1
     Susan A. David, David Clutterbuck, David Megginson, and
     Christina Congleton

2   Goals in Coaching and Mentoring: The Current State of Play   21
     David Clutterbuck and Susan A. David

3   Researching Goals in Coaching   37
     Susan A. David, David Megginson, and Christina Congleton

4   New Perspectives on Goal Setting in Coaching Practice:
     An Integrated Model of Goal-focused Coaching   55
     Anthony M. Grant

5   Self-determination Theory Within Coaching Contexts:
     Supporting Motives and Goals that Promote Optimal
     Functioning and Well-being   85
     Gordon B. Spence and Edward L. Deci

6   A Social Neuroscience Approach to Goal Setting for Coaches   109
       Elliot Berkman, Ruth Donde, and David Rock

7   Putting Goals to Work in Coaching: The Complexities of
       Implementation   125
       Siegfried Greif

8   The Coaching Engagement in the Twenty-first Century:
       New Paradigms for Complex Times   151
       Michael J. Cavanagh

9   Goal Setting: A Chaos Theory of Careers Approach   185
       Jim E.H. Bright and Robert G.L. Pryor

10   When Goal Setting Helps and Hinders Sustained, Desired Change   211
       Richard E. Boyatzis and Anita Howard

11   The Goals Behind the Goals: Pursuing Adult Development in the
       Coaching Enterprise   229
       Robert Kegan, Christina Congleton, and Susan A. David

12   GROW Grows Up: From Winning the Game to Pursuing
       Transpersonal Goals   245
       Sir John Whitmore, Carol Kauffman, and Susan A. David

13   Goals in Mentoring Relationships and Developmental Networks   261
       Kathy E. Kram, Susan A. David, and Christina Congleton

14   Emergent Goals in Mentoring and Coaching   275
       Laura Gail Lunsford

15   Goal Setting in a Layered Relationship Mentoring Model   289
       Maggie Clarke and Sarah Powell

16   Working With Emergent Goals: A Pragmatic Approach   311
       David Clutterbuck

17   The Way Forward: Perspectives from the Editors   327
       Susan A. David, David Clutterbuck, and David Megginson

Index   *339*

List of Figures

1.1	From Benjamin Franklin's book of virtues	4
1.2	Benjamin Franklin's daily schedule	5
1.3	Essential elements of goal setting theory and the high-performance cycle	10
2.1	Goal evolution	32
3.1	Average goal orientation score by region	43
3.2	Average goal orientation score by education	44
3.3	Goal orientation and coaching experience by region	45
3.4	Average goal orientation score by response to "We are surprised by topics that come up during a coaching assignment"	46
4.1	Generic model of goal-directed self-regulation	60
4.2	Goal hierarchy	66
4.3	Goal neglect	68
4.4	Integrative model of coach-facilitated goal attainment	70
6.1	The social cognitive neuroscience of goal setting	110
7.1	Extended Rubicon phase model	133
7.2	The Stacey agreement/certainty matrix	140
8.1	Four phase states of complex systems	157
8.2	Two types of development and the developmental trajectory	167
8.3	The four factor model of leadership	169
8.4	Critical choices in dialogue	175
8.5	The coaching field—a dynamic dialogical model of the coaching conversation	177
9.1	Goal setting strategy for short-term situations	201
9.2	Long-term goal setting	202
10.1	Intentional Change Theory	212
11.1	Three plateaus in adult mental development	236
11.2	A junior partner's immunity X-ray	241
12.1	Why a shift of focus occurs during a coaching engagement	248
12.2	Developmental journey	255
13.1	Structure of the network	270

15.1   Layered Relationship Mentoring Model   295
15.2   Goal setting and the Layered Relationship Mentoring Model   297
16.1   The goal chain: The position of goals in the process of change 324

List of Tables

2.1   Whitmore's GROW sequence of questioning in coaching   22
2.2   Ten questions to ask before setting goals (Ordóñez et al., 2009)   29
3.1   Coaching goal orientation questionnaire   42
5.1   Overview of SDT mini-theories   91
5.2   Varying levels of integration and ownership associated with extrinsic motivation   93
7.1   The Rubicon phase model of motivation   128
9.1   Examples of slow and fast shift   187
9.2   System attractors   190
10.1   Two attractors   221
13.1   Functions of the mentoring relationship   262
13.2   Phases of the mentoring relationship   262
13.3   Past and present conceptualizations of mentoring (Higgins and Kram, 2001)   270
14.1   SMART goals   283
15.1   Examples of characteristics of types of mentoring relationships   294
15.2   Characteristics and outcomes of each of the layers in the Layered Relationship Mentoring Model (Clarke, 2004)   298
16.1   Goals in different coaching and mentoring contexts   315

About the Editors

Dr Susan A. David is a leading expert on leadership development, people strategy, employee engagement, and emotional intelligence. She is a founder and co-director of the Institute of Coaching at McLean Hospital of Harvard Medical School and an Instructor in Psychology at Harvard University. As the co-chair of the Institute of Coaching's Research Forum, she convenes an annual gathering of global leaders in coaching, with the objective of advancing the research and application of coaching. She was an invited member of the Harvard/World Economic Forum Breakthrough Ideas meeting, and is a frequent contributor to the best practice articles of the online *Harvard Business Review*. She is principal editor of the comprehensive and definitive *Oxford Handbook of Happiness* (2013). Dr David is the founding partner of Evidence Based Psychology, a leadership development and management consultancy created to provide strategic advice and help senior executives to foster positive and sustainable outcomes for themselves and their organizations. Her clients are leading organizations across the globe. (http://www.evidencebasedpsychology.com; http://www.instituteofcoaching.org).

Professor David Clutterbuck is Visiting Professor in the Coaching and Mentoring faculties of both Oxford Brookes and Sheffield Hallam Universities in the UK and he is Special Ambassador for the European Mentoring and Coaching Council (EMCC). Professor Clutterbuck has been responsible for the implementation, monitoring, and evaluation of highly successful mentoring and coaching programmes in numerous organizations around the world, including Standard Chartered Bank, Goldman Sachs, Lloyds-TSB, World Bank and Nokia, and has worked with the Audit Commission in the UK. He has been listed as one of the top 25 most influential thinkers in the field of Human Resources by *HR* magazine, and was placed by *The Independent on Sunday* as second in the list of top business coaches in the UK. Clutterbuck has authored, co-authored, or edited 55 books to date. David Clutterbuck completed the first longitudinal, cross-sectional, intra-dyadic study of developmental mentoring, in which goal orientation was a principal element of analysis.

David Megginson is Emeritus Professor of Human Resource Development at Sheffield Hallam University, UK, where he founded the Coaching and Mentoring Research Group. He has been Chair of the European Mentoring and Coaching Council (EMCC), which he founded with David Clutterbuck in 1992. David Megginson is a well-established author who was one of the first to query the role of goals in coaching and mentoring. He contributes to teaching the MSc in Coaching and Mentoring at Sheffield Business School, and supervises doctoral dissertations in coaching and mentoring. He founded the EMCC's research conference which has provided opportunities for researchers from a range of countries, research traditions and levels of experience to come together in a collegial way to share their work, their learning and their dreams.

Notes on Contributors

Elliot Berkman is Assistant Professor of Psychology at the University of Oregon. He attained his PhD at University of California, and MA's at both UCLA and Stanford Universities. Elliot's research interest is in the motivational, cognitive, and neural underpinnings of goal pursuit. His current projects utilize techniques from social cognition, social psychology, and neuroscience to investigate these processes as embedded in real-world goal pursuit. He is also involved in ongoing laboratory studies primarily focused on inhibition of "temptations" or counter-goal responses in the context of health-relevant behavior such as cigarette smoking cessation and dieting. Elliot is also a guest faculty member at the NeuroLeadership Institute, delivering educational programs about the brain to HR and learning professionals, coaches, consultants and change agents. For more information on his research visit his Social and Affective Neuroscience Laboratory on the web at: http://sanlab.uoregon.edu.

Richard E. Boyatzis is Distinguished University Professor, professor in Departments of Organizational Behavior, Psychology, and Cognitive Science at Case Western Reserve University, Adjunct Professor at ESADE. Having authored more than 150 articles about competency development, coaching and change, his books include *The Competent Manager*, and two international best-sellers: *Primal Leadership* with Daniel Goleman and Annie McKee; and *Resonant Leadership*, with McKee.

Jim E.H. Bright is a coach and organizational psychologist. He has a portfolio career running Bright and Associates, a Career Management company, as well as being Professor of Career Education and Development at Australian Catholic University. He has worked with major organizations in the USA, Europe and Australia including Bosch, Philips, Vanderbilt University, Commonwealth Bank of Australia, Westpac, BHP, Lend Lease, Datacom, Tax Office, Sports Institute of Australia, and the NSW Audit Office. Jim has published 10 books on Career Development including most recently, *The Chaos Theory of Careers*.

He has published over 500 peer-reviewed papers, reports, tests, and newspaper articles. He holds a BA(Hons) and PhD in Psychology and is a Fellow of both the Australian Psychological Society and the Career Development Association of Australia. In recent years Jim has provided coach training and keynote speaking services in the USA, Canada, UK, Ireland, Portugal, Australia and New Zealand. He blogs at www.brightandassociates.com.au/wordpress.

Michael J. Cavanagh is both an Academic and Practitioner. He is currently the Deputy Director of the Coaching Psychology Unit at the University of Sydney (Australia) and Visiting Professor at the Institute of Work Based Learning at Middlesex University (UK). He has coached leaders and managers at all levels from a diverse range of public and private, national and multinational organizations. Michael's work and teaching focuses on coaching leaders and teams in complex settings. Michael has recently led a team of researchers in a 3.5 million dollar research project investigating leadership development and coaching in high stress workplaces. He is also the principal author of the Standards Australia Handbook of Organisational Coaching—one of the world's first ISO aligned National guidelines for the training of coaches and the provision of coaching services. A registered Psychologist, Michael is also the Australian Coordinating Editor of the International Coaching Psychology Review.

Dr Maggie Clarke is an Academic at the University of Western Sydney (UWS) in Australia. Her teaching at UWS is in the discipline of education, particularly in the areas of secondary education and pedagogies. Her teaching is grounded in research, and her scholarly activities have received recognition at a national and international level through her publications, professional relationships and long-term Executive role on the Australian Teacher Education Association (peak Teacher Education Association in Australia). Dr Clarke has received a number of awards recognizing the quality of her teaching including the UWS Vice Chancellor's Award for Excellence in Teaching (2012), an Australian Learning and Teaching Citation for Outstanding Contribution to Student Learning, "for leading quality change in teacher education and influencing improvement of teaching and learning practices through her scholarly work at the University of Western Sydney" in 2010 and a UWS College of Arts Award for her outstanding contribution to student learning in 2009. She is currently co-writing an introductory higher education textbook *Becoming a Teacher*.

Christina Congleton is a Research Associate at Evidence Based Psychology, a leadership development and management consultancy. She has practiced as a certified Integral Coach since 2006, focusing on the integration of personal and professional effectiveness. Christina holds an EdM in Human Development and Psychology from Harvard University's Graduate School of Education, where she studied leadership and adult development. Prior to this she worked in neuroimaging laboratories at Massachusetts General Hospital, co-authoring work on the effects of meditation practice on the brain. Christina graduated Phi Beta Kappa from Oberlin College where she was awarded high honors for her research on brain functioning and social behavior.

Edward L. Deci is Helen F. and Fred H. Gowen Professor in the Social Sciences and Professor of Psychology at the University of Rochester. He holds a PhD in psychology from Carnegie–Mellon University and did an interdisciplinary post-doc at Stanford University. For more than 40 years Deci has been engaged in a program of research, much of it in collaboration with Richard M. Ryan, that has led to and been guided by Self-Determination Theory. Deci has published ten books, including *Intrinsic Motivation and Self-Determination in Human Behavior* (with Ryan, 1985) and *Why We Do What We Do* (1996). A grantee of the National Institute of Mental Health, the National Institute of Child Health and Human Development, the National Science Foundation, and the Institute of Education Sciences, he has lectured and consulted at more than 100 universities, as well as many businesses, government agencies, and other organizations around the world.

Ruth Donde (BPharm MBA) is a facilitator and consultant specializing in implementation of wide-scale coaching and leadership initiatives. She was the Regional Director for Neuroleadership Group, Asia Pacific and was Neuroleadership Group Leader of the Year 2011 and Thought Leader of the Year 2012. Ruth has completed her studies in the Neuroscience of Leadership. She has written and published papers and chapters on various topics including internal coaching, ROI of coaching, coaching culture, and mapping neuroscience to leadership behaviors and has presented papers at global conferences. She co-presented, with Elliot Berkman, the session on the Neuroscience of Goals at the Neuroleadership Summit 2011 in San Francisco.

Dr Anthony M. Grant is globally recognized as a key pioneer of Coaching Psychology and evidence-based approaches to coaching. Anthony left school at the age of fifteen with no qualifications beginning tertiary studies in 1993 as a mature age student in his 30s. He holds a BA (Hons) in Psychology, an MA in Behavioral Science and a PhD on the topic of Coaching Psychology. In January 2000 Anthony established the world's first Coaching Psychology Unit at Sydney University where he is the Director and holds an appointment as Associate Professor. He is also a Visiting Professor at Oxford Brookes University, Oxford, UK; a Senior Fellow at the Melbourne School of Business, Melbourne University; and a Visiting Scholar at the Säid School of Business, Oxford University. Anthony has considerable coaching experience at senior levels with leading Australian and global corporations. In 2007 Anthony was awarded the British Psychological Society Award for outstanding professional and scientific contribution to Coaching Psychology, and in 2009 he was awarded the "Vision of Excellence Award" from Harvard University for his pioneering work in helping to develop a scientific foundation to coaching.

Prof. Em. Dr Phil. Siegfried Greif, MSCP, is member of the University of Osnabrueck (Germany), and managing director of a consulting institute (www.iwfb.de). He was professor at the Free University of Berlin and had the chair of Work and Organizational Psychology at the University of Osnabrueck (Germany). Major fields of his research are stress at work, change management and coaching. He is editor of a book series on *Innovative Management* by the German Publisher Hogrefe (Goettingen). Among 14 books he has published one in German on Coaching (2008), many articles in journals, and diverse book chapters. He teaches coaching in universities and gives courses to practitioners. Homepage: www.home.uni-osnabrueck.de/sgreif/

Anita Howard is an adjunct professor at Case Western Reserve University (CWRU), an executive coach and organizational consultant with over 20 years of experience in corporate, non-profit and educational settings. She is a Master Coach in Weatherhead's Center for Executive Education, training and certifying new coaches. Before coming to Weatherhead, Anita co-founded a management consulting company where she developed training models to enhance the performance of multicultural professionals in corporate settings and African American students in US universities and secondary schools. Anita also has worked in university administration at Tufts University, Harvard University, and Radcliffe College. Anita's research program centers on the role of positive and negative emotion in professional learning and development, coaching intentional change, and use of emotional and social intelligence competencies in performance settings.

Carol Kauffman, PhD, ABPP, has taught for over twenty-five years at Harvard Medical School as an Assistant Clinical Professor, where she is also the Founding Director of the Institute of Coaching (InstituteofCoaching.org). In 2009 she received a two million dollar award to create the Institute and in 2010 the Institute of Coaching Professional Association was launched to support coaches' educational needs. The Institute awards $100,000 annually in coaching research grants. She was also founding Editor-in-Chief of the first academic peer-reviewed journal of coaching published by a major publisher. She directed and authored Harvard Business Review's first research project on executive coaching. Carol is an executive coach with over thirty years of experience helping leaders raise the bar on their performance and managing their success. She has worked with multi-national organizations, delivering training programs throughout the Americas, Europe and Asia. She has recently completed a leadership development program with the top 100 leaders of a Fortune 50 company.

Robert Kegan is the William and Miriam Meehan Professor of Adult Learning and Professional Development at the Harvard University Graduate School of Education. The recipient of numerous honorary degrees and awards, his thirty years of research and writing on adult development have influenced the practice of leadership development, executive coaching, and change management throughout the world. His seminal books, *The Evolving Self, In Over Our Heads, The Way We Talk,* and *Immunity to Change* (the latter two co-authored with Lisa Lahey) have been published in many languages. Bob has been on the faculty of the World Economic Forum's Davos Conference, and had his work featured in such diverse periodicals as *Harvard Business Review, The New York Times Sunday Business Section,* and *Oprah Magazine.* For the past several years, Bob has served as a trusted advisor to CEOs and senior leaders in the private and public sectors in the US, South America, Europe, and Asia. A husband, father, and grandfather, he is also an avid poker player, an airplane pilot, and the unheralded inventor of the "Base Average," a superior statistic for gauging offensive contribution in baseball.

Kathy E. Kram is the Shipley Professor in Management at the Boston University School of Management. Her primary interests are in the areas of adult development, relational learning, mentoring, diversity issues in executive development, leadership development, and organizational change processes. In addition to her book, *Mentoring at Work,* she has published in a wide range of journals. She is co-editor of *The Handbook of Mentoring at Work: Theory, Research and Practice* with Dr Belle Rose Ragins, and co-editor of *Extraordinary Leadership: Addressing the Gaps in Senior Executive Development* with Dr Kerry Bunker and Dr D.T. Hall. Dr Kram is a founding member of the Center for Research on Emotional Intelligence in Organizations (CREIO). During 2002–2009, she served as a member of the Board of Governors at the Center for Creative Leadership. She received her BS and MS degrees from M.I.T. Sloan School of

Management, and a PhD from Yale University. In 2011 she received the Everett Hughes Award for Outstanding Scholarship from the Careers Division of the Academy of Management.

Laura Gail Lunsford is an assistant professor of psychology at the University of Arizona South. Her work focuses on the psychological processes, e.g. professional identity and personality characteristics, involved in mentoring and coaching relationships. Dr Lunsford has published articles and chapters on mentoring in addition to presenting on the psychology of mentoring in the United States and Europe including at the American Psychological Association, Association for Psychological Science, the International Mentoring Association, and the European Mentoring and Coaching Council. Her current research is on mentoring behaviors and the costs associated with being a mentor. She is a recipient of the International Mentoring Association's Hope Richardson dissertation award.

Sarah Powell has a background in Music Education, completing her Undergraduate studies at the Sydney Conservatorium of Music, Sydney, Australia. She has taught in Primary and Secondary schools for 10 years. Sarah completed a Masters of Education in 2008 and the following year, a Master of Teaching Honors, for which she received First Class Honors. She began her Doctoral studies in 2011, focusing on males singing in choirs, identity and success, particularly in the context of education. Sarah has taught in the areas of Music and Education.

Professor Robert G.L. Pryor has worked in the field of vocational counseling and psychological assessment since 1974. He has worked both for government and a variety of private consultancies. Robert also is a director of an interdisciplinary medico-legal consultancy specializing in medico-legal assessment. He has published widely in assessment, counseling and career development theory. He has presented at numerous national and international conferences over the last 35 years. He has also lectured at several universities and was a Visiting Senior Research Fellow at the University of New South Wales for four years. As well he is the director of Congruence, a test construction and rehabilitation consultancy company. In addition he currently is an Adjunct Professor in the School of Education, Australian Catholic University National. In 2007 Robert was ranked in the top 10 international journal contributors to career development in the United States by the *Journal of Vocational Behavior*.

Dr David Rock coined the term 'NeuroLeadership' and is the director of the NeuroLeadership Institute, a global initiative bringing neuroscientists and leadership experts together to build a new science for leadership development. He is on the faculty and advisory board of CIMBA, an international business school based in Europe and a guest lecturer at several universities globally including Oxford's Saïd Business School. David received his professional doctorate (D. Prof.) in the Neuroscience of Leadership from Middlesex University in 2010. He is the author of four books including the business bestseller *Your Brain at Work* (2009). He co-edits the NeuroLeadership Journal, an annual peer reviewed journal at the nexus between neuroscience and leadership, and has written many of the seminal papers in that field. Based in the US, he also consults to large organizations globally, including NASA, Citibank, American Express, Juniper Networks and Nokia Siemens Networks. Over 12,000 executive and personal coaches learned to coach through his approach, and his models have been taught to over 75,000 executives around the globe.

Dr Gordon B. Spence is Program Director of the Master of Business Coaching at Sydney Business School, University of Wollongong. He holds a PhD in coaching psychology from the University of Sydney and lectures on the psychology of peak performance, leadership, evidence-based coaching, business well-being, and the application of positive psychology within organizational contexts. Gordon is an active researcher (with particular interests in autonomous motivation, mindfulness, employee engagement and workplace well-being) and is co-chair of the Scientific Advisory Council, Institute of Coaching, McLean Hospital/Harvard University. He is also a practicing executive and workplace coach, workshop facilitator, and author of numerous peer-reviewed journal articles and book chapters.

Sir John Whitmore is Chairman and Founder of Performance Consultants International. He is a pre-eminent thinker in leadership and organizational change and works globally with leading multinational corporations to establish coaching management cultures and leadership programs. He has written five books on leadership, coaching and sports, of which *Coaching for Performance* is the best known having sold 750,000 copies in 25 languages. Honored with the President's Award by International Coach Federation (ICF), rated as the Number One Business Coach by the Independent newspaper and as having had the most impact on the coaching profession by the Association for Coaching, John is one of the leading figures in the international coaching community with programs running globally in over 30 countries.

Foreword

It's my pleasure to write a Foreword for a book that critically examines and extends goal theory. You could say that my own views on goals are contradictory. On the one hand, I see them as necessary because people need a place to get started. They need to answer the question "what am I going to do tomorrow?" However, I have always found goal-setting exercises extraordinarily mechanical. They presume a static world. This doesn't leave room for learning and iteration, which is how the change process actually happens: through experimenting, tweaking, modifying, and ending up somewhere different from where you thought you were going.

My views are based in part on my research into working identity and the process of personal change during career transition. I've found that accurate self-knowledge is not easy to attain via introspection. You can't just sit there and think about the past— you have to generate new data. You need to experiment and then reflect on what you've learned. This makes sense, because people are not static. We change, we evolve; the world changes, it evolves. We have to find identity through experimentation, and when we're experimenting, crafting, and questioning, our goals change as well. It's a dynamic process.

In addition to my research, my ideas about goals are informed by my teaching experience, particularly in executive education. For a number of years I've taught a program designed for people who want to move into broader leadership roles—from those that are expert or functional in nature to those that are more strategic. These leaders are asked to stretch; to focus on areas where they would like to make changes.

The problem for most of them is that they either don't know what they want to accomplish, or what they want to accomplish is abstract. One person wants to be a better leader—what does that look like? Another wants to move into a more fulfilling career—what is that? For me, the question is how to help people learn by taking small steps, with each step defining the next, until they have a sense of the bigger picture.

Goal setting is a tool within this process, and we do sometimes use the SMART model in our leadership development program. However, this is such a small piece of the whole leadership and adult development puzzle. Goals can be problematic because, essentially, they are outcomes. They create a carrot and stick scenario, in which the stick is "I won't be seen as high potential", or "I'll get a bad evaluation", and the carrot is, "I'll get a promotion". What I've seen is that people are able to get started with these specific, measurable goals, but then they begin to think more broadly about the kind of person they want to become; what kind of life they want for the next ten years. They begin to shift from a system of carrot and stick to the motivation that comes from developing possible selves, from saying "I can do this, and I want to do this, because I am the kind of person who behaves this way." This orientation is infinitely more motivating than SMART goals, and as long as a leader grounds him or herself in behavioral experiments, as well as relationships that support exploration, it is quite effective in moving things forward. Therefore, in addition to the SMART model, I think we need to think about development in terms of this second, more nuanced process.

The scholarly volume you are now reading brings together some of the most prominent academics who are challenging and enriching the way we think about setting and pursuing goals. From Anthony Grant's integrated model, to Robert Kegan's description of the "goals behind the goals", the reader will find a wealth of information to stimulate his or her own thinking. I'm also pleased that Kathy Kram's chapter highlights the importance of developmental networks, because I've found that people are much more limited by their networks than they realize. As much as our networks love and support us, they can pigeon hole us and constrain us to who we've been, rather than open us to whom we might become. I've seen that once people start forging connections outside of their normal groups, their sense of what's possible and what kind of goals they want to set for themselves can change dramatically.

Finally, I appreciate the implications this book presents for organizations. I do a lot of teaching about leading organizational change, and I know that goal development can be difficult because the environment is so turbulent. Naturally, people in organizations would like to have very specific goals that allow them to tick boxes. However, similar to the process of change at the individual level, what's most motivating is to find a compelling orientation.

It's easy to set a goal based on something like return on investment. It's much harder to say, "This is the kind of organization we would like to be, and here are some indicators we can use to measure whether we're actually moving in that direction." This is different, but it's more appealing to people.

Like individual change, organizational change is also iterative and dynamic. I'm an avid student of Henry Mintzberg's work on organizational strategy.[1] He has a beautiful analogy to sculpture: you have your materials, and in the process of working with them you figure out how to deviate from your plan, to add and subtract. I think this depicts perfectly the process of leading change.

In the context of a complex world, we are due for a critical re-examination of the way we set and pursue goals. *Beyond Goals* is a wonderful resource for the coaching, mentoring, and organizational development communities as we engage in this conversation. I hope you enjoy taking part.

Herminia Ibarra
Paris, France
2013

---

1   Mintzberg, H. (1994). *The Rise and Fall of Strategic Planning*. New York: The Free Press.

Preface

In this book, we examine in depth the role of goals in coaching and mentoring. Our primary thesis is straightforward: simplistic assumptions about the role of goals in coaching and mentoring are not helpful to either the relationship or the learning process.

Goal theory has been the subject of extensive study in recent years and it is clear that having and pursuing goals are strongly associated with personal achievement in a wide range of contexts. Yet, in light of our own observations, as well as mounting evidence from the academic community, we believe it is important to challenge the assumption that every coaching or mentoring relationship must start with a precise goal. In many cases, the purpose of a developmental relationship is to help the learner acquire and shape goals—goals are therefore emergent. Indeed, starting a relationship with fixed goals can lead participants to focus blindly on the wrong objective. In our workshops with coaches of varying levels of experience, we've seen that it is often the coach or mentor, rather than the client, who feels the need to identify very clear goals at the beginning of the engagement. Is the coach in this case really acting in the client's best interest? And if not, what should the practitioner do differently?

We argue passionately that the role and nature of goal management in coaching and mentoring vary significantly depending on the kind of goal being pursued, and the purpose in pursuing it. Questions along the way include: What do we mean by goal? What do we mean by purpose? How can coaches become more insightful in helping clients to craft and work with goals?

To explore these questions and in an effort to move thinking "beyond goals", we invited expert scholars, including some of the most prominent names in coaching and mentoring, to contribute their knowledge and ideas. The result is a book that includes a wealth of information and cutting-edge perspectives for the practitioner, researcher, or student to consider.

We begin by setting the stage with historical and contemporary overviews of goal theory, as well as evidence from our own research on goals in coaching. The book then transitions into contributed chapters that present approaches from psychology, neuroscience, and motivation science. This content leads into a focus on complexity science and chaos theory—themes we did not anticipate, but that emerged clearly in the work of multiple authors. Later chapters include interviews from some of the greats in coaching and mentoring: Sir John Whitmore, Robert Kegan, and Kathy Kram. After shifting to a focus on mentoring, we conclude the book with a chapter on pragmatics in developmental relationships, as well as reflections from the editors. Of course, you, the reader, are enthusiastically encouraged to formulate your own.

At the end of your reading experience, if you feel better equipped to support clients in working with goals; if you feel more aware of the pitfalls of simplistic approaches and more able to challenge your own and your clients' assumptions about goals; and, perhaps most importantly, if you are alight with new questions and curiosities that you will take forward in your own practice or research; then we will have fulfilled our own goals in writing this book.

The Editors
Susan David, David Clutterbuck and David Megginson

Acknowledgements

This book is a testament to the teamwork, effort and encouragement of so many. The contributors—each a respected authority in his or her field—have dedicated hour upon hour to conceive of, write, and shape what are cutting-edge chapters on what they have discovered about goals over the course of their careers. It is to these experts—including my co-editors David Clutterbuck and David Megginson—that I extend my deepest thanks and appreciation.

This book would not have happened without Christina Congleton. It is remarkably rare to work with someone who brings a combination of unfailing organizational and editorial skills, creativity, calm, and downright niceness. Christina has all of these qualities and others, in spades. To the rest of the team at Evidence Based Psychology, especially Kimbette Fenol and Karen Monteiro, thank you for your encouragement, support and outstanding work on other projects, in a way that enabled me to focus on this one.

My clients—you are a daily reminder of how the effective use of goals can enable and inspire organizations and those within them. My colleagues at the Institute of Coaching, Carol Kauffman, Margaret Moore, Ruth Ann Harnisch, Laurel Doggett and the rest of the team, are fellow travelers, dedicated to using evidence to positively impact human experience. Thank you for the inspiration, foresight, and insight that you continue to provide.

My family—Veronica, my late father Sidney, Christopher, Madeleine, Liezel, Alex, Sam, Charlotte, Moshe, Robyn, and Richard have taught me so much about how to work with goals in the context of this ever-changing and wonderful journey. Anthony Samir my husband and life partner, Noah David, my beautiful son, and the "little baby sister", Sophie, who was born while the book was being finalized, you are proof that the most meaningful and generative experiences come when we willingly embrace life as it emerges.

Susan David, PhD

Reviews of *Beyond Goals*

We all know that goals are dreams with deadlines. We also know that setting goals enables us to turn the invisible into the visible. What's more, goals are the catalysts of change. If we set goals, and pursue these full heartedly, we are likely to arrive at remarkable places. Susan David, David Clutterbuck and David Megginson have been in pursuit of exactly the "remarkable" in their book Beyond Goals. Their contributions and the ones of their associates show us the road forward in making coaching and mentoring a highly successful endeavour. This book is a "must" for everyone interested in this rapidly expanding field of studies.

Manfred F. R. Kets de Vries, INSEAD, France

We have needed this considered and careful exploration of the use of goals in coaching to challenge any number of blithe assumptions. The range of perspectives and the depth of coverage in this volume will encourage more reflective and effective engagement to help clients change what matters. I'm adding it to our "must-read" list for coaching supervisors.

Douglas Riddle, Global Director Coaching Services & Assessment Portfolio, Center for Creative Leadership, USA

Beyond Goals is an educative, highly readable and compelling analysis of standard practices in goal setting for individuals and business. You are invited to challenge current thinking and traditional techniques for goal achievement and to engage with stimulating perspectives that have the potential to revolutionise the future of goal setting. An inspirational and invaluable resource for all those involved with mentoring and coaching.

Lise Lewis, International President of the European Mentoring and Coaching Council (EMCC)

This book is a jewel of an examination of goals, their rich colors and facets visible here as nowhere else I have seen. Leaders in the coaching field highlight the complexity of goals and the many ways to help clients reach them - and reach beyond them. In a field that is sometimes simplistic and sometimes bewildering, this book stands out as valuable to both practice and theory building.

> *Jennifer Garvey Berger, author* Changing on the Job: Developing Leaders for a Complex World *and co-editor,* Executive Coaching: Practices and Perspectives

Before coaching, I spent over 20 years in corporate America and dreaded annual goal development and reviews exactly for the reasons described in this book. I thought I was an oddity, and now I find the old paradigm shifting. Goals can be meaningful, purposeful, and useful for individuals and organisations. This book provides excellent information on the history and evolution of goals and goal setting, and deep insight into how we as coaches, mentors, and managers can support our clients in practice.

> *Diane Brennan MBA, MCC, Past President International Coach Federation*

What a relief. Finally an academically sound and engrossing recognition that goals in coaching are simultaneously central and irrelevant. Demonstrating life's elegant non-linearity, the authors ask us to question current coaching lore and to build an up-to-date understanding of the real nature of goals in coaching and mentoring. A mind-opening feast.

> *Nancy Kline, Founding President, Time To Think*

List of Abbreviations

ACC	Anterior cingulate cortex
BAS	Behavioral approach system
BIS	Behavioral inhibition system
BPNT	Basic psychological needs theory
CAS	Complex Adaptive Systems
CET	Cognitive evaluation theory
COT	Causality orientations theory
CTC	Chaos Theory of Careers
DASS	Depression Anxiety and Stress Scale
DMN	Default Mode Network
EOC	Edge of chaos
ERN	Error Related Negativity
fMRI	Functional magnetic resonance imaging
GCSQ	Goal-focused Coaching Skills Questionnaire
GCT	Goal contents theory
GROW	Goal, reality, options, will (also what, when and whom)
HRO	High Reliability Organization
ICT	Intentional Change Theory
MBO	Management by Objectives
MNS	Mirror neuron system
mPFC	Medial prefrontal cortex
NEA	Negative Emotional Attractor
OIT	Organismic integration theory
PASS	Perceived Autonomy Support Scale
PEA	Positive Emotional Attractor
PFC	Prefrontal cortex
PGH	Painful goal honesty
PNS	Parasympathetic Nervous System
PPT	Positive psychotherapy
PTC	Perspective Taking Capacity

RMT	Relationships motivation theory
rVLPFC	Right ventrolateral prefrontal cortex
SDT	Self-determination theory
SF	Solution-focused
SMART	Specific, measurable, attainable, realistic, time-bound (and variations)
SNS	Sympathetic nervous system
SRIS	Self-reflection and Insight Scale

Goals: A Long-term View

Susan A. David, David Clutterbuck, David Megginson,
and Christina Congleton

The fascination with goals and goal achievement is deep rooted in human history. What is it that makes one person adhere year upon year, with tremendous energy, to a goal for themselves or for others, while other people with similar goals give up at the first hurdle? What is it about the power of a shared goal that encourages and sustains whole groups of people or even nations in tasks and activities that require great personal sacrifice? These are questions that have puzzled philosophers for millennia. Consider Aristotle who, over 2,000 years ago, proposed actions that individuals and communities could take in pursuit of goodness (Irwin and Fine, 1996).

In more recent history, these questions have increasingly preoccupied behavioral scientists and human resource professionals. The link between individual, team and organizational performance has become both clearer and more important as a differentiator in the success of businesses and other organizations (Pfeffer and Veiga, 1999). The study of goals tends to follow two paths: (1) goal setting—how and why people and organizations set goals in the first place, and (2) goal management—how goals are pursued (Locke and Latham, 1990; Locke and Latham, 2002; Riediger, Freund, and Baltes, 2005; Shah, 2005). In this first chapter we examine goals in history, and provide descriptions of the theories and research that have shaped the way we understand goal setting and goal management today.

What is a Goal?

The *Oxford English Dictionary* defines a goal as "the object of a person's ambition or effort; a destination; an aim" (Allen, 1991, p. 505). This definition explicitly conveys that a goal requires the application of physical or mental energy over a period of time. However, another definition is "a boundary or limit". Indeed, this is the meaning of both the Old High German "zil", and the Middle English "gol", the root words for "goal" (Elliot and Fryer, 2008). This definition implies a very different set of concepts—among them that goals can be confining. It is an aspect that has not often been discussed, although, as we will see in the next chapter, the idea has been acknowledged by goal theorists and has recently come into greater prominence as a result of arguments between academics about the value of goal focus (Ordóñez et al., 2009).

A generally accepted academic definition of a goal is "a regulatory mechanism for monitoring, evaluating and adjusting one's behaviour" (Locke and Latham, 2009, p. 19). This implies that goals are internal rather than external functions, although they may be focused on achieving change in a person's environment and may be internally or externally motivated (Deci, 1975). Intrinsic (internal) and extrinsic (external) goal motivation are discussed further in Chapter 5.

Goal-addressed behaviors are fundamental to achievement in almost every aspect of human endeavor. Even infants recognize simple goal-oriented behaviors (Király et al., 2003), demonstrating that goal-related concepts take hold early in the human psyche. Just as we can trace goal orientation to initial stages of human development, we can recognize its existence in earlier periods of history. We consider this in the next section.

Goals in History

Over the centuries, people have found reasons to identify and pursue their ambitions. Dating back to antiquity, many religions have included a notion of a transcendent realm, or heaven, which has carried implications for human behavior (Ellwood and Alles, 2007). For example, in Hinduism, Buddhism, and Jainism, it is believed that people who have taken exceptionally good actions during their lives are reborn into heavenly realms. In Zoroastrianism, Christianity, and Islam people subscribe to a similar belief: those who are assessed favorably on the day of judgement will be granted entry to heaven.

In Western culture the belief in heaven as a reward for good behavior, bestowed in the after-life, was advanced by the Christian church and thus woven into the early social fabric. However, the Christian view of goals was complicated by the concept of grace, which has been defined as, "the unmerited favour of God; a divine saving and strengthening influence" (Allen, 1991, p. 511). Nonetheless, in the sixteenth century the Protestant reformation increased the importance of goal-directed behaviors: pursuing an occupation and excelling in worldly tasks was considered a demonstration of spiritual confidence, and evidence of one's salvation (Wren and Bedeian, 2009). Fundamental to this approach was the notion that we cannot be complacent—we need to prove or improve ourselves. The existence of goals provided a future orientation. This helped people focus on what change was needed most, and to work diligently towards this.

The Protestants' industriousness continued to impact the worldview of many Westerners in the centuries that followed, including the founding fathers of the United States. Benjamin Franklin is famous for his Puritan-inspired work ethic and thirteen self-proclaimed virtues, which included resolution (doing as you intend), and industry (always engaging in something useful) (Franklin, 1791/1896). From Franklin's autobiography, penned between 1771 and 1790, we know that he used a chart to monitor the virtuousness of his behavior, and that he kept a schedule of his daily activities. Franklin took advantage of the morning hours to reflect on his good intentions for the day, and he reviewed his accomplishments at night. His record-keeping offers a window into goal-directed behavior at the close of the eighteenth century (see Figures 1.1 and 1.2).

It was during this time that the Industrial Revolution was bringing sweeping changes to the way people lived and worked in a number of Western countries. The rise of the factory presented new challenges in organizing and coordinating goal-oriented behavior. The labor force consisted largely of those accustomed to farming, performing a trade in a small workshop, or helping their families. There were no established managerial practices or training regimes for factory life (Wren and Bedeian, 2009). The evolution of work life eventually brought management issues into the arena of science and academia, notably with Frederick Taylor's work on scientific management (Taylor, 1911). This was complemented by the development of scientific psychology in Europe, spurred by Wundt's pioneering laboratory experiments, as well as Freud's investigation of the human psyche (Hergenhahn, 2009). Goal-related behavior became a topic of interest for scholars, who began to generate theory and research to enhance our understanding of goal setting and pursuit.

FORM OF THE PAGES.

TEMPERANCE.						
EAT NOT TO DULLNESS; DRINK NOT TO ELEVATION.						
S.	M.	T.	W.	T.	F.	S.
T[emperance]						
S[ilence]	*	*		*		*	
O[rder]	**	*	*		*	*	*
R[esolution]			*			*	
F[rugality]		*			*		
I[ndustry]			*				
S[incerity]							
J[ustice]							
M[oderation]							
C[leanliness]							
T[ranquillity]							
C[hastity]							
H[umility]							

Figure 1.1   From Benjamin Franklin's book of virtues

Source: Franklin, 1791/1896, p. 99

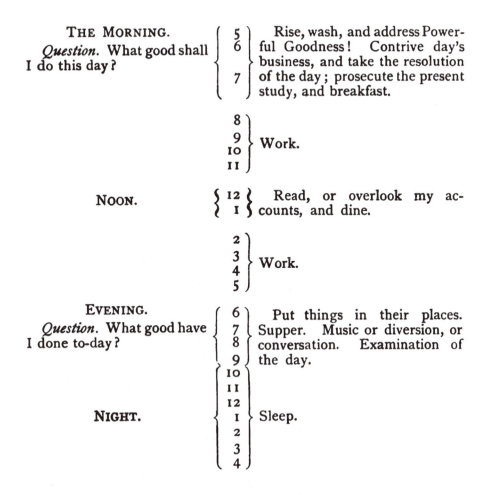

THE MORNING.
Question. What good shall I do this day?

5
6
7

Rise, wash, and address Powerful Goodness! Contrive day's business, and take the resolution of the day; prosecute the present study, and breakfast.

8
9
10
11

Work.

NOON.

12
1

Read, or overlook my accounts, and dine.

2
3
4
5

Work.

EVENING.
Question. What good have I done to-day?

6
7
8
9

Put things in their places. Supper. Music or diversion, or conversation. Examination of the day.

NIGHT.

10
11
12
1
2
3
4

Sleep.

Figure 1.2   Benjamin Franklin's daily schedule

Source: Franklin, 1791/1896, p. 101

Goal Theory, Research, and Practice

In this section we discuss the evolution of research on goals, in academia and in practice. Where appropriate, we link this research to key issues in coaching and mentoring. These topics are further explored in subsequent chapters.

The academic study of goals dates to the early 1900s, when psychologist Narziß Ach (1905/1951) began investigating volition and willpower at Germany's Würzburg School. He argued that *goal images* led to the formation of conscious or unconscious *determining tendencies*, and these in turn prompted people to take action (Ach, 1905/1951, 1935; Elliot and Fryer, 2008). Kurt Lewin (1926/1961)—best known for his law that behavior is a function of the person and the environment—built on Ach's work by studying the concept of *intention*. He went on to analyze forces that either helped or hindered people in their processes of goal pursuit.

The first known empirical research into goal setting was by Mace (1935), who also pioneered what we now call employee engagement. Mace showed that money was not the dominant work incentive, and maintained that people's will to work depended on circumstances and work environment. His experiments into goal setting laid the foundations for Drucker's (1954) Management by Objectives (MBO), and for the "giants" of goal theory, Edwin Locke and George Latham (1990), to eventually develop their theories and experiments.

MANAGEMENT BY OBJECTIVES

The technology of goal setting took a leap forward in the 1950s and 1960s with Peter Drucker's (1954) development of Management by Objectives (MBO). Its driving principle is that defining and focusing on specific goals improves the efficiency of resource use. Drucker observed that managers became trapped in activity, spending most of their time on tasks that contributed little benefit to the organization's overarching objectives. By focusing on fewer, more significant goals and ensuring that all employees were aware of both the overall goals and individual, specific goals, organizations could be more effective and productive. Clarifying goals thus became more important than controlling how employees achieved them, and negotiating individual goals played a significant part in gaining employee commitment.

The popularization of "stretch" goals has taken MBO theory a step further. A stretch goal is one that the pursuer does not know how to reach, and that may even seem unrealistic (Kerr and Landauer, 2004). The practice of setting stretch goals was popularized in the 1990s at General Electric by the former CEO, Jack Welch. Welch observed that in "reaching for the unattainable" (Krames, 2002, p. 46), people were able to achieve far more than they believed they could.

Today stretch goals continue to be frequent triggers for coaching and mentoring interventions. When faced with a difficult task, one that requires a change in thinking or new perspectives, individuals and teams can benefit from the rigorous processes that effective coaching entails. In particular, coaching and mentoring can help to counterbalance excessive optimism or unwillingness to consider failure—for example, by ensuring that resource issues are discussed.

Proponents of MBO see goal setting as helping organizations and individuals shift their attention from inputs to re-focus on outputs. This is viewed as a liberating process, providing individuals and teams the freedom to choose the means whereby they will achieve goals, and saving senior management from having to pay attention to the details of these means. Indeed, Drucker saw this as an emancipatory force in business (Drucker, 1954).

Many coaches and mentors today encounter busy leaders who are liberated when they step back from daily activity to reflect upon and prioritize tasks. Implicit in this stepping back is an opportunity to gain clarity on what is truly worth doing, and to focus energy on the important, rather than solely on the urgent. Goals make feasible the integration of the efforts of hundreds or indeed thousands of individuals, and so are inevitable and invaluable. With the growing complexity of the workplace, leaders are simply no longer able to master the details of individual jobs. They need to get hold of the outputs and to call for an account of progress towards achieving these. Following Drucker's MBO, leaders can set targets even when they do not know how they are to be achieved.

MBO has been widely embraced in organizations; however, many objections have been raised over the years. Critics of modern management methods (e.g. Foucault, 1975; Brewis, 1996; Jacques, 1996) have regarded the shift toward defining objectives as enlarging the degree of control exercisable by the leaders of organizations, by enabling them to hold firmly onto the levers of change. They have suggested that individuals in contemporary organizations will find their lives regulated by a cascade of goals from those senior to them, and these will be used to focus employees' efforts, measure their performance, and determine their financial and reputational rewards. These critics envision that goals will become the means by which a dominant group will exert power and "drive performance" — to use a common phrase in management discourse — in a non-dominant group. In this context, employees' commitment to the economic objectives of the business enterprise is protected and made subservient to the potentially joyful act of work in and of itself (Foucault, 1975; Brewis, 1996; Jacques, 1996; Peltonen, 2012).

Johnson and Bröms (2000) have critiqued the mechanistic mind-set that is seen as being promoted through MBO's goal orientation. Their research has demonstrated that targets set by the big three US automotive manufacturers had distorting effects on the flow of products through the manuafacturing process: the targets incentivized manufacturing divisions to produce and sales people to sell, regardless of the balance between supply and demand. Toyota, on the other hand, benefitted from having no targets beyond the call for continuous improvement, and with each car on the production line being manufactured in response to a specific order from a customer.

Johnson and Bröms have advocated for an approach that draws on the work of one of Drucker's contemporaries, William Edwards Deming, who formulated a contrasting perspective to MBO. Deming's leadership of the Quality Management movement is discussed in the next section.

DEMING AND THE QUALITY MANAGEMENT MOVEMENT

Deming began his work in Japan at the close of the 1940s, and later gained notoriety in the United States for his work at Ford Motor Company (Wren and Bedeian, 2009). Deming emphasized pride in work through continuous improvement, and freedom from the constraint of targets against which individuals and teams had to perform (Deming, 1986). The twelfth of Deming's famous fourteen principles was to:

> *Remove barriers that rob the hourly worker of his right to pride of workmanship. The responsibility of supervisors must be changed from sheer numbers to quality.*
>
> *Remove barriers that rob people in management and in engineering of their right to pride of workmanship. This means, inter alia, abolishment of the annual or merit rating and of management by objective. (Deming, 1986, p. 24)*

Deming (1986) also pointed out that statistical understanding was necessary to measure work, and that an appreciation of statistics would demonstrate that individual performance is at the mercy of a wide range of factors outside of the worker's control. Moreover, he maintained that the most important things could not be measured.

Drucker's MBO and Deming's Quality Management movement have offered contrasting theories and methodologies that have impacted the way organizations approach goals. Another important source of influence is the work of psychologists Edwin Locke and Gary Latham, who are responsible for generating what has become standard goal setting theory.

LOCKE AND LATHAM'S THEORY OF GOAL SETTING AND TASK PERFORMANCE

In the mid-1960s Locke began studying the relationship between goals and performance. Based on a review of goal setting literature, he concluded that more challenging goals were related to better performance (Locke, 1968). Latham subsequently helped to validate this claim by performing field studies with logging crews (Latham and Locke, 1975) and typists (Yukl and Latham, 1978). The positive relationship between goal difficulty and performance was replicated many times in laboratory settings (Locke et al., 1981).

Locke and Latham (1990, 2002) subsequently joined forces to generate goal setting theory. Building on Ryan's (1970) work on conscious goals, they described "the object or result being sought" (Locke and Latham, 1990, p. 25) as goal content, which breaks down into *specificity* (how precise, clear and measurable the goal is) and level or *difficulty* as perceived by the individual (how complex or hard the person considers achieving it to be). To be most effective, they argued, goals should be challenging and specific, and accompanied by appropriate levels of moderating factors including commitment (determination to achieve the goal) and feedback (a means to assess progress against the goal). They maintained that specific, challenging, goals led to higher performance than vague goals, such as "do your best".

Locke and Latham (2002) argued that goals increase performance because they direct and maintain attention on intended outcomes. They also motivate people to increase their efforts in proportion to goal difficulty, and to sustain those efforts until objectives are achieved. Finally, setting goals encourages people to use their existing knowledge and skills to formulate effective

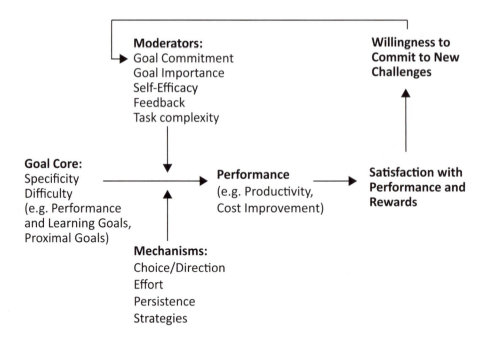

Figure 1.3   **Essential elements of goal setting theory and the high-performance cycle**

Source: Locke, E.A. & Latham, G.P. (2002). Building a practically useful theory of goal setting and task motivation: A 35-year odyssey. *American Psychologist, 57,* 705–17. Copyright © 2002 by the American Psychological Association. Reproduced with permission.

strategies for task completion. The main elements of their goal setting theory and what they call the "high-performance cycle" are depicted in Figure 1.3.

ADDITIONAL GOAL-RELATED THEORIES

Locke and Latham (2009) point out that, in addition to their own theory, goals are at the core of four well-known theories of motivation. These are Maslow's (1943, 1954) need hierarchy, Fishbein and Ajzen's (1975) theory of reason and action, Bandura's (1986) social cognitive theory, and Carver and Scheier's (1998) control theory. We will briefly explore each of these in turn.

MASLOW'S HIERARCHY OF NEEDS

Maslow (1954) maintained that people have two types of need: deficiency needs and growth needs. Deficiency needs, in ascending order of instinctive motivation, are physiological (need for sleep, food, water), safety and security (e.g. order, freedom from threat) and belongingness (being accepted by others). Growth needs are esteem and ego (status, self-respect) and self-actualization (self-fulfillment, having one's ability challenged). Maslow proposed this hierarchy as a theory of motivation, and considered needs to be the basis of goal setting. While Maslow's theory is widely known and has influenced the fields of organizational behavior and management, there has been little empirical evidence to support it (Wahba and Bridwell, 1976).

FISHBEIN AND AJZEN'S REASON AND ACTION THEORY

Fishbein and Ajzen (1975) explored the relationship between people's *behavioral intentions* and the factors that influence those intentions. They claimed that behavioral intentions were equivalent to a combination of people's *attitudes* toward the particular behavior, and *subjective norms*—their perception of how others view the behavior. This combination—of one's own attitudes with perceptions of other people's attitudes—was believed to determine the strength of one's intention to act. The theory has been tested on a number of behaviors including dieting (Sejwacz, Ajzen, and Fishbein, 1980) and the use of sun protection (Hoffmann, Rodrigue, and Johnson, 1999). However, scholars have disagreed about the implications of effect sizes in these studies (Hale, Householder, and Greene, 2003). Ajzen (1991) extended the model to include *perceived behavioral control*, which refers to the individual's experience of self-efficacy. He acknowledged that a person's belief in his ability to act influences the strength of his intention.

BANDURA'S SOCIAL COGNITIVE THEORY

In a spirit similar to Fishbein and Ajzen, Bandura (1986, 1991) broke with theorists who overemphasized external influences on behavior, claiming that, "If human behavior were regulated solely by external outcomes, people would behave like weathervanes, constantly shifting direction to conform to whatever momentary social influence happened to impinge upon them" (Bandura, 1991, p. 249). He suggested that people receive psychological rewards for achieving goals, and proposed a complex reciprocal interaction between three forces: (a) personal factors such as cognition, affect, and biological events, (b) behavior, and (c) environmental influences. The theory regards people as agents proactively engaged in their own development, possessing self-regulatory functions that enable them to exercise some control over their thoughts, feelings, and actions. Bandura claimed that self-efficacy beliefs were integral to goal setting. According to him, "The more capable people judge themselves to be, the higher the goals they set for themselves and the more firmly committed they remain to them" (Bandura, 1991, p. 258). His work also laid the foundation for discovering the distinction between performance and learning goals (see p. 13, this volume).

CARVER AND SCHEIER'S CONTROL THEORY

Carver and Scheier (1998, 2002) have studied the convergence of self-regulation and dynamic systems models. Their theory includes concepts that will be explored in greater detail in subsequent chapters (see Chapters 4, 6, 8, 9 and 10, this volume), including feedback processes, attractors and repellers, and self-organization. Carver and Scheier describe a goal as a reference point. Pursuing a goal requires determining one's current position in relationship to that reference point and "making changes to diminish the gap between present location and goal" (Carver and Scheier, 2002, p. 305). In this way, goals act as attractors for particular types of behavior. Carver and Scheier (2002) point out that self-organization leads to emergent properties, and this has implications for how goals change. To illustrate, they describe two colleagues having coffee with no goal other than to socialize. The conversation, however, leads to a plan to collaborate on a new project, and entirely new and unanticipated goals are set. Carver and Scheier claim that the process of changing goals is an emergent, self-organizing one. The notion of emergent goals is one we will explore throughout this book.

The various components of Locke and Latham's goal theory, as well as those described here, raise questions related to coaching and mentoring. For example, in terms of specificity, we know that even when a goal can be clearly articulated and its achievement measured, it is not necessarily appropriate for the client. In our experience, helping the client understand his or her context (the systems he or she is part of, personal values and so on) frequently results in a change of goals. Many coaches and mentors have observed that goals are far from static. As Carver and Scheier have proposed, goals can be emergent: they are prone to shifts, revisions, and transformations as the client's process unfolds over time.

Further experimentation has revealed nuances in Locke and Latham's goal setting theory (Winters and Latham, 1996), with important implications for practice. When a task is straightforward, a specific goal that demands high-performance leads to superior achievement. However, when the task is complex and requires the acquisition of knowledge, increases in performance are associated with setting *learning goals* rather than performance goals. According to Seijts et al. (2004, p. 229), "A learning goal shifts attention to the discovery and implementation of task-relevant strategies or procedures and away from task outcome achievement." This finding is related to an important distinction that has emerged in contemporary goals research, described in the next section.

PERFORMANCE VERSUS MASTERY GOALS

Much of the recent research into goal orientation stems from studies with schoolchildren (Dweck and Leggett, 1988; Elliott and Dweck, 1988) that have led researchers to identify a distinction between *performance goals* and *learning goals*. Performance goals are those in which individuals strive to demonstrate their competence and impress others with their achievements. These goals are focused on specific outcomes, and might be considered "pass/fail". In contrast, learning goals, also called mastery goals, are those in which individuals strive to build their competence. While performance goals are about *proving* competence, learning goals are about *improving* it.

Dweck and colleagues have shown that, "individuals' goals set up their pattern of responding, and these goals, in turn, are fostered by individuals' self-conceptions" (Dweck and Leggett, 1988). Specifically, those who implicitly believe their intelligence or their abilities are fixed entities—impervious to change through work or practice—tend to adopt performance goals. Those who regard their abilities as malleable, and therefore open to growth and development, are more likely to adopt learning goals (Dweck, 2006).

Diener and Dweck (1978) have shown that the fixed mindset, with its orientation toward performance goals, is a maladaptive pattern associated with helplessness. When children who exhibit this pattern encounter obstacles during goal pursuit they begin to think and speak negatively about themselves, and their performance declines. Mastery-oriented children, on the other hand, are able to maintain optimism, along with effective problem-solving strategies. In short, mastery-oriented individuals are better able to persist in the face of goal-related difficulties. Dweck and Leggett (1988) conclude, "whereas helpless individuals appear to view challenging problems as a threat to their self-esteem, mastery-oriented ones appear to view them as opportunities for learning something new" (p. 258). Indeed, Wood and Bandura (1989) replicated this phenomenon in business school students who were tasked with managing a simulated organization. Those who were encouraged to adopt a mastery mindset outperformed those encouraged toward a fixed mindset, including on measurements of organizational productivity.

Consistent with the importance of feedback in Locke and Latham's theory of goal setting, researchers have found that feedback plays an important role for those with learning goal orientations. They are more likely to seek and benefit from feedback in the pursuit of their goals than those with a performance goal orientation (VandeWalle et al., 2000).

We have found that feedback—internally or externally generated—plays an important role in coaching. Internally generated feedback comes from intrinsic observation by the client—noticing what happens in situations relevant to the coaching purpose, or maintaining a learning log. Externally generated feedback comes either from observation by the coach or from other parties, for example, through boss-subordinate or 360-degree appraisal. The goal orientation a client takes—whether mastery or performance—is likely to influence the willingness to undertake activities that result in intrinsic feedback, as well as openness to feedback from others. A challenge to be navigated by coaches is that even people with a strong learning orientation will make judgements on what feedback to listen to, on the basis of receptivity (willingness to hear messages incongruent with established beliefs or assumptions), the perceived credibility of the feedback source, individual differences (e.g. openness to experience, curiosity) and emotional skills (e.g. the ability to navigate and manage the emotions generated by the feedback).

FURTHER RESEARCH

Research into goals and goal management continues. Recent work includes a focus on implementation intentions, goal alignment, and the social impact of goal seeking behavior. These ideas are introduced below and where relevant are expanded upon in subsequent chapters.

Gollwitzer (1999) studies the concept of *implementation intentions*, volitional acts that precede and facilitate the execution of actions. Translating goal intentions into practice requires the actor to develop very precise anticipatory "If-then plans"—essentially firm intentions of where, when, and how to implement actions that will achieve the goal. A 2006 meta-analysis by Gollwitzer and Sheeran revealed that implementation intentions are effective in "promoting the initiation of goal striving, the shielding of ongoing goal pursuit from unwanted influences, disengagement from failing courses of action, and conservation of capability for future goal striving" (Gollwitzer and Sheeran, 2006, p. 69). Implementation intentions are discussed in more detail in Chapter 7.

Another approach has been to study manipulations of the underlying psychological processes in goal pursuit. In a 2010 study, Senay and colleagues examined the relationship between goal-directed behavior and introspective self-talk. Volunteers were asked to solve anagrams. In one exercise, the researchers asked volunteers to either consider working on the anagrams, or to think about actually doing the task. In another exercise, volunteers wrote down either "Will I work on anagrams?" or "I will work on anagrams." In each case the volunteers in the first condition, who were encouraged to keep their minds open by asking "Will I?", performed significantly better on the task. When the researchers applied these experiments to real world activities, the same pattern occurred. Participants were asked to either consider "Will I go to the gym?" or state "I will go to the gym." Those who asked the question (engaging in what the researchers call "interrogative" self-talk) reported stronger subsequent intentions to go to the gym. The researchers found that those people who had been primed with "I will" experienced extrinsic motivation, and talked about feeling guilty or ashamed if they did not succeed in getting fit. Those who had been primed with a question ("Will I?") were intrinsically motivated (e.g. "I want to take more responsibility for my health"). The researchers show that interrogative self-talk leads to intrinsic motivation, and this in turn increases behavioral intention.

We have found that asking questions about a goal opens up wider possibilities, leads to greater motivation from within (rather than adherence to a standard imposed or absorbed from elsewhere) and enhances the sense of freedom of choice. Should coaches put less emphasis on defining goals and assessing client commitment, than on deepening the quality of the client's reflection and imagination about goals? This is an idea we will explore throughout this book.

A second body of recent work has been on the concept of *goal alignment*, with organizations showing increasing concern about whether individuals' goals are congruent with wider organizational objectives (Nankervis et al., 2006).

This idea, which has its foundations in Drucker's MBO, tends to focus on task or performance goals rather than on learning goals. Where coaching is aimed at performance improvement, a key question in contracting may be "How does the goal that we are working on align with other goals, both for the client and for his or her organization?" Similarly, in the context of mentoring or career coaching, it can be argued that alignment between the client's career intentions and the organization's succession planning process is worth considering. At the same time, when learning goals are at the fore for the individual client, yet an organization is seeking alignment with performance or task goals, the coach, client and other stakeholders will need to navigate this so as to manage expectations and facilitate successful outcomes.

Third, recent attempts have been made to examine an often-overlooked issue in research and practice: the *social impact of goal-seeking behavior* or how goal-oriented behaviors impact on others. Poortvliet and Darnon (2010) for example, found that while learning or mastery goals are associated with positive behaviors towards others and openness to opinions, performance goals (which can involve striving to outperform those around one) may result in maladaptive behaviors that are harmful to the collective. Many coaches will have encountered driven managers, who place more importance on reaching targets than on how people reach them. An important outcome of coaching in this context can be to facilitate insight into how these behaviors are impacting others, and also, how they may paradoxically be counter to the client's stated goal. For example, a focus on reaching targets at the expense of relationships may work in the short-term, but if these behaviors are leading to demotivation and staff attrition, those same targets will likely be negatively impacted over the longer-term.

Conclusion

It is clear from history that goal setting and goal management are important issues to individuals and organizations. Over the years, the human tendency to strive toward future ideals has left the realm of the strictly metaphysical or existential, to become an increasingly nuanced and vital science. Our understanding of how people identify and work toward their goals, and how those processes are influenced, is of utmost importance to people who put theory and research into practice: those working as managers, coaches, and mentors.

Building on a rich background and history—from the Würzburg School, to Management by Objectives, to Locke and Latham's seminal work—our aim is to extend the conversation on goal pursuit. In the next chapter we examine current goal-related practices, and we review the recent heated debate over goals.

References

Ach, N. (1951). Determining tendencies: Awareness. In D. Rapaport (Ed.), *Organization and Pathology of Thought*, 15–38. New York: Columbia University Press. (Original work published 1905).

Ach, N. (1935). Analyse des Willens [Analysis of volitions]. In E. Abderhalden (Ed.), *Handbuch der biologischen Arbeitsmethoden* (Vol. 4) VI. Berlin: Urban & Schwarzenberg.

Ajzen, Icek (1991). The theory of planned behavior. *Organizational Behavior and Human Decision Processes, 50*(2), 179–211.

Allen, R.E. (Ed.). (1991). *The Concise Oxford Dictionary of Current English*. (8th ed.) London: Oxford University Press.

Bandura, A. (1986). *Social Foundations of Thought and Action: A Social-Cognitive View*. Englewood Cliffs, NJ: Prentice Hall.

Bandura, A. (1991). Social cognitive theory of self-regulation. *Organizational Behavior and Human Decision Processes, 50*, 248–87.

Brewis, J. (1996). The "making" of the "competent" manager: Competency development, personal effectiveness and Foucault. *Management Learning, 27*(1), 65–86.

Carver, C.S. & Scheier, M.F. (1998). *On the Self-regulation of Behaviour*. New York: Cambridge University Press.

Carver, C.S. & Scheier, M.F. (2002). Control processes and self-organization as complementary principles underlying behaviour. *Personality and Social Psychology Review, 6*(4), 304–15.

Deci, E.L. (1975). *Intrinsic Motivation*. New York: Plenum.

Deming, W.E. (1986). *Out of the Crisis*. Cambridge, MA: MIT Press.

Diener, C.L & Dweck, C.S. (1978). An analysis of learned helplessness: Continuous changes in performance, strategy and achievement cognitions following failure. *Journal of Personality and Social Psychology, 36*, 451–62.

Drucker, P (1954). *The Practice of Management*. New York: Harper & Brothers.

Dweck, C.S. (2006). *Mindset: The New Psychology of Success*. New York: Ballantine Books.

Dweck, C.S. & Leggett, E.L. (1988). A social-cognitive approach to motivation and personality. *Psychology Review, 95,* 256–73.

Elliott, E.S. & Dweck, C.S. (1988). Goals: An approach to motivation and achievement. *Journal of Personality and Social Psychology, 54,* 5–12.

Elliot, A.J. & Fryer, J.W. (2008). The Goal Construct in Psychology. In James Y. Shah & Wendi L. Gardner (Eds), *Handbook of Motivation Science,* 235–50. New York: The Guilford Press.

Ellwood, R.S. & Alles, G.D. (2007). *The Encyclopedia of World Religions, Revised Edition.* New York: DWJ Books, LLC.

Fishbein, M. & Ajzen, I. (1975). *Belief, Attitude, Intention and Behaviour: An Introduction to Theory and Research.* Reading, MA: Addison-Wesley.

Foucault, M. (1975). *Discipline and Punish: The Birth of the Prison.* New York: Random House.

Franklin, B. (1896). *The Autobiography of Benjamin Franklin.* New York: American Book Company. (Original work published in 1791).

Gollwitzer, P.M. (1999). Implementation intentions: Strong effects of simple plans. *American Psychologist, 54*(7), 493–503.

Gollwitzer, P.M. & Sheeran, S. (2006). Implementation intentions and goal achievement: A meta-analysis of effects and processes. *Advances in Experimental Social Psychology, 38,* 69–119.

Hale, J.L., Householder, B.J., & Greene, K.L. (2003). The theory of reasoned action. In J.P. Dillard & M. Pfau (Eds), *The Persuasion Handbook: Developments in Theory and Practice,* 259–86. Thousand Oaks, CA: Sage.

Hergenhahn, B.R. (2009). *An Introduction to the History of Psychology,* (6th ed.). Belmont, CA: Wadsworth.

Hoffmann, R.G., Rodrigue, J.R., & Johnson, J.H. (1999). Effectiveness of a school-based program to enhance knowledge of sun exposure: Attitudes toward sun exposure and sunscreen use among children. *Children's Health Care, 28,* 69–86.

Irwin, T. & Fine, G. (1996). *Aristotle: Introductory Readings.* Indianapolis: Hackett Publishing.

Jacques, R. (1996). *Manufacturing the Employee.* London: Sage.

Johnson, H.T. & Bröms, A. (2000). *Profit Beyond Measure.* New York: Free Press.

Király, I., Jovanovic, B., Prinz, W., Aschersleben, G., & Gergely, G. (2003) The early origins of goal attribution in infancy, *Consciousness and Cognition, 12*(4), 752–69.

Kerr, S. & Landauer, S. (2004). Using stretch goals to promote organizational effectiveness and personal growth: General Electric and Goldman Sachs. *Academy of Management Executive, 18*(4), 134–8.

Krames, J.A. (2002) *The Jack Welch Lexicon of Leadership*. New York: McGraw-Hill.

Latham, G.P. & Locke, E.A. (1975). Increasing productivity with decreasing time limits: A field replication of Parkinson's law. *Journal of Applied Psychology, 60,* 524–26.

Lewin, K. (1961). Intention, will and need. (D. Rapaport, Trans.). In T. Shipley (Ed.) *Classics in Psychology,* 1234–89. New York: Philosophical Library. (Original work published 1926).

Locke, E.A. (1968). Toward a theory of task motivation and incentives. *Organizational Behavior and Human Performance, 3*(2), 157–89.

Locke, E.A. & Latham, G.P. (1990). *A Theory of Goal Setting and Task Performance.* Englewood Cliffs, NJ: Prentice Hall.

Locke, E.A. & Latham, G.P. (2002). Building a practically useful theory of goal-setting and task motivation: A 35-year odyssey. *American Psychologist, 57,* 705–17.

Locke, E.A. & Latham G.P. (2009). Has goal setting gone wild, or have its attackers abandoned good scholarship? *Academy of Management Perspectives* (February),17–23.

Locke, E.A., Shaw, K.N., Saari, L.M., & Latham, G.P. (1981). Goal Setting and Task Performance: 1969–1980. *Psychological Bulletin, 90*(1), 125–52.

Mace, C.A. (1935). *Incentives: Some Experimental Studies (Report No. 72).* London: Industrial Health Research Board.

Maslow, A.H. (1943). A theory of human motivation. *Psychological Review, 50,* 370–96.

Maslow, A.H. (1954). *Motivation and Personality.* New York: Harper & Row.

Nankervis, A.R. & Compton, R. (2006). Performance management: Theory in practice? *Asia Pacific Journal of Human Resources, 44*(1), 83–101.

Ordóñez, L.D., Schweitzer, M.E., Galinsky, A.D., & Bazerman, M.H. (2009). Goals gone wild: The systematic side effects of overprescribing goal setting. *Academy of Management Perspectives, 23*(1), 6–16.

Peltonen, T. (2012). Critical approaches to international human resource management. In G.K. Stahl, I. Björkman, & S. Morris (Eds), *Handbook of Research in International Human Resource Management* (2nd ed.), 532–48. Northampton, MA: Edward Elgar Publishing.

Pfeffer, J. & Veiga, J.F. (1999). Putting people first for organizational success. *Academy of Management Executive, 13*(2), 37–48.

Poortvliet, P.M. & Darnon, C. (2010). Toward a More Social understanding of Achievement Goals: The Interpersonal effects of Mastery and Performance Goals. *Current Directions in Psychological Science, 19*(5), 324–28.

Riediger, M., Freund, A.M., & Baltes, P.B. (2005). Managing life through personal goals: intergoal facilitation and intensity of goal pursuit in younger and older adulthood. *Journal of Gerontology: Psychological Sciences, 60B*(2), 84–91.

Ryan, T.A. (1970). *Intentional Behavior.* New York: Ronald Press.

Seijts, G.H., Latham, G.P., Tasa, K., & Latham, B.W. (2004). Goal setting and goal orientation: An integration of two different if related literatures. *Academy of Management Journal, 47*(2), 227–39.

Sejwacz, D., Ajzen, I., & Fishbein, M. (1980). Predicting and understanding weight loss: Intentions, behaviors, and outcomes. In I. Ajzen & M. Fishbein (Eds), *Understanding Attitudes and Predicting Social Behaviour,* 101–12. Englewood Cliffs, NJ: Prentice Hall.

Senay, I., Albarracin, D., & Noguchi, K. (2010). Motivating Goal-Directed Behavior through Introspective Self-Talk: The Role of the Interrogative Form of Simple Future Tense. *Psychological Science, 21*(4), 499–504.

Shah, J.Y. (2005). The automatic pursuit and management of goals. *Current Directions in Psychological Science, 14*(1), 10–13.

Taylor, F.W. (1911). *The Principles of Scientific Management.* New York: Harper & Brothers.

VandeWalle, D., Ganesan, S., Challagalla, G.N., & Brown, S.P. (2000). An integrated model of feedback seeking behaviour: Disposition, context and cognition. *Journal of Applied Psychology, 85*(6), 996–1003.

Wahba, M.A. & Bridwell, L.G. (1976). Maslow reconsidered: A review of research on the need hierarchy theory. *Organizational Behavior and Human Performance, 15*(2), 212–40.

Winters, D. & Latham, G.P. (1996). The effect of learning outcome goals on a simple versus a complex task. *Group and Organization Management, 21,* 235–50.

Wood, R. & Bandura, A. (1989). Impact of conceptions of ability on self-regulatory mechanisms and complex decision making. *Journal of Personality and Social Psychology, 56*(3), 407–15.

Wren, D.A. & Bedeian, A.G. (2009). *The Evolution of Management Thought.* Hoboken, NJ: Wiley.

Yukl, G.A. & Latham, G.P. (1978). Interrelationships among employee participation, individual differences, goal difficulty, goal acceptance, goal instrumentality, and performance. *Personnel Psychology, 31,* 305–23.

2

Goals in Coaching and Mentoring: The Current State of Play

David Clutterbuck and Susan A. David

Goals and goal setting are modus operandi in business, coaching and mentoring. So embedded are they in organizational life that we rarely stop to consider what we are doing when we set goals, why we are setting them, or how we can do this better. In recent years however, advances in the fields of neuroscience; the psychology of motivation, affect and change; and organizational behavior, have begun to offer new insights into goal setting. These demand a rethinking and a revision of goal setting theory and practice. This book invites leaders in the field to widen and expand the traditional perspective on goal setting, such that we can manage goals with greater levels of expertise and, ultimately, better serve our clients. In this chapter we examine current goal-related practices as well as recent debates over goal setting and management, and introduce new ways of thinking about the standard paradigm of goal pursuit.

Goals by Acronym: GROW and SMART

Today, two acronyms dominate the practice of goal pursuit. GROW is a sequence for goal management, while SMART is a framework for goal setting. Due to their popularity in the fields of coaching and mentoring, these acronyms appear frequently throughout this book. Here we describe them, and raise what we believe are critical questions in relation to current goal-related knowledge and practice.

GROW AND OTHER SEQUENCES FOR MANAGING GOALS

The GROW model of coaching was developed in the UK and gained popularity in the 1980s and 1990s. Among those identified as its originators are Graham Alexander, Alan Fine, Timothy Gallwey (1974, 2000), and Sir John Whitmore (2002; also see Chapter 12).

Table 2.1   Whitmore's GROW sequence of questioning in coaching

GOAL setting for the session as well as short- and long-term.
REALITY checking to explore the current situation.
OPTIONS and alternative strategies or courses of action.
WHAT is to be done, WHEN, by WHOM and the WILL to do it.

One way to think about the positioning of goals in the coaching or mentoring relationship is to explore where they occur in the sequence of a single coaching session. GROW places goals at the beginning, with Whitmore (2002) claiming that:

> ... goals based on current reality alone are liable to be negative, a response to the problem, limited by past performance, lacking in creativity due to a simple extrapolation, in smaller increments than what may be achievable, or even counterproductive ... Goals formed by ascertaining the ideal long-term solution, and then determining realistic steps toward that ideal, are generally far more inspiring, creative and motivating. (pp. 54–5)

Whitmore proposes that setting goals before considering the current reality allows mentees and clients to think beyond the constraints of their present circumstances.

Contrary to Whitmore's argument that goals are best set at the start, some models of coaching place goals later in the sequence. In his recent work, Grant (2011) emphasizes self-regulation and has developed a model, REGROW, where goals are only set after stages of Review and Evaluation. Coaching frameworks based on Egan's (2002) skilled helper model have goals or the change agenda as the fifth stage of a nine-stage process. Richard Kilburg (2000) places goals as the fourth of a seven-stage approach, which he describes as a fluid process, explaining that "sometimes the shift [to goals] is not clear and we just progressively deepen the discussion about a particular topic" (p. 82). Pemberton (2006) saves goals (or Targeting as she calls it) for the fifth of her seven-stage STARTED model.

Peseschkian's Positive Psychotherapy (PPT), with its focus on the patient's strengths and capacity to help him or herself (Peseschkian and Tritt, 1998) has much in common with some coaching approaches. PPT's treatment strategy involves five stages, with goals figuring into the last. In this final stage, the patient is asked, "What would you like to do, when no more problems are left to solve?" (Peseschkian and Tritt, 1998, p. 98). This "expansion of goals" stage is intended to encourage patients to look toward the future, but only after having engaged the therapeutic process.

These differing models lead us to raise a question: Are goals the starting point and the primary focus of coaching and mentoring conversations? Or do they emerge out of a lengthy, more open-ended exploration of the issues? This is a topic that will be touched on frequently in the chapters of this book.

SMART GOAL SETTING

A coach or mentor who has decided *where* to situate goals in the coaching sequence must also know *how* to approach goal setting. The most popular framework for goal setting in organizations is known by the acronym SMART. SMART is often attributed to Peter Drucker or Locke and Latham (see Chapter 1, p. 9), and while its use has presumably grown out of their work, its origins remain obscure. One of the first published uses of the term appears in a management article by Doran (1981).

The SMART framework defines effective goals as Specific, Measurable, Attainable, Realistic and Time-bound (Doran, 1981), with some variation in descriptions of what each letter stands for (for example, Whitmore (2002) uses "Agreed" rather than "Attainable"). The framework holds that goals lacking these SMART characteristics will be overly ambiguous and demotivating, and are thus unlikely to be achieved.

One of the questions we raise in this book is whether an overreliance on SMART goals hinders organizational effectiveness. Might the SMART framework be inappropriate for some, if not many, types of organizational challenges? Indeed, there is a growing and sophisticated rethinking of goals in coaching that suggests that goals of different kinds can suit differing circumstances. For example, Anthony Grant (2007; also see Chapter 4, pp. 60–63) suggests that goals can be:

- Proximal (close)   or   Distal (distant)

- Concrete   or   Abstract

- Approach   or   Avoidance

- Performance   or   Learning

Clarifying these distinctions serves to move the practice of crafting goals beyond the default SMART paradigm. We are able to recognize that distant goals may be difficult to define using time parameters; abstract goals are anything but specific or measurable; and avoidance goals may be "maintainable" rather than "attainable."

Further, it seems the SMART criteria are better suited to performance than learning goals. SMART includes performance criteria, such as measurement and time constraints, that may activate a fixed mindset (for more information on performance and learning goals, see Chapter 1, p. 13). While it may be useful to measure performance as people build competence over time, activating a fixed mindset in the initial stages of goal setting is counter-productive to learning goals. It encourages people to try to prove their competence, rather than to develop it.

Considering SMART at the organizational level, one of the possibilities we entertain in this book is that a preoccupation with SMART goals can dull responsiveness to the complex and emergent nature of organizational life, as well as the coaching and mentoring engagements that take place within it. This, in turn, can hinder performance. Weick and Sutcliffe's (2007) work on High Reliability Organizations (HROs) — organizations that successfully navigate complexity and avoid catastrophe — supports this hypothesis. They critique the use of overly scripted approaches to organizational issues, warning that rote protocols can lead to "mindlessness". They explain:

> *A tendency towards mindlessness is characterized by a style of mental functioning in which people follow recipes, impose old categories to classify what they see, act with some rigidity, operate on automatic pilot, and mislabel unfamiliar new contexts as familiar old ones.*

A mindless mental style works to conceal problems that are worsening.
(Weick and Sutcliffe, 2007, p. 89)

Mindfulness, on the other hand, involves a resistance to over-simplification, sensitivity to events as they unfold, and an "encouragement of a fluid decision-making system" (Weick and Sutcliffe, 2007, p. vii).

A concept that has gained considerable traction in recent years within the clinical and research communities, as well as popular culture, mindfulness has been defined as "bringing one's complete attention to the present experience on a moment-to-moment basis" (Marlatt and Kristeller, 1999, p. 68).

When SMART goals are used habitually, and perhaps mindlessly, circumstances are viewed through a narrow lens. This can lead client and coach down a path that is overly constrictive, and at worst, completely off course. While SMART clearly has its place in the realm of goal setting, we hope this book will call attention to its limitations, and support coaches and mentors in advancing the practice.

Goals Gone Wild

Until recently, the literature on coaching and mentoring has made the case for goals in general, and for SMART goals in particular, both consistently and uncritically (e.g. Zachary, 2000; Whitmore, 2002; Downey, 2003; Connor and Pokora, 2007). A significant development in goals research, and the one most relevant to coaching and mentoring, is the clash of Titans over whether goal theory, as described by Locke and Latham (1990), is actually effective.

The recent argument concerns an article written in 2009 by four academics, Lisa Ordóñez, from the University of Arizona, Maurice Schweitzer, from Wharton, Adam Galinsky, from Kellogg, and Max Bazerman, from Harvard, who collectively critique what they describe as "overprescribing goal setting" in organizations. In doing so, they have taken on the doyens of goal theory and research, Edwin Locke and Gary Latham, who provide a stinging rebuttal (2009) that questions the quality of the science behind Ordóñez and colleagues' challenge to established theories of goal management.

At the heart of the debate is the claim by Locke and Latham (2006) that "So long as a person is committed to the goal, has the required ability to attain it, and does not have conflicting goals, there is a positive, linear relationship between goal difficulty and task performance" (p. 265). Many writers on goals build on this relationship to infer that the more specific the goal is (the SMARTer it is), the more likely it is to be achieved (e.g. Whitmore, 2002; Downey, 2003).

Ordóñez and colleagues (2009) raise a host of concerns with organizational efforts to ensure that people set and pursue very specific, challenging goals. Here we summarize a number of their arguments and provide links to coaching and mentoring.

THE PROBLEM OF SPECIFICITY

Ordóñez's team contends that because goals focus attention, they reduce people's awareness of other factors that may be important to success. The lack of context makes it easier to focus on the *wrong* goals, and we would add that it also makes people less able to recognize when a goal has become inappropriate. Setting and pursuing specific goals, Ordóñez et al. (2009) say, "may cause people to ignore important dimensions of performance that are not specified by the goal-setting system" (p. 8).

In a working environment, coaches have a responsibility to help clients recognize and explore the big picture, and to understand the systemic nature of their dilemmas. Yet in many instances there is pressure to focus coaching on very specific goals, often set by a boss rather than the client. Unfortunately, the simplest things to measure are not necessarily the most important factors in achieving the overall purpose of a team. The coach can find himself or herself colluding in focusing on the wrong goals, or in avoiding goals that are more important, but more difficult to measure.

A second proposed problem with specificity is that narrow goals can promote "myopic, short-term behavior that harms the organization in the long run" (Ordóñez et al., 2009, p. 8). Ordóñez and her colleagues point to research that links organizations' short-term targets, such as quarterly earnings reports, with failure to invest in the research and development that would lead to long-term growth (Cheng, Subramanyam, and Zhang, 2005). This relates to another real dilemma in coaching. Particularly during assignments of short duration, it is tempting to measure the success of coaching in terms of whether the coach succeeds in helping the client hit short-term targets. But does this bring about durable change? Or does the coach's need to demonstrate his or her ability to deliver overshadow the client's need for lasting personal growth? Many of the experienced coaches we have spoken to express concerns about this potential conflict of interest, and it is an issue that is frequently raised during coach supervision.

THE RISKS OF CHALLENGE

Ordóñez and colleagues (2009) contend "People motivated by specific, challenging goals tend to adopt riskier strategies and choose riskier gambles than do those with less challenging or vague goals" (p. 9). This claim is supported by research: Larrick, Heath, and Wu (2009) showed that participants who were given specific, challenging goals in negotiation and gambling tasks adopted significantly riskier strategies than their counterparts who were encouraged to "do their best". In some cases, this led to poorer task outcomes.

These observations bring us to a second concern associated with challenging goals: they can induce unethical behavior, especially where people just miss difficult targets (Schweitzer, Ordóñez, and Douma, 2004). For example, Cadsby, Song, and Tapon (2010) found that people were significantly more likely to cheat on a simple task if they were challenged to perform at the high level of the 85th percentile, as compared to being paid with a direct pay-for-performance scheme, or a tournament-based scheme in which they were compared to other participants.

We believe that, like medical doctors, coaches should be expected to "do no harm". Part of a coach's role, therefore, is to help clients contextualize issues and recognize the nature and scale of risk. Coaches have a critical role to play in helping clients maintain contact with their personal values and to test goals and goal-oriented behaviors against their internal "ethical monitor". In our experience, the creation of reflective space is critical to this. Research indicates that impulses win when people have been working hard and exhaust their reservoirs of self-control (Baumeister, 2002). Creating opportunities for quiet reflection provides a balance.

THE DRAWBACKS OF COMPETITIVE PERFORMANCE

Ordóñez and colleagues (2009) propose "the narrow focus of specific goals can inspire performance but prevent learning" (p. 11). In some cases goals also promote competition while simultaneously discouraging cooperation, altruism, and extra-role behavior. Coaches can help clients and sponsors shift attention from performance goals to learning goals (see Chapter 1, p. 13), or adopt a combination of the two. Additionally, coaches can support pro-social workplace behaviors. It is important to consider the purpose of coaching. Is it for a narrow, performance-related objective, or does it have a wider learning purpose? What is the psychological contract between coach, client and sponsor?

THREATS TO MOTIVATION

Goals may increase extrinsic motivation, but also harm intrinsic motivation. As Ordóñez and colleagues (2009) observe, "Managers may think that others need to be motivated by specific, challenging goals far more often than they [subordinates] actually do" (p. 11). Shifting an employee's focus from internal to external rewards is likely to have negative effects on a host of important work-related phenomena, such as job engagement (Deci et al., 1999).

For coaches, identifying whether goals are intrinsically or extrinsically driven is critical in understanding a client's motivation. It can be argued that extrinsically driven goals may be much more difficult to link to personal values, which would tend to impel the style of coaching to a relatively mechanical form of skills acquisition or performance management. An issue to consider is how long a given change can last if it is driven mainly by extrinsic goals.

CONTINUING THE CONVERSATION ON GOALS

Locke and Latham (1984) themselves recognize the dark side of goals and have actively attempted to highlight the dangers of unintelligent or inappropriate goal-focus. Similar to Ordóñez et al. (2009), they identify a range of problems arising from goal setting—specifically, excessive risk-taking, increased stress, feelings of failure, using goals as a ceiling for performance, ignoring non-goal areas, short-range thinking, and dishonesty and cheating.

Whatever the rights and wrongs of this particular academic argument, Ordóñez and her colleagues have provided a valuable opportunity to challenge unintelligent or dangerous goal management and to bring attention to the down side of goal setting. They suggest ten questions to assess goals, each of which we find relevant to management, coaching, and mentoring.

Table 2.2   Ten questions to ask before setting goals (Ordóñez et al., 2009)

Question to ask before setting goals	Why is this important to ask?	Possible remediation
Are the goals too specific?	Narrow goals can blind people to important aspects of a problem.	Be sure that goals are comprehensive and include all of the critical components for firm success (e.g. quantity and quality).
Are the goals too challenging?	What will happen if goals are not met? How will individual employees and outcomes be evaluated? Will failure harm motivation and self-efficacy?	Provide skills and training to enable employees to reach goals. Avoid harsh punishment for failure to reach a goal.
Who sets the goals?	People will become more committed to goals they help to set. At the same time, people may be tempted to set easy-to-reach goals.	Allow transparency in the goal setting process and involve more than one person or unit.
Is the time horizon appropriate?	Short-term goals may harm long-term performance.	Be sure that short-term efforts to reach a goal do not harm investment in long-term outcomes.
How might goals influence risk taking?	Unmet goals may induce risk taking.	Be sure to articulate acceptable levels of risk.
How might goals motivate unethical behavior?	Goals narrow focus. Employees with goals are less likely to recognize ethical issues, and more likely to rationalize their unethical behavior.	Multiple safeguards may be necessary to ensure ethical behavior while attaining goals (e.g. leaders as exemplars of ethical behavior, making the costs of cheating far greater than the benefit, strong oversight).
Can goals be idiosyncratically tailored for individual abilities and circumstances while preserving fairness?	Individual differences may make standardized goals inappropriate, yet unequal goals may be unfair.	If possible, strive to set goals that use common standards and account for individual variation.
How will goals influence organizational culture?	Individual goals may harm cooperation and corrode organizational culture.	If cooperation is essential, consider setting team-based rather than individual goals. Think carefully about the values that the specific, challenging goals convey.
Are individuals intrinsically motivated?	Goal setting can harm intrinsic motivation.	Assess intrinsic motivation and avoid setting goals when intrinsic motivation is high.
What type of goal (performance or learning) is most appropriate given the ultimate objectives of the organization?	By focusing on performance goals, employees may fail to search for better strategies and fail to learn.	In complex, changing environments, learning goals may be more effective than performance goals.

We have found these questions to be useful in coaching and mentoring programs: they help the client and client sponsors reflect on what they want to achieve from the intervention. This observation reinforces our belief that goals in coaching should not be treated lightly or haphazardly, and that focusing too closely on goals before understanding context can be dangerous for the client and possibly unethical for the coach.

Lessons From Diversity of Concept

The considerable diversity of views about goal setting and management teaches us that the role of goals in coaching is more complex than it might initially appear. It is possible that the various theories about when and how to pursue goals are correct, but only some of the time. As we have reviewed in this chapter, goals can have a variety of characteristics, and not all of them are SMART. They can narrow or enlarge choices; focus on the short- or long-term; be ends to themselves, or stepping stones to other, perhaps less well-defined but more important goals.

In our own work we have observed that progress toward goals may be affected by many factors, such as:

- Motivation (How important is it to you?)

- Contextual awareness (How accurate is your picture of external factors that may help or hinder achievement?)

- Ownership (Who shares this goal and has a stake in its outcome?)

- Clarity (Are you able to envision the outcome?)

- Measurability (Will you be able to assess the outcome?)

- Stability (Is it a fixed or moving target?)

- Link to personal values (Is it aligned with an inner "sense of rightness"?)

- Previous experience of goal pursuit (Have you had success in the past?)

For the coach or mentor, the process of helping a client set and follow through on goals is not necessarily a straightforward one. To begin, it is important to establish the point to which the goal has evolved, in order to select an appropriate intervention strategy. It is also important to be clear about the kind of goal, as different strategies are indicated for different goal types. Finally, the coach or mentor needs to understand—and help the client understand—the context in which the goal is set, which may help or hinder its achievement.

Increasing emphasis is being placed on coaching and mentoring as systemic processes, where awareness of the client as influencing and being influenced by a number of systems is core to identifying and working with their issues (Hawkins, 2006; Whittington, 2010). This widens the view of goals beyond the level of the individual.

Goal Evolution: A Challenge to Current Theory

Traditional goal theory depicts goals as relatively static. You decide what you want to achieve, gather the necessary resources and motivation and take appropriate action. With apt, positive feedback you continue until the goal is achieved. Yet the way clients and mentees describe how they approach goals is very different from the theory—and certainly a lot messier.

The following is an attempt to capture the pattern of what actually happens in coaching and mentoring practice. It is not yet underpinned by empirical research, but our intention is that this model will spur empirical testing—our own and others'.

Firstly, this model recognizes that goals are not just formed spontaneously. There has to be a *stimulus*, which usually has both internal and external components—a combination of what others expect of you and what you expect of yourself.

From the stimulus emerges a *reactive goal*—an instinctive response that gives new purpose to our scanning of the environment. The reactive goal may be relatively ill defined at this stage. It may also be more motivated by avoiding pain (moving away from something rather than moving towards) and involve some instinctive steps towards achieving the reactive goal.

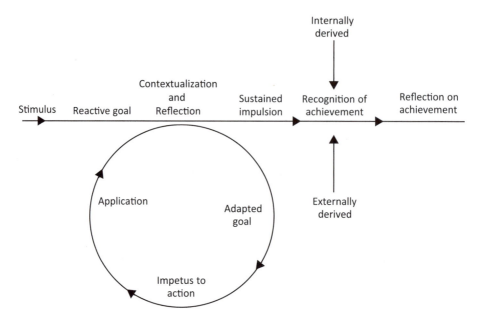

Figure 2.1   Goal evolution

With time to distance oneself from the stimulus, people can take a calmer, more rational look at the goal. *Reflection and contextualization* allow us to reposition and recast the goal in the light of the bigger picture and other goals we may be pursuing. This is also an opportunity to relate the goal more closely to our values. In many, if not most cases, the goal is substantially amended at this point, as we now see the issue from different perspectives.

From this process of reflection and contextualization, therefore, comes an *adapted goal*, modified to take account of our perception of internal and external realities. The process of adaptation is often very satisfying. People describe feeling more assured in their judgment and more confident in their ability to achieve the goal. Adapted goals are more likely to be "approach" goals, or a mixture of "approach" and "avoidance".

This new confidence provides an *impetus to action*—motivation to make the goal happen—which in turn leads to changes in behavior or processes, or *application*. Application does not necessarily mean that the change is sustained; rather that the individual feels able to experiment in ways that will, they hope, lead to achieving the goal. The experience of application may be either positive (making clear progress towards the adapted goal) or negative (making little or no progress, or making progress in the wrong direction).

Whether the experience is positive or negative, it leads (at least within a coaching or mentoring context) to a further period of *reflection and contextualization*. This either leads in turn to another adapted goal (repeating the cycle through impetus to action and application back to further reflection and contextualization); or the learner moves on, being sufficiently confident in the "rightness" of the goal and the path towards it. Success fuels success in what can be described as a *sustained impulsion*. An extra boost may come at key points from *recognition of achievement* as milestones are passed. This recognition may be internally generated (self-congratulation/self-satisfaction) or externally generated (for example, from feedback by peers or by the coach/mentor.)

Finally, an essential element in consolidating the gains appears to be another period of reflection, this time *reflection on achievement*. The goal, having been accomplished, takes on significance beyond its intrinsic value. It is a symbol of what we can achieve and hence a motivator to pursue other, perhaps more challenging goals.

Conclusion

Whether it is goals that have gone wild, or simply the academic conversations surrounding them, the recent debates call for new thinking and research to inform the practice of goals in coaching and mentoring. The next chapter reviews some of our own research on the practices and attitudes that coaches have adopted in relationship to goals.

References

Baumeister, R.F. (2002). Ego depletion and self-control failure: An energy model of the self's executive function. *Self and Identity, 1*, 129–36.

Cadsby, C.B., Song, F., & Tapon, F. (2010). Are you paying your employees to cheat? An experimental investigation. *The B.E. Journal of Economic Analysis & Policy, 10*(1), article 35.

Cheng, M., Subramanyam, K. R., & Zhang, Y. (2005). *Earnings Guidance and Managerial Myopia* (Working Paper). Los Angeles: University of Southern California.

Connor, M. & Pokora, J. (2007). *Coaching and Mentoring at Work*. Maidenhead: McGraw-Hill/Open University Press.

Deci, E.L., Koestner, R., & Ryan, R.M. (1999). A meta-analytic review of experiments examining the effects of extrinsic rewards on intrinsic motivation. *Psychological Bulletin, 125*(6), 627–68.

Doran, G.T. (1981). There's a S.M.A.R.T. way to write management's goals and objectives. *Management Review, 70*(11), 35–6.

Downey, M. (2003). *Effective Coaching: Lessons From the Coach's Coach*. Mason, OH: Texere.

Egan, G. (2002). *The Skilled Helper: A Problem-Management and Opportunity-Development Approach to Helping*. (7th ed.). Belmont, CA: Thomson/Wadsworth.

Gallwey, T. (1974). *The Inner Game of Tennis: The Classic Guide to the Mental Side of Peak Performance*. New York: Random House.

Gallwey, T. (2000). *The Inner Game of Work*. New York: Random House.

Grant, A.M. (2007). When own goals are a winner. *Coaching at Work, 2*(2), 32–5.

Grant, A.M. (2011). Is it time to REGROW the GROW model? Issues related to teaching coaching session structures. *The Coaching Psychologist, 7*(2), 118–26.

Hawkins, P. & Smith, N. (2006). *Coaching, Mentoring and Organizational Consultancy*. Berkshire: Open University Press.

Kilburg, R.R. (2000). *Executive Coaching: Developing Managerial Wisdom in a World of Chaos*. Washington, DC: American Psychological Association.

Larrick, R.P., Heath, C., & Wu, G. (2009). Goal-induced risk taking in negotiation and decision making. *Social Cognition, 27*, 342–64.

Locke, E.A. (1984). *Goal Setting for Individuals, Groups, and Organizations*. Chicago: Science Research Associates.

Locke, E.A. & Latham, G.P. (1990). *A Theory of Goal Setting and Task Performance*. Englewood Cliffs, NJ: Prentice Hall.

Locke, E.A. & Latham, G.P. (2006). New directions in goal-setting theory. *Current Directions in Psychological Science, 15*(5), 265–8.

Locke, E.A. & Latham, G.P. (2009). Has goal setting gone wild, or have its attackers abandoned good scholarship? *Academy of Management Perspectives, 23*(1), 17–23.

Marlatt, G.A. & Kristeller, J.L. (1999). Mindfulness and meditation. In W.R. Miller (Ed.). *Integrating Spirituality in Treatment: Resources for Practitioners*, 67–84. Washington, DC: American Psychological Association.

Ordóñez, L.D., Schweitzer, M.E., Galinsky, A.E., & Bazerman, M.H. (2009). Goals gone wild: The systematic side effects of overprescribing goal setting. *Academy of Management Perspectives, 23*(1), 6–16.

Pemberton, C. (2006). *Coaching to Solutions: A Manager's Toolkit for Performance Delivery*. Oxford: Butterworth-Heinemann.

Peseschkian, N. & Tritt, K. (1998). Positive Psychotherapy: Effectiveness study and quality assurance. *The European Journal of Psychotherapy, Counselling & Health, 1*(1), 93–104.

Schweitzer, M.E., Ordóñez, L., & Douma, B. (2004). Goal setting as a motivator of unethical behaviour. *Academy of Management Journal, 47*(3), 422–32.

Weick, K.E. & Sutcliffe, K.M. (2007). *Managing the Unexpected.* (2nd ed.). San Francisco: Jossey-Bass.

Whitmore, J. (2002). *Coaching for Performance: GROWing People, Performance, and Purpose.* (3rd ed.). London: Nicholas Brealey.

Whittington, J. (2010). *Coaching Constellations: A Practical Guide to a Profound Methodology.* London: Kogan Page.

Zachary, L.J. (2000). *The Mentor's Guide.* San Francisco: Jossey-Bass.

3

Researching Goals in Coaching

Susan A. David, David Megginson, and Christina Congleton

It is clear that models such as GROW and SMART are popular in the areas of management, coaching, and mentoring. How are these models and others like them implemented in practice? What outcomes do coaches, mentors, and their clients observe? Research helps us to find answers to these questions, as well as continue to refine coaching theory and practice. Indeed, calls for rigorous coaching research are plentiful, with visions for establishing clearer definitions of coaching; elucidating the scope, structure, and content of coaching engagements; and professionalizing the field (e.g. Feldman and Lankau, 2005; Stober and Perry, 2005; Bennett, 2006; Linley, 2006).

One source of information is through the analysis of quantitative data from surveys and psychological assessments. Another is through analyzing qualitative data collected in interviews, focus groups, or by making observations in the field. In this chapter we describe our own research on goals in coaching, and explore what this new evidence may mean.

Reviewing the Literature

We conducted a secondary analysis of Anthony Grant's (2010) compilation of abstracts from quality articles and theses on coaching. We searched these 635 articles for the term "goal", and found it mentioned in 83 of them. Only two of these however, Hughes (2003) and Stelter (2009), include any critique of the practice of goal setting. The remaining articles treat goal setting as a given—what we as coaches do. Goals are described as making a difference to performance, giving purpose to conversations, matching the expectations of the individualistic Western worker, and meeting the needs of clients and sponsors (Grant, 2010). The concerns presented by Ordóñez et al. (2009) have yet to reach the realm of coaching and mentoring.

IDENTIFYING THEMES

We also performed an analysis of the contemporary and classic coaching literature. We selected ten books that were diverse in their orientation or root discipline, and noted themes and issues related to goal orientation (Bachkirova, 2011; de Haan, 2008; Driver, 2011; Garvey, 2011; Hunt and Weintraub, 2002; Sandler, 2011; Starr, 2012; Szabó and Meier, 2009; Whitmore, 2002; Wilson, 2007). We identified the following as significant themes in goal pursuit:

- client-centeredness

- alignment

- ownership

- personal meaning

- holism

- clarity

- control

- positivity

- challenge

- prioritization

- action

- relationship

- completion

Each of these points is discussed below. They represent a summary of conventional best practice in goal orientation, in the context of coaching and mentoring.

Client-centeredness

Many writers on coaching stress the primacy of the client's agenda. It is the client who defines what he or she wants to achieve, at which point the coach and client can agree on desired outcomes (Whitmore, 2002; Driver 2011; Starr, 2012).

Alignment

Some authors emphasize the need for multiple parties to identify and align with the goals of coaching. Sandler (2011) focuses on the three-way contract between coach, client and line manager. Hunter and Weintraub (2002) include the client's work group, and Whitmore (2002) suggests that "all the parties involved" (p. 62) should agree on goals.

Ownership

A number of authors contend that for coaching to be effective, clients need to take ownership of goals. Starr (2012) recommends that coaches encourage clients to declare what it is they want, and Wilson (2007) argues that this should be done to reinforce motivation even when goals are mandated by others. Downey (2003, p. 142) says that there is always room for private as well as public goals in coaching. Driver (2011) adds that coaches should have clients ask themselves whether the goals are truly their own.

Personal meaning

Goal orientation and in particular goal setting can be seen as a dull routine. Writers challenge this stereotype, however, asserting that a goal can be a "personal dream, a vision that ignites action" (Whitmore, 2002, p. 59), and that goals should be deeply desired (Wilson, 2007).

Holism

While Wilson (2007) encourages setting holistic goals, a number of writers contend that even when goals are very specific, coaching should embrace the whole person. Bachkirova (2011) and Garvey (2011) advocate for holism, rather than narrow focus on the client's skills and knowledge. Hunt and Weintraub (2002) stress that holistic does not mean complicated: however comprehensive the coaching approach, only a small number of goals should be set.

Clarity

Wilson (2007) and Szabó and Meier (2009) advocate for helping clients establish a clear picture of their desired lives. Like Szabó and Meier, Starr (2012) explains this can be accomplished by inviting clients to explore their purpose in detail, thus bringing their goals to life with precision and clarity.

Control

The attainment of goals needs to be within the sphere of influence of the client. Both Whitmore (2002) and Wilson (2007) assert that it is crucial to choose performance goals that fall within the client's sphere of control. Driver (2011) takes a psychological approach, focusing on the client's expectation of success. High expectation of success leads to motivated, persistent effort to achieve.

Positivity

Elsewhere in this book we make a distinction between approach and avoidance goals (see Chapters 1 and 4), and we see a place for both. However, many authors seem to focus on approach goals. Whitmore (2002) and Wilson (2007) say goals should be expressed positively. Solutions-focused coaches Szabó and Meier (2009) suggest that this is done by starting with the end in mind.

Challenge

Consistent with Locke and Latham's (1990) theory of goal setting, coaching authors such as Whitmore (2002) describe challenge as a crucial characteristic of effective goals. Wilson (2007) encourages coaches to motivate clients to set their sights higher, and Hunt and Weintraub (2002) state that goals should be appropriately challenging.

Prioritization

Wilson (2007) advocates for prioritizing goals. Her somewhat mechanistic model contrasts with Driver's (2011) psychological orientation, which encourages focus on intrinsically motivating goals.

Action

Coaches assist clients in identifying pathways to goal realization. In order to differentiate coaching from performance management, Hunt and Weintraub (2002) emphasize that the plan for implementation needs to be minimal, and Driver (2011) simply suggests that there should be a mechanism for goal achievement. The "O" in the GROW model (Whitmore, 2002) stands for "options", meaning that coach and client generate a range of potential goal-related action options.

Relationship

A number of authors emphasize the importance of the coaching relationship in goal pursuit. De Haan's (2008) book *Relational Coaching* focuses on this aspect of the change process. The relationship is not an end in itself but rather, as stated by Bachkirova (2011), a dimension of coaching that ultimately contributes to goal achievement. Sandler (2011) stresses the importance of what some authors call the "working alliance" in coaching.

Completion

Wilson (2007) notes that goals often linger for years, draining people of energy. She suggests that simply highlighting what needs to be done and getting it down on paper is enough to trigger action, as people feel satisfied by a sense of completion. Szabó and Meier (2009) emphasize the need to be ready to end a coaching engagement once the client is on his or her way (hence their reference to their process as brief coaching). Starr (2012) advocates for identifying end-points to conversations.

Surveying Practitioners

Because goals remain largely unquestioned in the coaching literature, we conducted a survey to examine the current role of goals in coach practice. Specifically, we wanted to test whether goal orientation differed according to the coach's geographical region, coaching education, or years of coaching experience. We composed a questionnaire that contained ten goal-related items, and asked coaches to rate these questions on a scale of 1 to 5, from "never" to "always". The questionnaire was distributed to coaches in the United States and Europe, who had a range of experience, and were active in their own development either through attending conferences or a higher education course. We received 194 responses—45 from Europe, and 149 from the United States.

DISCOVERIES

We analyzed the internal consistency of the questionnaire, and determined that all but one of the ten questions ("We are surprised by topics that come up during a coaching assignment"—reverse scored) could be retained to calculate a composite score. The questionnaire items that were included in the composite "goal orientation" score are listed in Table 3.1.

Table 3.1   Coaching goal orientation questionnaire*

Item	Question
1	I set goals with my coachees at the start of a coaching assignment.
2	At the start of a coaching assignment we set goals for the whole assignment.
3	In subsequent coaching sessions we refer back to the goals set at the start.
4	We determine when to finish a coaching assignment by checking whether goals have been achieved.
5	The goals help us to decide whether the coaching is appropriately focused.
6	Goals remain the same throughout the coaching assignment.
7	We set goals for each coaching session.
8	The goals are central to deciding the effectiveness of the coaching.
9	We have purposeful conversations without setting goals. (Reverse scored)

*   Cronbach's alpha = .82

Differences by region

We analyzed the results of the survey to determine the effects of geographical region, education, and coaching experience on goal orientation. The first significant finding was that US respondents score significantly higher on the measure of goal orientation than their European colleagues (see Figure 3.1). This indicates that US coaches are more likely to begin coaching by setting goals for the entire assignment, to preserve those goals throughout the engagement, to refer back to established goals in subsequent sessions, and to use them to determine the appropriateness and effectiveness of the coaching intervention, as well as when to conclude coaching.

This geographical and perhaps cultural difference is likely related to the unique traditions out of which coaching has developed in these regions. As described in Chapter 1, Drucker's Management by Objectives, as well as

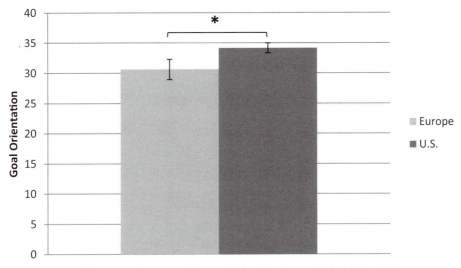

* Scores for U.S. and European coaches are significantly different; $t(185) = 4.856$, $p<.001$

Figure 3.1   Average goal orientation score by region

Locke and Latham's standard goal setting theory originated in the United States. This has undoubtedly contributed to the pervasiveness of goal setting and goal striving in the US coaching field. The field of European coaching, on the other hand, has been more strongly influenced by the founders of psychoanalysis and depth psychology: Freud and Jung, among others (Kets de Vries, 2006). The psychoanalytic tradition is concerned with surfacing elements of the unconscious, rather than pursuing pre-determined targets. These discrete histories may contribute to the significant difference in current goal orientation in these regions. Another difference in approaches to mentoring may be the willingness of US coaches to embrace sponsorship mentoring (see Kram, Chapter 13) compared with the reluctance of Europeans to set goals for career and income that sponsorship mentoring would imply (Gibb and Megginson, 1993).

Coaching education

The results of the survey also demonstrate that coaching education impacts the strength of coaches' goal orientation. Our sample included coaches who learned to coach through experience, and those who had taken either a short (less than five weeks), or a long (more than five weeks) training course. We found that those who have completed a long training course are significantly more goal-oriented than those who have learned through experience alone (see Figure 3.2). This suggests that coach training instills a goal orientation.

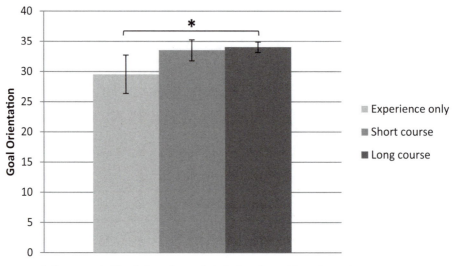

* Scores are significantly lower for coaches who have learned through experience than those who have taken a long course; $F(2) = 4.118$, $p = .018$

Figure 3.2   Average goal orientation score by education

It is likely that some courses provide explicit goal-related frameworks on which coaches base their subsequent work. It is also possible that, rather than being influenced by their training, coaches who are already goal-oriented are also most likely to enroll in longer courses. In other words, the finding may reflect an underlying variable, such as a personality trait, that leads people to be both highly goal-oriented and highly trained.

Coaching experience

The results demonstrate that, for the sample as a whole, years of coaching experience is unrelated to goal orientation. Examining the data by region, however, reveals a different pattern: while experience is unrelated to goal orientation for US coaches, there is a significant inverse relationship between goal orientation and experience for European coaches (see Figure 3.3). In other words, the longer a European coach has been practicing, the lower his or her score on goal orientation.

This may mean that in Europe, gaining experience as a coaching practitioner results in a loosening of adherence to goals. It is equally possible that these data represent a trend in the European coaching field, in which coaches who have been

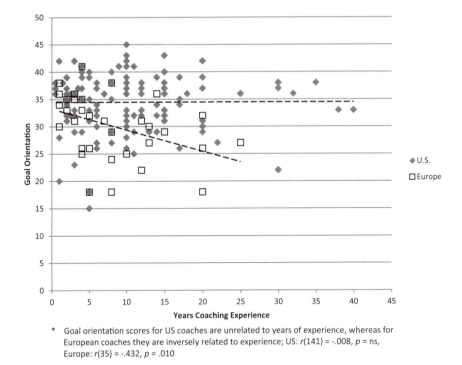

* Goal orientation scores for US coaches are unrelated to years of experience, whereas for European coaches they are inversely related to experience; US: $r(141) = -.008$, $p = $ ns, Europe: $r(35) = -.432$, $p = .010$

Figure 3.3   Goal orientation and coaching experience by region

newly trained or introduced to the field are more goal-focused than those who have been practicing for some time. Perhaps a more goal-oriented form of coaching is gaining popularity in Europe and newly trained coaches are exposed to this.

The meaning of these results can only be clarified through longitudinal research, in which coaching practitioners are followed over time. If European coaching practitioners continue to report declines in goal adherence as they gain experience, this would suggest that some attribute of the European coaching field tempers coaches' goal orientation as they gain expertise. If, on the other hand, novice European coaches retain current, relatively high, levels of goal orientation as they continue to practice, this would suggest a change in the European coaching field itself.

Goals and the element of surprise

It is worth noting that the questionnaire item we eliminated from the "goal orientation" score referred to the element of surprise in the coaching relationship.

If goal orientation and surprise were functioning in opposition to each other, anchoring two sides of a single scale, one would expect the reverse score of the item "We are surprised by topics that come up during a coaching assignment" to contribute to the overall goal orientation score. In other words, the more goal-oriented a coach, the less surprise he or she would experience in the coaching engagement. However, the data demonstrate that this is not the case.

To the contrary, we found that coaches who score lowest on surprise also score lowest on goal orientation—significantly lower than coaches who are surprised "sometimes" "often", or "always". This may indicate that rather than being mutually exclusive, orientation toward goals is related to the emergence of new and surprising topics in the coaching engagement.

An alternative explanation is that those least oriented towards setting goals are also least surprised by what comes up during coaching, due to their openness to emerging experience. Regardless of whether more or fewer topics emerge (as compared to those with high goal orientation), the characteristic of those with low goal orientation may be that they experience less surprise.

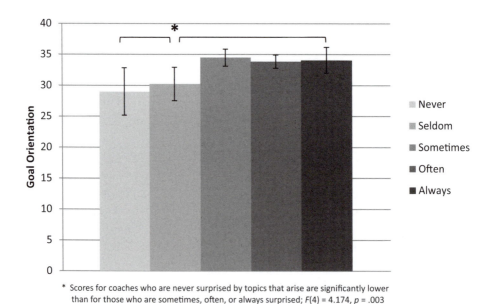

* Scores for coaches who are never surprised by topics that arise are significantly lower than for those who are sometimes, often, or always surprised; $F(4) = 4.174$, $p = .003$

Figure 3.4 **Average goal orientation score by response to "We are surprised by topics that come up during a coaching assignment"**

CONCLUSIONS FROM QUANTITATIVE RESEARCH

The use of goals is common in coaching practice, however US coaches are more strongly goal-oriented than those in Europe. Coach training is also related to goal orientation: those who have taken a long coach training course are significantly more goal-oriented than those who have taken no training course. The more experience a European coach has, the less he or she is oriented toward goals. This relationship does not hold for US coaches, where the use of goals is consistent across different levels of experience. Finally, orientation toward goals does not diminish the element of surprise in the coaching relationship.

This research sheds light on interesting patterns in the practice of goal setting and management. However, it does not tell the whole story. How do coaches make meaning about goals, and what do they see as the benefits and potential dangers of goal setting? To learn more about goals in coaching we conducted qualitative research, and gathered impressions and opinions from those who are active in the field.

Conducting Field Work

To gain more information about coaches' attitudes about goals, we identified 16 experienced coaches and asked them to discuss both benefits and barriers in one-to-one discussions. We also convened eight separate focus groups on this topic. A total of 125 coaches with a range of coaching experience participated. Finally, we interviewed 22 coaching clients, to find out what they had concluded about goals in coaching. The focus in all of these studies was to explore respondents' experience of negative effects of goals, in order to counteract the overwhelmingly positive, or unconsidered neutral references to, goals that we had encountered in the literature.

ANTI-GOAL THEMES

Two of us analyzed the results, and through an iterative process we identified a set of themes. We reviewed these with a third, independent coach and agreed on the following themes:

1.   reductionism

2.   narrowing focus

3.   superficial issues

4.   loss of present moment awareness

5.   unconsidered routine

6.   protecting the coach

7.   emergent nature of goals

8.   overloaded with goals

9.   undue pressure from goals

10.   conflict in who sets goals

Reductionism

Goals are criticized by a number of our respondents as reducing the richness, complexity and ambiguity of life. One participant said, "I refer to this movement toward numbers, set processes, and chiseling people down simplistically as 'the abandonment of life'." Some advocates of goals agree that goals reduce complexity and ambiguity, but stress that this reduction helps with focus. However, the anti-reductionism position contends that a more nuanced approach to what it means to be human is necessary in order for goals to be helpful.

Recently, we have noticed that organizations make well-meaning attempts to guide coaches and clients toward working on important areas for the organization by providing participants with competency frameworks. Many coaches and clients find these atomized skills or competencies too bland an expression of what is needed to perform complex and ambiguous roles. Sometimes our clients are in crisis and the format of the competency statements bears no relation to their existential state. One participant stated plainly, "Goals set within the context of the competency framework don't relate to what matters."

Narrowing focus

As one participant describes, "Goals tend to narrow down the focus for coaching onto specific, measurable areas." Some coaches and clients applaud such measures, while others see them as hindrances. According to one participant, "Goals inhibit dialogue that can open up new areas and insights that could help achieve real change." Another claims, "Plans, goals, formal processes and targets can blind us to the valuable information that is generated by the actions we take to implement them." Some participants emphasize the value of open dialogue in their coaching sessions, saying that in such exchanges deeper, more complex issues and material come to light. They believe that "Goals can limit what is covered, and prevent broad development." A participant reports, "Once, focusing on a career goal meant we didn't have time to address a very important personal goal." In these ways, coaches and clients see goals as limitations, rather than helpful anchors in the coaching program.

Superficial issues

It is often said that not everything that can be measured is important, and not everything that is important can be measured. A concern expressed by many of the clients we interviewed is the potential for coach and client to collude in order to avoid less comfortable lines of inquiry. According to one client, "Attention to goals hides the deeper issues." Another boldly states, "If I can set SMART goals, don't you think I would have sorted it [myself]? It's the messy, wicked issues I want to look at." This is echoed by one participant's question: "Do goals act as a crutch to avoid what would be painfully beneficial?"

We have found that many executives being coached will bridle if targets or goals are set for them. They want to use coaching to clarify their thoughts, and only then decide on a course of action. Additionally, we have observed that the goals managers set for their subordinates tend to be simplistic. According to one participant, "They can be a distraction; coach and coachee may overlook something important if too focused on goals."

Loss of present moment awareness

There is a strong movement towards mindfulness in coaching (Ehrlich, 2012; Ridings, 2012), and as one participant points out, "I am aware of a possible tension between goal setting and mindfulness." Stress, overwork and imbalanced lifestyles are pervasive in organizational life, and setting new goals in a coaching context may be contrary to the space for pause, reflection, and moment-to-moment attention a client needs. A participant says, "There is a case for valuing the experience of the moment and the process of growth rather than continuously striving towards goals", and another claims, "There are situations where 'relax', 'just be' or 'let go' are important." Exhausted clients—those in a state of "joyless depletion" (Casserley and Megginson, 2009), need to take on less, not more. "Out-there" activities like working towards new goals bring them farther from where they want and need to be. Similar to the impulse to move away from more difficult topics, coaches and clients may avoid present moment awareness because, as one participant acknowledges, "People feel discomfort about free space." We suggest that filling free space with specific goals may relieve discomfort, but not ultimately serve the coaching program.

Goals as an unconsidered routine

Some of our respondents noticed the habitual nature of goal setting in many organizations. One participant said, "People have the right to incubate, explore, create, realize; but they won't accept that right if the climate is one of drilling down to dull conformity." Another referred to the emphasis on goal setting in coaching education, stating, "Not setting goals does not correspond with my coach training, but it does with my non-directive Rogerian counseling training—and that makes a lot of sense to me."

Protection for the coach

Many of our respondents who were in training and relatively new to coaching have said that they see goals as a form of protection: if they have agreed on goals with the client, they are less likely to have to sink into deep waters or struggle with ambiguity in ways that might leave them uncomfortable or exposed. Participants made statements including, "I know I can defend my coaching if we can specify goals", "Not to make goals the key issue requires extra attention", and "Goals save the coach from having to be fully present." Another coach reflected, "In my coaching, goals are an aspect of my personal preferences for clarity and control. There are other ways which I fear I have not explored."

Emergent nature of goals

Another argument against goals raised by our respondents is that they are constantly shifting and do not have the solidity and stability that are often ascribed to them in coaching texts. As one of our participants noted, "One can set goals, but life is about constantly changing goal posts." Those who are critical of goals claim that goals shift between—or even within—sessions, so there is not much of a case for determining what they should be at the beginning of the coaching relationship. Aspirations have a quicksilver quality about them, which makes them hard to pin down. Participants state, "Goals are often predetermined, and then, by Session 3 have been redefined", and "Pre-set goals are usually vague and shift over time for everybody." Other participants suggest that the development of goals has a linear quality. Goals start in a standardized, conventional form— "improve work/life balance", "develop confidence in speaking out", etc. Over time, deeper, more explicit, and more personal aspirations can be voiced (i.e. "get home in time to read my kids a bedtime story", "deal with the way that Chris puts me down in front of my peers"). Sometimes, by the time these aspirations have been clarified, the coaching relationship has come to an end. Further, simply getting to a place where a person can articulate these goals may be all that is necessary. Our participants stressed the importance of allowing goals to surface over time, stating, "I don't know what I want to address yet—by the time I do, the goal will be a thing of the past", and "Goals could close the door on emergent opportunity and serendipity."

Overloaded by goals

One of our clients asked the striking question, "Do we have to set goals? I have 13 different organizations setting goals for me—I don't want coaching to be the 14th." Another observed that goals "Encourage 'do more' in a society where 'do less' may be more valuable." Having a multiplicity of goals can lead to a diffusion of effort as well as a neglect of other urgencies. Our research indicates that coaches and their clients can experience goals as overwhelming, and headed in the wrong direction. SMART criteria may contribute to this experience. As one participant asked, "Does the need for measurement demand excessive focus on goals?"

Undue pressure from goals

Some of our respondents reported that goal setting in coaching and mentoring could be used as a weapon in disguise: an instrument of social control that leads to illegitimate, or at least unhelpful, pressure on the client. A participant reported that for one project, "… destructive and preventative goals have been set." Others said that goals "… can put the coachee under undue pressure", and "… can be demotivating if not achieved." Another observed that, "Too much inexperienced insistence on the client setting goals in the early stages is one of the reasons why so many clients blow out." These data point to a potentially harmful effect of goal setting. It seems these types of situations are particularly prevalent in organizations or coaching engagements where the line manager of the client or the sponsor of the engagement is present at an initial goal setting meeting.

Conflict in who sets goals

When we, the authors, started working as mentors and coaches, as well as on researching the process, we found that the intent and aspirations in coaching were usually private to the participants and arose from their desires and needs. Over time, this privacy has been encroached upon by supervisors, sponsors, and HR professionals. Research respondents noted, "Goals are linked to business needs rather than the individual's own needs", and in one case, "360-degree feedback set an agenda that the client didn't want to address."

Participants expressed that what gave coaching and mentoring its power was that the time was dedicated to the client, on his or her own terms. The client has the final say in not only *what* is discussed, but *how* the conversation evolves. As one participant stated, "I know what my predecessor wants for me to achieve through the coaching, but I disagree—that is his way; I have mine." This raises questions about whether organization mandated 360-degree feedback, competency frameworks, performance appraisal reports, psychometric tests, etc. help or hinder the coaching process. Sometimes the third parties involved attempt to control the process, in order to justify the time and money dedicated to coaching and mentoring. Paradoxically, some of our respondents suggest that this diminishes the very features that make one-to-one development so powerful. As one respondent expressed, "Goals over-privilege the sponsor's agenda at the expense of the coachee's agenda."

CONCLUSIONS FROM QUALITATIVE RESEARCH

While goals are common in coaching programs, coaching practitioners and their clients express a host of reservations about their use. Some of these concerns relate to the client and the coaching topic: whether the complexity of coaching is minimized, the focus unhelpfully narrowed, or the topics kept unnecessarily simple. Regarding the coach and the coaching process, practitioners and clients express concerns about loss of mindful awareness and the perpetuation of habitual routines, and they speak in favor of allowing goals to emerge over time. Finally, participants raise concerns about goals in the context of organizations. Goals can overwhelm and exert pressure on clients, or be used to coerce them into fulfilling others' agendas. These themes raise many important questions about goals in coaching and mentoring, and call for further exploration of both the benefits and pitfalls.

Conclusion

Research can provide answers, but almost inevitably it raises a host of new questions to explore and puzzles to solve. Our research only scratches the surface of understanding goals in coaching and mentoring. To further our knowledge, we turn to esteemed colleagues who are extending theory and research on these topics. The chapters that follow bring together insights from leading-edge thinkers in coaching and mentoring, with the aim of generating new ideas and approaches to practice in goal pursuit.

References

Bachkirova, T. (2011). *Developmental Coaching: Working with the Self*. Maidenhead: McGraw-Hill/Open UP.

Bennett, J.L. (2006). An agenda for coaching-related research: A challenge for researchers. *Consulting Psychology Journal: Practice and Research, 58*(4), 240–49.

Casserley, T. & Megginson, D. (2009). *Learning from Burnout: Developing Sustainable Leaders and Avoiding Career Derailment*. Oxford: Butterworth-Heinemann.

Downey, M. (2003). *Effective Coaching: Lessons From the Coach's Coach*. Mason, OH: Texere.

de Haan, E. (2008). *Relational Coaching: Journeys Towards Mastering One-to-one Learning*. Chichester: Wiley.

Driver, M. (2011). *Coaching Positively: Lessons for Coaches from Positive Psychology*. Maidenhead: McGraw-Hill/Open UP.

Ehrlich, J. (2012). *Mindshifting: Focus for Performance*. New York: Steiner.

Feldman, D.C. & Lankau, M.J. (2005). Executive coaching: A review and agenda for future Research. *Journal of Management, 31*, 829–48.

Garvey, B. (2011). *A Very Short, Fairly Interesting and Reasonably Cheap Book About Coaching and Mentoring*. London: Sage.

Gibb, S. & Megginson, D. (1993). Inside corporate mentoring schemes: a new agenda of concerns. *Personnel Review, 22*(1), 40–54.

Grant, A.M. (2010). Workplace, executive and life coaching: An annotated bibliography from the behavioural science and business literature. Sydney, New South Wales: University of Sydney.

Hughes, J.L. (2003). *Adjusting the Mirror: Strategies for Coaching Executives with Narcissistic Personality Features*. Doctoral dissertation, Rutgers, the State University of New Jersey, Graduate School of Applied and Professional Psychology.

Hunt, J.M. & Weintraub, J.R. (2002). *The Coaching Manager: Developing Top Talent in Business.* Thousand Oaks, CA: Sage.

Kets de Vries, M. (2006). *The Leader on the Couch: A Clinical Approach to Changing People and Organizations.* West Sussex: John Wiley & Sons.

Linley, P.A. (2006). Coaching Research: who? what? where? when? why? *International Journal of Evidence Based Coaching and Mentoring,* 4(2), 1–7.

Ordóñez, L.D., Schweitzer, M.E., Galinsky, A.D., & Bazerman, M.H. (2009). Goals gone wild: The systematic side effects of overprescribing goal setting. *Academy of Management Perspectives,* 23(1), 6–16.

Ridings, A. (2011). *Pause for Breath: Bringing the Practices of Mindfulness and Dialogue to Leadership Conversations.* London: Live It Publishing.

Sandler, C. (2011). *Executive Coaching: A Psychodynamic Approach.* Maidenhead: McGraw-Hill/Open UP.

Starr, J. (2012). *Brilliant Coaching: How to be a Brilliant Coach in Your Workplace.* (2nd ed.). London: Prentice Hall.

Stelter, R. (2009). Coaching as a reflective space in a society of growing diversity—towards a narrative, postmodern paradigm. *International Coaching Psychology Review,* 4(2), 207–17.

Stober, D. & Perry, C. (2005). Current challenges and future directions in coaching research. In M. Cavanagh, A.M. Grant, & T. Kemp (Eds), *Evidence-based Coaching, Volume 1: Theory, Research and Practice from the Behavioural Sciences,* 13–19. Bowen Hills: Australian Academic Press.

Szabó, P. & Meier, D. (2009). *Coaching Plain and Simple: Solution-Focused Brief Coaching Essentials.* New York: W.W. Norton.

Whitmore, J. (2002). *Coaching for Performance: GROWing People, Performance, and Purpose.* (3rd ed.). London: Nicholas Brealey.

Wilson, C. (2007). *Best Practice in Performance Coaching.* London: Kogan Page.

New Perspectives on Goal Setting in Coaching Practice: An Integrated Model of Goal-focused Coaching

Anthony M. Grant

Strangely, the use of goals in coaching is sometimes seen as controversial. Those opposed to goal setting in coaching argue that setting goals constricts the coaching conversation and acts as a barrier to working with emergent issues, or that goal setting typically focuses on issues that may be relatively easily measured, but are of no real import. Others argue that goal setting is too often associated with coaches cajoling coachees in the blind pursuit of a previously-set but inappropriate goal, leading to "lazy" mechanistic coaching. Some coaches say they never use goals in coaching, and rather they help clients explore their values, clarify their intentions, and then work to help them to achieve their personal aspirations. Yet others talk about helping clients chart a course, navigate the waters of life, re-author personal narratives or foster transformational change.

Goal setting has even gained a bad reputation in some sections of the academic psychology press, with authors asking if goal setting has gone wild, and decrying the supposed over-prescription of goal setting (Ordóñez, Schweitzer, Galinsky, and Bazerman, 2009). There has also been discussion about the limitations of goal setting in the scholarly coaching press (Clutterbuck, 2008, 2010).

The above points have some merit. Yet goal theory potentially has much to offer coaching research and practice. There is a vast body of work on goals and goal setting. A search of the database PsycINFO in April 2012 using the keyword "goals" found over 59,000 citations. Yet the academic literature on the use of goals within the area of executive coaching is far smaller, with the keywords "goals" and "executive coaching" producing only 30 citations. Most of these report on the various uses of goal setting in executive coaching practice (e.g. Bono, Purvanova, Towler, and Peterson, 2009; Lewis-Duarte, 2010; McKenna and Davis, 2009b; Stern, 2009), with a few empirical studies examining how executive coaching facilitates goal attainment (e.g. Benavides, 2009; Burke and Linley, 2007; Freedman and Perry, 2010; Grant, Curtayne, and Burton, 2009; Milare and Yoshida, 2009; Schnell, 2005; Smither, London, Flautt, Vargas, and Kucine, 2003; Turner, 2004).

There have been surprisingly few articles discussing theoretical frameworks that explicitly link goal theory to executive coaching. For example, Gregory, Beck, and Carr's (2011) work argues that control theory (in which goals and feedback are two crucial elements) can provide an important framework for coaching, and Grant (2006) describes an integrative goal-focused approach to executive coaching.

This chapter draws on and extends my previous work (Grant, 2002, 2006; Grant, 2012a, 2012b) and, drawing on the goal setting, self-determination and personality literature from the behavioral sciences, discusses the concept of goals, presents a definition of goals that can be helpful in coaching practice and describes a new model of goal-focused coaching. It also describes new research that highlights the vital role that coaches' goal-focused skills play in determining successful coaching outcomes.

Do SMART Goals Encourage Scruffy Thinking in Coaching?

Because goals and goal constructs have been extensively debated and researched within academic psychology (Moskowitz and Grant, 2009), sophisticated understandings of goals and their role in human behavior have emerged over time within the wider psychological literature. This is not the case within the literature specifically associated with coaching practice. From an overview of coaching literature it is clear that many coaches' understanding of goals would be limited to acronyms such as SMART (originally delineated by Doran, 1981; Raia, 1965)—an acronym which equates goals with being specific, measurable, attainable, relevant and timeframed action plans (note: the exact articulation of the SMART acronym may vary between commentators).

Whilst the concepts embodied in the acronym SMART are indeed broadly supported by goal theory (e.g. Locke, 1996) and may well be useful in some instances in coaching practice, I think that the widespread belief that goals are synonymous with SMART action plans has done much to stifle the development of a more sophisticated understanding and use of goal theory within the coaching community. It is worth reflecting that acronyms such as SMART may well provide useful mnemonics—mnemonics being memorable surface markers of deeper knowledge structures. However, the use of such mnemonics without a clear understanding of the deeper underpinning knowledge may well result in "scruffy" thinking—that is, ill-informed decision making and the cultivation of inaccurate practice doctrines and mythologies, which may make it even more difficult for practitioners to engage with the broader knowledge-base. I hope that this chapter is able to make some headway in addressing this issue.

What are Goals?

If this chapter is to make a meaningful contribution in terms of the more sophisticated use of goals and goal theory in coaching, we need a clear understanding of what goals are. The term "goal" is generally understood as being "the purpose toward which an endeavor is directed; an objective or outcome" (see for example www.thefreedictionary.com). However, although such understandings are sufficient for everyday use, a more nuanced understanding of the goal construct is needed in coaching. In attempting to develop greater sophistication of the goal construct a range of other terms have been proposed by researchers over the years including "reference values" (Carver and Scheier, 1998), "self-guides" (Higgins, 1987), "personal strivings" (Emmons, 1992), or "personal projects" (Little, 1993). However, such broad definitions make it hard to distinguish between "aims", "objectives", "desires" or "outcomes" and also fail to capture the essence of the goal construct.

As previously mentioned, the purpose of goals is understood in relation to a change process in which goals are characterized as playing a role in the transition from an existing state to a desired state or outcome (e.g. Klinger, 1975; Spence, 2007). As such the goal construct has been described in terms of cognitions (Locke, 2000), behavior (Bargh, Gollwitzer, Lee-Chai, Barndollar, and Trötschel, 2001; Warshaw and Davis, 1985) and affect (Pervin, 1982) (for further discussion on these points see Street, 2002). Because these three domains are of great relevance for coaching, I argue that a definition of goals for use in coaching should encompass all three domains.

Cochran and Tesser (1996) present a comprehensive description of a goal as "a cognitive image of an ideal stored in memory for comparison to an actual state; a representation of the future that influences the present; a desire (pleasure and satisfaction are expected from goal success); a source of motivation, an incentive to action" (p. 100 as cited in Street, 2002). This understanding of goals may be particularly useful for coaching because, as Street (2002) argues, it emphasizes the role of cognition (in terms of cognitive imagery), as well as affect and behavior. In addition, and also of great relevance for coaching, is that the purpose of a goal as "a source of motivation and an incentive" is made explicit.

However, whilst this description is a clear advance on the notion that goals are synonymous with SMART action plans, it is still somewhat unwieldy as a working definition. One definition that is succinct, captures the essence of the above issues and is clearly applicable to coaching is Austin and Vancouver's (1996) notion of goals as being "internal representations of desired states or outcomes" (p. 388).

Goals are Central to Coaching

Definitions of coaching abound. The International Coach Federation defines coaching as "partnering with clients in a thought-provoking and creative process that inspires them to maximize their personal and professional potential" (ICF, 2012). The Association for Coaching defines coaching as "A collaborative solution-focused, results-orientated and systematic process in which the coach facilitates the enhancement of work performance, life experience, self-directed learning and personal growth of the coachee" (AC, 2012). The World Association of Business Coaches defines business coaching as structured conversation designed to "enhance the client's awareness and behavior so as to achieve business objectives for both the client and their organization" (WABC, 2012). The European Mentoring and Coaching Council states that coaching (and mentoring) "are activities within the area of professional and personal development ... to help clients ... see and test alternative ways for improvement of competence, decision making and enhancement of quality of life ... with the purpose of serving the clients to improve their performance or enhance their personal development or both ..." (EMCC, 2011).

Clearly there is considerable agreement within professional coaching bodies about the nature of coaching. All of these definitions of coaching indicate that the process of coaching is essentially about helping individuals regulate and direct their interpersonal and intrapersonal resources to create purposeful and positive change in their personal or business lives. In essence then, coaching is about helping clients enhance their self-regulatory skills so as to better create purposeful positive change in their lives.

Self-regulation Sits at the Core of the Coaching Process

The core constructs of such self-regulation are a series of processes in which the individual sets a goal, develops a plan of action, begins action, monitors their performance, evaluates their performance by comparison to a standard, and based on this evaluation changes their actions to further enhance their performance and better reach their goals (Carver and Scheier, 1998). In relation to coaching, the coach's role is to facilitate the coachee's movement through the self-regulatory cycle. Figure 4.1 depicts a generic model of self-regulation.

In practice, the steps in the self-regulatory cycle do not have clearly separate stages. Rather each stage overlaps with the next. Ideally the coaching in each stage should aim to facilitate the process of the next. For example, goal setting should be done in such a way as to facilitate the development and implementation of an action plan; the action plan should be designed to motivate the individual into action, and should also incorporate means of monitoring and evaluating performance, thus providing information on which to base follow-up coaching sessions.

This process is clearly at the core of the coaching process, and it is also clear from the above professional bodies' definitions of coaching that an active orientation towards purposefully creating positive change is a central part of the coaching conversation. Hence all coaching conversations are either explicitly or implicitly goal-focused.

Knowing when and how to set goals in coaching, knowing how to gauge the client's readiness to engage in a robust and explicitly goal-focused conversation or when to work with more vaguely defined or more abstract goals, is a skill set that distinguishes the novice or beginner coach from more advanced or expert practitioners (Grant, 2011; Peterson, 2011). Having a solid understanding of the multi-faceted nature of goals is thus useful in making the novice–expert shift. It is to this issue that we now turn.

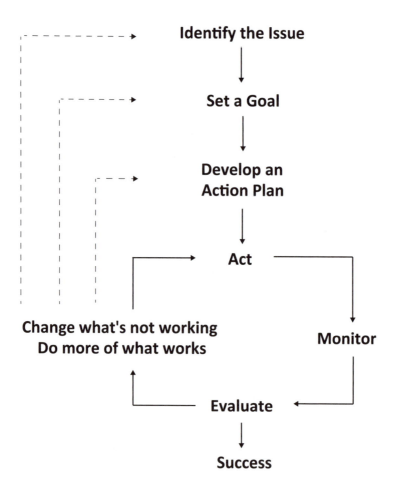

Figure 4.1   Generic model of goal-directed self-regulation

Source: © Anthony M. Grant 2012

The Multifaceted Nature of Goals

Goals are not a monolithic construct. If we are to understand coaching through the lens of goal theory, it is important to distinguish between different types of goals. There are over twenty types of goals that can be used in coaching, including outcome, distal and proximal goals, approach and avoidance goals, performance and learning goals, and higher and lower order goals, and the actual concrete results which the coachee aims to achieve. These are important distinctions as different types of goals differently impact on coachee's performance and experience of the goal striving process.

Time Framing

The time framing of goals is an important part of the goal setting process, and can influence the coachee's perception of the attainability of the goal (Karniol and Ross, 1996). *Distal* goals are longer-term goals, and are somewhat akin to the broad vision statements often referred to in business or management literature, or the "broad fuzzy visions" referred to in the life-coaching literature (Grant and Green, 2004) . *Proximal* goals are shorter-term and tend to stimulate more detailed planning than distal goals (Manderlink and Harackiewicz, 1984), and hence are important goals to be used in action planning. In essence, the action steps typically derived in coaching sessions are a series of proximal goals. Combining both distal and proximal goals into the coaching process can lead to enhanced strategy development and better long-term performance (Weldon and Yun, 2000).

Outcome Goals

Many coaching programs explicitly focus on setting *outcome* goals. These tend to be a straightforward statement of some desired outcome (Hudson, 1999); for example, "to increase sales of widgets by 15 percent in the next three months". This is a useful approach to goal setting, because for individuals who are committed and have the necessary ability and knowledge, outcome goals that are difficult and are specifically and explicitly defined allow performance to be precisely regulated, and thus lead to high performance (Locke, 1996). Indeed, many coaching programs focus purely on the setting of specific "SMART" goals and this approach is supported by some of the goal setting literature (Locke and Latham, 2002).

However, there are times when overly-specific outcome goals will alienate the coachee, and may actually result in a decline in performance (Winters and Latham, 1996). For individuals who are in a highly deliberative mindset or in a contemplation stage of change (Gollwitzer, 1999), it may be more useful to purposefully set more *abstract* or quite vague goals and focus on developing a broad fuzzy vision, rather than drilling down into specific details and setting more *concrete* goals. For individuals at this point in the change process, vague goals are often perceived as being less threatening and less demanding (Dweck, 1986).

Avoidance and Approach Goals

Avoidance goals are expressed as a movement away from an undesirable state, for example, "to be less stressed about work". Although this is an outcome goal, as an avoidance goal it does not provide a specific outcome target or detail which behaviors might be most useful in attaining the goal. In contrast an *approach* goal is expressed as a movement towards a specific state or outcome, for example, "to enjoy a fulfilling balance between work demands and personal relaxation". Not surprisingly, there are differential effects associated with avoidance or approach goals. Coats, Janoff-Bulman, and Alpert (1996) found that people who tended to set avoidance goals had higher levels of depression and lower levels of well-being. Other studies have found that the long-term pursuit of avoidance goals is associated with decreases in well-being (Elliot, Sheldon, and Church, 1997), and that approach goals are associated with both higher levels of academic performance and increased well-being (Elliot and McGregor, 2001).

Performance and Learning Goals

Performance goals focus on task execution. Performance goals are often competitive goals. The aim here is to perform well on a specific task, or to receive positive evaluations from others or outperform others. Performance goals tend to focus the coachee on issues of personal ability (Gresham, Evans, and Elliott, 1988). An example of a performance goal in executive or workplace coaching might be "to be the very best lawyer in my area of practice". Performance goals can be very powerful motivators, especially where the individual experiences success early in the goal attainment process. However, performance goals can actually impede performance. This is particularly the case when the task is very complex, or the goal is perceived as highly challenging, and the individual is not skilled or is low in self-efficacy, or where resources are scarce. Furthermore, in highly competitive situations or when there are very high stakes, performance goals can foster cheating and a reluctance to cooperate with peers. The corporate world is replete with such examples (Midgley, Kaplan, and Middleton, 2001).

In many cases *learning* goals may better facilitate task performance (Seijts and Latham, 2001). Learning goals (sometimes referred to as mastery goals) focus attention on the learning associated with task mastery, rather than the performance of the task. An example of a learning goal in executive or workplace coaching might be "learn how to be the best lawyer in my area of practice". Learning goals tend to be associated with a range of positive processes including perception of a complex task as a positive challenge rather than a threat, greater absorption in actual task performance (Deci and Ryan, 2002), and enhanced memory and well-being (Linnenbrink, Ryan, and Pintrich, 1999). Furthermore, individual performance can be enhanced in highly complex situations when team goals are framed as being learning goals, and these can foster enhanced cooperation between team members (Kristof-Brown and Stevens, 2001). One benefit of setting learning goals is that they tend to be associated with higher levels of intrinsic motivation which in turn is associated with performance (Sarrazin, Vallerand, Guillet, Pelletier, and Cury, 2002).

Although the differences in the articulation of these different types of goals may appear to be a mere matter of semantics, in fact the way a goal is expressed is very important (Rawsthorne and Elliott, 1999) and coaches need to be attuned to such nuances if they are to work effectively within a goal-focused coaching paradigm.

Complementary and Competing Goals

Coaches also need to be attuned to the existence of *competing or conflicting* goals. These exist where the pursuit of one goal interferes with the pursuit of another goal. Sometimes goal conflict is easy to identify, for example in the case of the two goals "to spend more time with my family" and "to put more time into work in order to get a promotion". However, the conflict between goals may not always be immediately evident. For example, the goal "to get my sales force to sell more widgets" may be in perceived conflict with the goal "to have a more hands-off leadership style" if the coachee (a sales manager) finds delegation difficult and is used to a more controlling management style in dealing with the sales force.

The skill of the coach here is to help the coachee find ways to align seemingly conflicting goals and develop complementary goals. Sheldon and Kasser (1995) have argued that such congruence is important in facilitating goal attainment and well-being.

Unconscious Goals?

Human beings are goal-orientated organisms. Without goals we could not exist as conscious sentient beings. Indeed, Carver and Scheier (1998) argue that all human behavior is a continual process of moving towards or away from mental goal representations. This is not to say that all goals are consciously held. Under many conditions, we enact complex outcome-directed behaviors even though we may not have consciously set specific goals.

For example, I might be sitting at home and decide to walk to the corner store to buy some biscuits so I can enjoy afternoon tea and biscuits at home. My overarching and consciously set goals are to get biscuits and then make and enjoy afternoon tea. With this goal in mind, I put on my shoes, check my wallet, and walk to the store taking care to look both ways as I cross the road. There I select my biscuits, chat with the store-keeper, purchase my biscuits, return home safely and put the kettle on. All of these actions themselves involve a goal, yet hardly any of these goals were consciously set. Because such goal-states do influence our behavior even though we may not have consciously set specific goals, goal theory can help coaches be attuned to such dynamics and can provide a framework from which to help clients explore, identify and then change unhelpful implicit goals in order to better facilitate purposeful positive change (for an informed discussion on how actions are initiated even though we are unconscious of the goals to be attained or their motivating effect on our behavior see Custers and Aarts, 2010).

Self-concordant Goals

Goals that are self-congruent and in alignment with the coachee's core personal values or developing interests are more likely to be engaging and associated with greater effort. Self-concordance theory (Sheldon and Elliot, 1998) offers the coach a useful framework from which to understand and work with the reasons and motivations underpinning goal selection and goal strivings.

Self-concordance refers to the degree to which a goal is aligned with an individual's intrinsic interests, motivations and values. This can be a simple and powerful framework for understanding the link between values and goals. Derived from self-determination theory (Deci and Ryan, 1980; see also Chapter 5, p. 90) the self-concordance model emphasizes the extent to which individuals perceive their goals as being determined by their authentic self, rather than compelled by external forces.

The self-concordance approach delineates the perceived locus of causality as varying on a continuum from controlled (external) factors to internal (autonomous) facets. It is important to note that it is the individual's perception of the locus of causality that is the key issue in determining the extent to which the goals are deemed to be self-integrated and where they sit on the external-internal continuum. It is important that coachee's goals are as self-congruent as possible, and in the coaching process coaches may need to play an active role in helping their coachees to align goals in order to make them personal and congruent. There are at least four factors that may influence successful goal alignment from this perspective (Sheldon and Elliot, 1999).

First, the coachee needs to be able to identify the enduring and authentic from transitory or superficial whims or desires, thereby more effectively focusing their efforts. Secondly, the coachee needs to be able to distinguish between goals that represent their own interests and goals that represent the interests of others (Sheldon, 2002). Such insight is contingent on a high level of self-awareness. Given that there are significant individual variations in levels of self-awareness (Church, 1997), some coachees may find this quite hard. Thirdly, the goal content needs to be expressed in a way that aligns the goals with the coachee's internal needs and values. Fourthly, the coach needs to have the ability to recognize when a goal is not self-concordant, and then be able to re-language and reframe the goal so that it does align with the coachee's needs and values.

Goal Hierarchies

Goal hierarchy frameworks are one way of operationalizing the notion of goal self-concordance whilst also making explicit links between values, goals and specific action steps. Goals can be also considered as being ordered hierarchically with concrete specific goals being subsumed under *higher order* and broader, more abstract goals (Chulef, Read, and Walsh, 2001) in a fashion similar to the "Big Five" personality traits (Costa and McCrae, 1992). Hence, abstract goals such as "to be a great business leader" can be understood as being vertically higher than the *lower order* and more specific goal "to increase business profits by 25 percent in the next quarter", and there is some empirical support for this notion (Chulef, et al., 2001; Oishi, Schimmack, Diener, and Suh, 1998).

Higher order goals from this perspective equate to values. A valuable model for using goal theory in coaching involves thinking of values as higher order abstract goals that are superordinate to lower order, more specific goals, which in turn are superordinate to specific action steps.

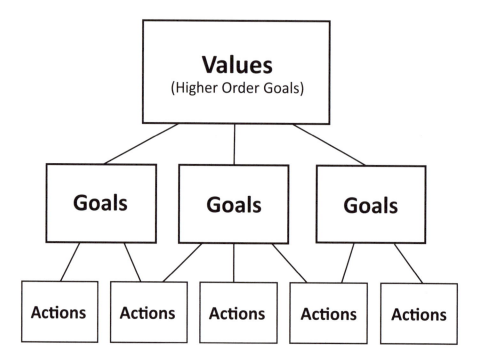

Figure 4.2   Goal hierarchy

Indeed, visualizing values, goals and actions as being part of a hierarchy in this way provides coaches with an extremely useful case conceptualization framework for coaching practice.

In using this model in coaching practice, it is important to try to ensure both vertical and horizontal congruency. That is, to ensure that goals are aligned with the client's higher order values, and that any actions designed to operationalize the goals are themselves similarly aligned (vertical alignment). It is also important to try to ensure horizontal alignment so that goals complement, support and energize each other rather than being, as previously mentioned, *competing or conflicting* goals. This would result in the pursuit of one goal interfering with the pursuit of another. Of course, such alignment may not be possible. Nevertheless, simply drawing a coachee's attention to the existence of any competing or conflicting goals, and highlighting any disconnect between goals and values can provide the coachee with important insights and alternative perspectives, which may in turn facilitate more useful ways of facilitating change.

Goal Neglect

The hierarchical model is also very useful to coaches as it can be used to illustrate the effect of goal neglect. The notion of goal neglect is not well-known in the coaching literature, but has very useful implications for coaching practice. It refers to the disregard of a goal or a task requirement despite the fact that it has been understood or is recognized as being important (Duncan, Emslie, Williams, Johnson, and Freer, 1996). In essence goal neglect occurs when we fail to pay attention to a specific goal of importance, but instead focus our attention on some other goal or task, resulting in a mismatch between the actions required to attain the original goal, and the actions that are actually performed.

Human beings are essentially goal-directed organisms (Deci and Ryan, 2000). All behavior (behavior here is broadly defined to include thoughts, feelings and physical actions) is shaped and given direction, purpose and meaning by the goals that we hold, and of course much of our behavior is shaped and directed by goals and values which are outside of our immediate conscious awareness. In relation to the goal hierarchy model, it is the higher order (or superordinate) values that give direction, meaning and purpose to the lower order goals and actions.

When self-regulation at upper levels of a goal hierarchy has been suspended (for example, by not enough attention being paid to those values), the goals at a lower level become functionally superordinate in guiding overt behavior and actions (Carver and Scheier, 1998). That is to say that the guidance of the human system defaults (regresses) to lower levels.

This seemingly technical psychological point has important implications for coaching practice. This is because, typically, the lower order goals in the hierarchy are not in themselves relatively meaningful in comparison to the higher order values. In fact, in many cases the lower order goals and actions are not pleasant activities at all. They are often made palatable by the notion that reaching those lower order goals will activate the higher order value.

When we fail to consistently pay attention to the higher order values in the goal hierarchy system, and overly focus on attaining lower order goals, the lower order goals become the superordinate or dominant values. These lower order goals are often inherently dissatisfying in themselves.

In the example below, the higher order value is "to be an outstanding lawyer", and many individuals would enter the law profession with the intention of becoming an outstanding lawyer and contributing to justice for their clients. In order to become an outstanding lawyer they would need to work hard, make explicit contributions to their firm or practice and build a revenue stream. The attainment of these mid-level goals are in turn made possible only by the enactment of lower order goals and actions such as dealing with administration, documenting billing hours and the like. However, all too frequently individuals place too much attention on their lower order goals (e.g. revenue building or documenting billing hours), neglecting their higher order values, and this can easily result in goal dissatisfaction and disengagement.

This framework can give coaches and their coachees useful insights into the psychological mechanics underlying goal dissatisfaction, and can be used to develop tools and techniques to help clients in the coaching process. For example, by helping clients purposefully re-focus their attention on more abstract goals, we help them reconnect with their higher order values. They may end up redefining their goals, and in doing so feel revitalized and re-engaged in the enactment of purposeful positive change.

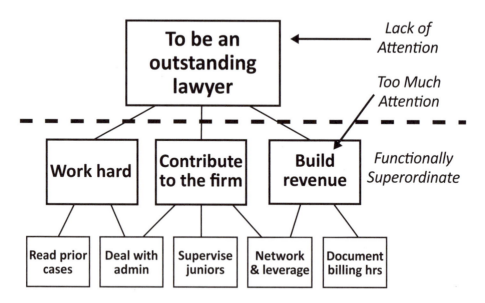

Figure 4.3   Goal neglect

Putting This All Together

As can be seen from this brief overview of some of the relevant constructs, goal theory has much to offer coaching practice. The question is then, how can we organize all this information in a way that is accessible and useful in coaching practice?

One way of integrating this diverse body of knowledge is to develop a visual representation or model of the various factors related to goal-focused coaching, and such a model is presented in Figure 4.4. A word of caution: as with all models, this is only a representation of some possible ways that these factors relate in the coaching process. This model represents my own personal experience and understanding, and I would encourage readers to explore the limitations of this model by reference to their own understanding and coaching experience, and then adapt and extend this model in order to create their own frameworks.

In reference to this model, which attempts to capture the key aspects involved in the goal-focused approach to coaching and highlights some of the factors that a coach may consider during the coaching engagement, the coaching process is driven by certain needs (represented on the left hand side of the model). Both individual and contextual/organizational factors play a role in determining the perceived need for coaching, which gives rise to the individual's intentions to participate in the goal selection process. Individual factors at play here include perceived deficits and opportunities, psychological needs, personality style and available resources (or lack thereof). Contextual or organizational factors include system complexity, the social and psychological contracts, rewards and punishments, and available resources (or lack thereof).

The goal selection process is often not straightforward. Even where coaching has been mandated by an organization with specific outcomes in mind, the goal setting process can be convoluted and complex. The rush to seize and set a specific goal too early in the coaching process is a key derailer. Certainly key issues and broad initial goals should be discussed very early in the coaching process in order to give the conversation direction and purpose, but the coach should also be paying attention to a number of factors during the goal selection process. These include the coachee's understanding of, and engagement with, the coaching process.

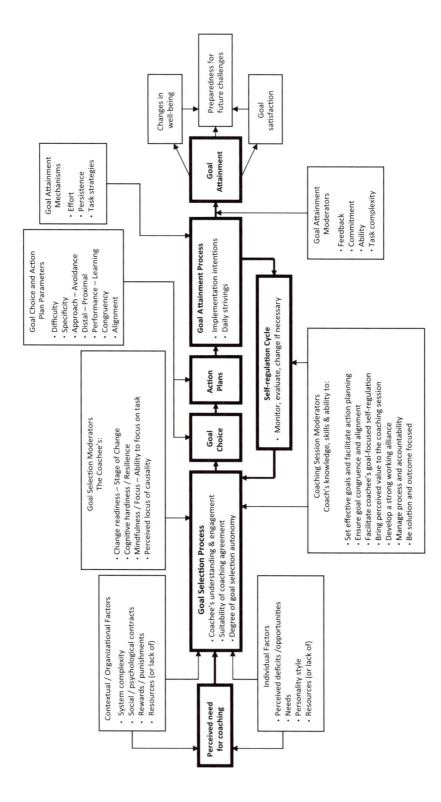

Figure 4.4　Integrative model of coach-facilitated goal attainment
© Anthony M. Grant 2012

Some coachees arrive for their first coaching session with little idea of the nature of coaching. The suitability and clarity of the coaching agreement (be that formal or informal) will play an important role in engaging the coachee in the goal selection process, as will the degree of autonomy the coachee has in goal selection.

Goal Selection Moderators: The Coachee's Characteristics

Other factors that will impact on the goal selection process include the coachee's readiness to change. Coaches need to consider if the coachee is in the pre-contemplation, preparation or action stage of change (for a useful reference on applying the Transtheoretical Model of Change to a wide range of goals see Prochaska, Norcross, and DiClemente, 1994). The Transtheoretical Model of Change posits that change involves transition through a series of identifiable, although somewhat overlapping stages. Five of these stages have direct relevance for goal setting in coaching. These stages are:

1. *Precontemplation:* No intention to change in the foreseeable future.

2. *Contemplation:* Considering making stages, but have not yet made any changes.

3. *Preparation:* Increased commitment to change, intend to make changes in the near future and often have started to make small changes.

4. *Action:* Engaging in the new behaviors, but have made such changes for only a short period of time (usually less than six months).

5. *Maintenance:* Consistently engaging in the new behavior over a period of time (usually six months).

Stage-specific Coaching Strategies

For individuals in the *Pre-contemplation stage* the general principle is to raise awareness, increasing the amount of information available to the coachee so that they can move forward into action. There are many ways of raising awareness including multi-rater feedback scales, qualitative feedback, sales or performance data, or other relevant information.

The key characteristic of the *Contemplation stage* is ambivalence; the conjoint holding of two or more conflicting desires, emotions, beliefs or opinions. The general principle for individuals in the *contemplation* stage is to help the coachee explore their ambivalence, rather than pushing them into setting a goal before they are ready. Setting specific or stretching goals too soon in this stage often results in the coachee disengaging from the goal selection process.

In the *Preparation stage* the coachee is getting ready to make change. Here the aim is to build commitment to change. In terms of goals, the coach should be helping the coachee focus on developing a clear vision of the future (abstract goals) and using goal setting that involves small, easily attainable but consistent action steps. Progress throughout this stage should be monitored closely and new desired behaviors positively reinforced by acknowledging and celebrating the attainment of small sub-goals.

In the *Action* and *Maintenance stages* the key is to build on past successes and maximize self-directed change, working on using more stretching goals and developing strategies to sustain the change over time.

Clearly, there is a considerable art to the effective use of goals in coaching. Other factors that impact on the goal selection process include the coachee's ability to focus on the tasks at hand, their ability to adapt in the face of adversity, and the perceived purpose of the goal and the extent to which they feel that they have agency and autonomy in the goal selection process.

Coaching Session Moderators

There are also a number of factors related to the coaching session itself that impact on the goal selection process. These include the coach's ability to set effective goals and facilitate action planning, and the coach's ability to maximize goal congruency and goal alignment whilst facilitating the coachee's goal-focused self-regulation.

The success of the above is also dependent on the coach's ability to bring perceived value to the coaching session and develop a strong working alliance with the coachee (Gray, 2007). All the theoretical knowledge about goal theory is of no import, unless the coach can put this theory into action, managing the goal striving process, holding the coachee accountable and being solution and outcome focused.

Goal Choice and Action Planning

Goal choice and action planning are outcomes of the goal selection process. It is important to note that although the model represents these as linear processes, in reality these are iterative, with a certain amount of back and forth movement between stages. The goal choice and action planning parameters include goal difficulty and specificity, whether the goals are approach or avoidance goals, time framing (distal or proximal), and a performance or learning orientation.

Goal choice is a necessary, but not sufficient part of the coaching process — plans must be developed and enacted. Action planning is the process of developing a systemic means of attaining goals and is particularly important for individuals who have low self-regulatory skills (Kirschenbaum, Humphrey, and Malett, 1981). The coach's role is to develop the coachee's ability to create a realistic and workable plan of action and task strategies that facilitate the goal striving process and promote effort and persistence in the face of adversity.

One key outcome of successful action planning is the facilitation of the coachee's transition from a *deliberative* mindset to an *implementational* mindset (Gollwitzer, 1999; Heckhausen and Gollwitzer, 1987; see also Chapter 7). The deliberative mindset is characterized by a careful weighing of the pros and cons of action and a careful examination of competing goals or courses of action (Carver and Scheier, 1998). The implementational mindset is engaged once the decision to act has been made. This mindset has a determined, focused quality, and is biased in favor of thinking about success rather than failure — clearly an important point for coaching.

The shift from the deliberative to the implementational mindset is also important because individuals in implementation see themselves as being more in control of their outcomes (Gollwitzer and Kinney, 1989) and tend to hold a positive, optimistic view of their ability to succeed (Gollwitzer, 1999). These factors are associated with higher levels of self-efficacy, self-regulation and goal attainment (Bandura, 1982).

The Self-regulation Cycle, Feedback and Goal Satisfaction

The monitoring and evaluation of actions and the generation of feedback as the coachee moves through the self-regulation cycle is a vital part of the coaching process. However, many people are not naturally self-reflective (Jordan and

Troth, 2002) and so the coach may need to find ways to develop action plans that focus on observable, easily monitored behaviors.

What is monitored will, of course, vary according to the coachee's goal and situation. Some behaviors will be easier to monitor than others. Exercise or activity-based actions can be relatively straightforward to monitor. Interpersonal skills or communication patterns in the workplace may be more difficult to monitor, and the coach and coachee may have to be creative in devising means of monitoring and evaluating.

Care should be taken to set the kinds of goals that will generate useful feedback, because the right feedback is vital in providing information about how (or if) subsequent goals and associated actions should be modified. This process, if done well, eventuates in successful goal attainment. Goals that have been well-aligned will be satisfying when achieved, and the positive emotions associated with such goal satisfaction may play an important role in priming the coachee for engagement in future challenges.

So What? Does Goal Theory Matter in Practice?

Although it is clear from the above discussion that goal theory can inform what happens within coaching sessions and also has great relevance for the broader coaching process, the question arises: does goal theory really matter in actual practice? Is the coach's ability to be goal-focused related to coaching outcomes? This is a key question for the further development of evidence-based coaching practice.

A significant body of research within the psychotherapeutic literature holds that the most important factors in determining therapeutic outcomes are the so-called "common factors" — the ability of the therapist to develop a working alliance with the client that embodies trust, warmth and respect for the client's autonomy (Lampropoulos, 2000). Not surprisingly it is often assumed in the coaching literature that this is also the case for coaching (McKenna and Davis, 2009a). However, coaching is not therapy. The aims and process of coaching and therapy are different.

To date there have been few studies that have sought to explore the importance of goals in the coaching relationship, so I was interested to see which aspect of the coaching relationship was more positively related to coaching outcomes—a goal-focused approach to coaching, or the so-called "common-factors" associated with the person-centered approach (Grant, 2012a). To explore this issue I designed a within-subjects (pre-post) coaching study, in which forty-nine mature age coachees (males = 12; females = 37; mean age = 37.5 yrs) set personal goals and completed a 10 to 12 week, five-session, solution-focused cognitive-behavioral personal coaching program using the GROW model (Whitmore, 1992).[1]

Participants were asked to identify their desired outcome for the coaching relationship (i.e. their goal), then rated the extent to which they had achieved this outcome on a scale from 0 percent (no attainment) to 100 percent (complete attainment). Psychological health was also assessed using the Depression Anxiety and Stress Scale (DASS-21: Lovibond and Lovibond, 1995), and an 18-item version of Ryff's Psychological Well-being Scales (Ryff and Keyes, 1995). In addition, self-insight was assessed using the Insight subscale of the Self-reflection and Insight Scale (SRIS; Grant, Franklin, and Langford, 2002).

In order to see which aspect of the coaching relationship was the better predictor of coaching success, two key measures of the coaching relationship were used. The goal-focused aspect of the coaching relationship was measured using an adaptation of the Goal-focused Coaching Skills Questionnaire (GCSQ; Grant and Cavanagh, 2007). Items on this scale include: "The coach was very good at helping me develop clear, simple and achievable action plans"; "We discussed any failures on my part to complete agreed actions steps"; "The goals we set during coaching were very important to me"; "My coach asked me about progress towards my goals"; "The goals we set were stretching but attainable".

The "common factors" aspect was assessed using an adaption of Deci and Ryan's (2005) Perceived Autonomy Support Scale (PASS). Items on this scale included: "My coach listened to how I would like to do things"; "I feel that my coach cares about me as a person"; "My coach encouraged me to ask questions"; "I feel that my coach accepts me"; "I felt understood by my coach"; "I feel a lot of trust in my coach".

---

1   The GROW model is a commonly-used way of structuring the coaching conversation by setting a goal for the coaching session, then discussing the reality of the situation, exploring options and finally wrapping up the session by delineating some action steps. Although this may appear to be a simplistic linear process, in fact the GROW model can be used in a sophisticated and iterative fashion, with the conversation cycling back and forth between steps. For an extended discussion on the use of the GROW model see Grant (2011).

The coaching program appeared to be effective and successful in helping the clients reach their desired outcomes for the coaching relationship: there was a significant increase in goal attainment following the coaching program ($t_{1,48}$ (11.43); $p <.001$), as well as insight ($t_{1,48}$ (2.61); $p <.05$), and significant decreases in anxiety ($t_{1,48}$ (2.89); $p <.01$) and stress ($t_{1,48}$ (2.13); $p <.05$). No changes in levels of depression or psychological well-being were observed.

The main area of interest was the relationship between coaching successes and the various aspects of the coaching styles used by the coaches. There was a significant correlation between coaching success as defined by the extent to which the client had achieved their desired outcome (i.e. goal attainment) and the GCSQ ($r = .43$; $p <.01$), and there was also a significant correlation between coaching success (as defined by the extent to which the client had achieved their desired outcome) and the PASS ($r = .29$; $p <.05$). Not surprisingly there was also a significant correlation between the GCSQ and the PASS ($r = .61$; $p <.001$). This suggests that both a goal-focused coaching style and a "common factors" person-centered coaching style contribute to coaching success.

However, and this is a key point, the correlation between coaching success (goal attainment) and the goal-focused coaching style measured by the GCSQ remained significant even when statistically controlling for a "common factors" person-centered coaching style as measured by the PASS ($r = .31$; $p <.05$). It should be noted that, when controlling for the goal-focused coaching style as measured by the GCSQ, the relationship between the PASS and coaching success (goal attainment) was not significant ($r = .03$; $p = .81$).

These findings strongly suggest that the use of goals in coaching is indeed of practical importance in that the use of a goal-focused coaching style is more effective than a "common factors" person-centered coaching style in the coaching context. This is not to say that a person-centered relationship is not important. Rather, this reminds us that the coaching relationship differs from the counseling or therapeutic relationship, and that coaches need to be mindful of the fact that they are employed by their clients to help make purposeful positive change in their personal and professional lives.

Conclusion

Coaches may see themselves as helping clients explore their values, clarify their intentions, and then working to help them to achieve their personal aspirations.

We may use metaphors such as helping clients chart a course, navigate the waters of life or re-author their lived narratives. However, regardless of such semantics, coaching is necessarily a goal-directed activity.

The integrative goal-focused approach to coaching presented in this chapter is a multifaceted methodology for helping individuals and organizations create and sustain change. The key issue for coaches is one of informed flexibility in goal setting. By understanding the different types of goals and their relationship to the process of change, and through facilitating the goal alignment process, professional coaches can work more efficiently with their clients, helping them to achieve insight and behavioral change that enhances their workplace performance, their professional working lives and, most importantly, their own personal well-being and sense of self.

References

AC. (2012). Association of coaching definition of coaching. [Retrieved April 19, 2012, from] http://www.associationforcoaching.com/about/about03.htm

Austin, J.T. & Vancouver, J.B. (1996). Goal constructs in psychology: Structure, process, and content. *Psychological Bulletin, 120*(3), 338–75.

Bargh, J.A., Gollwitzer, P.M., Lee-Chai, A., Barndollar, K., & Trötschel, R. (2001). The automated will: Nonconscious activation and pursuit of behavioral goals. *Journal of Personality and Social Psychology, 81*(6), 1014.

Benavides, L. (2009). *The Relationship Between Executive Coaching and Organizational Performance of Female Executives as a Predictor for Organizational Success.* Benavides, Lily: University of San Francisco.

Bandura, A. (1982). Self-efficacy mechanism in human agency. *American Psychologist, 37*(2), 122–47.

Bono, J.E., Purvanova, R.K., Towler, A.J., & Peterson, D.B. (2009). A survey of executive coaching practices. *Personnel Psychology, 62*(2), 361–404.

Burke, D. & Linley, P. (2007). Enhancing goal self-concordance through coaching. *International Coaching Psychology Review, 2*(1), 62–9.

Carver, C.S. & Scheier, M.F. (1998). *On the Self-Regulation of Behavior.* Cambridge: Cambridge University Press.

Chulef, A.S., Read, S.J., & Walsh, D.A. (2001). A hierarchical taxonomy of human goals. *Motivation & Emotion, 25*(3), 191–232.

Church, A.H. (1997). Managerial self-awareness in high-performing individuals in organizations. *Journal of Applied Psychology, 82*(2), 281–92.

Clutterbuck, D. (2008). What's happening in coaching and mentoring? And what is the difference between them? *Development and Learning in Organizations, 22*(4), 8–10.

Clutterbuck, D. (2010). Coaching reflection: The liberated coach. *Coaching: An International Journal of Theory, Research and Practice, 3*(1), 73–81.

Coats, E.J., Janoff-Bulman, R., & Alpert, N. (1996). Approach versus avoidance goals: Differences in self-evaluation and well-being. *Personality and Social Psychology Bulletin, 22*(10), 1057–67.

Cochran, W. & Tesser, A. (1996). The "What the hell" Effect: Some effects of goal proximity and goal framing on performance. In L. Martin & A. Tesser (Eds), *Striving and Feeling,* 99–123. New Jersey: LEA.

Costa, P.T. & McCrae, R.R. (1992). *Revised NEO Personality Inventory and NEO Five-Factor Inventory: Professional Manual.* Florida: Psychological Assessment Resources.

Custers, R. & Aarts, H. (2010). The unconscious will: How the pursuit of goals operates outside of conscious awareness. *Science, 329*(5987), 47.

Deci, E.L. & Ryan, R.M. (1980). Self-determination theory: When mind mediates behavior. *Journal of Mind & Behavior, 1*(1), 33–43.

Deci, E.L. & Ryan, R.M. (2005). Perceived autonomy support scale. [Retrieved August 5, 2006 from] http://www.psych.rochester.edu/SDT/measures/needs_scl.html

Deci, E.L. & Ryan, R.M. (Eds). (2002). *Handbook of Self-determination Research.* Rochester, NY: University of Rochester Press.

Dweck, C.S. (1986). Motivational processes affecting learning. *American Psychologist, 41*(10), 1040–48.

Doran, G.T. (1981). There's a S.M.A.R.T. Way to write management's goals and objectives. *Management Review, 70*(11), 35–6.

Duncan, J., Emslie, H., Williams, P., Johnson, R., & Freer, C. (1996). Intelligence and the frontal lobe: The organization of goal-directed behavior. *Cognitive Psychology, 30*(3), 257–303.

Elliot, A.J. & McGregor, H.A. (2001). A 2 × 2 achievement goal framework. *Journal of Personality and Social Psychology, 80*(3), 501–19.

Elliot, A.J., Sheldon, K.M., & Church, M.A. (1997). Avoidance personal goals and subjective well-being. *Personality & Social Psychology Bulletin, 23*(9), 915–27.

EMCC. (2011). European mentoring and coaching council code of conduct for coaching and mentoring. [Retrieved 19th April 2012, from] http://www.emccouncil.org/src/ultimo/models/Download/4.pdf

Emmons, R.A. (1992). Abstract versus concrete goals: Personal striving level, physical illness and psychological wellbeing. *Journal of Personality and Social Psychology, 62,* 292–300.

Freedman, A.M. & Perry, J.A. (2010). Executive consulting under pressure: A case study. *Consulting Psychology Journal: Practice and Research, 62*(3), 189–202.

Gollwitzer, P.M. (1999). Implementation intentions: Simple effects of simple plans. *American Psychologist, 54*(7), 493–503.

Gollwitzer, P.M. & Kinney, R.F. (1989). Effects of deliberative and implementational mindsets on illusion of control. *Journal of Personality and Social Psychology, 73*, 186–99.

Grant, A.M. (2002). Towards a psychology of coaching: The impact of coaching on metacognition, mental health and goal attainment. *Dissertation Abstracts International Section A: Humanities and Social Sciences, 63/12*, p. 6094 (June).

Grant, A.M. (2006). An integrative goal-focused approach to executive coaching. In D. Stober & A.M. Grant (Eds), *Evidence based Coaching Handbook*, 153–92. New York: Wiley.

Grant, A.M. (2011). Is it time to REGROW the GROW model? Issues related to teaching coaching session structures. *The Coaching Psychologist, 7*(2), 118–26.

Grant, A.M. (2012a). *Making a Real Difference: Insights and Applications from Evidence-based Coaching Research in the Lab, Workplace and Reality TV.* Paper presented at the Second International Congress of Coaching Psychology, Sydney, Australia.

Grant, A.M. (2012b). An integrated model of goal-focused coaching: An evidence-based framework for teaching and practice. *International Coaching Psychology Review, 7*(2), 146–65.

Grant, A.M. & Cavanagh, M. (2007). The goal-focused coaching skill questionnaire: Preliminarily findings. *Social Behavior and Personality: An International Journal, 35*(6), 751–60.

Grant, A.M., Curtayne, L., & Burton, G. (2009). Executive coaching enhances goal attainment, resilience and workplace well-being: A randomised controlled study. *The Journal of Positive Psychology, 4*(5), 396–407.

Grant, A.M., Franklin, J., & Langford, P. (2002). The self-reflection and insight scale: A new measure of private self-consciousness. *Social Behavior and Personality, 30*(8), 821–36.

Grant, A.M. & Green, J. (2004). *Coach Yourself.* London: Pearson.

Gray, D.E. (2007). Towards a systemic model of coaching supervision: Some lessons from psychotherapeutic and counselling models. *Australian Psychologist, 42*(4), 300–309.

Gregory, J.B., Beck, J.W., & Carr, A.E. (2011). Goals, feedback, and self-regulation: Control theory as a natural framework for executive coaching. *Consulting Psychology Journal: Practice and Research, 63*(1), 26.

Gresham, F.M., Evans, S., & Elliott, S.N. (1988). Academic and social self-efficacy scale: Development and initial validation. *Journal of Psychoeducational Assessment, 6*(2), 125–38.

Heckhausen, H. & Gollwitzer, P.M. (1987). Thought content and cognitive functioning in motivational versus volitional states of mind. *Motivation and Emotion, 11*, 101–20.

Higgins, E.T. (1987). Self-discrepancy: A theory relating self and affect. *Psychological Review, 94*, 319–40.

Hudson, F.M. (1999). *The Handbook of Coaching*. San Francisco: Jossey-Bass.

ICF. (2012). International coach federation code of ethics. [Retrieved 19th April 2012, from] http://www.coachfederation.org/ethics/

Jordan, P.J. & Troth, A.C. (2002). Emotional intelligence and conflict resolution: Implications for human resource development. *Advances in Developing Human Resources, 4*(1), 62–79.

Karniol, R. & Ross, M. (1996). The motivational impact of temporal focus: Thinking about the future and the past. *Annual Review of Psychology, 47*, 593–620.

Kirschenbaum, D.S., Humphrey, L.L., & Malett, S.D. (1981). Specificity of planning in adult self-control: An applied investigation. *Journal of Personality & Social Psychology, 40*(5), 941–50.

Klinger, E. (1975). Consequences of commitment to and disengagement from incentives. *Psychological Review, 82*, 1–25.

Kristof-Brown, A.L. & Stevens, C.K. (2001). Goal congruence in project teams: Does the fit between members' personal mastery and performance goals matter? *Journal of Applied Psychology, 86*(6), 1083–95.

Lampropoulos, G.K. (2000). Definitional and research issues in the common factors approach to psychotherapy integration: Misconceptions, clarifications, and proposals. *Journal of Psychotherapy Integration, 10*(4), 415–38.

Lewis-Duarte, M. (2010). *Executive Coaching: A Study of Coaches' Use of Influence Tactics*. Lewis-Duarte, Melissa: The Claremont Graduate University, US.

Linnenbrink, E.A., Ryan, A.M., & Pintrich, P.R. (1999). The role of goals and affect in working memory functioning. *Learning & Individual Differences, 11*(2), 213–30.

Little, B.R. (1993). Personal projects: A rationale and method for investigation. *Environment and Behavior, 15*, 273–309.

Locke, E.A. (2000). Motivation, cognition, and action: An analysis of studies of task goals and knowledge. *Applied Psychology, 49*(3), 408–29.

Locke, E.A. (1996). Motivation through conscious goal setting. *Applied & Preventive Psychology, 5*(2), 117–24.

Locke, E.A. & Latham, G.P. (2002). Building a practically useful theory of goal setting and task motivation. *American Psychologist, 57*(9), 705–17.

Lovibond, S.H. & Lovibond, P.F. (1995). *Manual for the Depression Anxiety Stress Scales*. Sydney: Psychology Foundation of Australia.

Manderlink, G. & Harackiewicz, J.M. (1984). Proximal versus distal goal setting and intrinsic motivation. *Journal of Personality & Social Psychology, 47*(4), 918–28.

McKenna, D. & Davis, S.L. (2009a). Hidden in plain sight: The active ingredients of executive coaching. *Industrial and Organizational Psychology: Perspectives on Science and Practice, 2*(3), 244–60.

McKenna, D. & Davis, S.L. (2009b). What is the active ingredients equation for success in executive coaching? *Industrial and Organizational Psychology: Perspectives on Science and Practice, 2*(3), 297–304.

Midgley, C., Kaplan, A., & Middleton, M. (2001). Performance-approach goals: Good for what, for whom, under what circumstances, and at what cost? *Journal of Educational Psychology, 93*(1), 77–86.

Milare, S.A. & Yoshida, E.M.P. (2009). Brief intervention in organizations: Change in executive coaching. *Psicologia em Estudo, 14*(4), 717–27.

Moskowitz, G.B. & Grant, H. (Eds). (2009). *The Psychology of Goals*. New York: The Guilford Press.

Oishi, S., Schimmack, U., Diener, E., & Suh, E.M. (1998). The measurement of values and individualism-collectivism. *Personality & Social Psychology Bulletin, 24*(11), 1177–89.

Ordóñez, L.D., Schweitzer, M.E., Galinsky, A.D., & Bazerman, M.H. (2009). Goals gone wild: The systematic side effects of overprescribing goal setting. *Academy of Management Perspectives, 23*(1), 6–16.

Pervin, L.A. (1983). *The Stasis and Flow of Behavior: Toward a Theory Of Goals*. In *Nebraska Symposium on Motivation, 38*, 1–53. Lincoln: University of Nebraska Press.

Peterson, D.B. (2011). Good to great coaching. In G. Hernez-Broome & L.A. Boyce (Eds), *Advancing Executive Coaching: Setting the Course of Successful Leadership Coaching*, 83–102. San Francisco: Jossey-Bass.

Prochaska, J.O., Norcross, J.C., & DiClemente, C.C. (1994). *Changing for Good*. New York: Avon Books.

Raia, A.P. (1965). Goal setting and self-control: An empirical study. *Journal of Management Studies, 2*(1), 34–53.

Rawsthorne, L.J. & Elliott, A.J. (1999). Achievement goals and intrinsic motivation: A meta-analytic review. *Personality & Social Psychology Review, 3*(4), 326–44.

Ryff, C.D. & Keyes, C.L.M. (1995). The structure of psychological well-being revisited. *Journal of Personality and Social Psychology, 69*(4), 719–27.

Sarrazin, P., Vallerand, R., Guillet, E., Pelletier, L., & Cury, F. (2002). Motivation and dropout in female handballers: A 21-month prospective study. *European Journal of Social Psychology, 32*(3), 395–418.

Schnell, E.R. (2005). A case study of executive coaching as a support mechanism during organizational growth and evolution. *Consulting Psychology Journal: Practice and Research, 57*(1), 41–56.

Seijts, G.H. & Latham, G.P. (2001). The effect of distal learning, outcome, and proximal goals on a moderately complex task. *Journal of Organizational Behavior, 22*(3), 291–307.

Sheldon, K. & Elliot, A.J. (1999). Goal striving, need satisfaction and longitudinal well-being: The self-concordance model. *Journal of Personality and Social Psychology, 76*(3), 482–97.

Sheldon, K.M. (2002). The self-concordance model of healthy goal striving: When personal goals correctly represent the person. In E.L. Deci & R.M. Ryan (Eds), *Handbook of Self-determination Research*, 65–86. Rochester, NY: University of Rochester Press.

Sheldon, K.M. & Elliot, A.J. (1998). Not all personal goals are personal: Comparing autonomous and controlled reasons for goals as predictors of effort and attainment. *Personality & Social Psychology Bulletin, 24*(5), 546–57.

Sheldon, K.M. & Kasser, T. (1995). Coherence and congruence: Two aspects of personality integration. *Journal of Personality & Social Psychology, 68*(3), 531–43.

Smither, J.W., London, M., Flautt, R., Vargas, Y., & Kucine, I. (2003). Can working with an executive coach improve multisource feedback ratings over time? A quasi-experimental field study. *Personnel Psychology, 56*(1), 23–44.

Spence, G.B. (2007). Gas powered coaching: Goal attainment scaling and its use in coaching research and practice. *International Coaching Psychology Review, 2*(2), 155–67.

Stern, L.R. (2009). Challenging some basic assumptions about psychology and executive coaching: Who knows best, who is the client, and what are the goals of executive coaching? *Industrial and Organizational Psychology: Perspectives on Science and Practice, 2*(3), 268–71.

Street, H. (2002). Exploring relationships between goal setting, goal pursuit and depression: A review. *Australian Psychologist 37*(2), 95–103.

Turner, C.A. (2004). *Executive Coaching: The Perception of Executive Coaching from the Executive's Perspective.* Turner, Carol Ann: Pepperdine U, US.

WABC. (2012). Worldwide assoication of business coaches definition of business coaching. [Retrieved April 19, 2012, from] http://www.wabccoaches.com/includes/popups/definition.html

Warshaw, P.R. & Davis, F.D. (1985). The accuracy of behavioral intention versus behavioral expectation for predicting behavioral goals. *The Journal of Psychology, 119*(6), 599–602.

Weldon, E. & Yun, S. (2000). The effects of proximal and distal goals on goal level, strategy development, and group performance. *Journal of Applied Behavioral Science, 36*(3), 336–44.

Whitmore, J. (1992). *Coaching for Performance*. London: Nicholas Brealey.

Winters, D. & Latham, G.P. (1996). The effect of learning versus outcome goals on a simple versus a complex task. *Group & Organization Management, 21*(2), 236–50.

5

Self-determination Theory Within Coaching Contexts: Supporting Motives and Goals that Promote Optimal Functioning and Well-being

Gordon B. Spence and Edward L. Deci

Coaching is an activity that is inherently motivational as it deals with the processes of facilitating goal setting (Grant and Cavanagh, 2011) and strengthening motives that are linked to effective functioning and well-being (Spence and Grant, 2013). In other words, it is about providing the interpersonal supports for the intrapersonal processes that energize and direct behavior toward healthier and more successful human functioning. It is somewhat surprising, therefore, that theories of motivation have not occupied a more prominent place in the scholarly coaching literature (Spence and Oades, 2011). Whilst coaching practice is explicitly and implicitly informed by a variety of different theoretical approaches (for discussions see Barner and Higgins, 2007; Peltier, 2001; Spence and Oades, 2011; Stober and Grant, 2006), including theories of self-regulation (e.g. Carver and Scheier, 1998) and goal setting (e.g. Latham and Locke, 1991), coaching has yet to capitalize on many of the insights that have emerged from the scientific study of motivation.

In this chapter we focus on one such theory, namely, self-determination theory, (SDT; Deci and Ryan, 2000; Ryan and Deci, 2008a) and we both give an overview of its theoretical propositions and discuss its relevance to coaching. As such, the following pages, which respond to the ongoing call for coaching practice to be built upon firm theoretical and empirical foundations (Grant and Cavanagh, 2011), attempt to translate empirically validated theory into practice, capitalize on recent interest in SDT shown by coaching scholars (e.g. Burke and Linley, 2007; Govindji and Linley, 2007; Spence and Grant, 2013; Spence and Oades, 2011), and stimulate further advances in coaching practice and research.

Coaching: What's it Really About?

The literature is awash with definitions of coaching (Hawkins, 2008), that vary from the relatively generic, "a conversation, or series of conversations, one person has with another [relating to] the coachee's learning and progress" (Starr, 2011), to more domain-specific formulations, such as that offered by Hall, Otazo, and Hollenbeck (1999):

> ... a practical, goal-focused form of personal, one-on-one learning for busy executives and may be used to improve performance, or executive behavior, enhance a career or prevent derailment, and work through organizational issues or change initiatives. (p. 40)

This definition is typical of many presented in the coaching literature, as it emphasizes the enhancement of performance and is concerned primarily with gains made at the behavioral level. Indeed, of the nine definitions drawn from the literature by Hawkins (2008), seven were explicitly focused on "performance," which is not surprising because most workplaces assess the value of their employees based on their accomplishments.

Yet our sense from reading the coaching literature and interacting with coaches (and trainers of coaches) is that, at least implicitly, coaching is about much more than what people can *do*. Fundamentally, it seems to be strongly focused on "human potential": on unlocking and developing human capabilities (Whitmore, 1996), maximizing people's engagement (CIPD, 2007), and obtaining a greater contribution of one's latent abilities and strengths (Hawkins, 2008). In a sense, coaching seems, to a significant degree, to be about psychological well-being. Relatedly, concepts such as self-regulation, self-directed learning, and personal growth appear as strong themes (Caplan, 2003; Downey, 2003; Parsloe, 1999), and some definitions of coaching reflect a more holistic understanding of people, emphasizing the quality of life experiences and placing coachees' wellness alongside behavioral effectiveness as appropriate goals for coaching (e.g. Grant and Spence, 2010).

A MORE HOLISTIC CONCEPTUALIZATION

In this chapter, we opt for a holistic understanding of coaching, one cast in terms of the *optimal functioning* of individuals, with optimal functioning understood to be a construct with physiological, behavioral, cognitive, affective, and meaning components. The focus on these multiple outcomes evolves naturally from the organismic starting point of self-determination theory (Deci and Ryan, 1985). Unlike some psychological theories that have been considered relevant to coaching, such as cognitive (Auerbach, 2006) or psychodynamic (Allcorn, 2006) approaches, SDT assumes that people are proactive organisms, with an inherent growth tendency that is part of their genetic endowment. That is, the meta-theory maintains that people are by nature inclined toward acting on and engaging the environment in ways that satisfy their psychological needs and, in the process, develop mastery, connectedness, and empowerment as the bases for their continued engagement, self-elaboration, and coherence (Deci and Ryan, 1985). Such attempted growth, if it occurs within developmental contexts that provide necessary psychological nutrients, will facilitate flourishing. To the extent that it has not, people will be turning to coaches or other professionals for the supports they need to become more effective.

Accordingly, we consider excellence in coaching to be the implementation of a set of interpersonal processes that lead to the coachee experiencing enhanced physical health (physiological), engagement in effective, purposeful actions (behavioral), the possession of sufficient attentional control to process information effectively (cognitive), an ability to encounter a wider range of emotional states with equanimity and poise (affective), and the conscious linking of personal goals and commitments to important beliefs, core values, and/or developing interests (meaning).

We consider this understanding of coaching to be preferable to the more narrow behavioral and performance-oriented conceptualizations because knowing only what people can do and how well they can do it will yield an incomplete picture of their overall status. Indeed, it is not difficult for us to bring to mind examples of individuals who, by all external indicators (e.g. attainment of KPIs/performance goals, bonus payments, social status), appear to be doing extremely well, yet they report a hidden "dark" side that may be characterized by chronic physical illness, sub-optimal effort, poor concentration, elevated depression, stress or anxiety, and lack of meaning and purpose. Such "high performers" are in a perilous position. Whilst change is usually clearly indicated, ambivalence is often high and substantial enough to prevent meaningful change (Casserley and Megginson, 2009). So, the performer presses on: But for how long?

Optimal functioning is sustainable functioning

The utility of explicitly anchoring coaching to a holistic concept like optimal functioning is that it focuses both the coachee and coach (as well as other stakeholders) on the former's life experiences and sustained behavior change. This points toward enhancing self-regulation and, if done well, results in greater persistence even in the absence of specific coaching-related contingencies. Enhanced self-regulation can then be supplemented by supportive scaffolds such as simple practices (e.g. physical exercise routines) and structures (e.g. social support networks) to help maintain self-renewing motivation, effort, and well-being.

If, as we have just argued, coaching is about optimal functioning, then coaches will be well served by theories that elucidate the pre-conditions for optimal functioning and give guidance on what is required for those conditions to be created. SDT is specifically concerned with (1) the development of conditions that support greater self-reliance, vitality, task engagement, and effective learning; (2) the motivational (i.e. regulatory) processes that underlie and organize these indicators of optimal functioning; (3) the life goals whose pursuit and attainment are more aligned with achieving the outcomes; and (4) the human psychological needs that energize the motivated activity and goal pursuits that have been shown empirically in many studies across multiple domains to yield the desired life experiences, affects, persistence, willingness, and accomplishment (e.g. Deci and Ryan, 2000; Ryan and Deci, 2008b). However, as the theoretical knowledge base of coaching is still relatively underdeveloped, it appears that coaches may not yet have gained an understanding of this work, which appears to hold great potential for informing coaching practices. We will thus attempt to make the relevance of SDT to coaching ever clearer.

Bolstering the Evidence Base for Coaching using Self-determination Theory

Arguably the most dominant theme to emerge from the coaching literature in the past decade is "coaching needs more research." The rationale for this is fairly straightforward. The unregulated nature of the coaching industry, coupled with the widespread popularity of coaching, has attracted practitioners whose work is influenced by diverse professional and non-professional backgrounds (Spence, Cavanagh, and Grant, 2006). As such, it has typically been a difficult industry for consumers to navigate, with little agreement on what constitutes best practice—an issue the empirical investigation of coaching should help to clarify. Indeed, it has also been argued that the coaching industry needs to embrace rigorous empirical inquiry and seek greater professionalization if it is to secure its future (Spence, 2007).

Of course, research is only one part of the professionalization equation for the coaching industry. How research is used is also important, which is why calls for more research in coaching have often been accompanied by calls for more evidence-based coaching practices (Cavanagh and Grant, 2006). Stober and Grant (2006) define evidence-based coaching as "the intelligent and conscientious use of *best current knowledge* integrated with practitioner expertise in making decisions about how to deliver coaching", [with "best current knowledge" defined as] "up-to-date information from relevant, valid research, theory and practice" (p. 6, italics in original). As such, the present discussion is part of a larger dialogue currently occurring in the coaching literature about what constitutes firm foundations for coaching practice. For this contribution to the unfolding dialogue, we chose to focus on SDT because it has an extensive evidence base that can be readily adapted to specify interpersonal conditions (viz., coaches' orientations, behaviors, and supports) that facilitate coachees' sustained change toward optimal motivation, effective life goals, high-quality performance, and healthy functioning.

THE RELEVANCE OF SDT RESEARCH

While SDT researchers have yet to focus on coaching per se, literally hundreds of studies have examined the validity of SDT in the contexts where coaching is used (Spence and Oades, 2011). Hence, we argue that the extensive support both for the basic processes of SDT (e.g. Deci, Koestner, and Ryan, 1999; Ng, et al., 2012; Vansteenkiste, Ryan, and Deci, 2008b) and for its relevance to such domains as parenting (e.g. Grolnick, Deci, and Ryan, 1997), education (Ryan and Deci, 2009), management (Gagné and Deci, 2005), health care (Ryan, Patrick, Deci, and Williams, 2008), psychotherapy and counseling (Ryan, Lynch, Vansteenkiste, and Deci, 2011), and sport coaching (Ryan and Deci, 2007), makes the direct applicability of SDT to coaching extremely compelling. Through this research we have seen that there are substantial similarities in the kinds of responsiveness, behaviors, and supports that, when provided by a recognized authority such as a manager or psychotherapist, will promote effective growth, change, persistence, performance, and wellness among those with whom they are working. Of course, we still strongly support the idea of research programs applying SDT specifically to coaching.

Self-determination Theory: A Brief Overview

SDT is a macro-theory of human motivation that has evolved over four decades and encompasses six related mini-theories. Whilst each mini-theory has its own specific focus (see Table 5.1), all of them address interrelated psychological processes that are deemed important for psychological growth, development, and effective functioning (for a comprehensive review see Deci and Ryan, 2000).

BASIC PSYCHOLOGICAL NEEDS

According to Deci and Ryan (2000), "it is part of the adaptive design features of the human organism to engage in interesting activities, to exercise capacities, to pursue connectedness in social groups, and to integrate intrapsychic and interpersonal experiences into a relative unity" (p. 229). Stated differently, human beings have a set of universal, fundamental psychological needs, the satisfaction of which are essential for healthy development, vital engagement, effective behaving, and psychological well-being. Specifically, the quote is suggesting that people need to feel *competent* as they exercise and expand their capacities, *related* as they connect with others within collectives, and *autonomous* as they become more psychologically integrated and self-regulating. These three fundamental psychological nutrients are at the core of basic psychological needs theory (BPNT), which explains how satisfaction of these needs supports the development and operation of the most effective motivations and healthiest life goals, resulting in the range of outcomes outlined above. In contrast, thwarting of these basic needs will have a significant cost for the individual both developmentally and in contemporary circumstances, resulting in diminished wellness and performance outcomes.

Table 5.1   Overview of SDT mini-theories

Sub-theory	Scope
Basic Needs Theory (BPNT)	Links optimal functioning and well-being to the joint satisfaction of three basic psychological needs: autonomy, competence and relatedness.
Cognitive Evaluation Theory (CET)	Focuses on how intrinsic motivation (IM) is enhanced by social-cultural factors that lead people to feel effective (e.g. positive feedback) and autonomous (e.g. acknowledging feelings), and is diminished by factors that convey incompetence (e.g. negative feedback) or constrain personal choice (e.g. threats) and lead people to feel coerced or seduced into action.
Organismic Integration Theory (OIT)	Argues that the regulation and values of extrinsically motivated behaviors can be internalized and integrated to differing degrees, resulting in regulation with differing levels of volition and endorsement (viz. external, introjected, identified, integrated).
Causality Orientations Theory (COT)	Describes three general motivational orientations; *Autonomous Orientation* (influenced by one's interests and self-endorsed values), *Controlled Orientation* (influenced by controls that govern how one should behave), and *Impersonal Orientation* (influenced by beliefs that one's efforts will be ineffectual).
Relationships Motivation Theory (RMT)	Focuses on the importance of need satisfaction within close relationships, emphasizing that high-quality relationships require people to feel autonomous within the relationship and to support the autonomy of their partners.
Goal Contents Theory (GCT)	Proposes that the beneficial impact of personal goals is influenced by the degree to which effort invested in those goals results in the satisfaction of one's basic psychological needs.

Accordingly, the theory proposes that people's level of functioning and well-being depends upon the degree of satisfaction of three basic psychological needs (Deci and Ryan, 1985). People are expected to do well and feel their best when the socio-cultural *conditions* of their lives (i.e. family relationships, friendships, workplace culture, political systems, cultural norms) support the inherent needs for freely engaging in interesting activities (i.e. autonomy), producing valued outcomes through the use of their strengths and abilities (i.e. competence), and feeling closely and securely connected to significant others (i.e. relatedness).

INTRINSIC AND EXTRINSIC MOTIVATION

Central to self-determination theory is the assertion that it is important to differentiate types of motivation in order to understand and predict different qualities of experience and behavior. The primary distinction within the theory is between *autonomous motivation* and *controlled motivation*. Autonomous motivation involves acting with a full sense of choice, willingness, and volition. When autonomous, people will concur with that which they are doing, and they will experience positive affect, endorsement, and satisfaction. Autonomous motivation comprises two specific types of motivation—intrinsic motivation and well-internalized extrinsic motivation. Intrinsic motivation means engaging in an activity because the activity itself is interesting and enjoyable. Intrinsic motivation is the prototype of autonomous motivation, and perhaps the most delightful instance of it is children at play. The motivation is internal and inherent, and the satisfaction is significant. By contrast, extrinsic motivation refers to engaging in an activity in order to get some separate consequence. We will shortly explore how SDT addresses the issue of internalizing extrinsic motivation, which represents a movement towards greater levels of autonomous motivation.

Controlled motivation involves acting because people feel pressured to do so, whether through seduction (e.g. the offer of a reward) or coercion (e.g. the threat of punishment). When motivated in this way, people may comply with the controlling contingencies, which is the modal response, or they may defy the controls, doing the exact opposite of what was demanded. In both cases the behaviors are controlled because people are not making a true choice about how to behave based on their needs, goals, and values. The classic case of controlled motivation is the carrot and stick, which is a type of extrinsic motivation that we refer to as *external regulation* because people's behaviors are being controlled by external contingencies. However, as shown earlier in Table 5.1, *organismic integration theory* proposes that people can internalize the value and regulation of extrinsically motivated behaviors. The more fully internalized the behavioral regulations, the more autonomous the subsequent behavior.

INTERNALIZATION AND INTEGRATION: KEY DEVELOPMENTAL PROCESSES IN SDT

According to Deci and Ryan (1985) internalization refers to the process whereby people "take in" an external value or regulation but may or may not accept it as their own. The process of organismic integration, which is the fundamental developmental process, involves fuller internalization in which people accept the value and regulation of an extrinsically motivated behavior and integrate it with their own sense of self. More specifically, there are four types of extrinsic motivation that vary in the degree of internalization and integration and in the degree of autonomy of resulting behaviors (see Table 5.2).

As noted, external regulation is extrinsic motivation for which there has been no internalization of the regulation and value. Introjection results when people take in a controlling contingency and maintain it in a similar form such that they are then using it to control themselves. Within SDT the terms self-control and internal control refer to pressuring oneself to behave with ego-involved contingencies of self-esteem and guilt. This is very different from true self-regulation in which one acts with volition and choice rather than pressure and tension. Thus, and importantly, introjected regulation is not autonomous but is one of the two types of controlled motivation, the other being external regulation.

Table 5.2   Varying levels of integration and ownership associated with extrinsic motivation

Reason	Type	Motivation
External	Controlled	Striving because somebody else wants you to and you'll get some reward for doing it or get into trouble for not.
Introjected	Controlled	Striving because you would feel ashamed, guilty, or anxious if you didn't, or self-aggrandized if you did. You strive for this because you think you should and use internal sanctions to motivate the striving.
Identified	Autonomous	Striving because you personally accept the value of the behavior for yourself. Although the behavior or goal may have been acquired from others, you now endorse its utility for your own needs and goals.
Integrated	Autonomous	Striving because of the importance of the behavior as an integrated aspect of who you are. This motivation is not about the activity being interesting or fun but rather about it being deeply important for behaving with integrity and respect.

Source: Adapted from Deci and Ryan (2000).

Autonomous extrinsic motivation

Further, people can internalize a regulation more fully by identifying with its importance for their own needs and self-selected goals. When this has occurred, they have accepted the regulation as their own and are relatively autonomous when enacting it. This type of extrinsic motivation is referred to as *identified regulation*. Finally, when people have integrated an identification into their sense of self, the extrinsic motivation is referred to as *integrated regulation*, which is the most mature form of extrinsic motivation and represents the most successful type of socialization. Identified regulation and integrated regulation are both considered types of autonomous motivation, as, of course, is intrinsic motivation. Fully internalized extrinsic motivation is still different from intrinsic motivation, however, because intrinsic is about people's inherent interest in behaviors whereas integrated regulation is about the internalized importance of the behaviors for their plans, goals, or values.

Having now described autonomous and controlled motivations, we can point out that *cognitive evaluation theory* (CET) is the mini-theory that has guided the study of intrinsic motivation, of its sequelae, and of the socio-contextual conditions that maintain or enhance it (or alternatively diminish it). In contrast, organismic integration theory (OIT) has focused on the study of extrinsic motivation, the degrees of internalization that form different types of extrinsic regulations, the conditions that facilitate versus hinder fuller internalization, and of outcomes associated with the different types of extrinsic motivation.

THE ORGANISMIC DIALECTIC

As mentioned, the SDT perspective views humans as proactive and growth oriented, manifest in their intrinsic motivation and organismic integration. From that perspective, the self is viewed as an active processor of experience, a set of dynamic psychic processes and structures that continuously seeks to make meaning of the myriad internal and external events that comprise a person's life and to integrate them into a coherent, unified sense of self. As such it represents an inherently positive view of human nature. Nonetheless, SDT explicitly acknowledges, and focuses much of its empirical attention, on the *organismic dialectic* of human experience (Deci and Ryan, 1985). Simply put, a dialectic is the juxtaposition of conflicting forces or ideas. The dialectic that is central to SDT is the conflict that exists between people's natural orientation towards growth and development in interaction with the potentially disruptive power of various socio-contextual forces (e.g. parental control, peer pressure, restrictive legislation) that can block, impair, or stall these positive developmental tendencies and autonomous motivations (Ryan and Deci, 2000).

Needs and the dialectic

Internalization and integration, which represent one aspect of the organismic dialectic, are developmental processes that can be either catalyzed or impaired by the presence of different socio-cultural conditions, which constitute the other aspect of the dialectic. It is this nexus where the basic psychological needs once again come into play. SDT has postulated, and an enormous body of research has supported, that satisfaction of the three basic psychological needs serve to maintain intrinsic motivation and to facilitate internalization and integration of extrinsic motivation (Deci and Ryan, 1985). This implies that any social agents who in some way supervise, advise, or guide others (such as coaches) will be more effective to the degree that they relate to those others and provide support in ways that facilitate the satisfaction of their basic psychological needs. Through promoting the satisfaction of these needs in particular situations, social agents can support the autonomous motivation of the people with whom they are interacting.

Because the growth processes within people require basic psychological need satisfaction in order for them to master challenges encountered in the environment, the theory examines the degree to which individuals, in their ongoing interactions with the context, are able to satisfy versus thwart their needs. To the degree that their basic needs are thwarted, the darker side of the human experience becomes evident in the form of inactivity, negative affect, aggressive behaviors, and psychopathology. This point is, of course, crucially important for coaching because it highlights the necessity for coaches to provide need support within the coaching process. We will return to this issue later.

SUPPORTING AUTONOMOUS MOTIVATION

The orientations and skills involved in supporting need satisfaction have been delineated by research within the rubrics of BPNT, CET, and OIT. Need support begins with a socializing agent (like a coach) relating to others via their internal frame of reference. When doing so, the agent will often offer choice, provide positive feedback, facilitate problem-solving when difficulties arise, give meaningful rationales for engaging in various tasks, minimize use of controlling language (e.g. "should", "must", and "have to"), and refrain from using rewards, punishments, deadlines, and evaluations as ways of motivating people. Rewards may be necessary, but if they are treated simply as part of an agreement (rather than as an attempted motivator) they will be less detrimental.

We believe that these interpersonal skills, which are known to be need supportive in many domains (see Stone, Deci, and Ryan, 2009), closely resemble the skills that are essential for effective coaching (see Spence and Oades, 2011). Thus, SDT would strongly maintain that part of the job of coaches is to facilitate both intrinsic motivation and the internalization of extrinsic motivation. There is good reason to believe that if coaches relate to coachees in such empathic, responsive, and supportive ways, the positive motivational consequences will follow (De Haan, 2008).

Delving Deeper: Self-determination and the Importance of Personality, Relationships, and Life Goals

In our discussion of OIT we discussed autonomous and controlled types of motivation as they relate to specific behaviors (e.g. doing homework) or in some cases to life domains (e.g. work). Our focus was on the degree to which people's motivation for the behaviors or domains had been internalized and thus how autonomous the subsequent behaviors were likely to be. We now turn to a discussion of the influence that personality, relationships and goal selection have on personal functioning and well-being.

INDIVIDUAL DIFFERENCES IN MOTIVATION

Another of the mini-theories of SDT, referred to as *causality orientations theory* (COT), concerns general individual differences in autonomous and controlled motivation. It examines people's tendencies to experience the environment as either autonomy supportive or controlling, and correspondingly to function in either an autonomous or controlled way. COT refers to people's general motivations, regardless of their circumstances. The idea of general individual differences in causality orientations is that these orientations are formed during development and remain relatively stable over time.

Causality orientations, which are aspects of people's personalities, are generally considered independent variables. That is to say, they can be used to predict people's motivations for a behavior, as well as their degree of need satisfaction in a situation or domain. Thus, research on SDT frequently uses autonomous and controlled causality orientations (aspects of people) as well as the autonomy support and control in the social context (aspects of environments) to predict people's motivations and, in turn, a range of important outcomes.

It is worth noting that causality orientations are, in a sense, aggregates of motivations across behaviors and domains and can be distal targets for coaching interventions. Thus, although coaching interventions may tend to focus on motivations for specific behaviors or domains, it is possible that coaches, by providing the requisite need-supportive environments could to some degree be strengthening coachees' autonomous causality orientations, which would have implications for their lives more generally. For example, coaching is often used in organizations to help newly promoted managers develop the skills required to effectively lead others. For managers whose default is to internalize the preferences of others for the purpose of decision-making and goal setting (a controlled orientation), this transition can be a distressing experience. In such a circumstance, a coach can help the person by creating conditions that allow him or her to (i) become aware of this interpersonal tendency, and (ii) get better (and progressively more comfortable) at making decisions grounded in his or her own values, preferences or past experiences (and finding ways to manage the relationship implications of this more autonomous approach).

THE IMPORTANCE OF RELATIONSHIPS

Relationships motivation theory (RMT) is a theory concerned with the promotion of high-quality close personal relationships. Its focus highlights the importance of need satisfaction for both partners within a close relationship, thus differing in a very important regard from the foci of the other SDT mini-theories insofar as the other theories are concerned largely with relationships that have a differential in authority or expertise between the partners (e.g. parents and children, physicians and patients). Close personal relationships are by their very nature more mutual, and research has confirmed that the highest quality relationships are ones for which there are greater levels of mutuality. Indeed, research indicates that, for optimal relationships, each partner will be highly autonomy supportive toward the other (Deci, La Guardia, Moller, Scheiner, and Ryan, 2006). Of the SDT mini-theories, RMT is perhaps the least relevant to coaching and mentoring, as the nature of these relationships is not always mutual. It should be noted however that, in some circumstances (e.g. manager-as-coach), mutual learning does occur through the experience of working with the perspectives and insights of others. As such, an understanding of this critical characteristic of close relationships may be highly relevant when the coaching process addresses issues individuals are having in their relationships.

LIFE GOALS AND WELL-BEING

Goal contents theory (GCT) is the last of the SDT mini-theories and is focused primarily on people's life goals or aspirations. Specifically, the theory has proposed that "not all goals are created equal" (Ryan, Sheldon, Kasser, and Deci, 1996); that pursuit and attainment of life goals will be beneficial for performance and wellness only insofar as goal-directed efforts lead to the satisfaction of people's basic psychological needs. When coaching is conceptualized in terms of the optimization of personal functioning and well-being, a basic understanding of life goals, as well as motivations, should prove helpful for coaches in facilitating clients' optimal performance and well-being.

Research on GCT began with empirical work showing that people's aspirations tend to fall into two broad categories, referred to as *extrinsic aspirations* and *intrinsic aspirations* (Kasser and Ryan, 1993). Those that were labeled extrinsic included amassing wealth, being famous, and having a trendy, attractive image; those labeled intrinsic included personal growth, meaningful relationships, and community contributions. Research further showed that when people placed relatively strong importance on the extrinsic life goals they tended to be low in self-esteem and self-actualization and high in depression, anxiety, and narcissism; whereas those who placed relatively strong importance on intrinsic life goals tended to be high in the indicators of well-being and low in the indicators of ill-being (Kasser and Ryan, 1996).

Stated differently, people who strongly pursued wealth, fame, and image tended to evidence less wellness than those who strongly pursued growth, relationships, and community, because the intrinsic goals were more closely related to basic psychological need satisfaction. For example, people who spend a great deal of time trying to achieve wealth and fame are likely not to feel very autonomous (i.e. they become pawns to the goals) and further they are likely not to have much time to devote to, for example, their friends and families. Whenever this happens, the pursuit of extrinsic life goals "crowds out" (Frey, 1997) or makes it difficult for an individual to satisfy their basic needs for autonomy, relatedness and competence.

Other research has focused less on the relation of life goals to well-being but has instead linked extrinsic-goal pursuits to more negative learning and performance outcomes. In contrast, it has linked intrinsic-goal pursuits to more positive learning and performance outcomes (Vansteenkiste, Simons, Lens, Sheldon, and Deci, 2004) . This research by Vansteenkiste et al. (2004), as well as other research by Sheldon, Ryan, Deci, and Kasser (2004), has shown that not only does the content of goals (i.e. extrinsic versus intrinsic) relate to performance and well-being outcomes, but also the motives for pursuing them (i.e. controlled versus autonomous) explain independent variance in the outcomes. This is a vital finding because it indicates that the goals people pursue and their motives for pursuing them both make a difference. Hence, in the coaching process, working with both people's goal contents as well as their motives are important for facilitating meaningful change in people's lives.

Development of need substitutes

Satisfaction versus thwarting of basic needs is integrally involved with GCT, as it is with the other SDT sub-theories. As is the case with individual differences in causality orientations, individual differences in aspirations are influenced by the degree to which people's needs are met during their important developmental years. Studies have shown, for example, that when parents are controlling (i.e. low in autonomy support) and cold (i.e. low in relational support) their children tend to be more oriented toward extrinsic (relative to intrinsic) life goals (Kasser, Ryan, Zax, and Sameroff, 1995; Williams, Cox, Hedberg, and Deci, 2000). It is presumed that this occurs as a way to achieve external indicators of worth to compensate for their inner anxiety and low self-worth, effectively functioning as need substitutes for people who find it difficult to satisfy the basic needs themselves.

Further, the needs for competence, relatedness, and autonomy are also important with respect to goal attainment. For example, Niemiec and colleagues (2009) found that the well-being and ill-being outcomes associated with intrinsic and extrinsic aspirations were mediated by need satisfaction. That is, when people attained intrinsic aspirations, that attainment promoted satisfaction of the basic needs, which in turn led to greater well-being and less ill-being.

Coaching with Self-determination in Mind: Practical Applications

We now see that one way we might conceptualize coaching is as an interactive process that attempts to facilitate the *autonomous motivation* and *intrinsic aspirations* of coachees. Both are strongly associated with persistence, effective performance, well-being, and vitality—the kinds of outcomes that are important in coaching (Grant and Cavanagh, 2011). Further, abundant research has shown that when helping professionals support a client's needs for competence, relatedness, and autonomy, both autonomous motivation and intrinsic life goals are enhanced. This can be extrapolated to the field of coaching to propose that being need-supportive is central to how coaches help their clients to actualize efficacy and wellness.

As such, SDT appears to be a highly relevant theoretical framework for coaching. Spence and Oades (2011) suggest several reasons why it is a useful framework for coaching practice:

- It provides a "bigger picture" from which to understand what is being attempted in coaching through its macro-theoretical account of the growth tendencies, innate psychological needs, and socio-cultural factors that shape human personality, behavioral self-regulation, and well-being (Ryan and Deci, 2000).

- It places motivation at the center of behavior change efforts, rather than seeing it as a necessary pre-requisite for change or something that occasionally needs to be elicited from clients.

- The different mini-theories can be used as a basis for case conceptualizations or other efforts focused on building a nuanced understanding of the coachee. This is useful because it can help to guide questioning in the early stages of coaching and support a purposeful, theory-guided exploration of psychological need satisfaction that can help both the coach and the coachee see when, where, and how the latter's needs are (or are not) being satisfied.

Finally, SDT can help coaches develop a more nuanced appreciation of the working alliance (De Haan, 2008) and how, through the process of *relating*, conditions can be created that contribute to optimal growth and development. More specifically, it suggests that the use of core coaching skills such as active listening, expressing empathy, exploring successes, identifying personal strengths, encouraging volitional acts, and other supportive gestures are important because of their potential to enliven the developmental processes that are central to human flourishing.

To illustrate how SDT can be useful from a practice perspective, the following section will be organized into two parts. The first will focus on how the coaching relationship, and the conversations that comprise it, can function as a partial satisfier of the basic psychological needs in the coaching context. The second will focus on how the coaching process (which often unfolds over several months) can stimulate coachees' autonomous functioning by giving continuity to need satisfaction and can also help coachees examine how to achieve greater ongoing satisfaction in their lives.

BASIC NEED SATISFACTION DURING COACHING CONVERSATIONS

As mentioned, SDT recognizes that the socio-cultural conditions of a person's life often stifle human development and growth. Based on this observation, the presence of a coach can be understood as representing a general improvement in these conditions, provided the coach relates to coachees in a way that supports autonomy, relatedness and competence.

It should be noted that whilst the SDT model of change assigns importance to the satisfaction of all three basic needs, the satisfaction of autonomy is considered primary. As Ryan et al. (2011) point out, "once people are volitionally engaged and have a high degree of willingness to act, they are then most apt to learn and apply new strategies and competencies" (p. 231) and, more generally, act in ways that lead to satisfying psychological outcomes (Deci, 1995). To put it another way, as people's sense of autonomy increases, so does the likelihood they will make decisions to "engage in interesting activities, exercise capacities, and pursue connectedness in social groups" (Deci and Ryan, 2000, p. 229).

We now briefly explore the question of how coaches can contribute to the satisfaction of coachees' basic psychological needs.

Autonomy support

Many coaching models place the coachee at the center of decision making processes as a way of encouraging client ownership of development and growth (Grant, 2006). Whilst coaches will typically look to the coachee to provide impetus for any goals set throughout the course of a coaching engagement, this principle is also applied within sessions. For example, the use of simple process models like the Goal-Reality-Options-Wrap up model (GROW; Whitmore, 1996) encourages coachees to take ownership of their behavior change process by inviting them to set the agenda for each conversation. This invitation can, however, be unsettling for some coachees either because they are: i) confused about what to focus on, ii) not used to being asked to take ownership for their own development, iii) suspicious of the coaching process or fearful it might not work, or iv) holding an expectation that the coach is the expert who will decide (and direct) what needs to be done (Spence and Oades, 2011). Whatever the reason, coaching models like GROW are autonomy supportive insofar as they emphasize respecting a coachee's current perspective, conveying that coachees are free to choose what gets done, and respecting and valuing the choices that are made.

Competence support

Coaching assumes that people are essentially capable and possess potential that will emerge in the presence of supportive conditions (Grant, 2003).

An approach widely used in coaching to uncover latent potential is the solution focused (SF) approach (Berg and Szabo, 2005). This approach assumes that people are not only capable and doing their best, but also that some aspect of the change they seek is already present in their lives (even if it is only small). SF coaching techniques tend to orient people towards what is working or going well and, in so doing, can create conditions that foster feelings of competence. It is also important, however, that coachees be engaged in an active process of developing their own plan for acquiring needed skills, as this helps to affirm abilities related to problem-solving and personal development.

Relatedness support

Coaching is generally considered to be founded on core Rogerian, person-centered principles (Stober and Grant, 2006) that are reinforced through the use of key micro-skills such as active listening, empathy, unconditional positive regard, attentive and responsive body language, etc. (Starr, 2011; Zeus and Skiffington, 2002). In SDT terms these skills create an atmosphere conducive to satisfying the need for relatedness, through the development of a warm, trusting relationship focused on the coachee's salient concerns. Further, Spence and Oades (2011) point out that "whilst coachees may have close relationships outside coaching, they may not consistently feel heard, understood, valued and/or genuinely supported within those relationships" (p. 46). If not, they are unlikely to feel strongly and positively connected to others and in an attempt to satisfy this basic need, they may attempt to connect by acting in accordance with the preferences of others, rather than their own. For example, an employee may decide not to pursue an exciting internal promotion due to his concern that his line manager of three years might see it as an act of betrayal. In situations like this, coaching may help an insecurely connected person to feel safe enough to explore more self-concordant forms of action (and to manage the relational implications of these).

BASIC NEED SATISFACTION THROUGHOUT THE COACHING PROCESS

For coaching to be successful it is important that both parties establish a good working alliance (Peltier, 2001) and remain attentive to the degree to which people are getting their needs satisfied in their ongoing lives. To the extent that they are not, a relationship with a coach is not an adequate substitute, so it is important that the coaching process engage in problem-solving with respect to attaining greater need satisfaction. An interesting topic of conversation might then be how the coachee's behavior interferes with need satisfaction at work or elsewhere.

Goal setting and goal striving

The coaching process can be understood as a self-regulatory cycle that commences with the establishment of a goal, the articulation of an action plan, and participation in an ongoing reflective cycle based on actions taken between one coaching session and the next (Spence and Grant, 2007). Typically individuals come to coaching seeking help to attain personal and professional goals. Whilst some goals are clear and obvious, for many they are not, and a coach can support the coachee in resolving a variety of concerns such as not knowing what goals to set, struggling to strive towards goals set by others, and/or managing fluctuations in goal-related motivation.

SDT research has important implications for coaches because numerous studies have shown it is possible to facilitate helpful shifts in the underlying motivation for particular goals (e.g. Williams et al., 2006). This is particularly salient for individuals faced with the challenge of working towards imposed goals (i.e. goals that are not self-generated), which often occurs in organizational settings. As these goals are frequently associated with a diminished sense of ownership, the use of autonomy-supportive strategies can help coachees to better understand both the goal and their relationship to it. In line with Deci et al. (1994), this might include the coach assisting the coachee: (1) to understand what credible *rationales* might exist for such goals; (2) to feel genuinely *acknowledged as well as acknowledging their own* feelings about the goals; and (3) to engage their circumstances with a greater sense of *choice*.

Supporting more self-determined living

The developmental trajectory described above suggests that by helping coachees through the process of internalization and integration, they will likely become better not only at being aware of the *quality* of their goal motivation (i.e. the reasons for adoption) but also, potentially, at transforming how they experience their goal striving. This can occur either as they more fully internalize the regulation of externally imposed goals, or by deciding to disengage from goals that are neither intrinsically interesting, nor personally important. Such decisions are likely to be associated not only with a greater sense of perceived autonomy, but also with greater feelings of competence, due either to the unveiling of latent abilities or to the subsequent acquisition of new skills and abilities that are supported by the coach.

Conclusion

In this chapter we set out to provide a detailed description of SDT and a discussion of its application within coaching contexts. Throughout we have drawn on the theory's extensive theoretical and empirical literature to show that SDT has considerable relevance for practitioners interested in the optimization of human functioning. We have also shown the relevance of certain coaching frameworks (e.g. GROW, Solution-Focus) and core micro skills (e.g. active listening) to the enhancement of functioning via the satisfaction of basic psychological needs. We hope this presentation of SDT will provide practicing coaches with enough understanding to permit what Stober and Grant (2006) refer to as the "intelligent and conscientious use" of the theory, and to do that in ways that assist coachees in attaining their most satisfying outcomes (Stober and Grant, 2006). We also hope that this stimulates the interest of both coaching and non-coaching researchers, and leads to the formulation of research questions and studies that help to clarify how coaching works in the way that it does.

References

Allcorn, S. (2006). Psychoanalytically informed executive coaching. In D. Stober & A.M. Grant (Eds), *Evidence Based Coaching Handbook: Putting Best Practices to Work for your Clients*, 129–52. New York: Wiley.

Auerbach, J.E. (2006). Cognitive coaching. In D. Stober & A.M. Grant (Eds), *Evidence Based Coaching Handbook: Putting Best Practices to Work for your Clients*, 103–28. New York: Wiley.

Barner, R. & Higgins, J. (2007). Understanding implicit models that guide the coaching process. *Journal of Management Development*, 26(2), 148–58.

Berg, I.K. & Szabo, P. (2005). *Brief Coaching for Lasting Solutions*. New York: Norton.

Burke, D. & Linley, P.A. (2007). Enhancing goal self-concordance through coaching. *International Coaching Psychology Review*, 2(1), 62–9.

Caplan, J. (2003). *Coaching for the Future: How Smart Companies use Coaching and Mentoring*. London: CIPD.

Carver, C.S. & Scheier, M.F. (1998). *On the Self-regulation of Behavior*. Cambridge: Cambridge University Press.

Casserley, T. & Megginson, D. (2009). *Learning from Burnout: Developing Sustainable Leaders and Avoiding Career Derailment*. Oxford: Butterworth-Heinemann.

Cavanagh, M. & Grant, A.M. (2006). Coaching psychology and the scientist-practitioner model. In D.A. Lane & S. Corrie (Eds), *The Modern Scientist-Practitioner: A Guide to Practice in Psychology*, 146–57. Hove, UK: Routledge.

CIPD. (2007). *Coaching in Organisations*. London: CIPD.

De Haan, E. (2008). *Relational Coaching: Journeys Towards Mastering One-to-one Learning*. Chichester: Wiley & Sons.

Deci, E.L. (1995). *Why We Do What We Do: Understanding Self-Motivation*. New York: Penguin.

Deci, E.L., Eghrari, H., Patrick, B.C., & Leone, D. (1994). Facilitating internalization: The self-determination theory perspective. *Journal of Personality, 62*, 119–42.

Deci, E.L., Koestner, R., & Ryan, R.M. (1999). A meta-analytic review of experiments examining the effects of extrinsic rewards on intrinsic motivation. *Psychological Bulletin, 125*, 627–68.

Deci, E.L., La Guardia, J.G., Moller, A.C., Scheiner, M.J., & Ryan, R.M. (2006). On the benefits of giving as well as receiving autonomy support: Mutuality in close friendships. *Personality and Social Psychology Bulletin, 32*, 313–27.

Deci, E.L. & Ryan, R.M. (1985). *Intrinsic Motivation and Self-Determination in Human Behaviour*. New York: Plenum Press.

Deci, E.L. & Ryan, R.M. (2000). The "what" and "why" of goal pursuits: Human needs and the self-determination of behavior. *Psychological Inquiry, 11*(4), 227–68.

Downey, M. (2003). *Effective Coaching: Lessons From the Coach's Couch*. New York: Texere/Thomson.

Frey, B.S. (1997). *Not Just for the Money: An Economic Theory of Personal Motivation*. Northampton, MA.: Edward Elgar.

Gagné, M. & Deci, E.L. (2005). Self-determination theory and work motivation. *Journal of Organizational Behavior, 26*, 331–62.

Govindji, R. & Linley, P.A. (2007). Strengths use, self-concordance and well-being: Implications for strengths coaching and coaching psychologists. *International Coaching Psychology Review, 2*(2), 143–53.

Grant, A.M. (2003). *Solution-focused Coaching: Managing People in a Complex World*. Harlow, UK: Pearson Education.

Grant, A.M. (2006). An integrative goal-focused approach to executive coaching. In D.R. Stober & A.M. Grant (Eds), *Evidence Based Coaching Handbook: Putting Best Practices to Work for your Clients*, 153–92. Hoboken, NJ: Wiley & Sons.

Grant, A.M. & Cavanagh, M.J. (2011). Coaching and positive psychology. In K.M. Sheldon, T.B. Kashdan, & M.F. Steger (Eds), *Designing Positive Psychology: Taking Stock and Moving Forward*, 293–309. New York: Oxford University Press.

Grant, A.M. & Spence, G.B. (Eds). (2010). *Using Coaching and Positive Psychology to Promote a Flourishing Workforce: A Model of Goal-Striving and Mental Health.* Oxford: Oxford University Press.

Grolnick, W.S., Deci, E.L., & Ryan, R.M. (1997). Internalization within the family. In J.E. Grusec & L. Kuczynski (Eds), *Parenting and Children's Internalization of Values: A Handbook of Contemporary Theory,* 135–61. New York: Wiley.

Hall, D.T., Otazo, K.L., & Hollenbeck, G.P. (1999). Behind closed doors: What really happens in executive coaching. *Organizational Dynamics, 27*(3), 39–53.

Hawkins, P. (2008). The coaching profession: Some of the key challenges. *Coaching: An International Journal of Theory, Research and Practice, 1*(1), 28–38.

Kasser, T. & Ryan, R.M. (1993). The dark side of the American dream: Correlates of financial success as a central life aspiration. *Journal of Personality and Social Psychology, 65,* 410–22.

Kasser, T. & Ryan, R.M. (1996). Further examining the American dream: Differential correlates of intrinsic and extrinsic goals. *Personality and Social Psychology Bulletin, 22,* 80–87.

Kasser, T., Ryan, R.M., Zax, M., & Sameroff, A.J. (1995). The relations of maternal and social environments to late adolescents' materialistic and prosocial values. *Developmental Psychology, 31,* 907–14.

Latham, G.P. & Locke, E.A. (1991). Self-regulation through goal setting. *Organizational Behavior and Human Decision Processes, 50*(2), 212–47.

Ng, J.Y.Y., Ntoumanis, N., Thøgersen-Ntoumani, C., Deci, E.L., Ryan, R.M., Duda, J., et al. (2012). Self-determination theory applied to health contexts: A meta-analysis. *Perspectives on Psychological Science., 7,* 325–40.

Niemiec, C.P., Ryan, R.M., Deci, E.L., & Williams, G.C. (2009). Aspiring to physical health: The role of aspirations for physical health in facilitating long-term tobacco abstinence. *Patient Education and Counseling, 74,* 250–57.

Parsloe, E. (1999). *The Manager as Coach and Mentor* London: CIPD.

Peltier, B. (2001). *The Psychology of Executive Coaching.* New York: Brunner-Routledge.

Ryan, R.M. & Deci, E. (2000). Self-determination theory and the facilitation of intrinsic motivation, social development, and well-being. *American Psychologist, 55*(1), 68–78.

Ryan, R.M. & Deci, E.L. (2007). Active human nature: Self-determination theory and the promotion and maintenance of sport, exercise, and health. In M.S. Hagger & N.L.D. Chatzisarantis (Eds), *Self-determination in Sport and Exercise,* 1–19. New York: Human Kinetics.

Ryan, R.M. & Deci, E.L. (2008a). A self-determination approach to psychotherapy: The motivational basis for effective change. *Canadian Psychology, 49,* 186–93.

Ryan, R.M. & Deci, E.L. (2008b). From ego depletion to vitality: Theory and findings concerning the facilitation of energy available to the self. *Social and Personality Psychology Compass, 2*(2), 702–17.

Ryan, R.M. & Deci, E.L. (2009). Promoting self-determined school engagement: Motivation, learning, and well-being. In K.R. Wentzel & A. Wigfield (Eds), *Handbook on Motivation at School*, 171–95. New York: Routledge.

Ryan, R.M., Lynch, M.F., Vansteenkiste, M., & Deci, E.L. (2011). Motivation and autonomy in counseling, psychotherapy, and behavior change: A look at theory and practice. *The Counseling Psychologist, 39*(2), 193–260.

Ryan, R.M., Patrick, H., Deci, E.L., & Williams, G.C. (2008). Facilitating health behavior change and its maintenance: Interventions based on self-determination theory. *The European Health Psychologist, 10*, 2–5.

Ryan, R.M., Sheldon, K.M., Kasser, T., & Deci, E.L. (1996). All goals are not created equal: An organismic perspective on the nature of goals and their regulation. In P.M. Gollwitzer & J.A. Bargh (Eds), *The Psychology of Action: Linking Cognition and Motivation to Behavior*, 7–26. New York: The Guilford Press.

Sheldon, K.M., Ryan, R.M., Deci, E.L., & Kasser, T. (2004). The independent effects of goal contents and motives on well-being: It's both what you pursue and why you pursue it. *Personality and Social Psychology Bulletin, 30*, 475–86.

Spence, G.B. (2007). Historical support for the further development of evidence-based coaching: The rise and fall of the human potential movement. *Australian Psychologist, 42*(4), 255–65.

Spence, G.B., Cavanagh, M.J., & Grant, A.M. (2006). Duty of care in an unregulated industry: Initial findings on the diversity and practices of Australian coaches. *International Coaching Psychology Review, 1*(1), 71–85.

Spence, G.B. & Grant, A.M. (2007). Professional and peer life coaching and the enhancement of goal striving and well-being: An exploratory study. *Journal of Positive Psychology, 2*(3), 185–94.

Spence, G.B. & Grant, A.M. (2013). Coaching and well-being: A brief review of existing evidence, relevant theory and implications for practitioners. In S. David, I. Boniwell, & A. Ayers (Eds), *Oxford Handbook of Happiness*, 1009–25. London: Oxford University Press.

Spence, G.B. & Oades, L.G. (2011). Coaching with self-determination in mind: Using theory to advance evidence-based coaching practice. *International Journal of Evidence Based Coaching and Mentoring, 9*(2), 37–55.

Starr, J. (2011). *The Coaching Manual: The Definitive Guide to the Process, Principles and Skills of Personal Coaching*. Harlow, UK: Pearson.

Stober, D.R. & Grant, A.M. (Eds). (2006). *Evidence Based Coaching Handbook: Putting Best Practices to Work for your Clients*. Hoboken, NY: Wiley.

Stone, D., Deci, E.L., & Ryan, R.M. (2009). Beyond talk: Creating autonomous motivation through self-determination theory. *Journal of General Management, 34*(3), 75–91.

Vansteenkiste, M., Ryan, R.M., & Deci, E.L. (2008). Self-determination theory and the explanatory role of psychological needs in human well-being. In L. Bruni, F. Comim, & M. Pugno (Eds), *Capabilities and Happiness*, 187–223. Oxford: Oxford University Press.

Vansteenkiste, M., Simons, J., Lens, W., Sheldon, K.M., & Deci, E.L. (2004). Motivating learning, performance, and persistence: The synergistic effects of intrinsic goal contents and autonomy-supportive contexts. *Journal of Personality and Social Psychology, 87*, 246–60.

Whitmore, J. (1996). *Coaching for Performance*. London: Nicholas Brealey.

Williams, G.C., Cox, E.M., Hedberg, V., & Deci, E.L. (2006). Extrinsic life goals and health risk behaviors in adolescents. *Journal of Applied Social Psychology, 30*, 1756–71.

Zeus, P. & Skiffington, S. (2002). *The Coaching at Work Toolkit: A Complete Guide to Techniques and Practices*. Sydney: McGraw-Hill.

6

A Social Neuroscience Approach to Goal Setting for Coaches

Elliot Berkman, Ruth Donde, and David Rock

Setting goals—creating a future desired state—is one of the central foundations of effective coaching. To date, the literature on goal setting has largely focused on particular qualities of goals such as measurability or specificity, with models such as "SMART" and "GROW" being popular. While these guidelines to setting goals appear to generate value, little has been done to understand what goes on in the brain in relationship to goal management.

This chapter aims to provide some theoretical understanding of what works and doesn't work in the pursuit of goals through the lens of combined social psychological theory and neuroscience methods. This lens is an amalgamation of what we see behaviorally, over a longer timeframe, and what we see mechanistically, focused on processes in the brain over a shorter period. For example, in the famous marshmallow experiment, Mischel (1972) determined that children who were able to exhibit self-control by delaying gratification and not eating marshmallows had higher grades and earnings years later. A neuroscientific approach to this behavioral experiment would be to attempt to identify the mechanisms involved in self-control and isolate one of those, and then to determine what we see in the brains of those exhibiting self-control as compared to those who don't. For example, the children who delayed gratification in the Mischel study showed greater recruitment of self-control regions of the brain 40 years later (Casey et al., 2011). This chapter considers both behavioral and mechanistic perspectives—a social neuroscience approach—with the purpose of translating insights into useful application in practical goal setting.

Figure 6.1   The social cognitive neuroscience of goal setting

A number of cognitive processes are necessary to goal pursuit (Berkman and Lieberman, 2009). First, is *goal representation*—the mental process of holding a goal in mind. This involves assimilating extrinsic goals as an internal representation (if the goal is extrinsic), and bringing the goal to the forefront of conscious awareness at times when the goal is relevant. This representation can be the image of our immediate desire (e.g. finding food to assuage the hunger), or a more distant mental image of our desired self (e.g. as a grandparent), together with some notion of the steps required to get there. Second, is *intention* to pursue the goal which includes *motivation* and *planning* (that is, a *will* and a *way*). Implementation intention provides a bridge from more abstract to more concrete aspects of the goal (Vallacher and Wegner, 1987). It is a way of translating abstract long-term goals into more tangible and actionable short-term tasks. Direct *goal action* follows from intention. Goal action involves the interplay of several sub-components: *attention, self-control and inhibition, social context* and *progress monitoring*. Progress monitoring is particularly useful when encountering new situations. This allows us to detect when we are going off track and apply error detection and discrepancy reduction processes. The brain's neural alarm, the anterior cingulate cortex (ACC) is activated when an error is detected, such as when a conflict arises between our intention and action (Botvinick, 2001). In essence, in order to achieve one goal, multiple higher-order mental processes are involved.

A full discussion of each of these processes is beyond the scope of this chapter. Instead, we focus on four:

- *motivation*—in particular, approach and avoidance motivation, and psychological distance to goal;

- *planning*—goal hierarchy;

- *social context*—shared goals; and

- *self-control*.

Our rationale for choosing these four processes include that they are: particularly relevant to coaching and to leaders in the workplace; relatively unknown and therefore tend to be overlooked (although they may be considered intuitively); and generally not included as part of traditional goal setting practice (e.g. setting SMART goals).

Motivation

One of the oldest theories in motivation neuroscience is approach and avoidance motivation. Jeffrey Gray (1970) postulated that all behavior is driven by two neurobiological motivational systems—one that responds to rewards and one that responds to threats or punishment. According to Gray, the sensitivities in these systems are present at birth and over time determine the level of the personality traits of extraversion (for the reward system) or neuroticism (for the threat system). People who are more reward sensitive (which roughly corresponds to increased sensitivity of the midbrain dopaminergic system) tend to experience and be motivated by positive, high arousal kinds of emotions like hope and elation, whereas those who are more sensitive to punishment (corresponding to increased sensitivity of the septo-hippocampal serotonergic system), are more motivated by fear and anxiety. Of course, all people have both systems and can respond to both rewards and threats. But the relative balance between the two varies from person to person and is what gives us our individual motivational signature.

More recently psychologists have tried to isolate the neurobiological basis of the reward and threat systems and have found a broad cortical asymmetry between the left and right prefrontal hemispheres. When people are in an approach state, there is greater activation in the left dorsolateral prefrontal cortex compared to the right. This asymmetry is observed in people who are typically motivated by rewards, even when they are at rest, (Davidson et al., 1990; Pizzagalli et al., 2005). In contrast, people in an avoidant motivated state or those at rest who are typically avoidant motivated demonstrate higher activation in the right prefrontal cortex.

In terms of goal pursuit, it is useful to identify whether people respond to the valence of a situation—is it good or bad—or rather the direction of moving towards or away from something. For the most part the direction of the action—approaching or avoiding—and the valance of the stimulus—positive or negative—are always confounded. It is rare to approach threat and avoid reward—except during goal pursuit. For example, engaging in a difficult conversation with a subordinate or denying oneself the pleasure of leaving early when there is still much work to be done are activities that are a routine part of being an effective and successful leader. In these cases, direction and valence are in opposition to one another. The feeling associated with the stimulus (the unpleasant conversation or the promise of an afternoon off) is incongruent with the desired action (to approach the conversation and to avoid skipping out).

Berkman and Lieberman (2010) modeled situations like this using cases where people might avoid food that looked appealing and approach food that did not. They found that approach *actions* were associated with left-sided asymmetry regardless of whether the food was positive or negative. This finding supports the idea that humans have the ability to override valence, making the stimulus itself irrelevant. What matters is the direction of behavior—which is determined only by one's current goals. The brain encodes the direction of the action, not the valence of the stimulus. Furthermore, in a situation where people were approaching something—even something bad—if they were more approach orientated (as leaders may well be), they tended to have more left hemispheric asymmetry.

What is the relevance of this to goal setting? People who are high in approach motivation might prefer situations to be framed as approach, and vice versa for people high in avoidance (Mann, Sherman, and Updegraff, 2004). It would make sense then to match these traits to the framing of goals.

How is a leader to tell whether someone is more approach (reward) or avoidance (threat) sensitive? Self-report scales such as the BIS/BAS (Carver and White, 1994) can also be used to determine trait levels of motivation. For example, "when I see an opportunity for something I like, I get excited right away" is an approach item, and, "I worry about making mistakes" is an avoidance item. Scores on these scales have been shown to correlate with brain asymmetry measures of motivation (Coan and Allen, 2004). Also, our dispositional approach or avoidance tendency will "leak" into our language, and this can give the astute listener some hints to our relative balance between these motivations. The way people speak and the words they choose can also be an easy identifier of tendency.

In goal setting, we can take any situation and frame it with an approach or an avoidance orientation. Those who are more approach motivated will respond more positively to an approach statement and those who are more avoidance motivated will be activated by a more avoidance goal statement. A basic laboratory example involved giving people messages to increase the amount of flossing. Two statements were used: 'Great breath, healthy gums, only a floss away' or 'Floss now and avoid bad breath and gum disease'. A couple of weeks later flossing behavior was measured. Who flossed more? As predicted by the "matching" theory, people who were more avoidance motivated were more motivated by the loss-framed article, and those who were more approach motivated were more motivated by the gain-framed article (Mann, Sherman, and Updegraff, 2004). We can improve outcomes by framing the goal in the most user-friendly way for the goal pursuer.

An example of an avoidance compared with an approach orientation in an organizational context, with the organization's objective of adding one percent of profit might be "prevent job losses by ensuring you contribute to increased profit" or as providing stability for our people e.g. "one percent retains our teams". They're not necessarily contradictory, so leaders don't have to pick one or the other. They can present both. In fact, studies have shown that individuals with different patterns of cortical asymmetry at rest tend to attend to different stimuli in the environment in the expected way (Coan and Allen, 2003; Davidson, 1992), suggesting that presenting both sides might peak the attention of people across the range of approach-avoidance motivation.

Projects may have many outcomes, so some of them might need to be more inherently loss or gain orientated, or to have two goals. In the workplace, it can be useful to have people articulate their own motivations. Many people may have the same goal, but different motivations for working toward it. There is power in allowing people to frame goals in ways that feel comfortable and motivate them, and also provide them with a sense of ownership. People are far more committed to a goal when they come to it on their own, or at least *believe* they came to it on their own (Ryan and Deci, 2001; Webb and Sheeran, 2006).

As a coach, it is helpful to understand your coachee's motivational direction; and also to be able to apply the skills of framing goals in approach and avoidance ways.

Goal Hierarchy

All goals are embedded in a hierarchy arranged from abstract (larger in scope and more distant in time) to concrete (smaller in scope and closer in time)

(Carver and Scheier, 2001). The abstract includes core values and our idealized self-image. We all have ideas in our head of who we would like to be and what we believe others would like us to be. What matters is the distance between those ideals and our sense of where we are right now. Where am I now, where would I like to be, and how do I get there? If, for example, part of my ideal self-image is to "be kind", but I don't see myself living up to that standard, how do I get there? "Being kind" is slightly more concrete than my overall ideal self-image, but it is still a fairly broad goal. So I must break it down into yet another smaller piece. How can I demonstrate being kind? I can go shopping for my elderly neighbor. That is a specific action that can be accomplished in an hour. The action may not be meaningful in itself—it is only meaningful because it's embedded in this bigger hierarchy (Kruglanski et al., 2002).

In order to move down the hierarchy we ask the question "how?". If I want to be a better me, how can I do that? Be more kind to others. How can I do that? Go shopping for my neighbor. The idea is that each of these is part of a many-to-one relationship. For each abstract (distant) goal there are many possible sub goals that answer the "how" question (Vallacher and Wegner, 1989).

Moving up the hierarchy answers the question "why?". Shopping for my neighbor—why? To be more kind. Why? So that I can be a better me.

The main insight from action identification theory (Vallacher and Wegner, 1989) is that goals are embedded in this hierarchy. The question "why?" moves you up and the question "how?" moves you down. Any action that you take can be represented within this framework. Higher levels of the hierarchy yield meaning; lower levels yield action.

Neuroscientific research shows that when we think about "how", the brain's motor planning system is activated, and in some cases motor activation itself is seen (Spunt, Satpute, and Lieberman, 2011). For example, when people think about how to brush their teeth, it is possible to observe activation in the same parts of the brain as the physical act of teeth brushing. That is, visualizing produces brain activation that is consistent with actually engaging in that action. This is the neural instantiation of observational learning. When we see someone acting (in other words, when we are visualizing), the motor system in our brain mimics that action. When we try to perform the action, the relevant brain regions have already had some practice.

In contrast, when we think about "why" a different, non-overlapping set of brain regions—the precuneus and medial prefrontal cortex (mPFC)—become activated (Spunt, Falk, and Lieberman, 2010; Spunt et al., 2011). These are the brain regions that are involved in thinking about one's own intentions or in trying to decipher those of another person—a task that involves determining what is being thought as opposed to what is being done.

In the context of organizational goal setting this suggests that the representation of how to do an action is separate from the representation of why you do that action. This is useful because sometimes we get stuck on the "how". For example, if I no longer have a car to go shopping for my neighbor, then it does not necessarily mean that I have to give up on the goal. In this case, what can be useful is to go up in the hierarchy to get a higher level perspective— to the "why" of going shopping for my neighbor, which is to be kind, and then explore alternative sub-goals that I can use to achieve the "how" of being kind. How else can I be kind? Perhaps I can borrow another neighbor's car to go shopping, or just do a shopping order online for this neighbor. This separation between the why and how on a neural level gives us more flexibility in terms of accomplishing our goals.

If you need to learn how to do something simple, or need to complete a task, focus on "how". If you want a more strategic focus, e.g. "What is important about engaging stakeholders", then answer the "why" question. It may be useful to frame this in terms of more abstract goals to engage the metalizing/ intention system. While this system cannot show exactly how to do it, it will provide the motivation as to why, which can then be used to motivate the action planning system to identify an appropriate "how".

From this summary, it should be apparent that the connection between the levels of the hierarchy is critical (Kruglanski et al., 2002). Often people spend so much time in the "how" routine, that the connection to the "why" is lost, and motivation erodes. Equally troublesome is when the focus is exclusively on the "why", the desired end state, to the exclusion of the "how", leaving one without a means to reach that end.

As discussed in the previous section, in organizations where there is an overarching "why", it can be useful to let individuals have the autonomy to select the "how". Then they'll have not only the motivation and understanding, but also ownership. Part of the breakdown that occurs when leaders micromanage is that they spend too much time on the "how" and lose sight of the "why", which is the direction they need to be providing. When provided with a convincing "why", many employees will self-generate their own "how". This helps them feel autonomous and also strengthens their understanding of the connection between the "how" and "why" levels (Ryan and Deci, 2001).

Transformative leaders, who are more conceptual, probably spend more time around "why" as compared to transactional leaders, who are more focused on how to get the job done. Mentalizing, like almost all cognitive skills, can be learned and the skill can be developed through practice. In other words, all leaders have the ability to learn to be more conceptual, regardless of their leadership style.

From a coaching perspective, an understanding of this hierarchy and comfort with navigating up and down its levels is crucial. The more adept the coach is here, the easier it will be to identify where in the hierarchy a coachee is and to support his or her progress when stuck.

Shared Goals

The concept of shared goals is highly relevant to those working in the social context of organizations. Shared goals refers to either many people individually working on their own though similar goals (e.g. a sales team) or many people working as a team on one goal (e.g. a production team).

In the first instance, if we think about a sales goal, the person's goal is to sell the product. They're not working as a team necessarily; they're all just expending effort, doing the same thing. In the second scenario however, where a team is working on a production goal we see a different effect: the *outsourcing of effort* (Fitzsimons and Finkel, 2011). When people know they're working in teams toward a common goal, they tend to *outsource*: to work less hard on the pieces of the goal that other people can help with, but not on those pieces that only they can accomplish. This is different from social loafing (Latane, Williams, and Harkins, 1979), a phenomenon evidenced in a classic social psychology experiment, where people playing tug-of-war on a team pull less hard than when playing on their own. Rather, outsourcing of effort is a specific kind of process that is very efficient in the context of teamwork: people allocate performance tasks to those most matched to them depending on their strengths, which is logical and done almost automatically (Fitzsimons and Finkel, 2010).

This effect was shown recently in a study of women, all of whom had a goal to exercise, amongst other goals (Fitzsimons and Finkel, 2011). All women were selected specifically because they exercised with their romantic partner, making exercise a shared goal. The investigators found that the women were less motivated to work knowing that their partners were going to help them. They conserved their resources in planning and executing the shared goal, expending them instead on other goals where they did not have their partner's assistance. Furthermore, women who relied on their partners for help on their own goals felt an increased level of commitment to those partners relative to women who didn't rely on their partners for goal support.

Shared goals alter goal-relevant reactions even at the neural level. There is a characteristic spike in an electroencephalography curve when a subject makes a mistake; this is called the Error Related Negativity (ERN). The ERN occurs almost simultaneously with the mistake being made—so quickly that it happens at least 100 ms before conscious recognition of the mistake. The magnitude of the ERN predicts our ability to learn from those mistakes by improving performance on subsequent trials following the error (Holroyd and Coles, 2002). In one study, researchers measured subjects' electroencephalographs (EEG's) while they performed a task and also while they watched either a friend or stranger perform the same task (Kang, Hirsh, and Chasteen, 2010). They found that, although there was an ERN spike in both cases, the ERN spike was larger when subjects viewed a friend making a mistake compared to when they viewed a stranger making that same mistake. This finding is related to those on the mirror neuron system (MNS), the network of brain regions that is shared between witnessing an action and performing that action (Iacoboni and Dapretto, 2006). In other words, these results show the overlap between your own intentions and other people's intentions. Taken together, the ERN that results from watching a friend make an error and studies on the MNS suggest that the overlap between your own mistakes and someone else's is even more extensive when you feel that person is similar to you.

From an organizational perspective, when you see other people as similar to yourself and/or trust them, it increases your motivation to work on shared goals. It may decrease your total effort but also increases your efficiency in your goal, and can enhance outcomes—less is more.

From the neuroscience data above, it is as though when we watch our friends, but not strangers, make progress, we learn from that progress, and we feel like their intentions are our intentions. We also feel that their errors are our errors. These kinds of overlapping intentions facilitate a coordination of effort. This links well into goal hierarchy where all team members can be doing different "how's" (working with their strengths), and still all be accomplishing the same "why". People don't necessarily commit to organizations, but rather to other people. We're fundamentally social creatures, so it makes sense that working together in groups increases commitment, which in turn increases affinity, which further increases commitment, and so forth.

Another relevant lesson from neuroscience is that similarity is relative (Van Bavel, Packer, and Cunningham, 2011). You don't have to actually be similar to other people for your brain to treat them as similar, you just need to have similarity on some dimension that is perceived to be relevant in the current situation. For example, assigning people to have the same color avatar (e.g. everyone on the team is blue) is all that is required to form a group identity (this is the so-called "minimal group paradigm" (Tajfel, 1982)). The blue team will perceive the other people in the group as more similar to them as compared to people with avatars of a different color. We like to be in groups, and we seek similarity with others to encourage this, even on superficial characteristics.

This lesson can be valuable in team coaching. Identify common identities and shared goals, then let individual team members determine their own sub-goals and work to their own strengths and motivations in order to more efficiently fulfill the goal.

Self-control

Self-control is a key part of goal pursuit. In psychology it is typically defined as the process of overriding or changing a habitual response or one that would otherwise occur without deliberate intervention (Baumeister, Heatherton, and Tice, 1994). Thus, by definition, self-control helps one to go against the path of least resistance. Very often, the reason goals are set is because they enable people to do something that they won't otherwise do. That is, goals are by their nature opposed to the path of least resistance. So, successful goal pursuit requires self-control to help people do something different than what they're currently doing.

Self-control is domain general: Different forms of self-control, e.g. emotional, physical, and cognitive, all draw upon a shared resource (Muraven, Tice, and Baumeister, 1998). As an example, if you give people a first task that involves strong attentional focus (e.g. a difficult word-search puzzle in a context with many distractors) and then after ten minutes ask them to engage in a totally different form of self-control (e.g. an emotion regulation task), they do worse on the subsequent tasks compared to people who engaged in a difficult first task that does not require self-control. The implications are that (1) self-control is a limited resource and (2) self-control is domain general because one form of self-control depletes another form of self-control (Baumeister, Vohs, and Tice, 2007).

Evidence shows that all these different forms of self-control (behavioral, emotional, cognitive) may be mediated through this same neural pathway (Cohen, Berkman, and Lieberman, 2013; Tabibnia et al., 2011), which explains why depletion of any type of self-control depletes them all. For example, researchers study motor control in the laboratory by teaching participants to habitually press a button when they see a cue, but to withhold the button press when they see a different (and infrequent) "stop" cue. Successful "stopping" on a task like this reliably recruits a variety of brain regions, including the right ventrolateral prefrontal cortex (rVLPFC). The rVLPFC is the only region that is also active when participants "withhold" an affective response through emotion regulation (Ochsner and Gross, 2005) or try to prevent an unwanted thought (Mitchell, et al., 2007). This is the brain's braking system.

Scholars have recently made the exciting discovery of *incidental* (or automatic) self-regulation. There seems to be a spillover effect between self-control domains—engaging in one form of self-control facilitates performance in others (Berkman, Burklund, and Lieberman, 2009). For example, it is possible that practising motor control (using a button pressing/stopping task) could be a great tool for improving emotional, attentional or cognitive self-control. In one study on this, how well subjects were able to regulate emotions was positively correlated with how much improvement they showed across eight training sessions of pressing and not pressing buttons (Morales, Berkman, and Lieberman, under review). We know that training in behavioral self-control generalizes to emotional self-control (Muraven, 2010). This may be mediated by changes in the right ventrolateral PFC (Berkman, Graham, and Fisher, 2012).

Coaches could use tools such as this behavioral training technique to assist coachees in improving domain general self-control. If a leader wants to learn better emotional control, practice on controlling something behaviorally may actually help him or her learn to improve on emotional regulation.

So what is the importance of this in goal pursuit? As stated earlier, goal pursuit is all about moving upstream, against the path of least resistance, in order to learn a new skill or to stretch. This is exactly what cognitive, behavioral and emotional forms of self-control are for.

Exercises like using your non-dominant hand for everyday tasks for two weeks can be helpful. This requires learning a new skill, having to suppress some motor patterns and learn new ones. People who do this have been shown to improve in self-control of emotions (Muraven, Baumeister, and Tice, 1999). Mindfulness training or meditation works on attention focus, which involves self-control and helps us to become more mindful generally. It has a number of clinical and general well-being benefits relevant to successful goal pursuit (Dickenson, Berkman, Arch, and Lieberman, 2013).

The more coachees practice self-control, the faster they will notice when they revert to habit and can then redirect themselves onto the new path towards goal attainment.

Further Components of Goal Pursuit

In this chapter we have covered some specific processes involved in goal pursuit from a social neuroscience perspective. There are many exciting topics in the field of motivational neuroleadership that are beyond the scope of this chapter, including brain-based attention training, implicit goal pursuit, and optimal goal planning. We hope that the applicability to coaching of the few topics we did cover will be clear, and that our broad framework of applying insights from social psychology and social neuroscience to coaching issues will prove useful for the reader. We eagerly anticipate learning about the new developments that are on the near horizon in this field.

Questions for Reflection by Readers

- How will the neuroscience of goal pursuit change your goal setting practice?

- What are the implications for setting goals in an organizational setting?

- How will this information change how you formulate goals?

- What other exercise can you think of to improve self-control?

- How would you structure team goals?

References

Baumeister, R.F., Heatherton, T.F., & Tice, D.M. (1994). *Losing Control: How and Why People Fail at Self-Regulation*. San Diego, CA: Academic Press.

Baumeister, R.F., Vohs, K.D., & Tice, D.M. (2007). The strength model of self-control. *Current Directions in Psychological Science*, *16*(6), 351–5.

Berkman, E.T., Burklund, L., & Lieberman, M.D. (2009). Inhibitory spillover: Intentional motor inhibition produces incidental limbic inhibition via right inferior frontal cortex. *NeuroImage*, *47*(2), 705–12.

Berkman, E.T., Graham, A.M., & Fisher, P.A. (2012). Training Self-Control: A Domain-General Translational Neuroscience Approach. *Child Development Perspectives*, *6*(4), 374–84.

Berkman, E.T. & Lieberman, M.D. (2009). The neuroscience of goal pursuit: Bridging gaps between theory and data. In G. Moskowitz & H. Grant (Eds), *The Psychology of Goals*, 98–126. New York: Guilford Press.

Berkman, E.T. & Lieberman, M.D. (2010). Approaching the bad and avoiding the good: Lateral prefrontal cortical asymmetry distinguishes between action and valence. *Journal of Cognitive Neuroscience*, *22*(9), 1970–79.

Botvinick, M.M., Braver, T.S., Barch, D.M., Carter, C.S., & Cohen, J.D. (2001). Conflict monitoring and cognitive control. *Psychological Review*, *108*(3), 624–52.

Carver, C.S. & White, T.L. (1994). Behavioral inhibition, behavioral activation, and affective responses to impending reward and punishment: The BIS/BAS scales. *Journal of Personality and Social Psychology*, *67*, 319–33.

Carver, C.S. & Scheier, M.F. (2001). *On the Self-Regulation of Behavior*. Cambridge: Cambridge University Press.

Casey, B.J., Somerville, L.H., Gotlib, I.H., Ayduk, O., Franklin, N.T., Askren, M.K., Jonides, J., et al. (2011). Behavioral and neural correlates of delay of gratification 40 years later. *Proceedings of the National Academy of Sciences*, *108*(36), 14998–15003.

Coan, J.A. & Allen, J.J. (2004). Frontal EEG asymmetry as a moderator and mediator of emotion. *Biological Psychology*, *67*(1), 7–50.

Coan, J.A. & Allen, J.J. (2003). Frontal EEG asymmetry and the behavioral activation and inhibition systems. *Psychophysiology*, *40*(1), 106–14.

Cohen, J.R., Berkman, E.T., & Lieberman, M.D. (2013). Intentional and Incidental Self control in Ventrolateral PFC. In D.T. Stuss & R.T. Knight, (Eds), *Principles of Frontal Lobe Functions* (2nd ed.), 417–40. London: Oxford University Press.

Davidson, R.J. (1992). Anterior cerebral asymmetry and the nature of emotion. *Brain and Cognition, 20*(1), 125–51.

Davidson, R.J., Ekman, P., Saron, C.D., Senulis, J.A., & Friesen, W.V. (1990). Approach-withdrawal and cerebral asymmetry: emotional expression and brain physiology. *Journal of Personality and Social Psychology, 58*(2), 330–41.

Dickenson, J., Berkman, E.T., Arch, J., & Lieberman, M.D. (2013). Neural correlates of focused attention during a brief mindfulness induction. *Social Cognitive and Affective Neuroscience, 8*, 40–47

Fitzsimons, G.M. & Finkel, E.J. (2010). Interpersonal influences on self-regulation. *Current Directions in Psychological Science, 19*(2), 101–5.

Fitzsimons, G.M. & Finkel, E.J. (2011). Outsourcing self-regulation. *Psychological Science, 22*(3), 369–75.

Gray, J.A. (1970). The psychophysiological basis of introversion-extraversion. *Behaviour Research & Therapy, 8*(3), 259–66.

Holroyd, C.B. & Coles, M.G. (2002). The neural basis of human error processing: reinforcement learning, dopamine, and the error-related negativity. *Psychological Review, 109*(4), 679–708.

Kang, S.K., Hirsh, J.B., & Chasteen, A.L. (2010). Your mistakes are mine: Self-other overlap predicts neural response to observed errors. *Journal of Experimental Social Psychology, 46*(1), 229–32.

Kruglanski, A.W., Shah, J.Y., Fishbach, A., Friedman, R., Chun, W.Y., Sleeth-Keppler, D. (2002) A theory of goal systems. *Advances in Experimental Social Psychology, 34*, 331–78.

Latane, B., Williams, K., & Harkins, S. (1979). Many hands make light the work: The causes and consequences of social loafing. *Key Readings in Social Psychology, 1*, 297.

Mann, T., Sherman, D., & Updegraff, J. (2004). Dispositional motivations and message framing: A test of the congruency hypothesis in college students. *Health Psychology, 23*(3), 330–34.

Mischel, W., Ebbesen, E.B., & Zeiss, A.R. (1972). Cognitive and attentional mechanisms in delay of gratification. *Journal of Personality and Social Psychology 21*(2), 204–18. doi:10.1037/h0032198. ISSN 0022-3514.

Mitchell, J., Heatherton, T., Kelley, W., Wyland, C., Wegner, D., & Neil Macrae, C. (2007). Separating sustained from transient aspects of cognitive control during thought suppression. *Psychological Science, 18*(4), 292–7.

Morales, J.I., Berkman, E.T., & Lieberman, M.D. (under review). Improving self control across domains: Increase emotion regulation ability through motor inhibition training.

Muraven, M. (2010). Building self-control strength: Practicing self-control leads to improved self-control performance. *Journal of Experimental Social Psychology*, 46(2), 465–8.

Muraven, M., Baumeister, R.F., & Tice, D.M. (1999). Longitudinal improvement of self-regulation through practice: Building self-control strength through repeated exercise. *The Journal of Social Psychology*, 139(4), 446–57.

Muraven, M., Tice, D.M., & Baumeister, R.F. (1998). Self-control as limited resource: Regulatory depletion patterns. *Journal of Personality and Social Psychology*, 74, 774–89.

Ochsner, K.N. & Gross, J.J. (2005). The cognitive control of emotion. *Trends in Cognitive Sciences*, 9(5), 242–9.

Pizzagalli, D.A., Sherwood, R.J., Henriques, J.B., & Davidson, R.J. (2005). Frontal brain asymmetry and reward responsiveness: a source-localization study. *Psychological Science, 16*(10), 805–13.

Ryan, R.M. & Deci, E.L. (2001). On happiness and human potential: A review of research on hedonic and eudaimonic well-being. *Annual Review of Psychology,* 52, 141–66.

Spunt, R.P., Falk, E.B., & Lieberman, M.D. (2010). Dissociable neural systems support retrieval of how and why action knowledge. *Psychological Science,* 21(11), 1593–98.

Spunt, R.P., Satpute, A.B., & Lieberman, M.D. (2011). Identifying the what, why, and how of an observed action: an fMRI study of mentalizing and mechanizing during action observation. *Journal of Cognitive Neuroscience*, 23(1), 6374.

Tabibnia, G., Monterosso, J.R., Baicy, K., Aron, A.R., Poldrack, R.A., Chakrapani, S., & .London, E.D. (2011). Different forms of self control share a neurocognitive substrate. *Journal of Neuroscience, 31*(13), 4805–10.

Tajfel, H. (1982). Social psychology of intergroup relations. *Annual Review of Psychology, 33*(1), 1–39.

Vallacher, R.R. & Wegner, D.M. (1987). What do people think they're doing? Action identification and human behavior. *Psychological Review, 94*(1), 3–15.

Vallacher, R.R. & Wegner, D.M. (1989). Levels of personal agency: Individual variation in action identification. *Journal of Personality and Social Psychology,* 57(4), 660–71.

Van Bavel, J.J., Packer, D.J., & Cunningham, W.A. (2011). Modulation of the fusiform face area following minimal exposure to motivationally relevant faces: evidence of in-group enhancement (not out-group disregard). *Journal of Cognitive Neuroscience*, 23(11), 3343–54.

Webb, T.L. & Sheeran, P. (2006). Does changing behavioral intentions engender behavior change? A meta-analysis of the experimental evidence. *Psychological Bulletin, 132,* 249–68.

7

Putting Goals to Work in Coaching: The Complexities of Implementation

Siegfried Greif

Goal Attainment can be Difficult

We have all had the experience of not implementing a behavior or change, despite its importance to our goals. Consider a leader who, in an effort to increase achievement motivation, plans to praise his team at their next meeting. Instead, he forgets and finds himself criticizing them for not performing an urgent task, and afterwards feels guilty for demotivating them yet again. People neglect to implement behaviors that at first glance seem to be simple and even life-saving. For example, the majority of heart failure patients who are directed to adhere to a healthy diet and engage in regular physical activity give up on their rehabilitation plan within three months (Tierney et al., 2011).

How can we explain inconsistent behavior implementation and how can we improve behavior modification in coaching? In the examples of both the leader and the heart patients, goal commitment is high and the subjects are able to behave as desired. In both cases, all of the criteria of goal setting theory (Locke and Latham, 2002) and its SMART goal approach (specific, measurable, achievable, realistic and time-framed) are met, but the goal is not achieved. In the first example, the leader might explain away his lack of praise as him having forgotten and being overtaken by the urgency of the incomplete task. In the second example, people may rationalize their lack of adherence by suggesting that it is difficult to change habits and to maintain the energy necessary to do so. How do these explanations fit with the scientific theory? This chapter explores motivation theory and the complexities of implementing goals in coaching.

The Rubicon Phase Model and Coaching: The Relevance of Implementation Intentions

This chapter focuses on a core question of modern motivation and volition theory that has high relevance for practical interventions in coaching and other fields: Why don't people do what they have planned? Why do clients not start to act immediately after reflecting on and deciding which goals they want to pursue and developing a plan of action? Gollwitzer's (1999) explanation is that these people have not formed a definite *implementation intention*. His work builds on Heckhausen's (1991) theory of motivation and action, which was an extension of basic models from Atkinson (1957) and Vroom (1964). Heckhausen and his colleagues noted that these models focused solely on the phase leading up to goal setting, while ignoring volitional processes in the following phase (Heckhausen and Gollwitzer, 1987; Heckhausen and Kuhl, 1985). The concept of implementation intentions has often been illustrated by the following historical example.

THE HISTORY OF THE CROSSING OF THE RUBICON

The model presented below includes implementation intentions and therefore is called the *Rubicon phase model* (Gollwitzer, 1999). The name refers to an action intention expressed by the Roman Julius Caesar in a famous speech to his army legion. Supposedly, on January 10 in 49 BC at the river Rubicon, Caesar declared that he intended to cross the river with his troops and march towards Rome. The small river marked the boundary between the Roman province of Cisalpine Gaul and the region directly controlled by Rome. Generals were forbidden to cross this river with their legions, as this would threaten the independence of the Roman senate. A general or soldier who violated this law automatically became an outlaw and was condemned to death (Abbott, 2012, p. 59). According to the historian Suetonius, Caesar uttered the famous phrase *alea iacta est* ("The die is cast.") to express his irrevocable decision, and to this day "crossing the Rubicon" serves as an idiom for decisions that have passed "the point of no return". Later, we will return to this story and consider the events that occurred after the crossing of the Rubicon.

RUBICON PHASE MODEL

The Rubicon phase model, as shown in Table 7.1 (Gollwitzer, 1999), proposes that an executed action is preceded by two phases. In the first of these, the pre-decisional phase A, the person deliberates on the costs and benefits of different possible goals. The phase ends with the selection of a goal, the so-called *goal intention*. An example of a team leader's goal intention might be: "In the future, I intend to give my team members more credit for good performance". Goal intentions resemble the behavioral intentions of the Fishbein and Ajzen prediction model of behavior (Ajzen and Fishbein, 1972; Fishbein and Ajzen, 2010). Results of empirical studies show that such goal intentions account for only 20 percent to 30 percent of the variance in future behavior (Ajzen, 1991). To raise the overall probability of correctly predicted behavioral outcomes, it is necessary to analyze additional contributions from the phase following the formation of the goal intention.

In the second phase, B, the will of the individual is activated. Through pre-actional planning, the individual plans how to perform actions in order to reach the intended goal. The volitional acts that precede and facilitate the execution of actions are referred to as *implementation intentions* (Gollwitzer, 1999). This phase parallels Ach's classical Volition Psychology (Ach, 1905) with its assumption that human will activates "determining tendencies" that are necessary to prompt actions. Empirical studies support his assumption that the transfer of goal intentions into practice depends on the development of precise anticipatory "If-then plans" as well as the firm intentions of where, when, and how to implement the actions (Gollwitzer and Sheeran, 2006, p. 31). Examples are: "Tomorrow morning, I will go to see John in his office and give him credit for the report that he produced", or "If I meet John at work tomorrow, then I will tell him that I appreciate his report." Important here is the specification of the time, location, and manner in which the person intends to act, or the situational cues to which he will respond.

The implementation or attempt to perform the action belongs to phase B in the model presented in Table 7.1. In the final phase, C, the individual evaluates his or her performance, reactions from the environment, and the resulting consequences in comparison to the original motives and goals. If the goals were not achieved, the individual may undertake a modified phase cycle.

Table 7.1   The Rubicon phase model of motivation

Basic constructs	Phases
(A) Motivation	Pre-decisional deliberation and goal intention
	↓
(B) Volition	Pre-actional planning
	↓
	Implementation intention
	↓
	Action
	↓
(C) Motivation	Post-actional evaluation

A meta-analysis of 94 studies by Gollwitzer and Sheeran (2006) compared the effects of goal intentions alone with the effects of goal intentions and additional respective implementation intentions. It demonstrates that this activation of implementation intentions adds a medium-to-large positive effect (mean d = .65, 95 percent confidence interval from .60 to .70) on a variety of desired outcomes, e.g. academic, personal and health goals.

HOW TO CROSS THE RUBICON

What practical conclusions can be derived from the phase model and studies on implementation intentions? How can they be used for coaching interventions? Phase A (pre-decisional deliberation and clarification of the goal intention) refers to motivational and goal reflection or clarification processes that are not new, but rather typical of many coaching approaches. For example, a client could set a target to remain calm in stressful situations, in order to improve his or her health and to avoid premature decision-making. The beginning of phase B (pre-actional planning) resembles the usual procedure of developing a plan for how the goal can be achieved. For example, the client might plan to spend time considering alternatives before making decisions. According to the Rubicon model, this planning shifts the focus toward implementation.

According to the phase model, at this juncture an additional intervention is beneficial: the activation of implementation intentions. Similar to the instructions to the subjects in the studies analyzed by Gollwitzer and Sheeran (2006), the coach asks the client to determine exactly what situation and cues will signal when to perform the intended behavior, and also to develop a self-instruction sentence. The standard self-instruction has the form of an

"If ..., then ...." sentence. For example: "If I observe that I have feelings of stress, then I will calm down and will not make decisions without considering alternatives." In addition, it is recommended that the coach helps the client develop a firm intention to perform the action in the next stressful situation. We have written a short guideline for our coaching education program that gives examples of how to encourage clients to take time and use their will to make decisions, how to visualize the future situation, or how to concentrate on the cues for the planned actions.

Storch (2004) describes how, through implementation intentions, we can cross our own psychological Rubicon in order to realize goals we wholeheartedly desire. She gives the example drawn from a coaching engagement of a female teacher who wants to avoid burn-out. The teacher plans to reduce her workload, but after several unsuccessful trials she consults her friendly school principal and complains: "Well, I know I should cut down on work, but somehow I don't want to. I'm not that old! I keep telling myself that I should say 'no' when the next project comes up ...". Obviously, as Storch highlights, the client has not yet crossed her Rubicon and is still captive to rumination and deliberation about her situation. If the client has crossed the personal Rubicon, he or she often shows a firm facial expression and talks about it without ambivalence.

Grant (2006, p. 159) refers to the Rubicon model and notes that "one key outcome of successful action planning is the facilitation of the coachee's transition from a *deliberative* mind-set to an *implementational* mind-set". In his early review of theories related to goal-oriented coaching (Grant, 2001, p. 31), he emphasizes that this transition implies a shift of the individual towards positive and optimistic views of the chances of success, and is associated with higher levels of self-regulation and goal attainment.

INTENTION MEMORY

Planned actions are performed only if the individual remembers his or her implementation intentions *in* the transfer situation. Kuhl (1984) suggests that humans possess a special intention memory that helps them to achieve long-term goals. Its function is similar to that of working memory (Baddeley, 1997), except that it represents action-related rather than sensory information. It specializes in implementation intentions, which are difficult from a motivational perspective to transfer into practice (for example, because they require a high level of energy or many action steps). The existence of this memory is derived from experimental and field research on the so-called *intention-superiority effect*

(Goschke and Kuhl, 1996; McDaniel and Einstein, 2007). It consistently shows that the recognition of words associated with intended execution of actions is faster and more sustained than that of words with no such associations.

People use external aids to activate their intention memory in daily life. Shopping lists at the supermarket; calendar systems; alarm clocks to remind us when to start a planned action; colored Post-it® notes and the like, are all examples of popular modern memory tools. In coaching, we can learn to apply similar reminders or be creative and invent new ones that can be used in the transfer situation. In the first example, where the team leader "forgot" to praise his team, it might have been helpful for him to bring a secret reminder (e.g. a little drawing of a smiley on his agenda notes) to the meeting.

Storch (2004) highlights the difficulty of changing habituated behavior. If, after self-directed efforts, a person is unable to convert resolution into action, Storch advocates for support through coaching. She also recommends using visualization techniques that facilitate memorizing intentions and that support the development of a clear mental image of the situational cues that are intended to activate the new behavior. I now move to the next question: What happens in the real transfer situation after crossing the Rubicon?

What Follows the Crossing of the Rubicon?

AN UNPREDICTED SITUATION AFTER CROSSING THE RUBICON

The phases of the Rubicon model of motivation do not tell the full story. For Caesar it was easy to cross the Rubicon as intended. No one hindered him or his legion as they marched into the city of Rome (Abbott, 2012, pp. 66 ff). However, his challenges were to come. Caesar had not foreseen that his adversary, the general and consul Gnaeus Pompeius Magnus (known as "Pompey"), had convinced the senate not to fight against Caesar immediately, but rather to leave Rome with all the rich Romans, taking all food and valuable goods with them. His plan was to organize a large army against Caesar in Greece. So, Caesar and his hungry soldiers, who were waiting for the pay that Caesar had promised them in Rome, arrived to a nearly abandoned city (Abbott, 2012, pp. 66 ff).

Instead of immediately reaching his goal of winning power over the Roman Empire, Caesar had to cope with many conflicts in his own legion, and develop a completely different action plan. He won several battles against the legions of Pompey in Spain and lost one in Dyrrachium. He adapted to new problem situations flexibly, despite nearly overstraining his military resources. Ultimately, he won the war and power over the Roman Empire in the *Battle of Pharsalia* on August 9 in 48 BC. Caesar defeated Pompey, who commanded twice the number of soldiers, by means of a superior strategy and his charismatic leadership.

This is a good example of a long and difficult process of goal-oriented, flexible actions that demand the strategic management of many unpredicted situations. It was necessary to establish multiple implementation intentions, engage in continual resource activation, and find creative solutions after setbacks.

PHASES AFTER CROSSING THE RUBICON

The Rubicon Phase Model in Table 7.1 above has to be extended to include processes of preparing for and coping with difficult transfer problems. Two extensions are outlined in Figure 7.1. Storch and Krause (2007) have added a transfer planning phase, B2, and the author appends a transfer coping phase, C. The third column of the figure lists coaching methods that correspond with each phase. Several of these have been mentioned above. Those remaining will be described below. The arrows between the phases indicate that they do not necessarily follow in a sequence: people often seesaw between or skip phases. The model implies that people who endlessly ruminate about problems without acting are stuck in Phase A, and will not start goal-oriented actions.

Phase A: Transition from need to motive

According to Storch and Krause (2007) a good headline for the Motivation Phase (A) is "Transition from need to motive". Coaching methods that are helpful here are those that help to facilitate problem- and self-reflection and goal clarification. As Storch (2004) points out, a first step in psychotherapy or coaching that enables a clarification of motives and initial goals is exploring the client's feelings that are associated with the goals. Self-congruent goals are often associated with positive bodily feelings, so-called somatic markers (Damásio, 1998). From studies of brain lesion patients and experimental research (see review of Reimann and Bechara, 2010), Damásio derived the hypothesis that individuals learn to associate the consequences of decisions with positive or negative emotional body reactions. These emotions serve as gut instinct evaluations and support decisions based on individual experiences. Storch and Krause (2007) recommend observing nonverbal emotional reactions (e.g. face expressions, tension of the limbs or stomach, etc.). They suppose that their strength indicates the strength of goal intentions. If the client does not show or feel positive somatic reactions associated with the goal, the goal intention should be reconsidered.

In addition, for Phase A Storch (2004) recommends focusing and activating the strengths and other resources of the client in coaching or therapy (e.g. through questions exploring strengths, and visualization of past experiences of success). In general, two classes of resources are distinguished: (1) an individual's internal or personal resources (e.g. motivation and energy, traits, abilities, skills, knowledge and potentials) and (2) external resources (e.g. support from people in the occupational or private environment and technical support or knowledge systems). Studies show that *resource activation*, as assessed through behavioral observation by therapists (Gassmann and Grawe, 2006) and coaches (Behrendt, 2006; Greif, 2010), predicts goal attainment of the clients and desired behavior modification. It is therefore assumed to be a general success factor in both psychotherapy and coaching, and one that can be trained systematically (Storch and Krause, 2007).

Phase B1: "Crossing the rubicon", and B2: "We shall prevail"

An extension of the Rubicon model by Storch (2004) is a division of the pre-actional preparation Phase B into two parts. The first, Volition (B1), is the classical phase of "Crossing the Rubicon" i.e. forming implementation intentions. The second, (B2), is the planning of the resource pool to support the client's self-management in the transfer situation (i.e. figuratively speaking a pool or set of resources that can be shared by the client in the transfer process). Coaching methods to support this second part include: a reflection on how to overcome internal and external obstacles (e.g. change resistance) that may hinder the transfer; resource activation (recalled from Phase A); and the development of a plan on how to apply the resources and transfer coaching in the next, action phase. Since the client is not left alone while mentally trying to convert the intended actions or changes into practice, "We shall prevail!" is an appropriate headline for Phase B2.

Phase C: "If it doesn't work, I will try again in a different way!"

In the standard Rubicon Phase Model not enough attention has been paid to the action phase after crossing the Rubicon: the *transfer* of difficult action intentions into real-world practice. Therefore, the author has extended the model with Phase C (transfer process coping) in Figure 7.1.

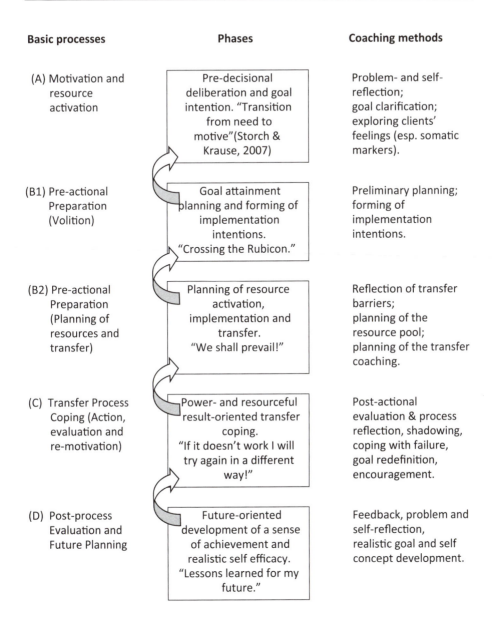

Basic processes	Phases	Coaching methods
(A) Motivation and resource activation	Pre-decisional deliberation and goal intention. "Transition from need to motive"(Storch & Krause, 2007)	Problem- and self-reflection; goal clarification; exploring clients' feelings (esp. somatic markers).
(B1) Pre-actional Preparation (Volition)	Goal attainment planning and forming of implementation intentions. "Crossing the Rubicon."	Preliminary planning; forming of implementation intentions.
(B2) Pre-actional Preparation (Planning of resources and transfer)	Planning of resource activation, implementation and transfer. "We shall prevail!"	Reflection of transfer barriers; planning of the resource pool; planning of the transfer coaching.
(C) Transfer Process Coping (Action, evaluation and re-motivation)	Power- and resourceful result-oriented transfer coping. "If it doesn't work I will try again in a different way!"	Post-actional evaluation & process reflection, shadowing, coping with failure, goal redefinition, encouragement.
(D) Post-process Evaluation and Future Planning	Future-oriented development of a sense of achievement and realistic self efficacy. "Lessons learned for my future."	Feedback, problem and self-reflection, realistic goal and self concept development.

Figure 7.1   Extended Rubicon phase model

Studies show that rigid implementation intentions may be problematic in transfer situations that require flexibility (Gollwitzer, Fujita, and Oettingen, 2004). As these studies imply, perfectionists who prefer high levels of control should be discouraged from adopting inflexible implementation intentions.

Coaches should also be aware that high occupational stress diminishes the effects of implementation intentions (Budden and Sagarin, 2007).

It is helpful for coaches to anticipate unexpected difficulties and obstacles — as in the example of Caesar after crossing the Rubicon. Clients may not be able to perform the intended actions, or even if they are successful in execution, their actions may not lead to the expected outcomes. Below I will describe examples of both seemingly simple coaching engagements where the clients know what they need to do, and where the outcomes are predictable, as well as ones where actions and changes produce unpredictable outcomes, and where there is low agreement on what to do.

Phase D: Post-process evaluation and future planning

The last phase shown in Figure 7.1 resembles the final phase of the original phase model in Table 7.1. It highlights as an extension, that even after successful performance of the action and high goal attainment rate it might be useful to reflect on the lessons learned, enjoy the success, develop a future oriented, realistic sense of self-efficacy and achievement, and plan future actions. Corresponding coaching methods are goal attainment ratings and other feedback-techniques, or methods that activate problem- and self-reflections or evaluation of the self-development of the client.

TRANSFER PROCESS COACHING IN PREDICTABLE OUTCOME SITUATIONS

Sometimes coaching is simple. The client knows what he or she wants and what to do to reach the goal. One or two coaching sessions allow sufficient time to concentrate on what to do and to form an action intention. The client succeeds in performing the action in the transfer situation and the outcome of the action is as positive as expected. But practical experience tells us that such simple coaching engagements are rare. Very often, clients underestimate the difficulties involved in changing their habitual behavior. Self-efficacy expectations sometimes are too optimistic, and the clients are not prepared to cope with unexpected inner resistances or external obstacles that may hinder the execution of planned behavior. It is easy to find good reasons for postponing our intention to promote our health by jogging regularly after work. There is an urgent telephone call to make or the day was too hard and we need a rest ...

Support of transfer into practice in phase C of the extended Rubicon phase model in Figure 7.1 seems to be an important success factor in the process of coaching (Greif, 2010). Standard books of coaching techniques (Megginson and Clutterbuck, 2005, 2009; Rauen, 2007, 2011) comprise valuable information how to support the client's transfer, but do not contain methods that are specifically applicable in phase C between coaching sessions, or address how to overcome difficulties in the transfer of intended actions into practice. An approach is the telephone transfer coaching of Geißler (2011) which is similar to the telephone shadowing technique that will be explained below.

Shadowing

Shadowing involves "nonparticipant observation" of a person performing actions. It is the counterpart of "participant observation" and therefore belongs to the core observation methods applied in field studies (Czarniawska, 2007). However, as a research method it has received little attention. *Job or performance shadowing* is a technique of observational learning, where a learner accompanies an experienced practitioner in his or her daily routines and observes performance (e.g. in an internship). Vice-versa, an experienced person may shadow someone who is trying to implement new or difficult actions in a real-life situation.

Job or performance shadowing is sometimes called *shadow consultation* (Resnick and King, 1985) or *solution monitoring* (Mumford and Connelly, 1991). A survey shows that it is rated as one of the most effective of different personnel development interventions (Jarvis, Lane, and Filler-Travis, 2006). Kilburg (2002, p. 92) concludes that:

> ... *when done well, shadow consultation creates a safe, interpersonal containment in which a consultant and a colleague can reflect carefully on any and all dimensions that may be creating impacts on a project. It can lead to dramatic improvements in the ability to be self-aware and therefore self-managing and self-confident in consulting assignments. It also creates a safety net through which a mature practitioner is unlikely to fall when the inevitable problems occur in our very difficult work. For new or less experienced practitioners, it is a wonderful way to stretch the learning curve and to do so quickly with live material that has immediate impact on performance.*

Kilburg (2002) found that shadowing is widely practiced in the field of organizational development, but that there was little research on the technique.

There are even fewer studies that examine it in coaching. Probably the most systematic of these was published by Kaufel et al. (2006). These researchers studied the outcome of voluntary coaching for German Military officers following 360-degree feedback. After goal clarification in the preliminary coaching sessions, "leadership accompaniment" was offered to 160 officers. The trained coaches accompanied up to ten officers on the job for several days and observed their goal-related behavior. These observations were closely followed by coaching sessions, in which the coach reflected with the officer on what they had seen. The combination of 360-degree feedback and coaching with this shadowing resulted in statistically significant ($p < .05$) pre-post-effects ($.14 < d > .50$), measured by improvements of their 360-degree ratings. The increases were higher than those for groups without shadowing.

Practical experience suggests that coaching clients tend to give up quickly after their first unsuccessful attempts to execute their action intentions. With shadowing, client and coach can immediately start to reflect on their observations of the external and internal barriers, while the situation is still mentally present. From practical observation, I infer that it is psychologically important to process negative emotions and feelings of helplessness by means of re-motivation and encouraging the client to try again directly after the situation, perhaps in a different, more adaptive way. If several days pass before the coach is able to intervene, re-motivation can become difficult. However, since a possible danger of shadowing is that clients may depend too much on the presence of the consultant or coach, it is necessary to support the client in learning how to monitor and reflect on their transfer trials in a result-oriented and autonomous way and to use self-motivation techniques without assistance. This belongs to the "lessons learned" in phase D of the model in Figure 7.1.

Telephone shadowing

In the field of sports coaching, nobody would consider it abnormal for the coach to monitor the coachee in the transfer situation. In business coaching, however, shadowing can be negatively viewed. The coach is therefore sometimes introduced as an expert or consultant who is participating in the situation. Where the face-to-face presence of the coach is not acceptable or too expensive, *telephone shadowing* is an alternative (see box). In coaching relating to organizational change processes, continual telephone shadowing can be the only possible coaching intervention in phase C of the model in Figure 7.1, since processes are dynamic and quick, with many critical situations and decisions that have to follow directly after unexpected situations and outcomes.

TELEPHONE SHADOWING
Telephone Appointments

Coach and client plan telephone coaching sessions at appointed times or when considered necessary by the client. Normally, it is recommended that telephone shadowing be carried out as shortly as possible after the transfer situation.

Internal and External Barriers of Transfer

If internal or external barriers are strong, an additional brief, encouraging telephone call can be arranged for shortly before the situation. In the telephone call after the transfer trial, client and coach reflect on the performance of the client in the situation, and on possible internal and external difficulties that may have hindered the client from acting as intended, along with how she or he can overcome these obstacles next time.

Psychological Essentials

Since the coach is not present in the situation itself, the process-reflection and feedback depends on the client's own observations of the situation and self-monitoring. If the client failed to effectively execute the intended actions, encouragement and re-motivation directly after the experiences of frustration or helplessness derived from practical experiences seem to be psychologically essential. Clients often give up immediately after failure. It is more difficult to encourage a renewed attempt when the coaching session takes place after several days. If the inner or external obstacles were unexpected or if the outcome of the actions were not as positive as predicted, it may be necessary to redefine the goals, adapt the planned actions and implementation intentions and to retry in the next possible situation.

The author has developed guidelines for the telephone shadowing coaching technique along with a short training program. The following example illustrates how to apply the technique in a seemingly simple case with high predictability of outcome. Later we will describe complex situations with unpredictable outcomes.

Case example: One year of procrastination in writing a master's thesis

The client was a postgraduate psychology student in a coaching seminar focused on procrastination. He was a member of one of the triads that had been assigned the task of practicing coaching sequences. The group came to tell me that they did not know how to coach one of their members, who was struggling with a severe procrastination problem. For a whole year he had postponed writing the Master's thesis that he had agreed upon with his professor. He had collected and read ample literature, completed his study and analyzed the data, but his repeated attempts to write petered out. Whenever he formed the intention to begin work on his thesis, he found himself coming up with reasons to postpone the start.

In a brief coaching session I confirmed that he had the ability to write short scientific texts. He worked on a scientific project as a student assistant and had written several reports without problems. One external barrier to finding time for the thesis was that he had assumed too many responsibilities along with related tasks. His major inner resistance seemed to be his high achievement motive: he wanted to write an excellent thesis that qualified him for a scientific career. Whenever he tried to start, he brooded about how to write an exceptional text. When he did not find a solution that satisfied his aspirations, in frustration he developed a routine that involved suppressing his brooding and procrastinating by taking on more and more seemingly urgent tasks.

I asked him when he would be able to organize a free day for the next attempt and he proposed the following Monday. I also suggested a telephone call in the early afternoon, after he had tried to start. He accepted unhesitatingly. We then talked about what might be an easy next step for the Monday, and came to the conclusion that he should avoid the ambitious sections of the thesis, and start with a description of the sample and realization of his study. Our work was in the spirit of the phrase, "Keep your ambition, but start with a small step".

In the telephone shadowing session on the Monday, he was distraught. He told me that when he had tried to get started, his computer did not work and he had been unable to reboot it. He feared that his hard disk had crashed. I empathized and helped him to reflect on his external resources, i.e. who could help him to diagnose and repair the technical problem. He formed a new intention and plan to restart his writing directly after the repair. He solved the technical problem faster than expected and started to write on the following day. During the next telephone call he told me that he was relieved that he had started well, but still felt insecure about whether he would be able to work consistently. He asked me to support him through further telephone communication. I reinforced his successful first trial and we agreed on several calls after the next trials.

After only five calls, he developed the routine and self-motivation techniques necessary for him to write continually. After the third, the calls became very short, since he reported no problems and his self-efficacy was growing. In the last call we reflected on the process and techniques that he could use autonomously in order to surmount barriers and remind himself to execute his action intentions in the future. He sent me the completed chapters by email to show me that his thesis was progressing. In the end, I received a copy of his thesis with a grateful dedication. He earned a top grade and his professor offered him a research assistant position.

Practical experience of telephone shadowing shows that it can be a quick and effective intervention. In some cases it is necessary to have telephone shadowing over a long period. An example of a longer case was a student who failed his Master's examination at a London university and had only one more chance to repeat it. His goals were to improve his learning and memorizing techniques, read and memorize the recommended comprehensive literature, and improve his written English for the answers to the open examination questions. In addition, he wanted to stop his incessant rumination on his failure and to learn how to control his examination anxiety before and during the examination. We worked successfully on each of these goals and he received a "merit". Telephone shadowing was used to continually re-motivate him and to support his persistence in keeping up with his voluminous and long-term learning demands. Most of the telephone sessions were between ten and twenty minutes.

As the examples demonstrate, telephone shadowing is a technique that supports the goal-oriented self-regulation of the client who is performing difficult transfer tasks: executing their action intentions on time, and achieving concrete results. On the basis of practical experience we assume that it is a powerful technique that substantially increases the implementation rate. We have started a randomized controlled study in which we hope to verify our observation. Kreggenfeld and Reckert (2008) applied a similar telephone technique developed by Geißler (2011) to support the transfer. They found that the goal attainment rate exceeded 80 percent.

COACHING THE UNEXPECTED AND CHAOS THEORY

Professional coaches know from experience that their clients, not unlike Caesar, often face unpredicted, turbulent situations while trying to implement their planned actions in phase C of the extended Rubicon phase model, shown in Figure 7.1. In such cases the coaching work is not as simple as in the cases above. For coaching people in high-stress leadership positions, Cavanagh (2010) refers to complexity science and a figure of Zimmerman, Lindberg and Plsek (1998), that refers to a matrix of situations developed by Stacey (1996). As shown in Figure 7.2, Stacey differentiates between situations with a low and high (1) predictability of the outcome of planned actions and (2) agreement between experienced people about what to do. According to this model, there is only a small zone in which rational, knowledge-based decisions lead to expected outcomes. Within this zone, both predictability and agreement are high, because the consequences of actions are linear. The case examples above belong in this zone.

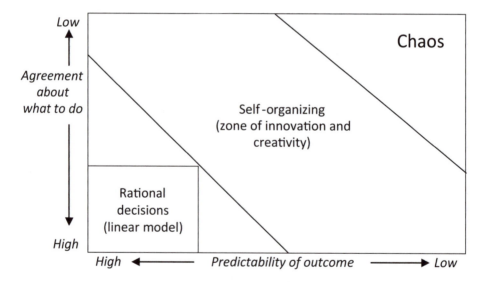

Figure 7.2   The Stacey agreement/certainty matrix
Source: Adapted from Zimmerman, Lindberg, and Plsek, 1998

If the predictability of action outcomes remains high, but agreement or knowledge about what to do is lacking, decisions are based on opinions. A situation in which both predictability and agreement are low is a zone of chaos. As people approach such situations at the "edge of chaos" (Cavanagh, 2010), they feel increasingly uncertain. According to Cavanagh, the zone between chaos and linear relations between actions and outcomes is characterized by mainly self-organizing processes (See also Cavanagh, Chapter 8; Bright and Pryor, Chapter 9, this volume.) Here solutions emerge by evolutionary selection amongst trials. Since this zone demands heretofore unconventional or unexpected solutions, it can be perceived as an area of creative and innovative solutions. According to complexity science, such complex and non-linear outcome situations should not be avoided, but accepted as opportunities for innovation.

Cavanagh (2010) challenges coaching theory and the profession, claiming that it focuses too heavily on linear processes and high predictive outcome. He suggests that the non-linear and unpredictable, even chaotic, environments of the client be taken into consideration. But how can we support our clients in coping with situations where the outcome of their actions is non-linear or unpredictable?

To answer this challenging question, we refer to chaos and self-organization theories (Gleick, 1987; Haken and Stadler, 1990; Kriz, 2009), as well as theories and research on successful goal-oriented problem-solving behavior in unpredictable situations (Dörner, 1990; Kriz, 2008; Osman, 2010). The following points summarize the essential principles that can be guidance for the coach and client in phase C of the extended Rubicon phase model in Figure 7.1, in the case of unpredictable consequences of actions:

- Expect the unexpected!

- Know how stable and chaotic states of systems differ and how transitions between these states are possible by means of self-organization.

- Analyze task and system or environment characteristics repeatedly.

- Be attentive to many small clues and learn how they relate to outcome criteria, even if the relations are minimal.

- Pay attention to time-lagged influences with non-linear growth.

- Do not adhere rigidly to solutions that are not working; change and try different solutions and improve your flexibility in solving problems.

- Clarify emotions and unwind negative feelings after experiences of failure.

Below is an illustrative case example of coaching related to organizational change.

Case: Coaching and shadowing a project manager

The following case refers to a company that belongs to the supply industry. The company provides a range of services (energy, logistics, maintenance, facility management, supply) to chemical and pharmaceutical plants in one of the largest locations in Germany (2.9 square miles and about 30,000 employees). The vision of the CEO and project manager was a radical customer-oriented reorganization of the core processes and structures and a substantial cost reduction in all services and sub-companies in comparison to the competitors.

I was asked to coach the CEO, the project manager and the core team for about one and a half years in all phases of the project. I participated in the selection of the consultancy, development of different strategy options, presentations to the heads of the firms that owned the company, negotiations with the powerful shop stewards, communications to the employees, initial sessions of the core team, analysis of the processes, customer interviews, planning and presentation of the complete reorganization concept to the owners, implementation and last but not least evaluation of the planned changes. From the beginning the project was beset with many hidden pitfalls, conflicts and power-plays between and amongst the top levels. At one point, a possible strike announced by the union threatened to stop the whole project.

In my coaching, I combined standard individual problem-solving coaching sessions with shadowing (starting with face-to-face and later, telephone) in phase C of the extended Rubicon phase model in Figure 7.1. For example, during a session the client might analyze the current as-is-state and develop a plan of action and implementation intentions. In the sessions we talked a lot about the dynamics of complex organizational changes, informal change resistance and conflicts, and how to manage uncertainty according to points mentioned in the summary above. Shadowing involved accompanying the client in anticipated critical situations (e.g. presentations to the owners, heads or lower leadership levels of the sub-companies and negotiations with the shop stewards), and observing the process and behavior. In an evaluation session that directly followed, we reflected on the process and analyzed the results. I facilitated problem- and self-reflection and eventually a goal redefinition, and the development of action plans and implementation intentions. The whole coaching process can be summarized by cycles of (1) reflection sessions, (2) goal re-definition, resource planning and action intentions, (3) implementation trials with or without shadowing and (4) evaluation sessions. As the coaching progressed I reflected with the clients on how they could replace the shadowing with self-monitoring and self-feedback. As a consequence, the number of shadowing situations was reduced and I made myself redundant as an observer and coach.

The job of managing uncertain organizational change is strenuous, not only for the client, but also for the coach. As coach in the example above, I too wished for encouragement in helping the clients to cope with many unexpected and seemingly unsolvable problems and the frustrating new conflicts that arose frequently. My question was how to keep my professional distance in the demanding coaching process and have enough time for reflection independently from my clients? I therefore asked the company to pay for a coach for me and they accepted. This "coaching of the coach" was very supportive, both for me directly and, I suspect, indirectly for the company. The goal attainment rates of the changes after the reorganization of the sub-companies (based on economic criteria and expert ratings) ranged from between 85 to 100 percent.

On the Way to a Better Understanding and Management of the Complexities of Goal Attainment

According to Heckhausen and Kuhl (1985) "The path from wishes to action is a long one" (p. 134). The Rubicon phase model of Gollwitzer (1999) follows the path from the pre-decisional and decisional phase, where individuals reflect and decide which goals they wish to reach. After having set their goal, in the post-decisional phase, they plan actions that lead to their goal and in the ideal case develop a firm implementation intention to perform the planned actions, similar to Julius Caesar, when he intended to cross the Rubicon. The Rubicon phase model has contributed to a better understanding of how individuals progress along the path from wishes to action. The results of meta-analysis of laboratory and field studies of Gollwitzer and Sheeran (2006) demonstrate that the instruction to form an implementation intention, in addition to mere goal intentions, increases the likelihood that planned actions will be carried out. The evidence from this basic and field research supports the practice of providing implementation instructions for coaching clients after they have decided on their goals and action plans. It is to be expected that this raises the transfer rates and goal attainment.

The original Rubicon phase model does not close the intention-doing gap completely. For example, if the goal is to break strong habits, research results show that this is not always successful if the habit strength is high (Webb, 2009) and that strong implementation intentions are necessary (Adriaanse, Gollwitzer, De Ridder, de Wit, and Kroese, 2011). Forming a new habit, e.g. drinking water every day at breakfast, takes between two and 36 weeks daily implementations until automaticity reaches a high level (Lally, Jaarsveld, Potts, and Wardle, 2010). As mentioned in the beginning of the chapter, patients with heart failure give up on their life-saving rehabilitation plan within three months (Tierney et al., 2011). If their health behavior plans conflict with strong habits or if stress at work suppresses the intention (Budden and Sagarin, 2007), implementation intentions probably will not change behavior sustainably. The author proposes to add another phase to the Rubicon phase model that focuses on coping with difficult transfer processes. Telephone shadowing is recommended here as a special coaching method that may help to close the intention-doing gap a bit further.

The methods mentioned have been tested in numerous coaching cases. However, in the field of coaching, research evidence of the usefulness of the theory-based implementation instruction or telephone shadowing is still missing. The same applies to other methods and tools, which have been transferred from other fields to coaching. We definitely need randomized controlled studies testing the effectiveness of separate and combined methods in coaching. We have started such research and the first results of our study show impressive transfer rates and goals attainment ratings after telephone shadowing. However, in general, coaches cannot wait for years until research produces reliable evidence that the methods, which they need for coaching, are effective. Reflective practitioners (Schön, 1983) who try to develop a better understanding of human functioning and more effective intervention methods by attentive observation and new insight, are not completely different from psychological scientists. The more specifically practitioners and scientists explicate their hypotheses in terms of observable results, the more it is possible to test them with practical observation. Based on the extended Rubicon model, the hypothesis can be derived that if a coaching client does not implement a planned behavior modification, the chances that he or she will perform the intended actions will rise if implementation intentions and telephone shadowing methods are applied in combination. In my view, coaches and their clients are ideal partners to conduct such tests and engage in reflective practice to explore the complexities of implementation.

The greatest challenge, not only for coaching of individuals, but also for managing organizations, lies in the question of how it might be possible to manage complex and unpredictable changes. Reflective coaching practitioners and scientists could help clients understand and navigate transitions and change processes by: expecting the unexpected, continually exploring, monitoring, and reflecting before deciding what to do, and managing uncertainty with flexibility and innovation. In unpredictable change processes, continuous reflective practice is an indispensable precondition for achieving positive results.

References

Abbott, J. (2012). *History of Julius Caesar*. Amazon Kindle Edition (online book).

Ach, N. (1905). *Über die Willenstätigkeit und das Denken*. Göttingen: Vandenhoeck & Ruprecht.

Adriaanse, M.A., Gollwitzer, P.M., De Ridder, D.T.D., de Wit, J.B.F., & Kroese, F.M. (2011). Breaking habits with implementation intentions: A test of underlying processes. *Personality and Social Psychology Bulletin, 37*(4), 502–13.

Ajzen, I. (1991). The theory of planned behavior. *Organizational Behavior and Human Decision Processes, 50*(2), 179–211.

Ajzen, I. & Fishbein, M. (1972). Attitudes and normative beliefs as factors influencing behavioral intentions. *Journal of Personality and Social Psychology, 21*(1), 1–9.

Atkinson, J.W. (1957). Motivational determinants of risk-taking behavior. *Psychological Review, 64*(6, Pt 1), 359–72.

Baddeley, A.D. (1997). *Human Memory: Theory and Practice* (10th ed.). Boston: Allyn & Bacon.

Behrendt, P. (2006). Wirkung und Wirkfaktoren von psychodramatischem Coaching—Eine experimentelle Evaluationsstudie. *Zeitschrift für Psychodrama und Soziometrie, 5*(1), 59–87.

Budden, J.S. & Sagarin, B.J. (2007). Implementation intentions, occupational stress, and the exercise intention-behavior relationship. *Journal of Occupational Health Psychology, 12*(4), 391–401.

Cavanagh, M.J. (2010). *Coaching High Stress Leaders.* Paper presented at the Third International Coaching Research Forum (13–14 December 2010) — Institute of Coaching Psychology and European School of Management and Technology (ESMT), Berlin (Germany).

Czarniawska, B. (2007). *Shadowing and Other Techniques for Doing Fieldwork in Modern Societies.* Malmö, Sweden: Liber AB–Copenhagen Business School Press.

Damásio, A. (1998). The somatic marker hypothesis and the possible functions of the prefrontal cortex. In A.C. Roberts, T.W. Robbins, & L. Weiskrantz (Eds), *The Prefrontal Cortex: Executive and Cognitive Functions,* 36–50. New York: Oxford University Press.

Dörner, D. (1990). The logic of failure. In D.E. Broadbent, J.T. Reason, & A.D. Baddeley (Hrsg.), *Human Factors in Hazardous Situations,* 15–36. New York: Clarendon Press/Oxford University Press.

Fishbein, M. & Ajzen, I. (2010). *Predicting and Changing Behavior: The Reasoned Action Approach.* New York: Psychology Press.

Gassmann, D. & Grawe, K. (2006). General change mechanisms: The relation between problem activation and resource activation in successful and unsuccessful therapeutic interactions. *Clinical Psychology & Psychotherapy,* 13(1), 1–11.

Geißler, H. (2011). Coaching meets Training — zur Lösung des Transferproblems durch "virtuelles Transfercoaching (VTC)". In M. Loebbert & R. Wegener (Eds), *Coaching entwickeln. Forschung und Praxis im Dialog,* 123–34. Göttingen: Vandenhoeck & Ruprecht.

Gleick, J. (1987). *Chaos: Making a New Science.* New York: Penguin.

Gollwitzer, P.M. (1999). Implementation intentions: Strong effects of simple plans. *American Psychologist,* 54(7), 493–503.

Gollwitzer, P.M., Fujita, K., & Oettingen, G. (2004). Planning and the implementation of goals. In R.F. Baumeister & K.D. Vohs (Eds), *Handbook of Self-Regulation: Research, Theory, and Applications,* 211–28. New York: Guilford Press.

Gollwitzer, P.M. & Sheeran, P. (2006). Implementation intentions and goal achievement: A meta-analysis of effects and processes. *Advances in Experimental Social Psychology,* 38, 69–120.

Goschke, T. & Kuhl, J. (1996). Remembering what to do: Explicit and implicit memory for intentions. In M. Brandimonte, G.O. Einstein & M.A. McDaniel (Eds), *Prospective Memory: Theory and applications,* 53–91. Mahwah, NJ: Erlbaum.

Grant, A.M. (2001). *Towards a Psychology of Coaching: The Impact of Coaching on Metacognition, Mental Health and Goal Attainment.* University of Sydney, Sydney, Australia.

Grant, A.M. (2006). An integrative goal-focused approach to executive coaching. In D.R. Stober & Grant, Anthony M. (Eds), *Evidence Based Coaching Handbook: Putting Best Practices to Work for your Clients,* 153–92. New York: John Wiley & Sons.

Greif, S. (2010). A new frontier of research and practice: Observation of coaching behaviour. *The Coaching Psychologist, 6*(2), 21–9.

Haken, H. & Stadler, M. (1990). *Synergetics of Cognition: Proceedings of the International Symposium at Schloß Elmau, Bavaria, June 4–8, 1989.* New York: Springer-Verlag Publishing.

Heckhausen, H. (1991). *Motivation and Action.* New York: Springer.

Heckhausen, H. & Gollwitzer, P.M. (1987). Thought contents and cognitive functioning in motivational versus volitional states of mind. *Motivation and Emotion, 11*(2), 101–20.

Heckhausen, H. & Kuhl, J. (1985). From wishes to action: The dead ends and short cuts on the long way to action. In M. Frese & J. Sabini (Eds), *Goal-directed Behavior: Psychological Theory and Research on Action,* 134–60. New Jersey: Erlbaum.

Jarvis, J., Lane, D., & Filler-Travis, A. (2006). *The Case for Coaching.* London: CIPD Books.

Kaufel, S., Scherer, S., Scherm, M., & Sauer, M. (2006). Führungbegleitung in der Bundeswehr—Coaching für militärische Führungskräfte. In W. Backhausen & J.-P. Thommsen (Eds), *Coaching. Durch systemisches Denken zur innovativen Personalentwicklung,* 419–38. Wiesbaden: Gabler.

Kilburg, R.R. (2002). Shadow consultation: A reflective approach for preventing practice disasters. *Consulting Psychology Journal: Practice and Research, 54*(2), 75–92.

Kreggenfeld, U. & Reckert, H.-W. (2008). 'Virtuelles Transfercoaching'. Die Transferquote verdreifachen. In H. Geißler (Ed.), *E-Coaching,* 217–24. Hohengehre: Schneider.

Kriz, J. (2008). *Self-Actualization: Person-Centred Approach and Systems Theory.* Ross-on-Wye, UK: PCCS-books.

Kriz, J. (2009). Cognitive and interactive patterning: Processes of creating meaning. In J. Valsiner, P.C.M. Molenaar, M.C.D.P. Lyra, & N. Chaudhary (Eds), *Dynamic Process Methodology in the Social and Developmental Sciences,* 619–50. New York: Springer Science + Business Media.

Kuhl, J. (1984). Volitional aspects of achievement motivation and learned helplessness: Toward a comprehensive theory of action-control. In B.A. Maher (Ed.), *Progress in Experimental Personality Research* (vol. 13), 99–171. New York: Academic Press.

Lally, P.V., Jaarsveld, C.H.M., Potts, H.W.W., & Wardle, J. (2010). How are habits formed: Modelling habit formation in the real world. *European Journal of Social Psychology, 40*(6), 998–1009.

Locke, E.A. & Latham, G.P. (2002). Building a practically useful theory of goal setting and task motivation. *American Psychologist, 57*(9), 705–17.

McDaniel, M.A. & Einstein, G.O. (2007). *Prospective Memory: An Overview and Synthesis of an Emerging Field.* Thousand Oaks, CA: Sage.

Megginson, D. & Clutterbuck, D.A. (Eds). (2005). *Techniques for Coaching and Mentoring.* Oxford: Butterworth-Heinemann.

Megginson, D. & Clutterbuck, D.A. (Eds). (2009). *Further Techniques for Coaching and Mentoring.* London: Elsevier.

Mumford, M.D. & Connelly, M.S. (1991). Leaders as creators: Leader performance and problem solving in ill-defined domains. *The Leadership Quarterly, 2*(4), 289–315.

Osman, M. (2010). Controlling uncertainty: A review of human behavior in complex dynamic environments. *Psychological Bulletin, 136*(1), 65–86.

Rauen, C. (Ed.). (2007). *Coaching-Tools II. Erfolgreiche Coaches präsentieren Interventionstechniken aus ihrer Coaching-Praxis.* Bonn: managerSeminare.

Rauen, C. (Ed.). (2011). *Coaching-Tools. Erfolgreiche Coaches präsentieren 60 Interventionstechniken aus ihrer Coaching-Praxis* (7th ed.). Bonn: manager Seminare.

Reimann, M. & Bechara, A. (2010). The somatic marker framework as a neurological theory of decision-making: Review, conceptual comparisons, and future neuroeconomics research. *Journal of Economic Psychology, 31*(5), 767–76.

Resnick, H. & King, J. (1985). Shadow Consultation: Intervention in Industry. *Social Work, 30*(5), 447.

Schön, D.A. (1983). *The Reflective Practitioner.* New York: Basic Books.

Stacey, R.D. (1996). Emerging Strategies for a Chaotic Environment. *Long Range Planning: International Journal of Strategic Management, 29*(2), 182–9.

Storch, M. (2004). Crossing Your Personal Rubicon. *Scientific American Mind, 14*(5), 94–5.

Storch, M. & Krause, F. (2007). *Selbstmanagement — ressourcenorientiert. Grundlagen und Trainingsmanual für die Arbeit mit dem Zürcher Ressourcen Modell ZRM* (4th ed.). Bern: Huber.

Tierney, S., Mamas, M., Skelton, D., Woods, S., Rutter, M.K., Gibson, M., et al. (2011). What can we learn from patients with heart failure about exercise adherence? A systematic review of qualitative papers. *Health Psychology, 30*(4), 401–10.

Vroom, V.H. (1964). *Work and Motivation.* New York: Wiley.

Webb, T.L S.P.A. (2009). Planning to break unwanted habits: Habit strength moderates implementation intention effects on behaviour change. *British Journal of Social Psychology, 48*(3), 507–23.

Zimmerman, B., Lindberg, C., & Plsek, P. (1998). *Edgeware: Insights from Complexity Science for Health Care Leaders*. Irving, TX: VHA Press.

Acknowledgements

The author acknowledges many helpful comments and English style improvements of an earlier version of the manuscript by Susan David, Christina Congleton, and David Clutterbuck.

8

The Coaching Engagement in the Twenty-first Century: New Paradigms for Complex Times

Michael J. Cavanagh

Introduction

The world is, and always has been, an unpredictable and uncertain place. It often unfolds in ways that defy our ability to anticipate and respond effectively. Much of the history of the human race has been concerned with attempts to make this unfolding world more predictable and safe. We have developed societies, organizations, and technologies (of which coaching is just one) aimed at securing access to food, shelter, community, information and other resources. From the perspective of wealthy societies, we have been remarkably successful in these endeavors.

However, the world continues to defy our attempts to control it, even despite our best efforts. It remains a paradoxical mix of stability and instability, harmony and conflict, regularity and unpredictability. Complex adaptive systems theorists call this paradoxical state *bounded instability*. It is also called the edge of chaos, and it is characteristic of all complex systems (Stacey, 2011; see also Chapter 9). In complex systems cause and effect is non-linear and it is this non-linearity that gives rise to bounded instability. It is what delights us with difference, stimulates growth, gives rise to astounding creativity and even enables life itself (Gribbien, 2004). Non-linearity has important consequences for how we conceptualize the coaching process, and particularly for how we understand goals and the goal setting process.

This chapter examines how models of coaching and goal setting might be developed that pay greater attention to the fact that people and systems are characterized by bounded instability and non-linearity. I will argue that many of the models used in both business and coaching assume linear cause and effect. This makes them useful in stable environments (i.e. times where predictability is high). But what happens when the expected regularities shift, when life does not go to plan, and the unexpected happens? Sometimes this is simply part of the normal fluctuation of life—instability within the usual boundaries. And sometimes this instability leads to tipping points which move the system to new states; where the old models do not serve us well, and where agreement about what to do is elusive. Science tells us that the world at large is going through just such a tipping point (or series of tipping points) (Barnosky, et al., 2012). The game is changing. New models of leadership and coaching—and a new relationship to goals—are needed to meet the complex novel challenges we are facing.

We Live in Game-changing Times

The world is entering a new era (Castells, 2010; Kumar, 1995). Each transition from one era to another (nomadic to agrarian; rural to city based; artisan manufacturing to modern industrial) has been accompanied by fundamental changes in the socioeconomic organization of human activity. New technologies in production, energy, transportation and communication have done more than simply enable us to produce and transport goods and information more efficiently. They have simultaneously had major impacts on the way we think and structure our understanding of the world (Castells, 2010).

As each new type of society and economic organization emerges, people are faced with new challenges for which their previous social structures have left them ill-prepared (Bernstein, 1977; Douglas, 1996). For example, in feudal times success was defined by following the rules of one's life station (being a good serf, or good lord). In comparison, with a move to city life dominated by trade and a growing middle class, these old regularities ceased to apply. Here, movement through the social strata became possible, and commercial success became equated with life success. Getting along in the world was more dependent on the individual's capacity to develop transportable skills and to manipulate thought, emotion and language, than it was on the dutiful fulfillment of a social role (Douglas, 1996). It is no coincidence that the provision of mass education through schools and universities coincided with the rise of the cities and capitalist modes of economic organization (Douglas, 1996; Filloux, 1993; Noble, 1977; Verhulst, 1999).

The transition that the world is currently experiencing is just as profound as the transition from rural feudal system to a city based industrial economy. Many have commented that we have moved from the Industrial Age into the Knowledge Age services (Despres and Hiltrop, 1995; Falk and Sheppard, 2006), and that what counts now is the ability of organizations to see change as the new stability, and to be more flexible, resilient and innovative in the production of knowledge, goods and services (Joiner and Josephs, 2007; Kumar, 1995; Castells, 2010). However, this analysis underplays the reality. The change that we are seeing is more fundamental.

Advances in the internet, mass transportation and telecommunications, have connected us in ways hitherto unimagined. They have given rise to new forms of business and social networking the long-term implication of which we cannot predict. Social networking, for example, has enabled groups to quickly form and mobilize in response to issues (as seen in the Arab Spring and 2011 London riots). At the same time researchers are finding concerning signs of personality changes, and even structural changes in the brains of those who have grown up with social networking and the internet (so called "internet natives": Gentile, Twenge, Freeman, and Campbell, 2012; Greenfield, 2011).

The impact of human population and resource usage has also led to a series of environmental issues and tipping points the impacts of which are equally unpredictable. Population growth, increasingly unstable weather patterns, a rise in sea level, and a loss of habitat and biodiversity are all threatening the viability of ecosystems, industries and communities. There is a growing recognition that many of the patterns of action that previously brought us success are now unsustainable, and indeed are positively destructive (Barnosky et al., 2012; Ehrlich, Kareiva, and Daily, 2012).

Rather than entering the knowledge age, I believe we are entering the Metasystematic Age, or the Age of Connectedness. The core challenge of the new era is not increasing the quantity, speed, agility, or even accessibility of knowledge, goods and services. Nor is it about creating more resilient workers. It is not about how to do more of what we are already doing. Our core challenge is to develop new paradigms that help us understand and work with the environmental, economic, and social challenges that are emerging in a hyper-connected world. This requires us to take a metasystematic perspective on the world—

to see the world as a complex interdependent system of systems. It will require leaders and coaches who are capable of stepping out of patterns of action grounded in a linear reductionistic understanding of the world, and developing new approaches to management and goal setting that are consistent with the emergent non-linear dynamics of the world we inhabit.

What will this look like for leaders and coaches? At one level this is a question that cannot be answered as the paradigm is itself emergent. However there is much work in management, the sciences, and the humanities that is seeking new systemic ways of ways of understanding the world. This includes Chaos theory, Catastrophe theory, and Complex Adaptive Systems approaches. What can be said is that these emerging theories and models take a different perspective in three related ways. They have:

1.   A greater focus on connectedness and process.

2.   A wider systemic horizon with more inclusive system boundaries.

3.   A broader temporal view.

Linear Approaches to Management and Coaching

Currently, the dominant model of business tends to focus leaders and coaches on a narrow "system of interest". They focus us on the interests of the organization, the individual or team and the local level. Stakeholders, such as customers, supply chain participants, competitors, the wider society and the environment receive attention to the degree that they impact key metrics such as productivity, engagement, profitability and market share (Dallas, 2011). This narrowing of system boundaries is also demonstrated in both what gets counted as a cost in business, and how costs are accounted for. Costs that are borne outside the defined system of interest are typically ignored or discounted. They are known as *externalities* (OECD, 2002). For example, the healthcare costs associated with smoking do not appear on the balance sheet of tobacco companies. The future costs of climate change or soil degradation are not accounted for in determining the productivity of energy production or farming methods.

The temporal horizon of business also tends to be narrow. Productivity, profitability and market share are measured across relatively brief periods of time, particularly in public companies dominated by the time frame of stock markets. Strategic planning typically has a time horizon of months, or perhaps a few years rather than decades.

Underpinning the dominant view of business is a linear reductionist paradigm. Each level of the system is effectively treated as an independent entity. We abstract the parts from the whole and draw strong boundaries around each part and ignore or underplay the ways in which the whole and the parts mutually affect each other over time. For example, a reductionist approach to the geopolitical world treats nations as relatively independent, each with the role of maximizing its own growth and well-being. Within organizations it sees business units in profit silos and regards teams simply as groups of individuals. Connections between system members are only weakly incorporated into an understanding of the behavior of those members or the behavior of the system as a whole. In contrast, a broader systemic orientation regards all system levels as intimately connected and focuses on the interdependence both within and across systems.

The reductionist world view is highly attractive in a complex and confusing world. It presents an illusion of predictability and control. If I want to improve the profits of my sales team, then I simply incentivize the members to improve their performance, or I headhunt star salespeople. Here, performance is regarded as a function of the individual but does not capture how performance emerges as a function of the relationships between the individual salespeople, the team, and the network in which the sales person is embedded. In Groysberg's (2010) report on over a decade of studies involving knowledge based workers such as equity analysts, he showed that it is not the characteristics of the "talented" individual that lead to high performance. Whether a person is a star performer or not depends on the complex interaction between features of the person, the nature of the team, organization and the network of relationships in which that person is embedded. In other words, performance is an emergent property of the whole system, not simply the individual. This helps us understand why external "star" hires often fail to meet expectations, and often underperform relative to internal hires (Groysberg, 2010).

The practice of coaching has largely adopted the linear, reductionist perspective. Common models such as GROW (Whitmore, 1992), and the CIGAR model (Grant, 2005) assume that the client can set a clear goal, understand the gap between the current and future desired states and work systematically toward that goal in a predictable fashion. The focus of change is typically the individual, and the pathways of change are regarded as rational and direct

(Carver and Scheier, 2001). Eoyang, Yellowthunder, and Ward (1998) highlight the problems associated with treating non-linear goal processes in this way:

> Everyone involved in making public policy can think about the process as if it were well regulated and linear. Their project plans and shared discourse may revolve around the orderly steps of the problem solving method, which is their espoused theory. In reality, however, they experience the process as a surprising, uncontrolled, and emergent phenomenon. This distinction between espoused theory and experience leads to a variety of unpleasant outcomes. Participants blame themselves or others when the process does not progress as it should. Resources are wasted in pursuit of the perfect and controlled response. Opportunities are missed when serendipity is damped or ignored because it does not fit in the expected scheme. Personal and professional frustration result when well laid plans prove ineffective. (p. 3)

The Metasystematic Perspective

A GREATER FOCUS ON CONNECTEDNESS AND PROCESS

The challenges facing business and the world in general require leaders to pay more attention to how system elements are connected, and the dynamics of interaction between them. In complex systems, these interactions are marked by recursive feedback loops that mean the system and its members, as a whole, are typically governed by complex non-linear cause and effect dynamics. This means that complex systems unfold in unexpected and unpredictable ways (Cavanagh, 2006). The further into the future we project, the less certain our predictions. The implication for coaches and leaders is that we cannot always simply decide on a preferred future and then, via the exercise of self-discipline or power, create that outcome. We rarely hold the power required for such an approach, no matter how well meant or rational our strategies might be.

What roles then are left to coaches and their clients? A more nuanced understanding of the nature of complex systems can assist us in recognizing and selecting effective pathways of action. Complex systems are not always uniformly complex or unpredictable. Researchers have distinguished between different types of systems, or phase states that different parts of a system might occupy at any given time. These are *simple, complicated, complex and chaotic* (see Glouberman and Zimmerman, 2002; Snowdon and Boone, 2007). (See Figure 8.1).

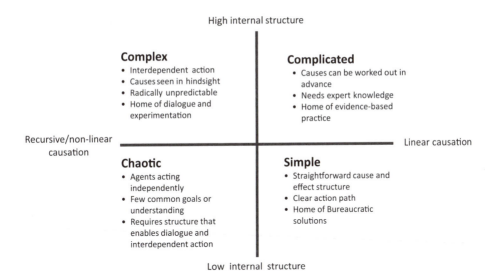

Figure 8.1   Four phase states of complex systems

A *simple system* is one in which the causal structure and interconnections are knowable in advance. A pendulum, for example, is a simple system. The functions and interrelationships between the parts are easily understandable and predicable. Its motion is governed by linear cause and effect. There are few, if any, truly simple systems in coaching. However, many short-term, straightforward goals and action steps can be treated as though they are simple systems (e.g. to book an appointment, make five phone calls, etc.). Activities where the outcome and process is clear and predictable effectively function as simple systems. Here straightforward planning and action processes fit well (Snowdon and Boon, 2007).

Some systems, even though predictable are *complicated*. A frequently used example here is a jet aircraft. The functions of each of the aircraft's components and their interrelationships are knowable and predictable, and for the most part are governed by linear cause and effect. The parts can't decide to change the way they operate. This means that an aircraft is (at least theoretically) a predictable system. However, one needs expert knowledge to be able to predict the impact of changes to the system.

In coaching, some aspects of an issue may function in relatively common or predictable ways. For example, the relationship between self-talk and behavior for an individual (although technically complex) may sometimes be treated as a predictable complicated system. In both simple and complicated systems, evidence-based approaches are very useful (Cavanagh and Lane, 2012). The cause and effect structures are stable enough to allow one to reliably deduce that the presenting situation has a similar structure to other past situations for which a particular intervention has been shown to be useful. Coaching and management practices such as data gathering, gap analysis, and strategic planning and the use of consultants to provide expert analysis and recommendation make sense for complicated issues or aspects of a system (Snowdon and Boon 2007).

Complex systems may have many parts (e.g. an organization), or as few as two (e.g. a marriage). Regardless of the number of parts they are different from simple and complicated systems in that responses and outcomes (cause and effect) are not stable, but change depending on what has gone before. Complex Adaptive Systems (CAS) is the name given by theorists to refer to complex systems in which the system members are agents in their own right and are able to adapt to system inputs in unpredictable and novel ways. For example, the flight crew of an aircraft is a complex adaptive system. The crew can move beyond the repetition of mechanical behaviors by choosing, altering and adapting their actions based on what has gone before and what is expected to happen in the future. The factors that shape their responses include their own goals, desires, states and predispositions alongside the operating processes, rules, and power dynamics. The history of the flight crew's action is itself part of what shapes ongoing action. This network of influences is an attractor space: a space in the system that gives rise to the emergence of the properties that characterize the system (see Cavanagh and Lane 2012, and Chapter 9, p. 190, for a fuller discussion of attractors).

> *Unlike the workings of a machine, a complex adaptive system may respond to a given set of circumstances in one way at one time, and very differently to those same circumstances at another time. For example, a co-pilot might challenge a decision made by the captain on one flight, but not do so in similar circumstances on another flight. A flight crew may choose to believe the accuracy of the cockpit instruments on one day, and ignore or disbelieve them on another. Importantly, these responses are not completely predictable nor are the conditions that govern them fully knowable. (Cavanagh and Lane 2012, p. 76)*

In complex systems, events are not random. However, the non-linear recursive causal structure of these systems means unexpected consequences may emerge as the impact of actions unfold over time. We see this causal chain in hindsight. For example, organizations' performance metrics, particularly when associated with remuneration, have been found to shape problematic and unethical behavior (Locke, 2004). Stretch goals similarly have been shown to lead to both motivation and demotivation depending on the initial conditions and expectations of the system members (Sitkin et al., 2011).

If outcomes cannot be fully predicted and the system evolves in unexpected ways, then setting specific longer-term goals and unitary linear pathways of goal achievement becomes problematic. Rather, in complex settings, the process of goal setting and goal pursuit should itself be emergent and adaptive over time. Typically, goals needs to be co-created among stakeholders and held loosely enough for them to develop and evolve over time. As shall be discussed at length later, the notion of purpose, rather than goals, may be a better organizing concept for coaching in complex settings.

This need for co-created and unfolding responses is evidenced by the recent focus in the academic leadership literature on dialogue and conversation (Boal and Schultz, 2007; Camison, 2010; Groysberg and Slind, 2012; Pine e Cunha and Rego, 2010; Stacey, 2007; Uhl-bien, Marion, and McKelvey, 2007). Dialogue in this context, is not simply a reinvigorated means of doing an old job (e.g. a more user friendly technique for influencing). Rather it is a process through which a coach or leader comes to understand what the job actually *is*.

For example, a coach may be engaged to assist a leader who is struggling with a team in conflict. There are two major tasks for working in a complex system such as this. The first task involves assisting the team to co-create a shared perspective that is able to support and enhance effective relationships and action among the team members. Attempts by the coach, leader, or any coalition of system members to impose a perspective that ignores or violates critical elements of other members' perspectives is likely to be unhelpful. When done well, the shared perspective will enable the players to see the events in a new way, and will also highlight potential pathways of action.

The second related task is to assist the team in co-creating new ways of working together to meet the challenges they face. Where cause and effect is complex or unstable, actions have uncertain outcomes. Here reliance on a single grand strategy is a poor response. Rather, the team should be supported in designing and implementing multiple small "safe-to-fail" experiments (Snowdon and Boon, 2007).

Safe-to-fail experiments enable the team to work with unpredictability and to capitalize on the innovation that results from engaging with the diverse perspectives found in contested space. Those experiments that produce desired outcomes are further nurtured and enabled; those that produce undesired outcome are terminated (Snowdon and Boon, 2007). Importantly, this desirability is not pre-judged. Rather, it is assessed in terms of its capacity to meet the needs of the system as it emerges and the possibilities it enables going forward. Companies like 3M and Google have long used collaborative exploratory processes in their research and design functions (Shor, n.d.). Indeed, 3M's *Post-it® Notes* is an example of a successful safe-to-fail experiment.

> *3M CEO William McKnight declared the company's rationale more than 50 years ago when he said that, "As our business grows, it becomes increasingly necessary to delegate responsibility and to encourage men and women to exercise their initiative. Mistakes will be made, but if a person is essentially right, the mistakes he or she makes are not as serious in the long run as the mistakes management will make if it is dictatorial and undertakes to tell those under its authority exactly how they must do their jobs." (Shor, n.d., p. 1)*

This does not mean that leaders simply empower their people and send them off. Rather, they, like coaches, need to stay engaged: watchful for new information and the emergence of both the expected and unexpected as the system unfolds. This ongoing iteration has led Stacey (2011) to regard systems, not as structures or entities, but as complex responsive processes.

This above dialogical process will at first glance appear quite familiar to coaches. After all, coaching is about creating an effective dialogue with the client. Indeed, I believe it is this that has made coaching so successful in today's world. However, while we might practice dialogue in a coaching session, it is often done in the service of non-dialogical goals.

Clients come to us in a variety of goal states ranging from holding clear predetermined goals to experiencing vague discontent. Typically, coaches employ dialogue to help the client clarify their goals and develop rational action plans to attain them. Metrics are set against goal attainment, and the coach works with the client to monitor and adapt the plan (e.g. Zeus and Skiffington, 2000; Green and Grant, 2003). External stakeholders and changing environments are not central to the coaching process. They may even be seen as sources of unwanted tension, conflict and confusion. The emergence of new unexpected goals for the client may similarly be seen as problematic and as a threat to the effectiveness of the coaching engagement.

However, a CAS perspective sees goals quite differently. In complex systems the outcomes of action are unpredictable particularly as time frames extend forward (Stacey, 2003). To the degree that longer-term goals are held, they need to be held in a very broad or high level way. The future is not viewed as an end game to be determined at a single point in time and then created through the implementation of rational strategies. Rather, it is a container of possibilities that will lead to other possibilities that lead to yet more possibilities. The choices we make enable and narrow the field of possibilities, but they do not determine the outcome in any predictable way. The outcomes, and our understanding of them, remain emergent and dynamic. As Stacey (2003, p. 423) states, "strategic direction is not set in advance but understood in hindsight as it is emerging or after it has emerged."

T.S. Eliot (1991, p. 201) expressed this view eloquently in his poem *Little Gidding*:

> *And what you thought you came for*
> *Is only a shell, a husk of meaning*
> *From which the purpose breaks only when it is fulfilled*
> *If at all. Either you had no purpose*
> *Or the purpose is beyond the end you figured*
> *And is altered in fulfilment.*

Chaotic systems are a type of complex system. More accurately, chaos is a phase that complex systems often go through. Contrary to the common understanding of the term chaos, *chaotic systems* are not without order. Rather, complex systems become chaotic when the behavior of the system's agents becomes independent rather than interdependent (Pina e Cunha and Rego, 2010).

While players on a football field form a complex system, a pitch invasion would be a chaotic system. The immediate reaction of nations and institutions to the failure of the subprime market would be an example of chaotic phase space.

The role of leadership and coaching in such spaces is to assist the stakeholders in the system to move back toward the complex space—to build perspectives and structures that enable the re-emergence of interdependent action (Cavanagh and Lane, 2012). Here the identification of perspectives that enable stakeholders to reconnect with the system in interdependent action is important. Coercive strategies that seek to impose simple or bureaucratic solutions in an attempt to escape the tension distress of chaos are likely to lead to lower levels of adaptability in the system over time. The search for simple solutions in chaotic times is not surprising. In times of distress we begin to draw stronger and narrower boundaries around ourselves and our thought action repertoires become restricted (Fredrickson, 2001). We narrow the horizon of our thinking when what is needed is bigger systemic perspective.

A WIDER SYSTEMIC HORIZON WITH MORE INCLUSIVE SYSTEM BOUNDARIES

The challenges the world is facing require us to extend the boundaries of the system we typically consider. The interconnectedness of the modern world means that what happens at any level of the system has impacts at all other levels. Companies can no longer be seen independently of the industries, societies and environments in which they are situated, and individuals and teams can no longer be thought of as productive units or resources to be utilized by the organization.

The size and interconnectedness of our systems also means that we can no longer treat impacts or costs, borne elsewhere in the system, or by future generations, as externalities. These need to be internalized (Goodwin, 2007). Cradle to grave accounting (or product life accounting), the introduction of triple bottom line reporting, and carbon trading schemes are all early indicators of a shift in the systemic horizon.

In conventional organizational models, extra-systemic impacts are typically seen as the domain of management. It is the leader's role to look outward, predict and deal with the wider system (Obolensky, 2010). However, in the emerging paradigm, leadership is an emergent property distributed across the whole system. The matrixed nature of our system connections also means that impacts are likely to show up at levels of the system in which leaders have little visibility. For example, finance staff may be the first to notice an impact on a supplier, or a team leader might notice a trend in the nature of presentations at a trade conference. This means there is a greater need for all system members to be able to notice, understand and explore cross system, or meta-systematic dynamics.

There is a tension here between a meta-systemic perspective and the limited perspective that any individual or group has by virtue of their place in the system. As Stacey (2007) suggests, all perspectives on a system are partial. It is not possible for anyone to have full view of the system, or to be able to fully model a complex system.

Fortunately, when one takes a dialogical approach, a full and objective understanding of the system is not what is necessary. Rather, organizational processes, rules and metrics need to be designed and implemented to assist people in being mindful of trends and the costs of action within and across systems. These processes scaffold people into a wider system view, so their careful selection is important. The metrics we currently choose tend to focus on outcomes relative to goals (Sitkin et al., 2011). They are selected because they are consistent with a linear reductionist perspective. Rather than focusing on the outcome measures of production and profitability, organizations may choose broad metrics of sustainability, innovation or system responsiveness. One such metric is Bhutan's Gross National Happiness index; measuring embedded carbon in products is another.

The valuing of diversity within and across systems is also a hallmark of an inclusive and open approach to boundaries. This is not for reasons of political correctness or because diversity is currently in vogue. Rather, diversity is seen as a critical enabler of system adaptation and change (Kauffman, 1993). The various perspectives and actions that arise due to people's different histories and positions within a system create contested space or tensions. In complex systems this tension can drive innovation and adaptation. Indeed empirical studies are demonstrating the critical role of diversity in maintaining adaptive and sustainable functioning in areas ranging from the environment to the economy (Cardinale, et al., 2012; Shediac, Abouchakra, Moujaes, and Naijar, 2008).

A BROADER TEMPORAL VIEW

The third way our paradigms need to change involves the breadth of time incorporated in our thinking and decision making. Rather than focusing only on the present and desired future goals, as is the case with traditional gap analysis, newer models take a longer view—one that draws from the past and extends toward the short-, medium- and long-term future. This broader temporal frame places greater emphasis on process, developmental dynamics and emergence.

In doing so they remain alive to the processes by which outcomes actually emerge, and the possibilities that are present when unexpected outcomes arise.

The recursive nature of causation in complex systems means the past is critical: where we have come from impacts on how we understand our present and our future (this phenomenon is known as sensitivity to initial conditions; see also Chapter 9, p. 188). A simple example can be seen in the effect of feedback on motivation and performance. A salesperson who received feedback that they were ranked third in the sales figures is likely to understand and react to that feedback very differently depending on whether s/he had previously been ranked first or fifth, the past patterns of fluctuation in ranks, and the historically generated shared story of what the ranks mean.

The meaning of an event or action is sensitive to both the past and the future— emergent meaning incorporates and transforms the meanings and conversations that precede the present moment. It also enables and constrains the future field of meanings and aspirations possible at the next iteration of the process. In this approach past, present and future are bound up together in the present moment. Failure to pay attention to the past or the hopes, fears and aspirations for the future is likely to create a dynamic where people feel stuck or unheard, leading to the emergence of reactionary, non-dialogical behavior. We see this in small ways where communication breaks down between individuals, and in broader social movements such as the Occupy Wall Street Movement.

In order to incorporate these three changes in thinking (a broader temporal perspective, a wider system frame, and greater attention to connectivity and process), we need to develop a range of systemically sensitive models that can practically inform our practice in the coaching engagement.

Systemically Sensitive Models for the Coaching Engagement

Developing frameworks of understanding and models of action in the following four areas may help coaches and leaders develop new ways of approaching complex challenges:

1.   identifying developmental need

2.   new models of leadership

3.   processes of dialogue

4.   systemic models of the coaching engagement

I would like to briefly discuss each of these areas, and present some models that I find useful in shaping effective coaching engagements that help clients meet complex challenges. In doing so I am not advocating that these are the only ones a coach need know, or that other ways of structuring coaching engagements in complex settings are ineffective. As we have seen, the models, theories and practices that have made coaching so successful up to now remain valid and useful approaches to many client issues.

IDENTIFYING DEVELOPMENTAL NEED

Coaching is fundamentally a developmental activity. In a recent study, 81 percent of coaches identified developmental coaching as a form of the coaching that they offer frequently or always (Standards Australia, 2011). Yet, in my experience, few coaches have a nuanced understanding of what differentiates it from other forms of coaching. The Standards Australia handbook on organizational coaching (Standards Australia, 2011) identifies four types of coaching based on the change that one is seeking.

- *Skills Coaching*: Coaching "aimed at acquiring or improving work-related skills" (p. 14).

- *Performance Coaching*: Coaching "aimed at improving the coachee's ability to achieve work-related goals such as specific metric-based organizational outcomes" (p. 12).

- *Developmental Coaching*: Coaching "aimed at enhancing a coachee's ability to meet current and future challenges more effectively via the development of increasingly complex understanding of the self, others and the systems in which the coachee is involved" (p. 11).

- *Remedial Coaching*: Coaching "aimed at the remediation of problematic attitudes or behaviours that interfere with the coachee's organizational performance" (p. 13).

Different theories, models and competencies and techniques are used in each of these different coaching interventions. It is not possible to give a detailed description of these here. (For a fuller description and discussion see Standards Australia, 2011.)

Given that both support and challenge are key tasks of leaders and coaches, the question of what type of coaching intervention is needed at any given time in the coaching engagement is important. What needs to be supported, and where might challenges be most usefully placed? Understanding the processes of development can help a coach approach these questions thoughtfully.

Almost 100 years ago Jean Piaget identified two processes of dealing with novel information and challenges. He named these *assimilation* and *accommodation* (Block, 1982). Assimilative responses attempt to incorporate the new information or challenge into pre-existing cognitive schemas. Assimilation then, involves learning a broader range of skills, techniques, and habits that fit with our current understanding of the world. This is sometimes called horizontal development (Cook-Greuter, 2004), and it is often what is being sought when a client asks, "How do I do X" or a manager states, "He needs to do Y".

Accommodation occurs when the person's cognitive schemas, or ways of seeing the world, need to change in order to understand the new information, or meet the new challenge. In accommodation, how we know and structure the world changes. We don't just know more, we know differently. This has sometimes been called vertical development (Cook-Greuter, 2004). While both types of development may be present in all the forms of coaching outlined above, accommodation or vertical development is a particular focus of developmental coaching, while skills and performance coaching typically focus more on assimilation.

While assimilation and accommodation are complementary types of development, they proceed at different rates. Learning new skills and techniques (assimilation) is often quite quick and results in clear and observable changes. Learning to understand one's relationship to self, others and the world differently is a process that emerges and is consolidated over time (Kegan 1994; Garvey Berger, 2012). As Figure 8.2 shows, accommodation typically occurs in punctuated stage transitions preceded by confusion and lower performance as our old ways of acting and interpreting the world fail us. As we develop new more effective ways of seeing the world, we need to renegotiate the application of previously learnt skills and build new ones consistent with our new understandings. This is an experimental and exploratory process in which tightly defined SMART goals may be counterproductive.

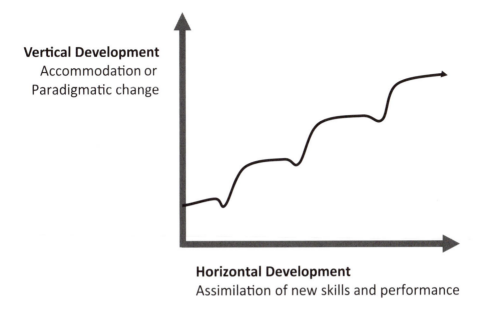

Vertical Development
Accommodation or
Paradigmatic change

Horizontal Development
Assimilation of new skills and performance

Figure 8.2   Two types of development and the developmental trajectory

A NEW LOOK AT LEADERSHIP

A complex adaptive systems view has important implications for our understanding of leadership. Heroic models that hold leadership to be a function of the individual, and that ignore context and relationships are likely to be inadequate. Similarly, models of leadership that focus only on context and relationship miss a key element of the system—the leader him or herself.

Many of the models of leadership currently being suggested take for granted the linear assumptions of command and control. For example, in their model of Transformational Leadership, Bass and Riggio (2006) suggest that transformational leaders articulate a compelling vision around which the system must organize. This approach leaves little room for the multiple diffuse goals that actually motivate and shape the behavior of agents in complex systems.

In contrast, in their definition of leadership, Kilburg and Donohue (2011) attend to mutual influences across multiple levels—personal, relational and systemic:

> *Leadership is a complex, multidimensional, emergent process in which the leader(s), follower(s), and other formal and informal stakeholders in a human enterprise use their characteristics, capabilities, thoughts, feelings, and behaviours to create mutually influencing relationships that enable them to co-evolve strategies, tactics, structures, processes, directions, and other methods of building and managing human enterprises with the goal of producing adaptive success in their chosen niche(s) in the competitive, evaluative, and evolving global ecology of organizations. (p. 15)*

While this is one of the best definitions of leadership in complex systems, it does not meet the important criterion of usability. It does not make clear how we should develop and support formal and informal leaders. Nor does it identify the characteristics, capabilities, thoughts, feelings and behaviors by which mutually influencing relationships are co-created. This is not surprising given that the interdependent and agentic nature of relationships means that a staggeringly wide range of characteristics can be usefully incorporated into effective relationships (Buckingham, 2012).

Below I propose a metasystematic model of leadership that identifies and integrates four capacities needed to notice, engage with, and influence attractors within and across systems (see Figure 8.3). These form a multi-layered triangular pyramid. The vertex of the pyramid, Perspective Taking Capacity (PTC) refers to the degree to which the leader is able to integrate competing system elements—the various needs, purposes, tensions and viewpoints that make up complex systems. The base of the pyramid is defined by Mindfulness, Purpose, and Positivity. These capacities highlight the broad level direction, reflexivity and the relational process elements needed for a leader to participate in a co-created unfolding dialogue. Higher levels of PTC enable the leader to coherently organize the information gleaned through mindful attention to what is emerging internally and externally, and to respond in ways that foster collaborative purposeful action in the midst of conflict.

Perspective taking capacity

Perspective Taking Capacity (PTC) is a person's capacity to understand, critically consider and integrate multiple competing perspectives into a more comprehensive perspective that enables adaptive action.

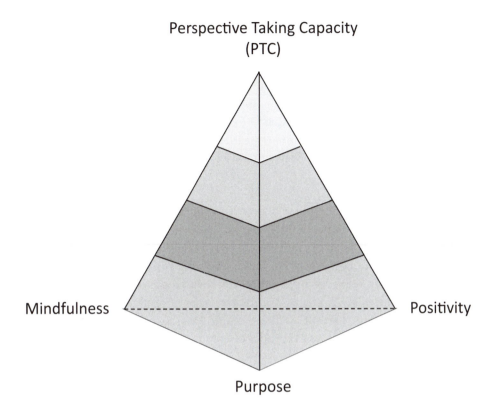

Figure 8.3   The four factor model of leadership

One can think of perspective taking capacity as a torch being carried in a dark landscape. All the stakeholders in that landscape are pointing their torches toward the ground in order to make sense of the path they are on and judge where next to put their feet. No-one's torch can see very far along the path. At best our torches can illuminate the choices immediately before us. How those choices will unfold is uncertain as the further into the future we try to project, the greater the number of twists, turns and bifurcations the path might take.

In this metaphor the height of the torch corresponds to the person's PTC. Higher level perspectives are able to throw a wider beam than lower level perspectives. They illuminate (or bring into view) more of the contested landscape. This bigger perspective enables those involved to more effectively assess the fitness for purpose of the range of possible actions before them, and to generate new more adaptive and meaningful responses. Einstein is often quoted to have said, "The significant problems we face cannot be solved at the same level of thinking with which we created them."

The creation of more expansive frames of reference requires the development of the requisite complexity of mind to be able to see the internal dynamics of systems. In other words, PTC is inextricably linked to the development of complexity of mind. Developmental theories such as Kegan's (1982, 1994) Constructive Developmental Theory (among others) can help us understand and operationalize PTC.

Constructive Developmental Theory is a hierarchical six stage theory of development. It holds that over the lifespan we develop more complex ways of understanding events, others and the self in the world. Each stage represents a different way of making meaning in the world (or different orders of mind), with each higher stage incorporating and extending or transforming the meaning making of lower stages. For the purposes of organizational coaching, only stages 2–4 are relevant as these stages can be observed in the adult population. Stages 0 and 1 are typically only demonstrated in infants and very young children. (For good discussions of the application of Kegan's theory to coaching see Chapter 11, this volume; Garvey Berger, 2012; Garvey Berger and Fitzgerald, 2002. See also Eriksen, 2006; Kegan and Lahey, 2009.)

For the purposes of this chapter, meaning making at each successive stage is organized by an increasing systemic breadth of perspective. In the pre-conventional stage (stage 2) meaning making is organized by the needs and desires of the individual. The conventional stage (stage 3) incorporates the perspective of the group as the organizing principle in meaning making. In the systemic stage (stage 4), the group and the individual are seen as interacting systems but not as fully interdependent. In the metasystematic stage (stage 5), the self, others and the world are seen as a co-evolving system of systems in which the developmental trajectory of each entity affects the others.

A progression through the stages involves an increase in the *complexity* of meaning making. There is also an increase in the permeability of the boundaries of *how* meaning is made. With openness to a wider range of information and feedback, comes a lesser need to defend one's position: one is more able to take an observer stance and to have a stable sense of self that is less dependent on and reactive to what is happening around one. In these ways, PTC supports the capacity of the second factor in the model—Mindfulness.

Mindfulness

A leader's capacity to develop more comprehensive perspectives depends on noticing new information and adopting a stance of curiosity and openness toward it. These are key features of mindfulness (Cavanagh and Spence, 2012; Marianetti and Passmore, 2010; Kabat-Zinn, 1990). Mindfulness is defined as "a motivated state of decentered awareness brought about by receptive attending to present moment experience" (Cavanagh and Spence, 2012 p. 117). Mindfulness represents a person's capacity to deliberately turn one's attention toward the present moment and to dispassionately notice what is happening, as opposed to seeing it through the filter of the past, or fears and desires associated with the future (Kabat-Zinn, 1990).

As coaches we have all had clients who seem disconnected from their own emotions or internal reactions, or oblivious of the reactions and perspectives of others. Sometimes this is because their meaning making structures make certain information irrelevant to them. At other times they are so caught up in their own perspectives and foci of attention that they do not notice what is happening. Indeed we should all be able to identify these processes in our own lives.

While a person's meaning making structures (PTC) condition what information may be seen as relevant, mindfulness can soften the boundaries around one's perspective—making them more permeable to new information. In doing so, it provides the raw data for the development of more adaptive perspectives (Cavanagh and Spence, 2012; Kabat-Zinn, 1990).

Purpose

Purpose is critical to all complex systems. Shared purpose (or at least compatible purposes) creates the foundation needed for interdependent, collaborative problem-solving and action. When system members are at cross purposes, tension, conflict and anxiety is likely to lead to chaotic behavior and system dissolution. The term "purpose" is used rather than "goal" because goals tend to be conceived of as relatively clear unitary states, the achievement of which is identifiable and measurable. Purpose, as it is used here, denotes the pattern of commitments (i.e. desires, higher order values, hopes, fears and responsibilities) that give meaning to human activity. Rather than a clear end state, purpose can be thought of as the set of criteria by which one judges, in hindsight, the degree to which something of value has been achieved.

For example, giving clear performance feedback is a common goal in business coaching. However a range of purposes might make this goal meaningful. For one leader this goal may be driven by their desire to "see the person flourish, improve team profitability, create a better world and be true to the promises I have made". Another leader may hope that such feedback will encourage the employee to seek alternative employment. The purpose may include reduction of managerial workload due to the poor performer, the desire to demonstrate proactive leadership to other team members, and a need to reduce the complexity of the issues faced by the leader. In each case, whether the goal has been successful will depend on the degree to which the leader judges his/her purpose has been met.

Purpose, then, is a spacious concept, but often a space of paradox and competing tensions. It can organize a person's behavior (and frequently does) in the absence of clearly articulated goals. Part of the role of coaches, particularly when engaging in developmental coaching, involves assisting the client to explore and adapt that network of commitments from which their responses emerge (Garvey Berger, 2012; Kegan, 1994). By focusing on purpose, rather than specific (or even fuzzy) goals, coaching enables the client to remain alive to the dynamics of their responses and inclinations. This both opens a wider range of possible responses and pathways to the person, and makes selection of particular pathways more meaningful.

Purpose, at an organizational level, is also a contested space. Organizations have multiple purposes and different stakeholders bring different purposes to the organization. Leaders have a particularly important role in the development and articulation of shared purpose. In complex systems leaders should not simply determine the purpose of the organization as if by *fiat*. Nor should they allow it to be defined in the interests of a narrow group of stakeholders. Rather, leadership from a metasystematic perspective involves the creation of purpose that is spacious enough to enable all key stakeholders to connect their purpose to those of the team, business unit or organization. At the same time their role is also to hold the organization in the tension created when these multiple purposes meet with the bigger systemic question, "What is it the world needs from us, and what does this mean for our purpose together?" Leaders' own voices and perspectives are important contributors to this dialogue.

Once purpose has been created, the leader has a role in challenging the system to not let go of its purpose cheaply in the face of difficulty and distress. At the same time leaders need to be open to rearticulating, adapting and relinquishing system goals, or even changing purposes, as the wider landscape changes. To do all of this, they need to hold systemically useful purposes at the level of complexity that is required to stimulate collaborative dialogue, development and engagement.

Positivity

Challenge and diversity introduces anxiety, tension and conflict into interactions. When these are at extreme levels, people can experience a lack of safety that leads individuals or groups of system members to engage in independent defensive action, rather than interdependent action that is aimed at adaptively meeting the challenge.

The dimension of positivity within the model, speaks to the quality of the interaction needed to develop in shared perspectives and purpose. Broaden and Build theory, (Fredrickson, 2001; Waugh and Fredrickson, 2006) maintains that people explore their world, build new connections and engage in innovation and experimentation in the context of expansive emotional spaces. The importance of positivity in communication to desired performance outcomes is well documented (see Fredrickson and Losada, 2005; Losada, 1999; Losada and Heaphy, 2004). For example, Losada and Heaphy (2004) found that positivity of communication could reliably distinguish high-performing teams from their low- and medium-performing counterparts. Similar results have been found in marital research by John Gottman (1994), who found that the positivity of a couple's communication on conflictual topics predicted the longevity and health of the relationship.

The above research also suggests that perfect harmony is not the aim of leaders in complex systems. Environments where nothing may be contested and no dissent or deviance is allowed produce stultifying and deadening emotional spaces. Some criticism and friction is needed for healthy communication. Losada and Heaphy (2004) showed that the beneficial effects of positivity only occur where positivity to negativity ratios fall between 2.9:1 and 8:1. Teams within this band demonstrated conversation patterns that were non-repetitive, able to both contribute information and explore positions, and consider both internal and external stakeholders. These ratios seem to mark the respectful, valuing, and responsive behaviors that create the psychological safety needed to explore and experiment within contested space.

Positivity then refers to the leader's capacity to collaboratively create, shape and support processes marked by sufficient psychological challenge and safety to enable ongoing stakeholder participation in dialogue over complex and contested issues.

PROCESSES OF DIALOGUE

I have already discussed the importance of dialogue in complex adaptive systems. While many processes have been identified to support dialogue (e.g. de Bono's (1985) Six Thinking Hats and Otto Scharmer's (2009) Theory U), at core they all focus on facilitating three objectives: suspending entrained thinking (suspense); positively engaging the tension between perspectives (dialectic); and creating new more spacious perspectives that guide common action (synthesis). A fourth stage, generative dialogue, focuses on action generation.

Figure 8.4 below represents these objectives as involving a series of critical choices. Participants typically come to contested spaces with entrained thinking. Here they face the choice of whether or not to defend this thinking. If one chooses to defend his or her thinking and pursue one's current frame of reference, two basic forms of conversation remain open: debate or discussion. In debate (from the Old French *débattre*—"to beat down") the person is focused on communicating his or her own position and undermining any opposing perspectives. The outcome is win vs. lose. In discussion (from the Latin *discutere*—"to dash to pieces" or "agitate") there is greater participation with each party seeking to have his or her perspective understood and accepted. As the root of the word suggests, discussions tend to end in win vs. lose outcomes too. However, they can also result in compromise positions in which both parties win a bit, and lose a bit. The key feature of both debate and discussion is an assimilative response to a challenge. While assimilative responses can provide solutions in contested space (at least for one party), these solutions tend to be suboptimal and beset with unintended consequences.

If, however, a person decides to suspend their frame of reference then a different pathway of conversation is opened. Suspend here has two meanings: (1) to bar for a period from a privilege, office, or position, and (2) to cause to be hung or held up. Both of these meanings are relevant in dialogue. First, the person temporarily sets to one side his or her position so as to understand the other perspectives operating in the contested space. Second, the person holds his or her perspective up for examination and consideration as a contribution to facilitating an understanding of the key issues, assumptions and values in the contested space.

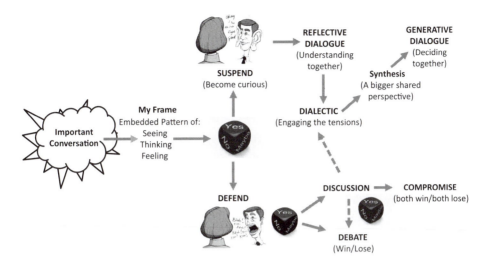

Figure 8.4   Critical choices in dialogue

Source: Adapted from Isaacs, 1999

By doing this, the contested space becomes a shared one in which the tensions between perspectives are positively engaged and can be explored and understood (dialectic). This is the stage of reflective or exploratory dialogue.

In conditions that require or allow interdependence and where there is a "good enough" holding of anxiety (Stacey, 2011, p. 345), this unresolved tension provides both the energy and information needed for the development of new shared perspectives (synthesis). The key characteristic of synthetic perspectives is that they are capable of including and adaptively organizing more of the issues, needs and values that gave rise to the conflict. They are not 'either/or', or compromise solutions like those generated in debate and discussion. They are also not additive (yours plus mine), or lowest common denominator (general consensus) solutions. Rather, synthetic solutions reflect interdependence: where before there was independence (me and you, or me vs. you), there is now a genuine "we". Synthetic solutions not only incorporate the critical needs, goals and values of the stakeholders, they organize and transform them so that new meaning and understanding can emerge.

The final stage is generative dialogue. Here dialogue moves from exploration to action based on the shared meaning created in reflective dialogue. Where the shared understanding incorporates uncertainty and complexity, multiple safe-to-fail experiments can be appropriate actions; where there is predictability and agreement, implementing rational action plans is useful. No matter what action is decided upon, an iterative process of dialogue is required to stay alive to additional patterns as they emerge.

The following model of the coaching engagement attempts to reflect a systemic, iterative dialogical approach to the change process.

A GENERIC SYSTEMIC MODEL OF THE COACHING ENGAGEMENT

In this chapter I have argued that the linear models used to guide coaching engagements struggle to meet the challenges faced in modern complex environments. A new model of the coaching engagement is needed: one that is sensitive to the dynamics, interactions and systems with which the coaching client is involved. Within such a model, information flow within and across system levels is key to eliciting the multiple rich perspectives. These perspectives provide the contested frames and points of tension that are essential to the development of higher order perspectives and effective adaptive behavior.

Shared understanding of the purpose, processes and roles involved in the coaching engagement remains important, as is an appreciation of the unpredictability, ambiguity and tension that will undoubtedly be encountered. This will help stakeholders manage the anxiety of working complex spaces, and prevent it from overwhelming the dialogue.

Figure 8.5 below is a model of the coaching process that incorporates the systemic complexity just discussed. It highlights the importance of multiple perspectives, i.e. a flow of information across and within system levels, a broader temporal focus, and iterative dialogue that facilitates meaning making and strategic action. It is itself the result of iterative development, having been built on an earlier model of systemic coaching (Cavanagh, 2006). It is presented here, not as a finished product, but as the next step in this ongoing iterative process.

The model is generic in that it can accommodate a host of psychological and organizational approaches, including cognitive behavioral, constructive developmental, psychodynamic, narrative, etc. Indeed, a diversity of perspectives and voices is encouraged as each will point to different values, strategies, and outcomes (Moberg, 2006). The tensions among these approaches may enable a more adaptive and situationally sensitive response to be developed.

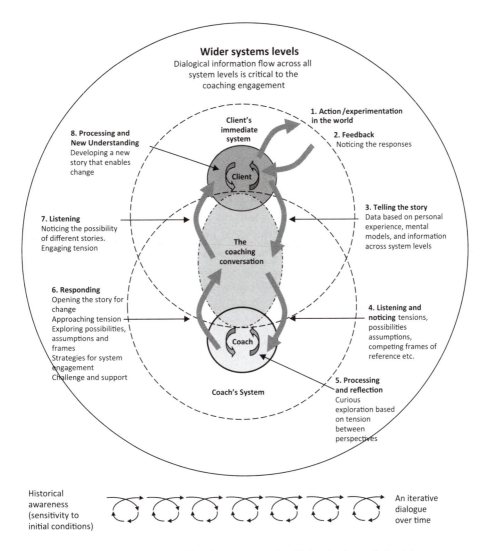

Figure 8.5   **The coaching field—a dynamic dialogical model of the coaching conversation**

As can be seen in the figure, the process of dialogue involves multiple iterative steps. Since the model is generic and dialogue is emergent, it is not possible to articulate all of the roles and responses that might come into play. However, three critical coach-related roles deserve mention.

First, the coach has an important role in *enabling and evoking rich perspectives*. Here questions that encourage the client to reflect on his or her experience more deeply and broadly are important. What are the competing voices within the client? What frames of reference are active, and what assumptions, rules and patterns are in play? The coach also has a role in eliciting a rich understanding on the perspectives of others, both within and outside the client's immediate system. This may involve the development of information and feedback processes, environmental scanning, and dialogue with other stakeholders. However it is done, exploration of multiple perspectives needs to be conducted in a manner that is genuinely curious and valuing.

The second critical role of the coach is *supporting and challenging the client to remain in the dialectic* (the place of tension and ambiguity between opposing perspectives) long enough for new more adaptive perspectives to emerge. Both support and challenge are necessary: support to prevent the client from being overwhelmed by anxiety and complexity; challenge to stimulate accommodative development as opposed to simply reverting to a less adaptive assimilative strategy.

Last, the coach has a role in *noticing repetitive patterns* and encouraging an exploration of these. Repetitive patterns of behavior, outcome, process or meaning making indicate the possible presence of attractors that keep people and systems stuck.

Conclusion

The old Chinese saying, "May you live in interesting times" is apt. It is sometimes thought of as a blessing and sometimes as a curse. That we live in interesting times there is no doubt. The challenges we face present great risks and great possibilities, and the linear, technologically driven solutions of the industrial age, are unlikely to serve us in this unstable, complex world. Coaching is a dialogical form of leadership and as such, it is particularly suited to these complex challenges. If we, as coaches, can step out of our own past patterns of action and understanding we can make a difference. By collaboratively developing more systemically sensitive models and processes with our clients, we are well placed to make a useful contribution to the greatest of human enterprises: the task of nurturing a sustainable and life-giving world for ourselves and for future generations.

References

Barnosky, A., Hadly, E., Bascompte, J., Berlow, E., Brown, J., Fortelius, M., Getz, W., Harte, J., Hastings, A., Marquet, P., Martinez, N., Mooers, A., Roopnarine, P., Vermeij, G., Williams, J., Gillespie, R., Kitzes, J., Marshall, C., Matzke, N., Mindell, D., Revilla, E., & Smith, A. (2012). Approaching a State Shift in Earth's Biosphere. *Nature, 486*, 52–8.

Bass, B. & Riggio, R., (2006). *Transformational Leadership*. Mahwah, NJ: Lawrence Erlbaum and associates.

Bernstein, B. (1977). *Class, Codes and Control*. London: Routledge.

Block, J. (1982). Assimilation, Accommodation, and the Dynamics of Personality Development. *Child Development, 53*(2), 281–95.

Boal, K. & Schultz, P. (2007). Storytelling, time, and evolution: The role of strategic leadership in complex adaptive systems. *The Leadership Quarterly, 18*, 411–28.

Buckingham, M. (2012). Leadership development in the age of algorithm. *Harvard Business Review*, June 2012, 86–94.

Camison, C. (2010). Effects of coercive regulation versus voluntary and cooperative auto-regulation on environmental adaptation and performance: Empirical evidence in Spain. *European Management Journal, 28*, 346–61.

Cardinale, et al. (2012). Biodiversity loss and its impact on humanity. *Nature, 486*, 59–67.

Carver, C.S. & Scheier, M.F. (2001). *On the self-regulation of Behaviour*. Cambridge: Cambridge University Press.

Castells, M. (2010). *The Information Age: Economy, Society and Culture, Volume 1: The Rise of the Network Society.* (2nd ed.). Oxford: Wiley-Blackwell.

Cavanagh, M. (2006). Coaching from a Systemic Perspective: A Complex Adaptive Conversation. In D. Stober & A.M. Grant (Eds), *Evidence Based Coaching Handbook*, 313–44. Hoboken, NJ: John Wiley & Sons.

Cavanagh, M. & Lane, D. (2012). Coaching Psychology Coming of Age: The challenges we face in the messy world of complexity. *International Coaching Psychology Review, 7*, 75–90.

Cavanagh, M. & Spence, G. (2012). Mindfulness in coaching: Philosophy, psychology or just a useful skill? In J. Passmore, D. Peterson, & T. Freire (Eds), *The Wiley-Blackwell Handbook of Psychology of Coaching and Mentoring*, 112–34. London: Wiley-Blackwell.

Cook-Greuter, S. (2004). Making the Case for a Developmental Perspective. *Industrial and Commercial Training, 36*(7), 275–81.

Dallas, L. (2011). Short-Termism, the Financial Crisis, and Corporate Governance. *Journal of Corporation Law, 37*, 264.

de Bono, Edward. (1985). *Six Thinking Hats: An Essential Approach to Business Management*. Boston: Little, Brown, & Company.

Despres, C. & Hiltrop, J-M. (1995). Human resource management in the knowledge age: Current practice and perspectives on the future. *Employee Relations, 17*(1), 9–23.

Douglas, M. (1996). *Natural Symbols: Explorations in Cosmology* (2nd ed.). London: Routledge.

Ehrlich, P., Kareiva, P., & Daily, G. (2012). Securing natural capital and expanding equity to rescale civilization. *Nature, 486*(7), 68–73.

Eliot, T.S. (1991). *T.S. Eliot: Collected Poems, 1909–1962 (The Centenary Edition)*. London: Harcourt Brace Jovanovich.

Eoyang, G., Yellowthunder, L., & Ward, V. (1998). *A Complex Adaptive Systems (CAS) Approach to Public Policy Decision Making*, paper presented to the Society for Chaos Theory in Psychology in the Life Sciences, August 1998.

Eriksen, K. (2006). The Constructive Developmental Theory of Robert Kegan. *The Family Journal, 14*, 290–98.

Falk, J. & Sheppard, B. (2006). *Thriving in the Knowledge Age: New Business Models for Museums and Other Cultural Institutions*. Oxford: Altamira Press.

Filloux, J-C. (1993). Emile Durkheim (1858–1917). *Prospects: The Quarterly Review of Comparative Education, 23*(1/2), 303–20.

Fredrickson, B.L. (2001). The role of positive emotions in positive psychology. *American Psychologist, 56*(3), 218–26.

Fredrickson, B.L. & Losada, M. (2005). Positive affect and the complex dynamics of human flourishing. *American Psychologist, 60*(7), 678–86.

Garvey Berger, J., (2012). *Changing on the Job: Developing Leaders for a Complex World*. Stanford, CA: Stanford Business Books.

Garvey Berger, J. & Fitzgerald, C. (2002). Leadership and complexity of mind: The role of executive coaching. In C. Fitzgerald & J. Garvey Berger, (Eds), *Executive Coaching Practices and Perspectives*, 27–57. Palo Alto, Ca: Davies-Black.

Gentile, B., Twenge, J., Freeman, E., & Campbell, W.K. (2012). The effect of social networking websites on positive self-views: An experimental investigation. *Computers in Human Behavior, 28*(5), 1929–33.

Glouberman, S. & Zimmerman, B. (2002). *Complicated and Complex Systems: What Would Successful Reform Of Medicare Look Like?* Discussion paper No. 8, Commision on the future of health care in Canada. [Accessed 15/9/2012] http://c.ymcdn.com/sites/www.plexusinstitute.org/resource/collection/6528ED29-9907-4BC7-8D00-8DC907679FED/ComplicatedAndComplexSystems-ZimmermanReport_Medicare_reform.pdf

Goodwin, N. (2007). Internalizing externalities: making markets and societies work better. *Opinionsur, 52,* 1–6. http://ase.tufts.edu/gdae/Pubs/te/OpinionSur_NevaGoodwin_Dec07eng.pdf [Accessed 15/6/2012].

Gottman, J.M. (1994). *What Predicts Divorce: The Relationship Between Marital Processes and Marital Outcomes.* New York: Lawrence Erlbaum.

Grant, A.M. (2005). What is evidence-based executive, workplace and life coaching? In, M. Cavanagh, A.M. Grant, & T. Kemp (Eds). *Evidence-based Coaching: Contributions from the Behavioral Sciences, Vol. 1,* 1–13. Bowen Hills, QLD: Australian Academic Press.

Green, J. & Grant, A.M. (2003). *Solution-focused Coaching: Managing People in a Complex World.* Harlow, UK: Pearson Education Limited.

Greenfield, S. (2011). Computers may be altering our brains. *The Independent,* August 12, 2011. [Accessed 24/9/2012] http://www.independent.co.uk/voices/commentators/susan-greenfield-computers-may-be-altering-our-brains-2336059.html

Gribbin, J. (2004). *Deep Simplicity, Chaos, Complexity and the Emergence of Life.* London: Penguin, Allen Lane.

Groysberg, B. (2010). *Chasing Stars: The Myth of Talent and the Portability of Performance.* Princeton: Princeton University Press.

Groysberg, B. & Slind, M. (2012). Leadership Is a Conversation. *Harvard Business Review, 90*(6), 76–84.

Isaacs, W. (1999). Dialogic Leadership. *The Systems Thinker, 10*(1), 1–5.

Joiner, B. & Josephs, S. (2007). *Leadership Agility.* San Francisco, CA: John Wiley & Sons, Inc.

Kabat-Zinn, J. (1990). *Full Catastrophe Living: Using the Wisdom of Your Body and Mind to Face Stress, Pain, and Illness.* New York: Delacorte.

Kauffman, S. (1993). *The Origins of Order: Self-Organisation and Selection in Evolution.* Oxford: Oxford University Press.

Kegan, R. (1982). *The Evolving Self.* Cambridge, MA: Harvard University Press.

Kegan, R. (1994). *In Over Our Heads.* Cambridge, MA: Harvard University Press.

Kegan, R. & Lahey, L.L. (2009). *Immunity to Change.* Cambridge, MA: Harvard Business School Publishing Corp.

Kilburg, R. & Donohue, M. (2011). Toward a "grand unifying theory" of leadership: Implications for consulting psychology. *Consulting Psychology Journal: Practice and Research, 63*(1), 6–25.

Kumar, K. (1995). *From Post-industrial to Post-modern Society: New Theories of the Contemporary World.* Malden, MA: Blackwell.

Locke, E.A. (2004). Linking goals to monetary incentives. *Academy of Management Executive, 18*(4), 130–33.

Losada, M. (1999). The complex dynamics of high performance teams. *Mathematical and Computer Modelling, 30*(9–10), 179–92.

Losada, M. & Heaphy, E. (2004). The role of positivity and connectivity in the performance of business teams: A nonlinear dynamics model. *American Behavioral Scientist, 47*(6), 740–65.

Marianetti, O. & Passmore, J. (2010). Mindfulness at work: Paying attention to enhance well-being and performance. In P.A. Linley, S. Harrington, & N. Garcea (Eds), *Oxford Handbook of Positive Psychology and Work*, 189–200. Oxford: Oxford University Press.

Moberg, D.J. (2006). Ethics blind spots in organizations: How systematic errors in person perception undermine moral agency. *Organization Studies, 27*(3), 413–28.

Noble, D. (1977). *America by Design: Science, Technology, and the Rise of Corporate Capitalism*. Oxford: Oxford University Press.

Obolensky, N. (2010). *Complex Adaptive Leadership: Embracing Paradox and Uncertainty*. Farnham: Gower.

OECD. (2002). Glossary of statistical terms—Externalities. http://stats.oecd.org/glossary/detail.asp?ID=3215 [Accessed 5/6/2012].

Pina e Cunha, M. & Rego, A. (2010). Complexity, simplicity, simplexity. *European Management Journal, 28*, 85–94.

Scharmer, C.O. (2009). *Theory U: Leading from the Future as it Emerges*. San Francisco: Berrett-Koehler Publishers.

Shediac, R., Abouchakra, R., Moujaes, C., & Naijar, M. (2008). *Economic Diversification: The Road to Sustainable Development*. http://www.ideationcenter.com/media/file/Economic_diversification2.pdf [Accessed 1/6/12].

Shor, R. (n.d.). Managed Innovation: 3M's Latest Model For New Products. *Manufacturing and Technology News*. http://www.manufacturingnews.com/news/editorials/shor.html [Accessed, 6/7/2012].

Sitkin, S., See, K., Miller, C., Lawless, M., & Carton, A. (2011). The paradox of stretch goals: Organizations in pursuit of the seemingly impossible. *Academy of Management Review, 36*(3), 544–66.

Snowdon, D. & Boone, M. (2007). A leader's framework for decision making. *Harvard Business Review, November 2007*, 69–76.

Stacey, R.D. (2003). *Strategic Management and Organisational Dynamics: The Challenge of Complexity*, (4th ed.). Harlow, UK: Financial Times/Prentice Hall.

Stacey, R. (2007). The challenge of human interdependence: Consequences for thinking about the day to day practice of management in organizations. *European Business Review, 19*(4), 292–302.

Stacey, R.D. (2011). Strategic Management and Organisational Dynamics: The Challenge of Complexity, (6th ed.). Harlow, UK: Financial Times Press.

Standards Australia. (2011). *Handbook Coaching in Organization.* Sydney, Australia: SAI Global Limited.

Uhl-Bien, M., Marion, R., & McKelvey, B. (2007). Complexity Leadership Theory: Shifting leadership from the industrial age to the knowledge era. *The Leadership Quarterly 18,* 298–318.

Verhulst, A. (1999). *The Rise of Cities in North-West Europe.* Cambridge: Cambridge University Press.

Waugh, C.E. & Fredrickson, B.L. (2006). Nice to know you: Positive emotions, self-other overlap, and complex understanding in the formation of a new relationship. *The Journal of Positive Psychology, 1*(2), 93–106.

Whitmore, J. (1992). *Coaching for Performance: GROWing People, Performance, and Purpose.* London: Nicholas Brealey Publishing.

Zeus, P. & Skiffington, S. (2000). *The Complete Guide to Coaching at Work.* Roseville, NSW, Australia: McGraw-Hill.

9

Goal Setting: A Chaos Theory of Careers Approach

Jim E.H. Bright and Robert G.L. Pryor

Goal setting and attainment has been popularly presented as the sine qua non of personal, career and organizational change (e.g. Covey, 1989). To a large extent this view has been uncritically accepted and embraced. However, chaos theory, and the Chaos Theory of Careers (CTC) in particular (e.g. Bright and Pryor, 2005; Pryor and Bright, 2003ab; Pryor and Bright, 2011) provides a new perspective on goal setting that can help us understand more fully what we are doing when we set goals, and what we are gaining and losing by so doing.

In this chapter we will briefly set out the Chaos Theory of Careers and in particular focus on the concept of Attractors to show how goal setting as it is commonly understood can be seen as a complexity reduction method that has limited effectiveness. While it plays a valuable role in facilitating short-term behavior change, it is less valuable when longer-term change is considered. Alternative conceptualizations of goal setting that de-emphasize elements such as focus, specificity and measurability may be more appropriate, but in becoming all inclusive in their purview they risk losing explanatory power. If all behavior is goal-directed, then there is nothing that is not goal-directed, and therefore the term "goal" explains nothing over and beyond the term "behavior".

Chaos Theory of Careers

The Chaos Theory of Careers was developed towards the end of the 1990s and arose out of the authors' dissatisfaction with extant career development theory. In particular classical career theory fails to provide an adequate account of:

- Change in people and careers;

- Chance events;

- Complexity of influences; and

- Constructedness (making sense) of people's experience of career.

The Chaos Theory of Careers views individuals as complex dynamical[1] systems that exist and function in a web of other complex dynamical systems which themselves vary in terms of complexity and changeability. All such systems are dynamical in the sense that they are continuously moving. These systems are complex because they are comprised of many different components (or influences) and because they are open systems—i.e. susceptible to external as well as internal influences (Pryor and Bright, 2007).

From these broad definitions we can identify and describe some key characteristics that are displayed by complex dynamical systems, including: Complexity; Change and non-linearity; Chance; Construction, and Attractors.

Complexity

We live in an interconnected world, where people have the potential to interact in unpredictable ways. We are influenced by complex arrays of factors, including our families, labor markets, organizational climate and culture, the economy, friends, media, cultural tradition, teachers, gender roles, issues of sexual orientation, politics, climate, and health (Bright, Pryor, Wilkenfeld, and Earl, 2005; Patton and McMahon, 2006).

Although such contextual factors are increasingly recognized in career and organizational development, the dynamic and interacting nature of these factors is often underemphasized. From a chaos perspective all of these influences are subject to continuous and unpredictable changes.

---

1   Dynamical refers to specific systems that change over time or dimension. A dynamical system is a mathematical formalization for any fixed "rule" which describes the time dependence of a point's position in its ambient space. Examples include the mathematical models that describe the swinging of a clock pendulum, the flow of water in a pipe, and the number of fish each spring in a lake.

Change and Non-linearity

Complex dynamical systems are sensitive to change because of their complex interconnections. Some of these changes are relatively minor, even trivial, when considered in isolation, but over time they have the capacity to cause a person to drift off course or to become stuck in a rut (i.e. slow shift; Bright and Pryor, 2008).

Table 9.1   Examples of slow and fast shift

Slow shift	Fast shift
Skills and knowledge becoming gradually outdated	Serious motor vehicle accident
Acquisition of skills or resources over time enabling a change of direction	Surprise meeting leading to a job offer
Gradually expanding service offering to clients by responding to their requests	Surprise arrival of a new technology e.g. iPad, opening up new possibilities for doing different work—e.g. App developer

At other times, we as individuals experience dramatic change that has the potential to rearrange much in our lives (i.e. fast shift). Although people and environments change continuously, traditional career and organizational change theories such as Holland (1959), Hultman (1998), Lewin (1951), Schein (1996) and Senge (1990) underestimate or ignore change.

Holland (1959) simply ignores change, asserting that people and occupations as well as the environment more generally do not change sufficiently to affect the fit between a person and an occupation. Hultman (1998), like many writing on organizational change, characterizes change as a discrete, one-off event as in "the change program"—and therefore underestimates the potential for continual and unpredictable change. Similarly, Lewin's (1951) unfreeze-change-refreeze notion is predicated on the idea that change happens in a linear and relatively orderly way. Furthermore, change is bedded down and frozen, implying periods of stasis between change events. This is a gross misrepresentation of the true continuous non-linear nature of change. Schein (1996) has more of a dynamic approach to change, but still underestimates the potential for continual change, as the process consultation model relies on establishing goals of "what kind of help is needed" and also considers change primarily as an event in "the change process" (p. 36). Senge's (1990) comes closest to embracing complexity and leveraging the power of a dynamical systems approach, however, Senge claims that applying systems theory to change will help us derive "laws" and "archetypes" and "microworlds" that will help us predict organizational behavior. While Senge's work provides the basis for thinking about organizational change in terms of dynamical systems theory, the chaos approach has the benefit of introducing very important change concepts like attractors, fractals, emergent patterns, non-linear change and phase-shifts.

Due to this fissure between theory and practice, coaches routinely have to confront shifts in their clients and their client's environments with little or insufficient guidance from traditional theories. This is one of the reasons why vocational rehabilitation has so seldom been coherently incorporated into past career development theories (Szymanski and Hershenson, 1998).

A characteristic of chaotic systems is that they display sensitivity to initial conditions, aka non-linearity (popularly known as "the butterfly effect"). Non-linearity has profound implications for attempts to model behavior, or to make long-term deterministic predictions because tiny differences in the initial conditions may result in enormous differences in outcome, and vice versa. In fields like organizational behavior and careers, measurements of behavior are relatively crude approximations more or less ruling out the possibility of being able to predict long-term behavior. Furthermore, it is not clear what the initial conditions might be for people and their environments. For instance, even the most reliable and robust personality measures correlate weakly with work performance and typically account for less than 10 percent of the variance in performance (e.g. Barrick, Mount, and Judge, 2001; Hurtz and Donovan, 2000; Minbashian, Bright and Bird, 2009). In other words, they leave us 90 percent unsure. Concepts in personality such as Extraversion are too broad to be measured precisely, and even the best scales will have standard errors of measurement in excess of three percent, some by a considerable margin. However in a dynamical system, as Lorenz (1993) has pointed out, changes of 0.000001 percent in initial conditions may be sufficient to dramatically alter the system's behavior.

Non-linear relationships are the norm, not the exception (Strogatz, 2003). Non-linearity illustrates that small changes in complex dynamical systems have the potential to result in disproportionate changes in other parts of the system. Small things can have profound effects on a career. For instance, meeting someone on a golf course with a common interest may give you a contact, which results in a job offer, which changes your career. The implication here is that we have to be very cautious of any approach that makes predictions about the future based upon the assumption that things will not change, or that they will change only gradually or in otherwise predictable ways. As we will see, non-linearity implies that goal setting is likely to be most effective over relatively short time periods.

Chance

The consequence of complex connected change and non-linearity is the inability to predict precisely and control comprehensively what happens within the system or in other systems with which the system interacts. As we have pointed out, although chance events have been relatively neglected in career development theories, there is good evidence to suggest that they are the norm, not the exception (e.g. Bright, Pryor, and Harpham, 2005; Krumboltz, 1998).

Chaos theory provides a conceptually integrated account of the existence of chance events; indeed, the theory suggests that in the absence of knowing the starting conditions of the system (which is the case for people), every event is a chance event in that we cannot have completely predicted it. The question then becomes one of seeing events in varying terms of uncertainty and recognizing that certainty (and hence complete predictability) is unobtainable. In this way randomness and random events can be understood as system fluctuations that cannot be fully, or perhaps even partially, explained from our vantage point within the system. Thus the Chaos Theory of Careers encourages people to embrace uncertainty.

Construction

To embrace uncertainty entails not fatalistic acceptance of the impact of other influences on individuals' lives and careers, but being responsible and active in influencing those things in one's life and environment that can be changed, and being constantly aware of the possibility of unforeseen changes and consequences. As a result, individuals' career development can be seen as a continual condition of meaning making in relation to themselves and their world (Pryor and Bright, 2011; Savickas, 1997).

Attractors

A system is defined as a group of components which form an integrated whole. As an integrated whole, each system has boundaries. Indeed, it is the boundaries of a system that effectively define its nature and function (Pryor and Bright, 2007). In chaos theory, attractors describe these limits. Attractors are like the invisible glue or force of gravity that holds a system together, thereby both limiting it and defining its identity in the process. There are four characteristic system attractors: *point*, *pendulum*, *torus*, and *strange*. The first three are characteristic of closed systems, and the last is characteristic of an open system.

Table 9.2   System attractors

Type of attractor	Type of system	Description
Point	Closed	System constrained to move predictably to a defined point or outcome
Pendulum (or Periodic)	Closed	System constrained to move predictably between two defined points
Torus	Closed	System constrained to move predictably between pre-determined number of points
Strange	Open	System exhibits self-similarity in movement over time, while continually changing in direction sometimes trivially, and sometimes in unpredictably dramatic ways

- **Point attractors** operate when a system is limited to move only toward a clearly defined point. When water runs out of a basin through a drain, the water is attracted to the drain. Focusing on one career goal is an example of a person captured by a point attractor.

- **Pendulum attractors** operate when a system is limited to move only between two defined points. People who simplify career decisions into either/or choices or swing between one choice and the other without considering other possibilities are captured within the pendulum attractor.

- **Torus attractors** operate when a system moves through a series of defined points that repeat over time. People who always follow the same rules and procedures or who fall into habitual patterns of working are captured by a torus attractor.

- **Strange attractors** are characteristic of chaotic systems. A strange attractor limits the system to exhibit the self-similar pattern, which is like old repeating patterns; however, because they are not totally closed, other factors can influence the system and its operation, sometimes dramatically. The system is in constant flux between the stability of closed systems and the susceptibility to varying degrees of change. This is described as being on "the edge of chaos" (EOC) (Pryor and Bright, 2004). The strange attractor operates when the system shows emergent stability over time, self-similarity, but also the possibility for radical non-linear change.

Some reflection will disclose that all of us actually live perpetually on the edge of chaos (i.e. in the strange attractor), but we often impose the three other attractors because they promise greater predictability and stability. Initially we may choose to impose the point, pendulum or torus attractor due to the predictability they offer in the short-term. This may result in us giving less attention to novelty and change, and missing opportunities to practice dealing with change. Over time, these attempts at reducing complexity to simple goals, alternatives, or rules are very likely to break down, because of human limitations of knowledge and control. Furthermore, given our attachment to these closed systems, we can find ourselves unprepared and unskilled to confront changes to our goals, roles and routines.

From a chaos perspective, goal setting can be seen as an attempt to simplify and tame open systems of complexity into simpler closed systems—in particular the point attractor. Using the attractors, goal setting acts by maximally reducing complexity to a consideration of how to get from the current point to the desired point. This simplicity may help explain the tremendous popularity of goal setting as a motivational coaching technique while at the same time it highlights what is being sacrificed (complexity).

Fractals are the trajectory or trace of a strange attractor's functioning and exhibit symmetry over time and scale; self-similar patterns emerge over time and can be seen at every level as we investigate deeper and deeper into the patterns. A coastline may appear as a large bay, but closer inspection reveals smaller inlets that resemble the larger bay; and closer-still may reveal small rock pools. The coastline consists of similar patterns of ever decreasing little bays. That is self-symmetry over scale. Individuals display fractal behavior in many different ways. For instance a person's smile or laugh is often self-similar over time and situations, but is not exactly identical. Traits such as Extraversion,

Conscientiousness, Agreeableness, Neuroticism and Openness to experience can be understood in fractal terms. A person's history of involvement in disputes with colleagues, or management style may be similarly fractal in nature. All of these components, and many more, collectively operate within each person's strange attractor, creating individuality, pattern and surprise.

Fractal patterns are dynamically stable — continually changing but generally in a self-similar pattern subject to occasional dramatic and unpredictable changes. A person's facial appearance over time demonstrates this fractal quality or self-similarity and change.

Furthermore, these fractal patterns are not simple, easily captured, or easily described by conventional methods such as psychometric testing, or even narrative. The Chaos Theory of Careers posits that people's behavior over time displays fractal patterns along the lines suggested in the previous paragraph. In CTC coaching, coaches try to help individuals gain a better understanding of their own unique fractals — their dynamic, complex, and ever-changing but self-similar patterns.

Goal Setting Theory

The basic propositions of goal setting as adumbrated by Locke and Latham (1990) are that: a) goals motivate us to exert effort commensurate with the demands of the goal or task; b) goals motivate us to be persistent over time; and c) goals direct our attention to relevant behaviors or outcomes and away from those which are not.

Goal setting is the most popular behavior change strategy employed by individuals and organizations. Ward (1995) argues that the use of goal setting is "widespread" (p. 9) and "much advocated in the literature" (p. 9). In complexity terms, goal setting involves reducing all of the complexity in a situation simply to the actor and the goal — from here to there. The strength of goal setting is that it demands a focus upon a clearly defined target, and very often it further demands movement toward that target within a specific time frame.

The essential weakness of all goal setting endeavors is the attempt to impose closed systems thinking on an open systems reality. In chaos attractor terms, the disciplined focus on specific behaviors and outcomes to the exclusion of other possibilities (distractions) is point attractor thinking. To seek to achieve competing goals through so-called "balance" strategies (e.g. work/life) is pendulum attractor thinking characterized typically by the assumption of roles such as the "professional", "parent", "spouse", "community participant" and so on. To try to organize time and resources as efficiently as possible in order to achieve particular goals is to think in terms of the torus attractor—everything in its place and a place for everything.

The limitations of such efforts at achieving control is that they cannot succeed in any long-term way with an open system reality, which is complex, non-linear, interconnected and ultimately unpredictable (Taleb, 2007). A focus that is too specific involves the risk of missing new opportunities. Dividing life into roles neglects the overlap, possible resonance effects, and conflicting priorities of such role demands. Trying to organize all of life is thwarted by the sheer number of possible outcomes from changing sets of circumstances, especially the consequences that could not be foreseen.

Put simply, humans can never know enough or control enough, to guarantee the outcomes of their thinking and behavior in all but the most trivial of circumstances. This does not mean that we have no knowledge or control. It does not mean that all goal setting founded on focus, persistence, determination, rule setting, role taking, bureaucratizing and routine instituting, is useless, but merely that it will never be sufficient. These are ways to introduce, establish and sometimes re-establish more stability into individual and organizational experience, but we still live and function in strange attractors on the edge of chaos, where the interplay of stability and change requires us to also confront and embrace uncertainty. What can the research data reveal about the role of goal setting within such a context?

Interpreting Empirical Data on Goal Setting Within a Chaos Perspective

Mark Tubbs (1986), examined 87 separate studies on goal setting, and found a clear pattern of results: under laboratory conditions goals worked; in real-life settings, they were far less effective. This is because real-life settings are more complex than a psychology laboratory. He concluded that "Given that laboratory studies usually used short trials, rather contrived tasks (most of which would seem to possess less of a performance ceiling than most actual work tasks), and a generally higher degree of control over alternate behaviors, this finding makes intuitive sense" (p. 478). As Stacey, Griffin, and Shaw (2003) point out, "If a system's specific long-term behavior is unpredictable, then setting specific goals for it is a questionable activity" (p. 91).

It is usually believed that goal setting will only be effective if you truly want to achieve your goals. This might help to partially explain why goals can be less effective in real-life settings: commitments wane over time (e.g. Tubbs, 1986). However, it may be that feedback is more important than commitment, and that feedback mechanisms are subject to interference and complexity over time in the less rarefied atmosphere found beyond psychology laboratories. Donovan and Radosevich (1998) conducted an examination of goal commitment and performance across 12 studies over 20 years, involving 2,000 participants, and found that goal commitment had very little effect on the levels of performance of the individuals studied. This can be explained within the CTC in terms of feedback.

Both goal setting theory and the CTC share an emphasis on feedback. Feedback is a central feature of complex systems (Briggs and Peat, 1989). It acts to accelerate or moderate processes, and can also be complex itself. Timing is a critical component of feedback and can determine whether the effect of the feedback is to accelerate or moderate system performance.

A practical difference between the CTC and goal setting theory with respect to feedback is that whereas the focus in goal setting is the goal, a CTC approach is to be committed to feedback rather than to goals per se. Thus one might focus not on trying to win an Olympic medal, but rather on improving performance on a particular skill. This entails being committed to establishing feedback mechanisms and attending to them.

As Pryor and Bright (2011) point out:

> Feedback mechanisms need to be both positive and negative, and continuous and intermittent. For instance, when seeking to increase sales of a product, the continuous feedback mechanisms might be the number of calls the sales representative makes every hour to prospective customers; positive feedback measures might include the number of new leads that they discover every day, and the negative feedback measures might include the number of rejections they receive each day. Intermittent measures might include comparing their monthly results to a colleague's sales figures. (p. 186)

The more feedback processes that are in place and monitored and the more varied they are, the better the picture of system performance one can build up.

Within the CTC, goal setting as typically characterized by the SMART formulation (Specific, Measurable, Achievable, Realistic and Time-based) is a point attractor. The challenge is to overcome or overturn conventional change management wisdom regarding the importance of the clarity of goals, and their precise measurability. Furthermore there exists empirical evidence to support a move toward fuzzier, less measurable, less immediately achievable, less apparently realistic and less time-based and more revisable goals (e.g. Abrahamson and Freedman, 2006; Shapiro, 2006; Tubbs, 1986; Donovan and Radosevich, 1998). For instance, Abrahamson and Freedman report that companies who engage in extensive strategic planning and goal setting are no more financially successful than companies that do not. Shapiro reports on the high failure rates of diets and New Year's resolutions—both activities that rely on goal setting.

Major Issues in Goal Setting

Ordóñez, Schweitzer, Galinsky, and Bazerman (2009) argue that goal setting often comes with a series of side-effects that are rarely considered and that can have a significant negative impact on individuals and organizations. Summarizing goal setting literature from the early 1970s to date, they highlight a range of serious problems with the overuse and uncritical use of goal setting and offer potential remedies. Chapter 2 provides a summary of their arguments. We provide a CTC perspective on each below.

1. **Are the goals too specific?**—Ordóñez et al. (2009) note that narrow goals can blind people to important aspects of a problem and suggest that, ideally, goals should be comprehensive and include all of the critical components for success (e.g. quantity and quality).

From a CTC perspective, even this remedy runs the risk of underestimating the changeability and complexity in a problem and our limits on knowing all the pertinent facts in advance. Goal setting is a narrowing down to the point attractor—this is simultaneously a strength and limitation of the technique. In recognition of this fact some authors (e.g. Pryor, Hesketh, and Gleitzman, 1989) have recommended the use of "fuzzy goals". Fuzzy goals recognize that for some people, being precisely able to formulate and articulate their most significant goals may be very difficult. In fact, they may not be able to express them clearly in words at all. Fuzzy goals identify arenas of significance for the person (such as "spiritual enlightenment") rather than a precise description of what it might actually mean. For some people life might be the constant exploration of what such a fuzzy goal might ultimately mean.

2. **Are the goals too challenging?** What will happen if goals are not met? How will individual employees and outcomes be evaluated? Will failure harm motivation and self-efficacy? Ordóñez et al. (2009) suggest we provide skills and training to enable employees to reach goals, and avoid harsh punishment for failure to reach a goal.

The CTC approach regards failure as almost inevitable due to complexity, and that it can be beneficial since it provides a framework for receiving feedback from the environment and discovering hidden contingencies. In complex situations, the relationships between things are not always evident. For instance we might discover the dress code of the golf club by inadvertently wearing colorful socks and being reprimanded by a petty official who takes his work very seriously indeed! Failure also creates an opportunity to practice recovery, and develop resilience and redemption behaviors (Pryor and Bright, 2011). An over-emphasis on goal setting runs the risk of encouraging people to try to eliminate failure, and to see failure in only negative terms, thus eliminating the opportunity to experience its potential benefits.

3. **Who sets the goals?** People will become more committed to goals they help to set (Ordóñez et al., 2009). At the same time, people may be tempted to set easy-to-reach goals. Ordóñez et al. (2009) recommend that we allow transparency in the goal setting process and involve more than one person or unit.

While developing personal efficacy in a situation is a desirable thing to do, it is also useful to assist clients to recognize the limits of their agency and control in some situations. It is a reality that events can and do overwhelm us despite the best laid plans or goals. Encouraging clients to embrace this reality provides an opportunity to work on developing resiliency, persistence, and creative problem-solving capacities as ongoing skills that will help them confront change with agility, opportunity, awareness, and optimism.

4. **Is the time horizon appropriate?** Ordóñez et al. (2009) recommend that we be sure that short-term efforts to reach a goal do not harm

investment in long-term outcomes. The implication is that these short-term goals may not be desirable.

However, from a CTC orientation this raises questions about long-term planning and predictability. How can we be sure that a short-term goal has moved us away from long-term outcomes until after the fact? If we consider the trajectories of strange attractors as represented in fractals, very often the trajectory at any one point will seem to contradict the overall "shape" that is emerging. The point attractor—a goal—constrains us to take the most direct linear route to the destination. However better destinations or outcomes might be discovered with broader exploration. Insisting too early that every activity be directed toward a particular destination may not be in the client's interests if in the process sufficient change results in the destination no longer being relevant or desirable.

5. **How might goals influence risk taking?** Ordóñez et al. (2009) voice the concern that unmet goals may induce risk taking, and recommend articulating acceptable levels of risk. Thus, the authors appear to view risk as negative and goals as having the potential to encourage such risk.

We would argue that risk taking is just as likely to be a desirable and positive aspect of goal setting. Also, the authors do not seem to anticipate the potential for goals to reduce risk taking, in the situation where conservative (unchallenging, unoriginal, stereotyped, familiar) goals are set, and any deviation from these goals would be associated with risk. From a CTC perspective, goal setting is more likely to induce conservatism and uncreative thinking, because the act of goal setting is usually an attempt to impose a closed-system point attractor on behavior in an open system.

6. **How might goals motivate unethical behavior?** Ordóñez et al. (2009) note that goals narrow focus, and that employees with goals are thus less likely to recognize ethical issues, and are more likely to rationalize their unethical behavior. To mitigate this they recommend multiple safeguards to ensure ethical behavior while attaining goals (e.g. leaders as exemplars of ethical behavior, making the costs of cheating far greater than the benefit, strong oversight). In essence the authors are arguing for a complexity solution, where the goals are understood within a more complex framework.

Within the CTC, the framework of the attractors provides a language for understanding goals as a simplification of a more complex reality in which meaning making occurs. Therefore, the goal is always subordinate to and in the service of that greater complex reality. This allows us to meaningfully consider bigger notions such as purpose, values and ethics which are located or represented via our strange attractor, and goals as simplifications of our purpose, values and ethics. Pryor and Bright (2007) characterize the nature of strange attractors as inter alia, the boundaries of their functioning and the end states to which such systems tend. For individuals these constitute the supervening goals of meaning and morality. Specific goals reflect particular ways in which individuals seek to move toward exploring and realizing the meaning and morality of their lives and careers within those lives. Consequently the attractors provide a coherent linkage between goals and bigger considerations.

7. **Can goals be idiosyncratically tailored for individual abilities and circumstances while preserving fairness?** Ordóñez et al. (2009) highlight that individual differences may make standardized goals inappropriate; yet unequal goals may be unfair. They suggest trying to set goals that use common standards and account for individual variation. It strikes us that this concern is not solely related to goal setting but applies to any organizational intervention or management approach.

8. **How will goals influence organizational culture?** Individual goals may harm cooperation and corrode organizational culture. Ordóñez et al. (2009) suggest that if cooperation is essential, team-based rather than individual goals should be considered, and careful thought should be given to the values goals convey.

Again, their argument is for a complexity oriented approach that is simultaneously specific and general in that they recognize the importance of bigger more complex group structures that may be impacted by narrowly focused individual goal setting. This is entirely consistent with a CTC approach.

9. **Are individuals intrinsically motivated?** Goal setting can harm intrinsic motivation. Ordóñez et al. (2009) recommend that we assess intrinsic motivation and avoid setting goals when intrinsic motivation is high.

From a CTC perspective, intrinsic motivation is likely to be an emergent feature of the complex interplay of many different factors (for instance past events, internalized views of self and past behavior, current interests, anxiety, self-efficacy, personality, personal narrative, current circumstances, health status, mood, peer pressure, societal values etc). Consequently, intrinsic motivation is a complex dynamical system—meaning it continually varies, is not completely predictable and is subject to non-linear effects. The imposition of an external goal on such a system essentially reduces an open complex system to a closed and simple system. In the short-term, we might "get lucky" and impose an extrinsic goal that aligns with the current trajectory of the intrinsic system—this will appear to the person as though they are following a natural and preferred course of action. However, the extrinsic goal may either not align or over time come out of alignment. Then the extrinsic goal may act as a brake, negative feedback or interference with the far more complex intrinsic motivational system, resulting in overall lower levels of motivation.

10. **What type of goal (performance or learning) is most appropriate given the ultimate objectives of the organization?** By focusing on performance goals, employees may fail to search for better strategies and fail to learn. Ordóñez et al. (2009) note that in complex, changing environments, learning goals may be more effective than performance goals. They point out: "An individual who is narrowly focused on a performance goal will be less likely to try alternative methods that could help her learn how to perform a task. As an example of this phenomenon, Locke and Latham (2002) described an air traffic controller simulation in which the performance goal interfered with learning in this complex domain (Kanfer and Ackerman, 1989)" (p. 11).

This is the most explicit linkage to the CTC approach to goal setting. By highlighting the complex and changing nature of many modern work environments, Ordóñez and colleagues make a case for a more complex approach to goal setting.

Setting Goals in an Open Systems World

Goals appear to be most effective in relatively unchanging environments, in the short-term and where the problem the goal is addressing is clear and relatively straightforward. The trouble is that these circumstances do not occur in real life as often as many people assume when they chose to set goals or blindly engage in goal setting.

Another problem is the type of goals that people try to set. We can distinguish between performance and learning goals. *Performance goals* are the ones we usually associate with goal setting, for instance, "I will increase my results on the test by 30 percent by the end of the quarter." Common versions of these are SMART goals, referred to above.

Learning goals generally refer to increased knowledge, skills, and abilities in a defined area. "Gaining a better understanding of decision making", "mastering the use of the comfy chair", "remembering your wife's recipe for lemon ice cream" are all examples of learning goals.

Changing circumstances mean that SMART performance goals can become less tenable, or even impossible as timeframes expand. Furthermore, the desirability of attaining such goals can become questionable as the scene changes over time. If your company's goal was to sell twice as much of the drug "Bug-shatterer-Pro" over the next 12 months, this goal might become inappropriate if during that time clinical trials demonstrated the drug to be a danger to the health of those taking it.

Learning goals are less susceptible to change in this way, and thus are more likely to be a useful strategy in a changing environment, or even over the longer-term. However outside of specific learning environments like schools, colleges and universities, the use of learning goals is less common.

Both forms of goal setting—Performance and Learning—still often suffer from inducing a form of selective blindness—to focus on one or two things at the expense of all else. There is little doubt that in the short-term, with relatively unchanging circumstances and with relatively straightforward problems, goals can under some circumstances be useful—the evidence points to this (Tubbs, 1986). However as Figure 9.1 shows, as problems get more complex and situations become more changeable, goal setting as a strategy becomes much more questionable.

Now consider the use of goals in the medium- to longer-term (i.e. any time horizon beyond a few months). The situation here is quite different. Even in relatively unchanging environments, the amount of time involved inevitably introduces some change, making goals less effective, and sometimes it

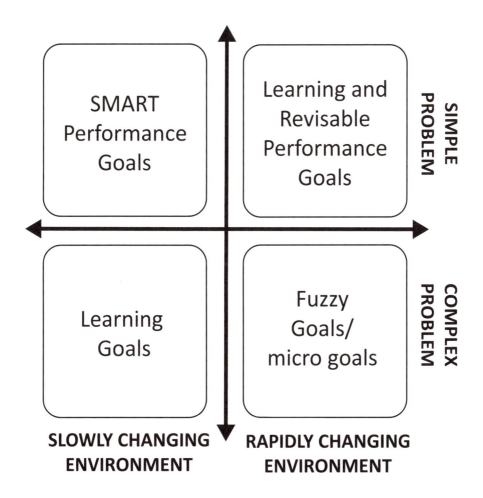

Figure 9.1   Goal setting strategy for short-term situations

can also make the problem more complex. Here we need "Fuzzy Goals"—goals that are more Situational, Multifaceted, Adaptable, Risk-Taking and Transformational—David Winter's alternative to the restrictive traditional SMART goal (Winter, 2010).

As circumstances become more complex and changeable, goal setting as a strategy becomes even more questionable and it would be more advisable to commence thinking in broader, more creative and flexible terms that permit more openness, and more of a wait-see-adapt-respond-try-fail-learn kind of methodology, something akin to the Beyond Personal Mastery® model of creativity (e.g. Pryor and Bright, 2011).

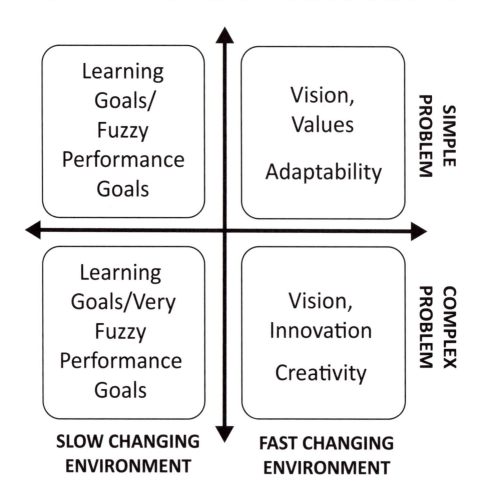

Figure 9.2   Long-term goal setting

What is instructive looking at Figures 9.1 and 9.2 is how traditional SMART goals may only be really effective in one of the situations out of the eight presented. This may provide a clue to the problems of goal setting — most problems are more complex, most situations are more changeable, and most people want to employ goal setting over too long a timeframe. This is why in the Chaos Theory of Careers goal setting is seen as a form of simplifying complexity and often oversimplifying complexity.

A Case Study Application

Kevin sought coaching assistance at the demise of his information technology company. He was the company director with a group of consultants and administrative staff. Kevin had left university four years earlier with excellent passes in various aspects of computing and information technology. From late high school he had dreamed of setting up his own company. After graduating Kevin devoted virtually all his time and resources into making his company successful. He specialized in tailored internet security systems. He took out a lease on an impressive suite of offices, hired several administrative staff and assembled a group of consultants mainly from his university student colleagues. He invested in several expensive information technology development systems since he wanted to provide "state-of-the-art" security solutions. Business was slow initially and then he secured several larger project contracts. However, in the last 18 months the competition had become fiercer, several consultants moved to other firms, Kevin under-quoted on two significant contracts and sustained major financial losses and one of his previously installed systems was breached by a hacker, damaging the company's credibility. Closing the company now was Kevin's only option and he was devastated. He had failed. His dream had somehow become just a mirage.

From a chaos theory perspective, Kevin's situation needed to be addressed in three ways:

1. **Do not be surprised by failure:** Kevin's emotional distress needed to be addressed. Chaos theory points to the complexity and unpredictability of outcomes. The human limitations of knowledge and control mean that even the very best organized efforts may result in failure. Business statistics clearly show that most firms fail (Pryor and Bright, 2012). In a chaos-filled reality risk and failure are virtually inevitable. While this does not make failure pleasant, it should also not be a cause for despair. Kevin may have made some business mistakes and the environment in which he did business may have become more cut-throat competitive. As a result he may have incurred financial losses. What could Kevin learn from his experience that would help him in his future endeavors?

2. **Point attractor thinking:** Chaos theory identifies Kevin's perspective as point attractor thinking, typical of narrow and focused goal setting. Kevin had only one goal and only one way of achieving that goal. His dedication to the goal was admirable but

in a world of complex dynamical systems, point attractor thinking is always going to be vulnerable to inflexibility of focus, tunnel vision about context and unforeseen changes. Kevin needed to start thinking more in terms of open systems perspectives as the way to formulate, monitor, explore and modify his goals.

3.   **Open systems (strange attractor) thinking:** The fractal of an individual's strange attractor is bounded by the purpose, meaning and values that the person consciously or unconsciously desires. Kevin was challenged to think about his goals in these terms as distinct from the very specific goal of running his own IT company. What purpose or meaning did this goal signify? Answering this question allowed Kevin to explore alternative ways of expressing, exploring, monitoring and realizing that goal.

It emerged that Kevin wanted to use his high level skills in IT, had an intrinsic interest in the whole information technology field (not just internet security), and sought the independence to be able to express his creativity through systems design and implementation.

Even though Kevin came to accept the likelihood of failure due to limits of predictability he was still personally sensitive to the issue. Therefore, since chaos theory strategies accept uncertainty and risk, the goal setting strategy for Kevin needed to aim at generating several options and attempting to keep these options open as further options emerged over time, as existing options came to be integrated, or as one option proved more preferable to all the others. Utilizing multiple options as the goal setting strategy had the advantage for risk-sensitive Kevin of reducing the likely incidence and impact of failure while exploring alternative ways to the attainment of his general supervening goals.

Among the options generated for Kevin to explore, combine and implement were:

a)   seeking further training in business management;

b)   seeking further training in financial systems;

c)   re-establishing a small business working from home to cut down infrastructure costs;

d)   establishing a partnership company with a broader IT service delivery base than internet security;

e)   joining an IT service franchise group as an independent service provider;

f)   working for a larger organization in an IT research team;

g)   undertaking computer consultancy work for another IT company for example in testing the integrity of firms internet security systems;

h)   working in his "spare time" on the development of new IT systems to market subsequently.

Kevin subsequently chose a combination of these options to implement and was encouraged to develop further his "luck readiness" (Pryor and Bright, 2005) as way to identify further opportunities as well as to test out the viability of the work and study options he had chosen on an ongoing basis.

Such a case study illustrates chaos theory perspectives in the following ways:

- Complexity implies limitations and limitations imply the possibility of failure. Failure is common and needs to be accepted, learnt from and incorporated as a possible outcome in all goal setting.

- Closed systems thinking may be an effective goal setting strategy in the short-term but in the longer-term it will be overtaken by non-linear change.

- Career fractality needs to be explored to uncover the person's current supervening goals.

- Uncertainty and risk need to be acknowledged and addressed in goal setting by flexibility in goal formulation, ongoing opportunity exploration and monitoring of progress and if necessary, goal adaptation or reformulation.

Conclusion

The valuable contribution that goal setting can make to the achievement of desired outcomes in individuals' lives and careers, and organizations' profitability and sustainability, is readily acknowledged. However, it has been argued that goal setting has been over-prescribed as a strategy for dealing with the realities of the twenty-first century. Goal setting is most effective in achieving outcomes in relatively stable contexts, where control is high and timeframes are comparatively short.

In practice, there are few such contexts. Rather, the world in which individuals and organizations operate is characterized by complexity of influences, non-linearity of change, systemic interconnectedness and randomness. Therefore there are dangers or at least limitations, as outlined above, in trying to impose closed systems thinking attractors in the form of goal setting strategies on such an open system world. In this chapter we have tried to demonstrate how the Chaos Theory of Careers can provide a conceptual framework for understanding both the strengths and limitations of goal setting strategies. Elsewhere we have provided alternative conceptualizations of how to function most effectively while embedded in the web of complex dynamical systems through "luck readiness" (Pryor and Bright, 2005) and "beyond personal mastery" (Pryor and Bright, 2011). While this chapter has focused on the constraints of human knowledge and control as it applies to goals, and despite the inherent uneasiness of living with uncertainty, we believe that the edge of chaos is also a place of opportunity, proactive change, personal growth, career development and organizational success. It is the place where each of us can find and/or create meaning and purpose, as well as assist others to live lives that matter and are worthwhile.

References

Abrahamson, E. & Freedman, D.H. (2007). *A Perfect Mess: The Hidden Benefits of Disorder*. New York: Little, Brown, & Co.

Barrick, M.R., Mount, M.K., & Judge, T.A. (2001). Personality and performance at the beginning of the new millennium: What do we know and where do we go next? *International Journal of Selection and Assessment, 9*, 9–30.

Briggs, J. & Peat, F.D. (1989). *Turbulent Mirror: An Illustrated Guide to Chaos Theory and the Science of Wholeness*. Grand Rapids, NY: Harper & Row.

Bright, J.E.H. & Pryor, R.G.L. (2005). The chaos theory of careers: A user's guide. *Career Development Quarterly, 53*(4), 291–305.

Bright, J.E.H., Pryor, R.G.L., & Harpham, L. (2005). The role of chance events in career decision making. *Journal of Vocational Behavior, 66*, 561–76.

Bright, J.E.H., Pryor, R.G.L., Wilkenfeld, S., & Earl, J. (2005). Influence of social context on career decision-making. *International Journal for Educational and Vocational Guidance, 5*(1), 19–36.

Bright, J.E.H. & Pryor, R.G.L. (2008). Shiftwork: A Chaos Theory Of Careers agenda for change in career counselling. *Australian Journal of Career Development, 17*(3), 63–72.

Covey, S.R. (1989). *The Seven Habits of Highly Effective People: Restoring the Character Ethic.* Melbourne: The Business Library.

Donovan, J.J. & Radosevich, D.J. (1998). The moderating role of goal commitment on the goal difficulty-performance relationship: A meta-analytic review and critical reanalysis. *Journal of Applied Psychology, 83*, 308–15.

Holland, J.L. (1959). A theory of vocational choice. *Journal of Counseling Psychology, 6*, 35–45.

Hultman, K. (1998). *Making Change Irresistible.* Palo Alto, CA: Davies-Black.

Hurtz, G.M. & Donovan, J.J. (2000). Personality and performance: The Big Five revisited. *Journal of Applied Psychology, 85*, 869–79.

Kanfer, R. & Ackerman, P.L. (1989). Motivation and cognitive abilities: An integrative/aptitude-treatment interaction approach to skill acquisition. *Journal of Applied Psychology, 74*(4), 657–90.

Krumboltz, J.D. (1998). Serendipity is not serendipitous. *Journal of Counseling Psychology, 4*, 390–92.

Lewin, K. (1951). *Field Theory in Social Science: Selected Theoretical Papers.* In D. Cartwright (Ed.). New York: Harper & Row.

Locke, E.A. & Latham, G.P. (1990). *A Theory of Goal Setting and Task Performance.* Englewood Cliffs, NJ: Prentice Hall.

Locke, E.A. & Latham, G.P. (2002). Building a practically useful theory of goal setting and task motivation: A 35-year odyssey. *American Psychologist, 57*(9), 705–17.

Lorenz, E. (1993). *The Essence of Chaos.* Seattle, WA: University of Washington Press.

Minbashian, A., Bright, J.E.H., & Bird, K. (2009). Complexity in the relationships among the subdimensions of extraversion and job performance in managerial occupations. *Journal of Occupational and Organizational Psychology, 82*, 537–49.

Ordóñez, L.D., Schweitzer, M.E., Galinsky, A.D., & Bazerman, M.H. (2009). Goals gone wild: The systematic side effects of overprescribing goal setting. *Academy of Management Perspectives, 23*(1), 6–16.

Patton, W. & McMahon, M. (2006). *Career Development and Systems Theory: Connecting Theory and Practice.* (2nd ed.). Rotterdam: Sense Publishers.

Pryor, R.G.L., Hesketh, B., & Gleitzman, M. (1989). Making things clearer by making them fuzzy: Counseling implications of fuzzy graphic rating scales. *Career Development Quarterly, 38*, 135–46.

Pryor, R.G.L. & Bright, J.E.H. (2003a). The chaos theory of careers. *Australian Journal of Career Development, 12*(2), 12–20.

Pryor, R.G.L. & Bright, J.E.H. (2003b). Order and chaos: a twenty-first century formulation of careers. *Australian Journal of Psychology, 55*(2), 121–8.

Pryor, R.G.L. & Bright, J.E.H. (2004). "I had seen order and chaos, but had thought they were different." The challenges of the Chaos Theory for career development. *Australian Journal of Career Development, 13*(2), 18–22.

Pryor, R.G.L. & Bright, J.E.H. (2005). *The Luck Readiness Index.* Sydney: Congruence Pty Ltd/Bright and Associates.

Pryor, R.G.L. & Bright, J.E.H. (2007). Applying chaos theory to careers: Attractors and attraction. *Journal of Vocational Behavior, 71*(3), 375–400.

Pryor, R.G.L. & Bright, J.E.H. (2011). *The Chaos Theory of Careers: A New Perspective on Working in the Twenty-First Century.* New York: Routledge.

Pryor, R.G.L. & Bright, J.E.H. (2012). The value of failing in career development: A chaos theory perspective. *International Journal for Educational and Vocational Guidance, 12*(1), 67–79.

Savickas, M.L. (1997). Career adaptability: An integrative construct for life-span, life-space theory. *Career Development Quarterly, 45*(3), 247–59.

Senge, P. (1990). *The Fifth Discipline: The Art and Practice of the Learning Organization.* Sydney, NSW: Random House.

Shapiro, S.M. (2006). *Goal Free Living: How to Have the Life You Want Now!* Hoboken, NJ: Wiley.

Schein, E.H. (1996). Career anchors revisited: Implications for career development in the 21st Century. *The Academy of Management Executive, 10*(4) 80–88.

Stacey, R., Griffin, D, & Shaw, P. (2000). *Complexity and Management: Fad or Radical Challenge to Systems Thinking?* London, UK: Routledge.

Strogatz, S.H. (2003). *Sync: The Emerging Science of Spontaneous Order.* New York: Hyperion.

Szymanski, E.M. & Hershenson, D.B. (1998). Career development of people with disabilities: An ecological model. In R.M. Parker & E.M. Szymanski (Eds), *Rehabilitation Counseling: Basics and Beyond.* (3rd ed.). Austin, TX: Pro-Ed.

Taleb, N.N. (2007). *The Black Swan: The Impact of the Highly Improbable.* New York: Random House.

Tubbs, M. (1986). Goal setting: A meta-analytic examination of the empirical evidence. *Journal of Applied Psychology, 71*(3), 474–83.

Winter, D.A. (2010). *How Smart is Smart?* [Downloaded from the http://careersintheory.wordpress.com/how-smart-is-smart/ on July 17, 2012].

Ward, A. (2005). *Whither Performance Management?* HR Network Paper MP52, September, 2005, Brighton: Institute for Employment Studies.

10

When Goal Setting Helps and Hinders Sustained, Desired Change

Richard E. Boyatzis and Anita Howard

Our lives move ahead in desired directions in large part as a result of intentionality (Kolb and Boyatzis, 1970; Boyatzis, 2008). Without intentionality, change is random, episodic or chaotic. This intentionality was first outlined in psychology by William James (1897). He called it "conscious volition" or what we would label as "will" today. To the ancient Greek philosophers, it was called "teleos," or purposiveness. The purposiveness of our acts is embedded in our intent, motivation, and drive (McClelland, 1985). In this chapter, we will explore how goal setting can help in the process of intentional, desired change *and* when it gets in the way of such change. The difference is the sustainability of the efforts. Do you join a health club after New Year's with the intent of losing weight and getting fit, and actually succeed in achieving your desired weight? Or do you, like many people, stop going to the health club sometime in February?

To be specific, we will explore three main points with regard to effective goal setting: (1) to be useful and helpful, the change effort must be sustained; (2) to be sustained, we must engage in goal setting in a way that predominantly engages the Positive Emotional Attractor (i.e. PEA which will be explained later), which is a more joyful and exciting experience; and (3) as a result of individual differences in a variety of factors, such as planning style, learning style, and such, there is a diverse array of conditions within which people will find goal setting energizing or demotivating.

Sustainability of Intent

Intentional Change Theory (Boyatzis, 2008) and Self-Determination Theory (Deci and Ryan, 1990) are among a set of theories in psychology that explain the need for and benefit of intentionality. Intentional Change Theory (ICT) explains how we identify a desired vision or purpose and convert it into a learning agenda, then practice the new acts, feelings, or thoughts, and build relationships that enable these discoveries. Through iterative cycles of these phases we achieve sustained, desired change, as shown in Figure 10.1. The experience within each of the states of the Positive Emotional Attractor (i.e. PEA) and the Negative Emotional Attractor (i.e. NEA) help a person work on the issues of each stage of ICT. The PEA relates to the personal hopes, possibilities, strengths, and optimism of the Ideal Self, while the NEA relates to the present reality, fears, shortcomings, and pessimism that constitute our Real Self (Howard, 2006; Fredrickson, 2009). The movement back and forth between the PEA and NEA are the tipping points that drive the sustained desired change effort forward or in reverse. These tipping points between the PEA and NEA are often experienced as the emergence of a new phase of change. They often feel discontinuous, like an epiphany or surprise. This discovery enables the next phase to emerge and evolve.

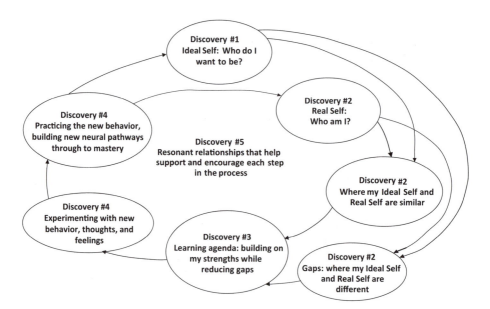

Figure 10.1   Intentional Change Theory

Source: From Goleman, Boyatzis, and McKee (2002) and Boyatzis (2008). Copyright © 2008 by the American Psychological Association. Reproduced with permission.

Performance Oriented Goals vs. Learning Oriented Goals

Goal setting is ubiquitous in today's fast-changing society. We routinely set goals in the workplace, in volunteer settings, and in personal life. But we may not be aware that goal setting is more likely to enhance performance and outcomes in some situations as compared to others. The positive effects of goal setting have been shown in situations where an individual's task is straightforward (Seijts and Latham, 2005). Positive outcomes also occur when a person believes in his or her own competence and/or a person's self-efficacy is high (Locke and Latham, 2002). Yet another scenario is when a person has a high need for achievement or a strong desire to impress others (Seijts, Latham, Tasa, and Latham, 2004). Goal setting in these types of settings is called performance oriented goal setting. Goal-based coaching seems to improve performance, but again, the duration of the sustainable effort is always a challenge (Bowles, Cunningham, De La Rosa, and Picano, 2007).

In their classic compendium of goal setting research, Locke and Latham (1990) synthesized their own and many others' research to support the concept that goal setting helps people move ahead in their lives and work. But the evolving stream of research on learning versus performance goal orientation suggested that goal setting had limited utility (Beaubien and Payne, 1999; Brett and VandeWalle, 1999; Chen, Gully, Whiteman, and Kilcullen, 2000). This research showed that setting specific goals invoked a performance goal orientation. This, in turn, aroused either avoidance or a proving goal orientation. Both of these were shown repeatedly to be less effective in sales, change, and creating purposiveness, as compared to a learning goal orientation.

Gary Latham took issue with these results and inspired a detailed study of goal setting and the learning orientation published by Seijts, Latham, Tasa, and Latham (2004). In this study, the authors showed that when the tasks were routine, specific goal setting created a clear purpose and direction, and a performance orientation worked best. But when the task required adaptation and learning, or was novel, a learning goal orientation was better.

A performance oriented goal might be: "I wish to lose 30 pounds and look good in my bathing suit by June 1." A learning oriented goal within the same arena might be: "I would like to feel better and look better going into the summer, when I can enjoy outside activities." One approach specifies a target (the performance oriented goal) and one focuses on a desire and direction (a learning oriented goal). These two approaches have different effects on people and settings in terms of helping or hindering sustained change.

Seijts and Latham (2005) claim that setting specific and challenging performance goals may lead to high performance on complex tasks for people who bring the requisite skills and experience to an endeavor. They propose that high-challenge performance goals increase attention to goal-relevant actions, raise the level of effort, increase persistence, and help people use knowledge to develop strategies for success. However, even in their earlier work in 2004, Seijts and Latham showed that specific high-learning oriented goals are indicated when individuals lack knowledge and experience, undertake a new venture, or discover that previous strategies no longer work. That is, learning oriented goals are more effective when the situation requires learning and adaptation, which is a persistent aspect of life in knowledge based work and professional services. Learning goals promote acquisition of new knowledge, environmental scanning, and seeking feedback—behaviors that help people change and adapt. This stream of research suggests that goal-oriented planning helps the most when organizing your day, for example, deciding how and when best to go to the grocery store. But when contemplating something new and complex, like getting a doctorate, learning oriented planning works best.

Research has shown that self-directed change is often facilitated by learning oriented goals (Seijts and Latham, 2005; Leonard, 2008). Goal setting can be a potent tool when used by those who make a conscious commitment to personal growth and desired change. For these individuals change is moved by personal vision, values, and standards—and by intrinsic interest in development and mastery. Leonard (2008) showed that MBA students developed significantly more on competencies for which they set learning goals than on other competencies (p. 109). Similarly, van Hooft and Noordzij (2009) found that pursuit of learning goals enhanced the outcomes of unemployed job seekers engaged in a job search process. Their use of learning oriented goals led to more search intentions, search behavior, and higher reemployment possibilities (p. 1581).

While change researchers have long understood that intentional change is a conscious process that occurs over time (Ford and Ford, 1994; Amis, Slack, and Hinings, 2004; Velicer and Prochaska, 2008), research on Intentional Change Theory (Boyatzis, 2008) is helping to identify periods in the change process when goal setting can be most helpful. As seen in Figure 10.1, ICT describes how goal setting facilitates desired change during Discovery #4 of the intentional change process—i.e. when people experiment and practice new behaviors in order to advance the goals and action steps outlined in their learning agenda (Discovery #3).

The learning agenda, in turn, is enabled by the Ideal Self and personal vision (Discovery #1) and informed by assessment of strengths that can be leveraged to build positive, sustained change—while also working to reduce identified gaps. As van Hooft and Noordzij (2009) uncovered in their examination of unemployed job seekers who set learning goals when looking for work, people are more motivated, persistent and lively when they set vision-centered learning goals—even if they face difficult challenges.

When Goal Setting Facilitates Desired Change

Intentional Change Theory proposes that goal setting works best when supported by mindful reflection on what matters most to the individual (i.e. by one's Ideal Self and personal vision). When intentional change begins by connecting to the Ideal Self, the change process becomes grounded in intrinsic motivation, personal passion, resonant meaning, and belief in possibility—this enables people to be more resilient and robust during work on development and change (Boyatzis, 2008). When the goal setting process and the experience of thinking about the goal is exciting and energizing, it can be said to be arousing the PEA. But when it is obligatory and a somewhat guilt inducing reminder of what a person "should" be doing, it arouses the NEA. The psychophysiological effects of each of these experiences are explored in the next section. For now, we shall focus on what keeps the change effort moving ahead.

Priming the Ideal Self has been shown to enhance motivational strength during goal pursuit (Spiegel, Grant-Pillow, and Higgins, 2004), while priming the Real Self, our conception of what we are in everyday life, has been shown to assist adaptive response to experiences and events that require us to improve or protect ourselves (French, 2001). A focus on the Ideal Self most often engages the PEA, while a focus on the Real Self most often engages the NEA (Boyatzis, 2008).

An ICT study on coaching intentional change (Howard, 2009) offered an interpretation as to when goal setting facilitates desired change. Howard examined the cognitive-emotional processing of mid-career dentists during their one-time executive coaching sessions on assessment of 360-degree feedback and exploration of change goals. Participants were randomly assigned to one of two coaching conditions: the Positive Emotional Attractor (PEA) or Negative Emotional Attractor (NEA) condition. The study measured the levels of positive versus negative emotion shown by participants during appraisal of 360-degree feedback results and discussion of change goals.

In the PEA condition the coach used the participant's own hopes, strengths, and desired future (the Ideal Self) as the anchoring framework for the coaching session. PEA sessions began with discussion on the coachee's personal vision—followed by the coach's provision of support to the coachee for interpretation of his or her 360-degree feedback (i.e. listening to the coachee's reactions to the survey results; responding to the coachee's questions and/or requests for the coach's feedback).

In the NEA condition the coach used the participant's perceived improvement needs, gaps, and current reality (Real Self) as the anchoring framework for the session. NEA sessions began with discussion on the coachee's day-to-day reality and desires for improvement—followed by the coach's provision of support to the coachee for interpretation of his or her 360-degree feedback (again, listening to the coachee's reactions to the survey results; responding to the coachee's questions and/or requests for the coach's feedback).

Toward the end of the coaching session participants in both coaching conditions were asked by their coach to share one or two change goals to pursue after the session. Time series analysis of the beginning, middle, and ending segments of the sessions showed that coachees shifted to negative emotional appraisal during discussion of change goals—and this occurred in both the Positive Emotional Attractor condition (primarily focused on the desired future) and the Negative Emotional Attractor condition (primarily focused on improvement goals). However, participants in the PEA condition demonstrated *significantly lower levels of negative emotion and focused more on personal interests and passions* as compared to those in the NEA condition.

Negative emotional appraisal facilitates assessment of situational requirements, recognition of obstacles and problems, minimization of losses, and other behaviors that help people plan and protect themselves (Lazarus, 1991; Silva, 2005; Brockner and Higgins, 2001). Results from this ICT coaching study suggest that engagement in goal setting after mindful reflection on personal desires, intentions, requirements, and improvement needs moved coachees to the next stage in the iterative cycle of intentional change (i.e. consideration of a learning plan and effective ways to work on change). These results also raise questions about the differential impact of coaching from the Ideal Self (promotion of a learning focus) as compared to the Real Self (promotion of a performance focus). But it is important to restate that coaching does not help when *always* focusing on the PEA. A person needs the NEA at times for activation (i.e. waking up), defending against threats, and adapting (i.e. as occurs in muscle building when you increase your exercise program to stress and stretch your muscles, thereby building muscle tissue).

In these conditions in Howard's study, as well in practical applications, the coach is attending to the psycho-physiological state of the coachee, monitoring whether they appear to be in the PEA or NEA, and watching for tipping points to indicate that the person has moved. The coach is attempting to bring the coachee into the PEA as often as possible to allow for relief from the pressure of the NEA *and* for the renewed openness to change that occurs in the PEA (Boyatzis, 2008). It is also important for the coach to monitor his/her own PEA/NEA state. The speed of emotional contagion means that the coach is unconsciously infecting the coachee with one attractor or the other, so emotional self-awareness is essential in the coach (Goleman, Boyatzis, and McKee, 2002; Boyatzis, Smith, and Blaize, 2006).

While purposiveness seems to be essential for desired change and growth, it also seems to deflect energy and motivation in some people and some situations. Nevertheless, three decades of research findings have established that goal setting positively impacts performance, and performance goals *and* learning goals each have a role to play (Seijts, Latham, Tasa, and Latham, 2004; Lock and Latham, 2006). If performance goals and learning goals are both important, the critical question is, *"when should each be used"* (Seijts and Latham, 2005, p.124)?

When Goal Setting Mutes the Motivating Power of Vision: Psycho-physiological Effects

Sustained, desired change is moved by vision. As indicated in Intentional Change Theory (Boyatzis, 2008), the Ideal Self or personal vision becomes a driver of change by focusing the person's attention and energizing the person both psychologically and physiologically. When engaging in visioning, a person activates parts of the visual cortex and Default Mode Network (DMN) that have been shown to be associated with imagining and being open to new ideas, people and emotions (Boyatzis, Jack, Cesaro, Passarelli, and Khawaja, 2010). By activating neural circuits associated with being open and scanning the environment for possibilities, and by arousing endocrine systems that are part of the Parasympathetic Nervous System (PNS), focusing on one's ideal future, dreams and personal vision, allows for renewal of the body and mind (i.e. reversing the damaging effects of chronic stress) which affects sustainability of the change effort. In a sense, it makes the goal setting process an exciting and energizing experience. Arousing the PNS is associated with more open and creative thinking (Boyatzis, Smith, and Blaize, 2006).

Boyatzis, Jack, Cesaro, Passarelli, and Khawaja (2010) conducted an fMRI study of two approaches to coaching. When a person was asked to dream about the future, and thus coached to the Positive Emotional Attractor (i.e. PEA), functional magnetic resonance imaging (fMRI) conducted several days later showed that neural regions associated with imagining (visual cortex) were activated. This activation was significantly greater than when the same people experienced a comparable coaching session that was instead focused on things they "should be" doing, thus arousing the Negative Emotional Attractor (i.e. NEA).

The arousal condition for each was a 30 minute coaching session (to the PEA or NEA on alternating days). The PEA coaching session for these college sophomores involved the coach asking one question, "What would your life be like 10 years in the future if everything were ideal?" The NEA coaching involved the coach asking about their current academic experience, "How are you doing on your courses? Are you doing all the readings and homework?" During the fMRI scan, the person was shown video statements by the two coaches. These statements were recreating, in a standardized form, the experience in the two coaching sessions. The subject then responded to their emotional disposition about each statement. Statements invoking the PEA coaching included, "I will be able to contribute to my community in the future because of my time at [this university]." Meanwhile, statements invoking the NEA coaching included, "It is no fun being at [this university]." Neutral statements were also used for comparison purposes, such as, "I am learning at [this university]." It was believed that since this was about their University experience, learning was a relatively neutral reminder. The 48 statements were randomly sequenced to allow for a within subjects differentiation of neural activation.

Another significant effect noted in this study was that the Posterior Cingulate Cortex (PCC) was more activated in the PEA condition than in the NEA condition. The PCC is part of two overlapping neural networks: the DMN, and what Jack, Dawson, Ciccia, Cesaro, Barry, Snyder, and Begany (2012) called the social network. Both of these networks are associated with more open scanning and perception. The social network is activated when a person is tuned into others, such as in an engaging coaching conversation. When the DMN is activated, a person is more capable of complex cognitive processing and is more cognitively, emotionally, and perceptually open (Jack et al., 2012).

Evidence suggests that discussing a person's personal vision results in neural activation associated with open thinking, imagining, and PNS arousal; therefore it is a process that helps the person prepare for possibilities and be open to them. The vision becomes energizing and motivating toward learning, change and adaptation. But there are other ways to bring a person being coached into the PEA: the coach can appeal to mindfulness through asking the coachee about their core values and virtues that they wish to enact (Boyatzis and McKee, 2005). The coach can also appeal to compassion by asking the coachee about people who have helped them in their life. Arousing gratitude arouses compassion, which in turn is usually a tipping point into the PEA (Boyatzis, Smith, and Blaize, 2006). Recent research suggests that being playful and engaging in laughter can also help a person move into the PEA (Ayan, 2009).

Goal setting creates a commitment to a specific target (Kolb and Boyatzis, 1970). In addition to creating a useful focus, it also may create a "should" or "ought" condition in which the person begins to sense an obligation to pursue something. Such an obligation might invoke the "ought self" and be less energizing than when arousing the Ideal Self (Higgins, 1987). The Ought Self is the Ideal Self that others in your life or work impose on you. This may or may not overlap with your own Ideal Self or personal vision. If it does, there is minimal deflation of motivation to change and to sustain such an effort. But if it creates a sense of guilt or obligation that is not consistent with your Ideal Self, then it activates the NEA. If this obligatory state is aroused, it is likely to stimulate defensiveness, which in turn activates the Sympathetic Nervous System (SNS). If this activation adds to other forms of stress already aroused, the intensity and severity of the stress becomes dysfunctional, and provokes a decrease in cognitive, perceptual and emotional openness (Boyatzis et al., 2006).

Arousal of the SNS has been shown to activate parts of the brain associated with executive functioning, known as the Task Positive Network. This neural network helps us focus our attention, solve problems, and make decisions (Boyatzis, et al., 2010). This is similar to the focusing aspect of pursuing a goal. But in focusing, we also decrease our openness to novelty and alternatives (Jack et al., 2012). By activating regions of the brain which are part of the Task Positive Network like the Anterior Cingulate Cortex, a person becomes engaged, but possibly limits consideration of new ideas and may not even be open to perceiving them. Therefore pursuing goals may simultaneously preclude noticing events, emotions and other people who might inhibit sustained progress toward the goal. The challenge for anyone is to cycle back and forth among these neural networks (Jack et al., 2012). But without explicit training and preparation for such cognitive cycling, a person may typically revert to repeatedly engaging the same neural networks, and thereby reduce their flexibility in sustaining the change effort over time or through changing circumstances.

Kayes (2006) described a situation in which focusing on a goal during a climbing expedition to Mount Everest resulted in the loss of lives. He tells the story of one deadly expedition, during which the desire to reach the summit led members of the climbing team to ignore emerging weather conditions. They had been told not to attempt the summit after 11 AM, in order to allow time to return. They were told by guides that bad weather was likely to come and block their safe return, but more influential members of the expedition were so focused on their goal of reaching the summit that they systemically denied each of the possible objections. Their narrow focus cost most of the expedition their lives, as the snowstorm arrived and blocked their path down from the summit. Although Kayes did not invoke neuroscience, nor the PEA/NEA argument in his analysis, he does make the point that when commitment to a goal or set of goals becomes exceedingly important, it involves a blindness to other possibilities, and the ignoring of potential threats. This is what we describe as the cognitive and perceptual limits of the NEA, which results in activation of the SNS and a likely reduction in openness to new information.

Under certain conditions, the goal setting process may shift a person away from the excitement and motivation emerging from a vision, and convert the person's actions into a fixation. Excitement turns into compulsion. Single minded stubbornness replaces reasoned thought.

This effect is well documented in the performance goal orientation versus learning goal orientation research cited earlier. The specification of a goal encourages a sense of needing to prove that the person can reach the goal. While this may work for some, a need to prove something to someone else can invoke defensiveness, with its associated reduction in cognitive and perceptual openness. A learning goal orientation, by encouraging more novelty and exploration, appears to promote better performance and actually exceeding the original goals by enabling more innovative activity (VandeWalle, Brown, Cron, and Slocum, 1999). Again, the difference in whether a performance oriented goal is motivating and improves performance toward the goal or inhibits such performance and progress depends in part on the person, whether the situation is arousing the PEA or the NEA, and the previous degree of arousal of the PEA and NEA. A strong prior PEA arousal may sustain openness through moments of NEA. It is a dosage challenge.

Some of these contrasting conditions are illustrated in Table 10.1. It shows when each stage of the ICT will be energizing (i.e. being in the PEA) or when it may become limiting or should be experienced in small doses (i.e. being in the NEA).

Table 10.1   Two attractors

	Positive Emotional Attractor	Negative Emotional Attractor
Neuro-endocrine	PNS Arousal	SNS arousal
Affect	Positive	Negative
Ideal Self	Possibilities, dreams, optimism, hope	Problems, expectations, pessimism, fear
Real Self	Strengths	Weaknesses
Learning Agenda	Excited about trying	Should do, performance, improvement plan
Experiment	Novelty, experiments	Actions expected, things you are supposed to do
Practice	Practice to mastery	Practice to comfort
Relationships	Resonant	Dissonant or annoying

When Goal Setting is Not Helpful

There are certain times when goal setting does not optimize the intentional change process, and instead undermines engagement in change. This can happen in a number of conditions: when goals do not align with the individual's own authentic values and vision (Boyatzis, 2008), when goals result largely from extrinsic requirements that activate the "ought self" and not the Ideal Self (Boyatzis, 2008), and when goals and/or action steps are inconsistent with the individual's learning style (Kolb, 1984) or planning style (McKee, Boyatzis, and Johnston, 2008). In a longitudinal study of MBA alumni, Annie McKee (1991) showed that only 25 percent of the sample were motivated by and planned using specific, measurable outcomes as goals. Another 25 percent preferred using "domain and direction" planning styles, meaning that they preferred to create an image of the desired direction for the work, more like a vision than specific targets or goals. Another 25 percent did not focus on the desired end state at all, but instead focused their planning on the actions or steps to move ahead. The remaining 25 percent appeared not to plan, and relied on a trust in higher powers or fortune. It appeared that in all but the goal-oriented planners, specific goal setting induces undue stress and people are less motivated, less creative, and less resilient during experimentation and practice of change behaviors (McKee, 1991).

Goal setting has also been shown to be less helpful when people engage the process without understanding what the job or task requires, and when the objective they are trying to achieve triggers high levels of anxiety (Seijts and Latham, 2005). The takeaway here is that right timing is essential. People are more effective when they use goal setting as a tool for moving intentional change that is driven by intrinsic belief and motivation. It also helps to set goals that fit one's developmental preferences and learning style—and to be aware of when performance goals would be more helpful and when learning goals are more effective.

This supports the observation that people "plan" and move forward in their lives and work in a wide variety of ways. Embracing this diversity of approaches can allow us, as coaches, to help others find the approach that is most exciting and motivating to them. The challenge continues to be how to manage the passion of one's Ideal Self with the obligations and needs of others, whether in our families or job. It calls for delicate weaving of elements of many Ought Selves into a mixture with the Ideal Self.

Implications for Coaching and Mentoring Practice

Findings from the goal setting and ICT literatures have implications for the practice of coaching and mentoring. First, coaches need to understand the psycho-physiological conditions that aid a person in pursuit of sustained, desired change, and those that inhibit it.

Second, a coach should understand the alternating needs of the PEA and NEA and what triggers a person's movement into each. We have pointed out that frequently bringing your coachee into the PEA will help by renewing his/her openness to the possibilities of change, new ideas, and even new emotions. It is inevitable and necessary to bring the coachee into the NEA, but because of some adverse consequences (i.e. possible reduction in cognitive, emotional and perceptual openness) this should be done in small doses and interspersed with longer periods in the PEA. Invoking thoughts and exploration of a person's dreams, values, passion, desired legacy, and strengths as part of a personal vision building process can help in this regard. But there are other ways to stimulate the PEA: through arousal of compassion and gratitude, through focusing on values, virtues, presence, oneness, and other aspects of mindfulness, and playfulness.

Meanwhile, sometimes a coach needs to provoke the NEA. In moments of denial, the coachee may need a wake-up call. Sometimes a person being coached is fearful and cannot see a desired future. They feel stuck. Some suggestions that might otherwise invoke the NEA, might arouse a sense of efficacy. For example, when coaching someone who appears to be creating an escape fantasy, looking for symptom relief or a break from current tension, they may identify a desired future that seems inappropriate or suboptimal to the coach.

For example, the vice president of IT at a company had written a personal vision and shared it with his coach (one of the authors of this chapter). The vision was thoughtful, sensitive, and comprehensive, except it did not say anything about work, job, or career. When asked about that omission, the person told the coach he was thinking how great it would be to drive a "big rig across country." The coach sensed this as an escape fantasy. Forty-five minutes later, after trying a number of the different exercises, some of which the coachee had done previously as homework, the coach asked, "You get home Friday night, take your shoes off and pour yourself a drink and sit with a smile, saying to yourself, 'This was a great week!' What happened in the past week?" He smiled and said, "I know what happened. I helped some teenagers realize that computers are their friend." He was referring to teenagers from an inner city high school that was in one of the least advantaged neighborhoods in the city. He had resisted the idea of doing this work because of his college tuition bills and alimony payments, and his life style. The coach realized that the coachee did not see how he could do this type of work part time, while maintaining his current job. When the coach mentioned this, it was an eye opening moment for the VP. His face changed. He entered the PEA. But it took the coach a bit of pushing in the NEA to get him to reveal enough to allow the coach to show him something he had not considered.

Third, coaches and mentors can pay attention to the timing within the coaching sessions. Such self-monitoring of their own PEA and NEA might help them be tuned in to the other person more acutely. The sustainability of the coach's sensitivity and effectiveness may be a function of his/her own ability to maintain a PEA. In addition, emotional contagion (Boyatzis, Smith, and Beveridge, 2012) explains how quickly and unconsciously the coach's mood will infect the coachee's mood (and vice versa). But because of the coach's increased influence position in the relationship, we believe the coach is more infectious than the coachee.

Fourth, coaches should be wary of slipping into a pattern of using any one approach to helping people identify their dreams, developing learning plans and goals, or maintaining their progress. Narrowness of methods may lead a coach to overlook the diverse planning and learning styles of people. Organizations often seem to slide into this mistake in search of standardization of their procedures and coaching or mentoring programs. Diversity within coachees requires pluralism of methods and techniques in the coach. The practice of coaching others to be excited about moving ahead in their lives and work often requires artistry in the relationship. Coaches need to rise above commitment to any one approach to planning, and embrace the diversity of others' approaches. It calls on coaches to be flexible, and to truly focus on the coachee's needs, motives, and stylistic distinctions, such as planning style and life stage.

Fifth, specific dosage or balance between PEA and NEA will vary by person, situation, and by even larger issues in the culture or economy. Experimenting with a variety of ways to identify and manage the best balance between PEA and NEA for a coachee takes time and an on-going relationship.

Sixth, beginning the coaching process and, where possible, each coaching session with discussion of the client's core vision equips individuals to be more open and resilient during discussion of the Real Self (i.e. personal gaps and improvement needs, environmental requirements, problems and obstacles, and strategies for change).

All of these possible applications of the concepts identified in this chapter should be studied carefully. Research is needed to understand the details of things like planning styles, tipping points between the PEA and NEA, other experiences that can invoke the PEA, and such. In addition, extensive outcome assessment is needed to examine the efficacy of any of these methods.

Conclusion

Decades of goal setting research and theory have established the benefits of goal setting as a tool for enhancing performance and fostering sustained intentional change. More recent work has explored the differential impacts of performance goals as compared to learning goals, and the times and conditions when performance goals are more effective or, alternatively, when learning goals bring superior outcomes. We have explored three main points with regard to effective goal setting: (1) to be useful and helpful, the change effort must be sustained; (2) to be sustained, we must engage in goal setting in a way that predominantly engages the Positive Emotional Attractor which is a more joyful and exciting experience; and (3) as a result of individual differences on a variety of factors, such as planning style, learning style, and such, there is a diverse array of conditions within which people will find goal setting energizing or demotivating.

Intentional Change Theory and research have documented the differential impact of PNS activation (through arousal of the Ideal Self and personal vision) as compared to SNS activation (through arousal of the Real Self and attention to current needs and requirements). More important, ICT findings on coaching to the PEA versus coaching to the NEA suggest that, depending on the timing of goal setting behavior, engagement in goal setting can either decrease creativity and openness to change (through SNS activation) or broaden creativity and openness (through PNS activation).

Goal setting is more likely to facilitate enhanced performance and desired outcomes when an individual is aware of the differential impacts of performance goals versus learning goals, is grounded in the Ideal Self and personal vision, uses goal setting approaches that are tailored to his or her learning style, and is able to employ the goal setting approach best suited to each unique situation. Goal setting is a tool that can lead to high success in the workplace and in life. But as in many human engagements and experiences, one approach is not sufficient and one style does not fit all.

Yes, goal setting is good, but it should be customized for use with the person and the stage of change. For goal setting to be motivational, it must help a person move into the joy and excitement of the Positive Emotional Attractor. But most approaches and methods fostering goal setting do the opposite — they arouse the Negative Emotional Attractor, a sense of guilt or obligation, and the resulting decrease in cognitive, emotional, and perceptual openness, as well as motivation to change. As is typical in change processes, it is always more complicated than any one panacea or method can provide.

References

Amis, J., Slack, T., & Hinings, C.R. (2004). The pace, sequence, and linearity of radical change. *Academy of Management Journal, 47*(1), 15–39.

Ayan, S. (2009). Laughing matters: Seeing the bright side of life may strengthen the psyche, ease pain, and tighten social bonds. *Scientific American Mind.* April/May, 24–31.

Beaubien, J.M. & Payne, S.C. (1999). *Individual Goal Orientation as a Predictor of Job and Academic Performance: A Meta-Analytic Review and Integration.* Paper presented at the meeting of the Society for Industrial and Organizational Psychology, Atlanta, GA. April, 1999.

Bowles, S., Cunningham, C.J.L., De La Rosa, G. M., & Picano, J. (2007). Coaching leaders in middle and executive management: goals, performance, buy-in. *Leadership and Organizational Development Journal, 28*(5), 388–408.

Boyatzis, R.E. (2008). Leadership development from a complexity perspective. *Consulting Psychology Journal, 60*(4), 298–313.

Boyatzis, R.E., Jack, A., Cesaro, R., Passarelli, A., & Khawaja, M. (2010). *Coaching with Compassion: An fMRI Study of Coaching to the Positive or Negative Emotional Attractor,* Proceedings of the Annual Meeting of the Academy of Management, Montreal.

Boyatzis, R.E. & McKee, A. (2005). *Resonant Leadership: Renewing Yourself and Connecting with Others through Mindfulness, Hope, and Compassion.* Boston: Harvard Business School Press.

Boyatzis, R.E., Smith, M.L., & Blaize, N. (2006). Developing sustainable leaders through coaching and compassion. *Academy of Management Journal on Learning and Education, 5,* 8–24.

Boyatzis, R.E., Smith, M.L., & Beveridge, A. (2012). Coaching with compassion: Inspiring health, well-being and development in organizations. *The Journal of Applied Behavioral Science,* first published on November 1, 2012. doi: 10.1177/0021886312462236.

Brett, J.F. & VandeWalle, D. (1999). Goal orientation and goal content as predictors of performance in a training program. *Journal of Applied Psychology, 84*(6), 863–87.

Brockner, J. & Higgins, E.T. (2001). Regulatory focus theory: Implications for the study of emotions at work. *Annual Review of Psychology, 86*(1), 35–66.

Chen, G., Gully, S.M., Whiteman, J.A., & Kilcullen, R.N. (2000). Examination of relationships among trait-like individual differences, state-like individual differences, and learning performance. *Journal of Applied Psychology, 85*(6), 835–47.

Deci, E.L., & Ryan, R.M. (1990). A motivational approach to self: Integration in personality. In R.D. Dienstbier (Ed.), *Nebraska Symposium on Motivation: Vol. 38, Perspectives on Motivation*, 237–88. Lincoln: University of Nebraska Press.

Ford, J.D. & Ford, L.W. (1994). Logistics of identity, contradiction, and attraction in change. *Academy of Management Review*, 19(4), 756–85.

Fredrickson, B. (2009). *Positivity: Groundbreaking Research Reveals How to Embrace the Hidden Strength of Positive Emotions, Overcome Negativity, and Thrive*. New York: Crown.

French, R. (2001). "Negative capability": Managing the confusing uncertainties of change. *Journal of Organizational Change*, 14(5), 480–92.

Goleman, D., Boyatzis, R.E., & McKee, A. (2002). *Primal Leadership: Realizing the Power of Emotional Intelligence*. Boston: Harvard Business School Press.

Higgins, E.T. (1987). Self-discrepancy: A theory relating self and effect. *Psychological Review*, 94, 319–40.

Howard, A. (2006). Positive and negative emotional attractors and intentional change. *Journal of Management Development*, 25(7), 657–70.

Howard, A. (2009). A theoretical and empirical examination of positive and negative emotional attractors' impact on coaching intentional change. An unpublished doctoral dissertation, Case Western Reserve University.

Jack, A.I., Dawson, A.J., Begany, K.L., Leckie, R.L., Barry, K.P., Ciccia, A.H., & Snyder, A.Z. (2012). fMRI reveals reciprocal inhibition between social and physical cognitive domains. *Neuroimage*, 66C, 385–401. doi: S1053-8119(12)01064-6 [pii], 10.1016/j.neuroimage.2012.10.061

Kayes, D.C. (2006). *Destructive Goal Pursuit: The Mt. Everest Disaster*. Basingstoke, Hampshire, UK: Palgrave Macmillan.

Kolb, D.A. (1984). *Experiential Learning: Experience as the Source of Learning and Development*. New Jersey: Prentice Hall.

Kolb, D.A. & Boyatzis, R.E. (1970). Goal-setting and self-directed behavior change. *Human Relations*, 23(5), 439–57.

Lazarus, R.L. (1991). Cognition and motivation in emotion. *American Psychologist*, 45(4), 352–67.

Leonard, D.C. (2008). The impact of learning goals on emotional, social, and cognitive intelligence competency development. *Journal of Management Development*, 27(1), 109–28.

Locke, E.A. & Latham, G.P. (1990). *A Theory of Goal Setting and Task Performance*. Englewood Cliffs, NJ: Prentice Hall.

Locke, E.A. & Latham, G.P. (2002). Building a practically useful theory of goal setting and task motivation: A 35-year odyssey. *American Psychologist*, 57, 705–17.

Locke, E.A. & Latham, G.P. (2006). New directions in goal-setting theory. *Current Directions in Psychological Science*, 15(5), 265–8.

McClelland, D.C. (1985). *Human Motivation*. Glenview, Il: Scott Foresman and Co.

McKee (London), A. (1991). *Individual Differences in Planning for the Future*. Unpublished PhD Dissertation. Case Western Reserve University.

McKee, A., Boyatzis, R.E., & Johnston, F. (2008). *Becoming a Resonant Leader: Develop Your Emotional Intelligence, Renew Your Relationships, Sustain Your Effectiveness*. Boston: Harvard Business School Press.

Seijts, G.H. & Latham, G.P. (2005). Learning versus performance goals: When should each be used. *Academy of Management Executive, 19*(1), 124–31.

Seijts, G.H., Latham, G.P.O., Tasa, K., & Latham, B.W. (2004). Goal setting and goal orientation: An integration of two different yet related literatures. *Academy of Management Journal, 47*(2), 227–39.

Silva, P.J. (2005). What is interesting? Exploring the appraisal structure of interest. *Emotion, 5*(1), 89–102.

Spiegel, S., Grant-Pillow, H., & Higgins, E.T. (2004). How regulatory fit enhances motivational strength during goal pursuit. *European Journal of Social Psychology, 34*, 39–54.

van Hooft, E.A.J. & Noordzij, G. (2009). The effects of goal orientation on job search and reemployment: A field experiment among unemployed job seekers. *Journal of Applied Psychology, 94*(6), 1581–90.

VandeWalle, D., Brown, S.P., Cron, W.L., & Slocum, J.W. Jr. (1999). The influence of goal orientation and self-regulation tactics on sales performance: A longitudinal field test. *Journal of Applied Psychology, 84*(2), 249–59.

Velicer, W.F. & Prochaska, J.O. (2008). Stage and non-stage theories of behavior and behavior change: A comment on Schwarzer. *Applied Psychology: An International Review, 57*(1), 75–83.

11

The Goals Behind the Goals: Pursuing Adult Development in the Coaching Enterprise

Robert Kegan, Christina Congleton, and Susan A. David

This chapter is based on an interview with Robert Kegan, the William and Miriam Meehan Professor in Adult Learning and Professional Development at the Harvard University Graduate School of Education. With Lisa Lahey, he is also the co-founder of Minds at Work, a consulting firm that helps individuals, teams, and organizations undergo learning and change. Dr Kegan is the author of numerous books, including *The Evolving Self*, *In Over Our Heads*, and (with Lisa Lahey) *Immunity to Change*. His work on development in adulthood is widely used in education, management, coaching, and organizational learning.

Introduction

Our motives to change or make improvements—what for shorthand purposes we might call goals—clearly arise out of the pinches and possibilities of daily experience. People find themselves running into certain problems in the context of their work or personal lives, or reaching for potentialities that remain just out of grasp. These are the immediate and fairly obvious motives that produce people's coaching goals.

However, there is a less obvious source of goals that has to do with how one *experiences* those challenges and possibilities. This involves the more general ways in which people make meaning; the deeper underlying assumptions that guide the way they generate a sense of themselves, the world, and their relationship to that world. In my own coaching practice, this dimension is often very vivid to me, and is in my mind a telling backdrop to what is going on for clients.

Of course, in general, people don't present themselves for coaching with the goal to "qualitatively transform my mindset" or "further my development as a person"—not even to me, a developmental psychologist. Most people come with very pressing, specific kinds of goals, and I respect the importance of those goals. However, it is possible for the coaching enterprise to follow a second path, in which the more immediate goal presents an opportunity for a person to take a much deeper kind of learning journey. In this case, the outcome of the coaching amounts to the person's explicit realization that they've been working on a much bigger goal than the one they came in with: that of their own development.

Goals and the Socialized Mind

To illustrate, I'll describe a scenario based on real experiences in coaching work. Consider a service professional who has shared with us his goal to be more excited, inspired, and passionate about his work. He wants to feel more connected and fully present in the work he is doing each day.

This person's goals have both an internal and external dimension: he wants to feel differently about the work, and he wants to carry it out in a different way. In the process of exploring his situation (using the Immunity to Change approach, described later on), we uncover his tendency to take all of the work that's given to him, exactly the way it is given to him, and to follow low-risk paths in completing it. This leads him to feel relatively unexcited, and disconnected from what he is doing.

In exploring more fully why this client behaves the way he does, it becomes clear that he feels it would be risky to turn down certain kinds of work, or to reconstruct what is handed to him. This is because it is tremendously important to him to be regarded highly by people in his work environment, and to be successful in their eyes. The path he's walking doesn't leave him very inspired, but it has led him to excel in a highly competitive firm. To him, it is a scary proposition to move toward an unknown or unproven trail.

One of the major constraints on his ability to change is that he is looking out onto the world through a particular epistemology—a way of knowing and constructing the world—that is characterized by what we call the socialized mind. Through the lens of this "macro mindset", the primary way in which he feels whole and safe is through his alignment with the set of values, expectations, and assessments that comes from his external context, in this case his work world. As for many people, that world is consuming for him, and it is the primary context in which he knows himself. Any risks to how he is seen within that world are not partial. They are ultimate. They raise the biggest questions about whether the psychological ground on which he's standing feels secure.

Even if you know a person is looking out onto the world through a socialized mind, you cannot know what his specific goals will be. You can know, however, that this mindset has significant implications for what lies behind his goals, and especially what will make it difficult to accomplish them. One way to help this person achieve his goals would be to convince him that were he to operate differently in his work life, he would be regarded just as highly, or perhaps more highly, by the people he considers to be important external references and evaluators. These people could reassure him that, should he begin working in a way that is more satisfying to him, he would have nothing to fear. This could have a significant influence on his ability to accomplish his goal, but in such a way that it wouldn't alter the basic terms of his meaning making system. He would still be looking outward, and still feeling whole based on how others evaluate him.

However, there's another possibility for how he might be able to accomplish his goal. It will seem like a longer way around, and a bigger kind of project, as it has to do with the further development of the mindset itself. He could come to regard and give more priority to his own emerging internal theory; his own set of convictions, and ideology. This internal framework will include his own metrics for success and satisfaction. As a capable and intelligent person, he's still going to recognize and be very sensitive to external standards, but those standards won't necessarily be so defining of his sense of who he is. He will begin to have loyalty and alignment now with his own internal system, and he may have to build allies or make the case that the new way in which he wants to operate is one that will be beneficial not only to him, but to his organization.

However he does it, he will be released a bit from having to be so continuously vigilant. Rather than monitoring other people's assessments, he'll be coming more from an internal system. This would enable him to alter his behavior, not because he's been given permission from external authorities, but because he trusts his own internal driver.

If he makes this kind of move, he is probably going to be liberated in a lot of other ways that go beyond the immediate goal he has set for himself. This is because his change is not just at the goal or the behavioral level, but rather underneath the goal, at the basic ground of the self.

Two Paths for Coaching: Identifying Technical and Adaptive Challenges

This example from the socialized mind reveals a kind of deep structure, which not only makes the goal or the barriers to the goal more intelligible, but lays out two very different coaching paths with respect to how we might help this person accomplish his goal. By the first path, we're not going to tamper with the basic operating system. We're just going to see if we can add new files, or new software, so to speak.

Following the second kind of coaching pathway, the goals become a type of Trojan Horse; a means by which a bigger change project is supported, and you're actually changing something of the operating system itself. This second path tends to implicate what we might call the "bigger goals behind the presenting goals", or the notion of implicit goals that come behind explicit goals. In this case, goal setting may not just be something that happens in the opening moments of a coaching process, but is something that could itself evolve.

A useful distinction between these two paths comes from Ron Heifetz's (1994) work on technical versus adaptive challenges. Heifetz's basic message is that the most common error people make is in trying to solve adaptive challenges through technical means. They don't realize that the reason the solution doesn't work is because the goal they have created is an adaptive one—one that would require the kind of transformation I've been describing, as opposed to simply new inputs or behavioral changes.

A common example is losing weight. For most people, I would say more than 90 percent of the population, losing weight is an adaptive challenge. There is a small percentage of people who can simply go on a diet and it will work. My sister is like this! About ten years ago she decided to cut out most desserts, and she immediately lost weight and never put it back on. She simply needed some kind of device to alter her behavior. For her, apparently, losing weight was a technical challenge.

For the rest of us, the vast majority, we are the ones who contribute to the common statistics about dieters who regain all of the weight they took off, and in fact usually add a bit more. Why does this happen? Because the diet is a perfect example of a technical fix. It goes directly at the behavior itself, providing a coaching support that involves a technical regimen, and also a kind of psychological support in the nature of a cheerleader who helps you celebrate success, or get back on your feet when you fall off the wagon or get discouraged. I'm being overly simple, but that is a way that coaching can be deployed on behalf of a technical goal. It will be successful if you are part of that small percentage of people for whom dieting is merely a technical challenge—but most people are going to need to get into the operating system. They're going to need to learn the reasons *why* they are inclined to overeat or never exercise, because if they don't get down to that bedrock level, the statistics demonstrate that their behavior will soon return to its original form.

If a person comes to me and I discover that he or she has never actually tried to make progress on the chosen goal, it makes sense to offer advice, suggest some behavioral changes, and see how well that goes. I often teach in Heifetz's course, where they've all been imbued with this idea of adaptive change. I come in irreverently and say, "You know, just forget all this adaptive stuff. It's very complicated and it takes a long time. If your goal is a technical challenge, go straight for the technical fix. The hell with Heifetz!"

Everyone laughs because, being bright and resourceful people, they have probably already tried many times to meet the goals they are interested in. In fact, most clients come to us with goals that are very important to them, at which they have made many prior attempts without success. To me, this is a good indication that we are in the world of adaptive challenges, which means that for the person to have any lasting success we're going to need to walk down that second, somewhat longer path.

I'm never reluctant to suggest this longer path because I know that it not only leads to much more lasting change, but that it *over-delivers*. That is to say, it's going to help people in ways that go far beyond the particular goals they've brought in. They've formulated those presenting goals with a lot of urgency, and as I said before, I respect their importance, but I consider that the coaching enterprise is most often an opportunity to use the particular urgently felt goal as a bit of a carrot or Trojan Horse. By leading clients through the immediate, urgent desire to accomplish a goal, it will actually provide for them the opportunity for a much bigger kind of change project—their own ongoing development. This will enable them to not only meet their goals, but also many others that haven't even occurred to them yet.

Goals and the Self-authoring Mind

Now we can turn to another illustration, to gain a fuller understanding of the coaching backdrop we are considering here. The socialized mind's preoccupation with the ways one is seen and valued, and the nature of one's reputation, and so on, is a robust way of looking out onto the world. It is a very widely occupied developmental position, and is commonly encountered in coaching work.

That being said, it is certainly not the only developmental position that people or coaches may be living out of, and therefore presenting goals from. I can illustrate by describing another service professional, who actually worked in the same firm as the first. His initial goal was to strengthen the "being" side of his life and his personality because he felt that the balance between his "being" and "doing" was widely out of whack.

This professional had become a super problem solver, who went at everything in life as an optimization problem. For example, when his wife presented some dilemma or challenge, he would respond in the ways that he had been well-trained. These were behaviors he had been well-rewarded for, and with which he had come to identify himself. However, his dissatisfied wife would say, "I didn't come to you for a solution to this problem, and I don't want you to be a strategy consultant with me. I want something else." This problem-solving orientation was causing issues for him in his most valued relationships.

He had come to see that that "something else" had to do with his being able to accompany another person; to travel alongside them and simply offer his curiosity, his support, and his understanding. That was his goal. Obviously he did not want to lose or completely separate himself from his orientation toward activity, solution, and execution, but he wanted to strengthen his ability to be more present; to not necessarily function as a problem solver.

Through the process of his coaching he came to see that he had a tendency to do anything *but that*. He was always trying to drive toward a solution; to jump in with the answers and save the day. He was even honest enough to see that he looked for, and in some cases tried to convert situations into ones where his abilities were needed. He recognized that once he had figured out in his own mind a future that everything should move toward, he stopped listening, and this obviously kept him from living in the present. These were the behaviors that stood in the way of accomplishing his goal.

We could think of a coaching approach that would just go directly at those behaviors. We could teach him how to breathe differently, or engage in some kind of meditative practice. We could find some equivalent to dieting, that is to say, some new regimen of behavior by which he would alter his own. Then we would check in with him and cheer for his success, and try to support him when he didn't feel he was succeeding, as a sort of external mind and conscience. This would all be a version of path number one; a technical coaching approach.

However, there's another whole possibility. He could come to see that the source of these obstructive behaviors is not just his habits, or how he was treated when he was seven years old, but how he constructs the world right now, today. He has already made the kind of change that the person in the first example has the opportunity to make. He has long since come to identify an internal system, or driver. In fact, he has done it so well, and for so long, that he now identifies himself and feels whole and stable, not by virtue of his getting continuous messages from the external world, but rather through his continuous identification with his own internal theory and ideology. It is this internal operating system that generates the "better answer" or solution—that is who he is.

I am describing an expression of the developmental stage that follows the socialized mind, which we call the self-authoring stage. We call it that because, whereas in the prior example the person is more "written upon" by the external culture and environment, in the self-authoring stage you seize the psychological pen in your own hand. You become the author, the writer, the maker of your way, and you experience yourself as the conduct of and consistency with your own internal system. Instead of looking to the external authority, you identify yourself as a kind of authority. That is to say, you are self-authorizing; self-authoring.

The person in our current example has experienced himself in this way, and it has been very satisfying. It's how he knows himself, and how he has achieved a lot of success. However, he's now seeing that his more immediate goal, to be more present with people, actually bespeaks the limitations of this very powerful developmental position. In fact, if he is going to have success with this goal, he has the opportunity to consider what we're calling here the second path; the longer way; the adaptive, developmental kind of journey.

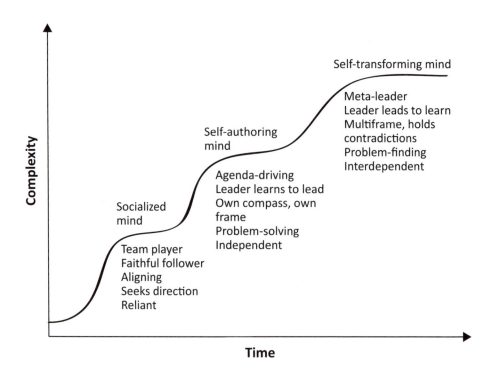

Figure 11.1   Three plateaus in adult mental development

Source: Kegan and Lahey, 2009, p. 15. Reprinted with permission from "Immunity to Change: How to Overcome It and Unlock the Potential in Yourself and Your Organization" by Robert Kegan and Lisa Laskow Lahey Copyright © 2009 by Harvard Business Publishing; all rights reserved.

He has the opportunity to move beyond even the self-authoring mind; the mind that puts such a premium on him being the agent and center of the action. The developmental position beyond self-authoring is what we call the self-transforming mind. It gradually leads to the identification of a new kind of self, where there are yet new metrics for success and satisfaction that don't always begin and end with setting your template down upon the world. You can have the experience of being part of a bigger whole, and recognize that your meaning system, however self-sealing or internally consistent it might be, inevitably has blind sides and leaves certain things out. From the self-transforming mind, looking at difference is not just a threat to your system or something that has to be incorporated into it, but an opportunity to see what you're missing, and observe your limitations. In this way, the system that you were previously so identified with, and therefore subject to, becomes something that you can look at and have a relationship to. You may love your theory and your system, but you aren't exactly identical to it. It becomes more of a cherished lens or tool that you can hold—and hold more lightly—rather than your being the lens itself.

This gives us a narrative from the self-authoring perspective. The story is similar to the first example, in that there's an explicit goal, but also a bigger back-drop, and an implicit goal that a person may not recognize. However, when people present themselves for coaching, they have the opportunity to support their ongoing, bigger development. Yes, coaching will enable them to meet their specific goals, but also to further their own evolutionary life project, and build an even more complex operating system. This will enable them to not only alter their behavior, but to see themselves and the world differently. Their behavior will change because they themselves will have changed.

Less Common Mindsets in Coaching

Now we have covered the major adult developmental stages that one encounters in coaching. The fully equilibrated self-transforming stage is relatively rare. That is to say, most of the research studies suggest that there might be 5–6 percent of the population that has entered the realm of the self-transforming mind. That's a small number, but I always tell my students there are 200 million adults in the United States alone, and this means *10 million* of them can construct the world this way. The 10 million are likely not all fully in the self-transforming stage, but they've begun to relativize the self-authoring stage enough so that there is beginning to be a bigger self. On the one hand you can say it is relatively rare, but on the other hand, with millions of people, it's hard to call it a rare phenomenon. You don't have to be Gandhi, or Martin Luther King.

Even for clients who are moving into the self-transforming stage, their goals generally implicate their aspiration to move further into that stage, rather than beyond it. More commonly, people's developmental paths involve the move from the socialized to the self-authoring mind.

There are developmental positions that precede the socialized mind, but these are generally occupied by children and adolescents rather than adults. If we look deeply into the mind of the ten-year-old, we see that they are just naturally transactional beings. Their meaning making system is characterized by what we call the instrumental mind, which precedes the socialized mind. We all recognize that even the sweetest ten-year-old will think to sell his mother on a hot day for a cold drink. Later he'll regret the sale because he'll have forgotten how much he gets from his mother, but at the moment it will have seemed like a good idea. Ten-year-olds can be very sweet if it serves their interests, or they can be Lord of the Flies, and you end up in a mob culture. There's nothing wrong with this mindset in a ten-year-old. We don't throw up our hands and say, "What's happened to the world; this child is evil." We expect them to grow out of it, and become socialized creatures.

There is something wrong with this mindset in thirty- or forty-year-old people, for whom there are all kinds of expectations about how they will conduct themselves. Are there lots of people running around in the bodies of adults who actually have completely self-interested, transactional minds? The answer to that is certainly "Yes, there are." Do we find them in coaching situations frequently? I'm not as sure about that one.

The true instrumental mindset should come across to any professional as being pretty simple, pretty concrete, often manipulative, and unable to partake in the forms of self-reflection and abstraction regarding basic motivations that are generally the lifeblood of coaching dialogues. If you were to find yourself with a client with whom you kept trying to take things to this level, and the person kept talking to you about the concreteness of it all and how this particular boss kept doing this, and the person seemed, not stubbornly unwilling, but rather absolutely *unable* to look at how he or she might have something to do with it, you may be in the presence of the instrumental mind. But I think that's relatively rare. If you happen to be a coach who works in a prison facility, for example, you might encounter this more often.

(Of course, we can't necessarily assume that every bad actor has the type of meaning making system that is more common to a ten-year-old. You start with the things we read in our newspapers, practically on a monthly basis, of people violating trust and operating in ways that look sociopathic. I suppose it would be natural to assume that if you manipulate the Libor rate, or defraud customers like Madoff, or any of these things that we see, that these people must be operating from a stage that is prior to the socialized mind. It isn't necessarily certain that these people are developmentally constrained, and never developed a social conscience (which is the sort of thing that happens as you move into the socialized mind). It's possible that they have left the world of the socialized mind; that they are no longer compelled by other's views, and have created an internal ideology that happens to be one that doesn't match our ethics. Perhaps they're even able to succeed as well as they do because they have fairly complex minds. However, their ideology would be considered immoral by the consensus.)

Revealing the Immunity to Change

Adult developmental theory suggests that there are overarching mindsets that may set the terms on people's goals, and may also set the terms on what gets in the way of meeting those goals. This introduces different options as to what coaching is about, and it raises the possibility that the coaching enterprise can support the broader project of adult development. If we as coaches actually want to walk down this second path, how do we develop specific approaches that rest on developmental theory, and support that bigger developmental possibility?

About 25 years ago, Lisa Lahey and I began deliberately asking ourselves whether there were ways to establish a helping relationship to specifically support developmental processes. We took a basic stance as educators, promoting processes of learning (rather than doctors, promoting a kind of cure to an illness). The Immunity to Change approach grew out of that inquiry.

At the heart of the Immunity to Change framework is the notion that these gradual qualitative transformations in mindset occur by actually shifting (broadening or expanding) our underlying knowing systems, or epistemologies—not *what* we know, but the *way* we know. As everyone who has suffered through a sophomore philosophy class knows, the basic structure of an epistemology is this very abstract thing called a subject–object relationship. Our knowing is shaped by those aspects of our thinking and feeling that we can look at, talk about, reflect on, and are therefore *object* for us, as well as those aspects of our thinking and feeling which we are run by, which we cannot look at because we're driven by them, and are therefore *subject* to them.

People talk about the thoughts and feelings that are object for them. They can talk about them; they can hold them; they are object. What's interesting about human beings is that while there are thoughts and feelings *we have*, there are also thoughts and feelings that *have us*, and that we're run by. We could consider this our blind side. Development is a process by which those things we are subject to gradually move to a place where we become bigger than them. They become elements or objects of our attention, where we can then do something with them.

That kind of development is promoted by living in a complex world, and hopefully finding enough support to stay with encountered differences rather than avoiding them. The differences prompt us and tempt us out of our current habits of mind, and this essentially moves things from subject to object. This kind of shift can happen naturally, over many years of life.

But from our point of view, the coaching enterprise is about incubating development. We fashion an intentional environment—an artificial and temporary environment—that has the purpose of helping facilitate these moves from subject to object. We protect a space, as well as the particular challenges, desires, and goals that people bring into the coaching relationship as pacers or drivers for this very development.

In particular, the Immunity to Change approach is a fast way of helping people see what is subject for them, and what is object. To go back to the examples of the service professionals' goals, the first person knew that he wanted to feel more alive in his work. That was object for him; he could see it. What the Immunity to Change approach does is to help the person see that in addition to these commitments he has, there are commitments that *have him*. These are commitments, or motives, he is subject to.

The first service professional was subject to his commitment to not risking his reputation, or endangering the way he was assessed by people in positions of authority at work. He wasn't aware of this; he wasn't getting up each morning and saying, "I am committed to preserving my reputation." The Immunity to Change process brings this situation out in stark relief. As one participant said to us, "It's a picture of me with one foot on the gas and one foot on the brake." The person in the first example had one foot on the gas, and wanted to be bolder in his work. He came to realize through the Immunity to Change process that he also had a foot on the brake. There was a commitment that had him; a commitment to not risking how other people regarded him.

The Immunity to Change process reveals a system that exists between two poles of commitment. It is based on the idea that the mind, like the body, has its own immune system. It is intelligent, quick, beautiful, and ceaseless, functioning to protect us twenty-four hours a day, mostly without our realizing it. But similar to our body's immune system, which protects us from bodily disease and external intruders, sometimes it gets us into trouble with its false alarms. Sometimes the immune system regards as an intruder something that we need to take in in order to thrive, and maybe even in order to live.

1 Visible Commitment	2 Doing/not doing Instead	3 Hidden competing commitments	4 Big assumptions
To be more excited and inspired in my work by connecting more with my own passions, and trusting more my own distinctiveness.	I work at things I am not that interested in (because I feel I must). I work in ways that are more routine, more established (because I feel that is what is expected).	To being well regarded by those who evaluate me. To not running any reputational, social, economic risks. To not looking unsuccessful. To not pushing an unknown/unproven trail.	I assume my safest route to success is to perform exceptionally well in ways that are expected and well established. I assume that if I am not highly regarded I will be a failure.

Figure 11.2   A junior partner's immunity X-ray

Source: Kegan and Lahey, 2009, p. 57. Reprinted with permission from "Immunity to Change: How to Overcome It and Unlock the Potential in Yourself and Your Organization" by Robert Kegan and Lisa Laskow Lahey Copyright © 2009 by Harvard Business Publishing; all rights reserved.

The simple example at the body's level is an organ transplant. The immune system sets up all of its energies to drive that new organ out. Even though it is operating as an ally, trying to protect and take care of us, it can actually put us at risk of great harm. The same is true for the mind's immune system. There are new ways of letting ourselves think and feel that may actually be necessary for our ongoing growth and development, but the immune system regards them as dangers.

For the person in our first example, he is protecting himself from being out of alignment with other people's high opinion and regard for him. His immune system treats as a virus anything that could lead people to have a less favorable opinion of him. The immune system's actions continue to generate the behaviors of going the safe way and taking the work that's assigned to him. It will continue to produce exactly the behaviors that prevent him from accomplishing his goal.

We could say the same thing for the second service professional. He has a commitment to being more present, but he realizes there is also a commitment that has him: to be a hero; to be the one who swoops in with the brilliant answer and solves the puzzle. If he doesn't do this he may feel useless, or that somehow life is less meaningful. He will encounter whatever particular kind of goblin hangs behind his doing other than what he has been doing.

The Immunity to Change process takes people through an exercise that, even in a couple of hours, shows them that they have constructed this brilliant system. The system protects you, but it also charges rent. The cost is that there's no real chance for you to succeed with your goal. The Immunity to Change process is a bit of a paradoxical move, because the first thing it does is show you that you are systematically constructed in such a way that it will be impossible for you to accomplish exactly the goal you're hoping for. This can be discouraging, but it is also very attention-grabbing. When people see that they have a foot on the gas and a foot on the brake relative to an important destination, the picture commands their interest, and creates a new kind of motivation. They ask, "How do I get out of this? It looks like I'm completely stuck."

This can prompt the construction of a bigger goal. A person may say, "I had a goal to be bolder and more innovative in my work, but now I have a bigger goal, which is taking my foot off the brake. How do I get out of this immune system so that I will not continue producing this behavior, but also stay safe?"

Goals start to change once you see the immune system. You see that you are producing the very behaviors that undermine your goals, so you start having a more systemic goal. You wonder how you are going to alter this system. This is beautiful, because it puts people in a stance where they're not just thinking, "How do I change my behavior?"—which is essentially the technical stance. They're asking "How can I change my mind?" This is the adaptive stance.

What I have described is the diagnostic half of the Immunity to Change approach. In showing people this picture of their system, it essentially moves that system from subject to object. They can literally see it on a page. This sets up the rest of the coaching journey, which is not just a kind of cheerleading around behavioral change, but is a process by which a person may actually come to change his mind.

References

Heifetz, R.A. (1994). *Leadership Without Easy Answers*. Cambridge, MA: The Belknap Press of Harvard University Press.

Kegan, R. & Lahey, L.L. (2009). *Immunity to Change*. Boston: Harvard Business Press.

12

GROW Grows Up:
From Winning the Game to
Pursuing Transpersonal Goals

*Sir John Whitmore, Carol Kauffman, and
Susan A. David*

Sir John Whitmore is a pre-eminent coach, consultant and author, and a leading thinker in leadership and organizational change. He is closely associated with the GROW Model, an acronym standing for (G)oals, (R)eality, (O)ptions and (W)ill (Whitmore, 1992). By working through these four key steps, individuals can gain clarity about their aspirations, understand their current situation, identify possibilities, and take targeted action toward achieving goals.

Sir John has commented that the GROW Model is often used in an overly rigid manner. His current interest is transpersonal coaching, an approach that involves focusing on what he calls "Bigger-than-self Goals". In this interview by Carol Kauffman, Director of the Harvard Institute for Coaching, he explores the implications of the latest thinking on goals as an opportunity to reposition GROW.

Goals and Responsibility in Coaching

Q: What are the origins of the GROW model?

Some early UK coaches, including me, had been using the GROW chronological sequence for some time before it was given that name. A staff member at a client site where Graham Alexander and I were working wanted a metaphorical word to represent that sequence. The staff member suggested "GROW", and we adopted it.

I don't want to claim any particular rights about GROW. I do want to say one thing, and that is: it doesn't say anything about coaching. It is a chronological sequence, and that's what is important about it. A brief definition of coaching that I believe has meaning is, "Coaching builds the Awareness and Responsibility of self and others." GROW is simply a questioning tool.

Q: The "G" in GROW stands for "goal". I remember once in a conversation you said, "Actually, it's not 'goal', it's 'vision', but 'VROW' wouldn't sell." Do you want to talk about that?

My background is in professional sports, and the goal in sports is to win the game. I always felt it was about winning, whatever "winning" means. Traditionally, winning means beating your opponent, but I think things have moved way beyond that. In fact, I believe that everyone should win.

A goal should be broader than just beating somebody else or some other company. It is doing the thing that is most valuable for everyone, and that includes the people working on the goal, and the people who gain by having it done. Goals are broader than the old meaning of the word, and I think more and more people are beginning to look at things that way.

Q: So goals, in the way you're describing them, can be intangible as well as tangible?

There are always intangible elements, since it's important that people doing the work have quality in their lives. They need to have satisfaction, and feel comfortable with what they are doing. You get a lot of willingness in organizations when people are invited to suggest their own goals. The corporation has a specific goal, but within that, the individual person is doing a particular aspect of that overall goal, with their smaller goals to achieve. They want to feel satisfied by doing a good job, so it's useful for them to have goals, and to know when they've met them.

Q: What is your view of the coach's responsibility for helping clients with goal processes?

When I'm coaching someone, I first ask, "What's the overall goal here for your department?", and "What is the goal you personally need to meet for your particular task?" This helps in defining the goal.

Then I ask questions like "How will we know if you have really achieved your goal? Is it a question of personal satisfaction? What would be the indicator that you've been successful?" That is getting more personal. It gets to the character, and structure or description of the goal. It must be very clear, not for me as a coach, but for the person being coached. That's the most important thing. My role is to help the person become clear about it.

Q: What are your thoughts about the coach's responsibility in the pursuit, management, and attainment of goals?

If I'm an on-going coach for someone, who has a goal that is a month or six months ahead, I say, "How often would you like me to check in with you to see how you are doing towards this goal?" I think people need some support along the way. It's one thing to establish a goal, but then do they remember it? Do other circumstances arise, causing that goal not to be the best goal?

The person may need to change the goal. Perhaps there is a new tool that could accomplish the goal more quickly—then you've got to raise the bar. There are many things that can change, and I think people ought to revisit their goals several times during pursuit. If they have a coach, the coach should question that along the way.

Q: When I did the survey for the *Harvard Business Review*,[1] we asked a couple hundred executive coaches "Do the goals shift during the encounter?" All but eight of them said yes. I like what you're saying about goal management: one thing is to keep revisiting goals, to see if the current reality means they have to shift.

What's your view on the coach's responsibility to help clients figure out if their goals are the right goals?

We have a high responsibility to support the individual in their clarity about it. I ask, "Who set the goal? What are the criteria, and who set them? Are you comfortable in that; do you have any doubts?" These are important questions to explore.

I don't pass great judgment myself on the answers, because I might have different answers, if I was in a similar situation. It's not right for the coach to take responsibility for actually achieving the goal—we shouldn't shift responsibility

---

1   See Kauffman and Coutu, 2009.

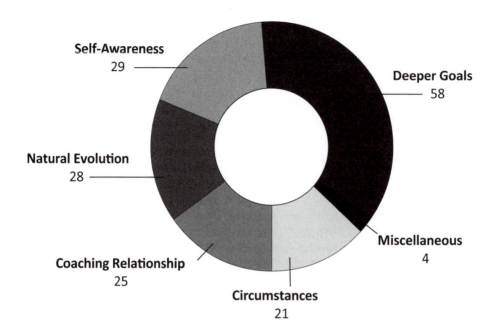

Figure 12.1   Why a shift of focus occurs during a coaching engagement
Source: Kauffman and Coutu, 2009, p.8. Reprinted by permission of *Harvard Business Review*. Exhibit from "The Realities of Executive Coaching" by Carol Kauffman and Diane Coutu, Harvard Business Review Research Report, January 2009. Copyright 2008 by the Harvard Business School Publishing Corporation; all rights reserved.

too much. I am honoring the person's own position, because then people take full responsibility for their lives. It works much better that way, and that's the point of coaching.

There is a hierarchy of responsibilities, and the coach has a responsibility to the person they are coaching. Even if a company asks a coach to work with a particular person, and even if the company is paying the bill, while I'm coaching that person, my commitment is to the individual. While I coach somebody, my commitment is to that person, so there is a correct consequence and behavior. I think that is very important.

Goals in the Context of the Organization and Society

Q: You've been talking about individual goals in the context of larger organizational goals. Can you say more about this?

There has to be a close relationship between the goals the individual has, and the goals the company has. There are some companies that have goals printed on the wall, but most people who walk past the sign don't know what it says. I think we really have to do better than that. These things need to be talked about in companies.

When I go in as a coach, I have the opportunity to work with this. I try to increase understanding between people in the organization—we can get a conversation going. A coach can ask questions that bring clarity. If you come in for a contract, even if you're coaching someone lower down in the organization, you can say you want to know about the company's objectives, and what they are shooting for.

It's important that the person you are coaching is clear about the company's purpose, or the purpose of the executive above. The person needs to know the purpose of the company's shareholders, and what they want to achieve. If the person is much lower hierarchically in the company, or the manager of a small team in a department, he or she may not be thinking an enormous amount about how good and useful the product is to humanity. But the person *is* looking at what the company wants to achieve in the short-term, from that department.

I had an extraordinary experience many years ago when working with a team of six people in a company. All were managers, and all had a few people underneath them. They did not think the company was doing the right thing in relation to the particular task they were given; they thought the company policy was wrong. We did quite deep coaching, and they realized that they either had to get themselves closer to agreement with the company, or they had to leave. Somewhat to my surprise, within six months all six of them left the company. Those things can happen. The company, thankfully, did not blame me for that, because they recognized that there was a conflict between the company and these people. They were good people, but they couldn't agree.

Q: Are there particular approaches or techniques you'd recommend to assess how well the goal resonates with the person, as well as with the external context? What do you do to help determine that the person is choosing the right goal for himself or herself—that it is intrinsic rather than extrinsic?

It is a matter of asking just that question: "How much are you committed to this goal, and to what extent does commitment to this goal come from the company?" Then I might follow up with, "What would you need to change, or what could be changed that would increase your commitment to it? What stands in the way of your commitment being higher?"

There are many questions about this, because some people come into a situation and say, "This is my goal." It's important to check that they put some thought into that part, and ask, "Where did that goal come from?" Some coaches say "What is your goal?", and leave it at that. But a lot of people, when asked, will be more specific about their goal, and often they realize there are some aspects they are not clear about.

Q: How do you think about the goal in the context of the business culture? Are there particular things that coaches can do to orient themselves?

You have to consider that there may be some goals the person isn't comfortable with for some reason. For example, they might feel they are not trained correctly. There is a lot to look at, and you can only make discoveries by talking to the person who is expected to meet the goal. My job is to make sure the person is as comfortable as possible with the goal. Sometimes it's simply a language issue. If a company has written down, "Our goal is ...," I might say, "If I'm going to coach some of your people, I want to know what you mean by that word." All that must be looked at.

I think those sort of things are the responsibility of coaches. Also, while it's important not to talk to a top executive about any individuals, if a coach sees a pattern emerging, he or she can say, "Of the people I've talked to, only 70 percent of them are satisfied with what they are doing. I need to tell you what I am hearing as the reason for their dissatisfaction."

Q: That's interesting—you can put the goals or the organization's agenda into a different perspective. Coaches in organizations do get together and, while keeping anonymity, they talk about patterns in goals and goal attainment. Then they can reflect that upward in the organization.

Organizational sponsors of executive coaching sometimes have a narrow view of the goals in the assignment. What has been your experience of this, and what kind of problems does it create?

I think one of the reasons that people get these rather narrow goals is because they are afraid to go wider. In our world today, where change is very much in the air, we have to think more in terms of whole systems. There are contextual issues that influence companies, countries, and all sorts of things.

I wouldn't tell a shoe manufacturer how to make shoes, but the company may be unaware of global circumstances that will affect the future of shoe manufacturing. There may be another country that's doing incredibly well with shoes, and making them for half the price because they have access to other materials. Does the company know about these global changes? Sometimes the answer is "No". Coaches have responsibilities today that they did not have ten years ago. They have a greater responsibility to ask relevant questions, to ask about things that are going on globally. It's a challenge to coaches, to suggest they should know something about the economy, the environment, and the global situation. They wonder, "How can I learn all about that?" I do feel it is a growing responsibility of coaches to have that broad ability to ask whole system questions.

Q: You're speaking about how goals, and our coaching work, are shaped by a complex set of forces related to the individual, the organization, as well as societal values and politics. What would help coaches understand and work with that complexity?

First of all, I would say it is about one's own personal development. Every single coach ought to be working on his or her personal development. How can coaching really be effective if the other person is more mature than they are? By "more mature", I mean further along the journey of personal development. Can you coach somebody who is further up than you are? I think you can, if you are a very skilled coach, but a lot of coaches would face difficulty and say, "This person knows more than I do; how can I coach them?"

Coaches have a responsibility to look more broadly and to ask broader questions, because some people in companies have a very narrow vision. I see politicians being incredibly simple in their decision-making. They have an inability to understand what's going on in the world because they are thinking in the short-term, focusing perhaps on what is going to affect them before the next election. The world is changing quickly now, in many ways, and that requires a different level of thinking.

I sometimes use the expression, "Coaching is more than just coaching". Coaching is not just asking questions. You must think for yourself; you must be savvy about these other things in the world, and what is changing.

I'll give you a rather extreme example. I'm involved in a huge project where we were looking into social aspects of the whole culture in China. Then the tsunami struck Japan, and all sorts of appalling things happened as a result of this extreme weather condition. The Chinese got a hold of us within a week or so, and said, "We always look at the Japanese as being expert in this area, because their island is on top of some sensitive tectonic plates. We're not very far away, and clearly this was bigger than they could cope with. We must look at this." They asked us to come to China immediately, which we did. It was interesting because they were already thinking more broadly and more contextually about how to deal with things. So it can happen at all levels, not just with individuals. It can happen to countries, as well as companies, and everything else.

Q: What helps coaches think about how goals fit into that wider systemic perspective?

The quality of your relationship with the people you are coaching is very important. Of course, if you are only having a three session coaching relationship it requires a lot of skill to be able to build that relationship and understanding quickly. If one has an on-going contract with the company, there may be times you can go have a cup of coffee with the person, as well as coaching in a more formal, structured way. You have to build a relationship, because when you have that relationship the person may acknowledge things that he or she was previously afraid to look at.

Sometimes I ask the question, "You say you have that goal, but who else might be affected by that goal? Are you going to tell them about it?" There are things that can take you a bit outside what might be considered a just and narrow goal.

I'll go one step further and say that in everything I am trying to achieve, whether it is in public service, healthcare, business or even sports, I believe goals should not be harmful in any way. I mean "harmful" in terms of the potential for people to get hurt, or become distressed when you achieve the goal. It's quite a serious issue in business, as many goals are achieved at a great expense to the environment. If someone said to me, "We as a company want to achieve this goal," and they had environmentally unhealthy equipment, I might say, "By producing these things, you are doing more harm to the environment. How can you do it in a way that is not harmful?" If they say, "I don't care," then I would choose not to coach that person.

A coach is expected to help people meet their goals, but just as there is a hierarchy of responsibility, I think there is a hierarchy in goals. I have my goals in a hierarchy, and I believe humanity is more important than a company. A company may have a goal that is absolutely fine for a narrow group of people, but harmful to other people. If the company's goal meets a lower ethical standard than my own, I always follow my own goal. It can get to the point where I say to a company, "I won't do that for you because that is harmful, and that is lower than I am willing to sink."

Goals in Transpersonal Coaching

Q: You're known for the transpersonal approach. How does transpersonal coaching relate to what we've been talking about, and how does it impact the way you work with goals?

Transpersonal means beyond the individual. Let me illustrate: it used to be that if you had a young child with psychological problems, you brought the child to a psychologist. Increasingly, we recognize if a child has a problem there are systemic issues within the family system. Family therapy is more successful than individual therapy, because it considers context.

A company has a particular goal of its own, but that's generally within the company. There may be contextual elements that are changing outside the company, such as the environment or the economy. The company needs to adjust to these external circumstances.

Business people are savvy about their own businesses. As I said before, I wouldn't tell a shoemaker how to make shoes, because I presume he or she knows better than I do. However, people in the company may be too busy to be aware of the external circumstances affecting them.

Q: What about on an individual level? I think of the transpersonal as relating to purpose and meaning. How do you help people connect that with their goals?

When we get to the transpersonal area, we are dealing with development of the person as a human being—as a more effective, more satisfied, more fulfilled human being. When people feel fulfilled, they are much more productive in the workplace, as well as in life. That sort of personal development element is quite important, certainly when we get to the executive level of people within organizations. It's important that they have that sense of satisfaction and fulfillment about what they're doing, which will include things within the organization, but also outside.

People say, "I have this or that problem at work," but when you start coaching them you often quickly get to the fact that they have a difficult relationship at home, or something like that. Obviously, that needs to be dealt with confidentially, but it needs to be dealt with, because if people are feeling unfulfilled or unhappy at home, they are not going to be as productive in the workplace. We have to address things, even if they are personal. The person's boss might say, "Look, you are being coached on your marriage problems. That shouldn't be paid for by the company." I would say, "This is between the company and that person," but I would tell the company that the coaching is extremely important for work reasons, as well as personal reasons.

Q: So what about the nitty-gritty of transpersonal coaching? What do you see as key steps in goal setting, and helping people manage their goals?

If I have an ongoing coaching contract with senior people in a company, I'm going to be asking them some deep personal questions quite early, because there may be difficulties based on some fundamental way of thinking. I'm going to explore questions about their lives, how they decided to work in the organization, what it means to them to be working there, where their fulfillment comes from, and so on.

The sequence in which I ask those questions, to get into that deeper, serious level, will depend on the person's personality. Some people are willing to open up quickly. Others may feel uncomfortable at the beginning; they have to know and trust you before they explore those things.

It's important for coaches to be variable, and perceptive enough to see when they need to change direction; when it's not quite right for the other person. They must be willing to ask the person, "Are we going in the right direction, or is there something else you'd rather look at?" These are all possibilities within coaching. But I'd certainly like to start with some deep questions like, "What do you see in terms of your personal development?"

The other thing that comes in, regarding personal development, is the spiritual side. In some parts of the eastern world little distinction is made between psychological progression and spiritual progression. But in the western world we say, "This is the domain of the psychologist, and this is the priest's in the church, and the two don't meet." But they do. They overlap, and the spiritual side does come into it. This is really what is implied by the transpersonal.

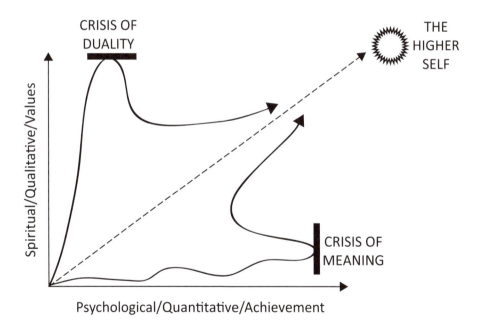

Figure 12.2   Developmental journey
Source: Whitmore and Einzig, 2006, p. 140

Q: So, in terms of goal setting and management, it's about going deep, and honoring the core of the person. There is an overlap of psychological, spiritual, and business, in a way. While you have an overall orientation that you're famous for, in fact what you do is iterative, and responsive to what the person is bringing you. Where does purpose come into this?

You've mentioned people having a feeling of purpose in their work, and this is a key point. One often puts the word together with meaning: meaning and purpose. What is the meaning and purpose of what you do?

Purpose is a sense of forward thinking. As people develop on their journey, a sequence of points occurs in the change process. One of those points is where they begin to feel they have some meaning or purpose in their lives. Very often, the purpose is not selfish. A person might say, "My real purpose is to produce this product because I think it makes people more happy, or healthy." That is the beginning of the spiritual part of the journey, when meaning and purpose come into it.

Q: What are your thoughts about evaluation of goal attainment? Do you think it is practical? Do you think it potentially distorts behavior?

Some things are fairly obvious. If you were to have coaches come in and work for the sales staff, success is going to be measured by the success of the sales. That's measurable, because you know you sold 400 products last year, and 550 this year. You are obviously doing better. But if you are dealing with something softer than that—for example, how comfortable people are in their jobs—that sort of thing that is much more difficult to measure.

Q: From a transpersonal perspective, what is good practice around evaluating goal achievement?

It depends. When you get into the transpersonal, you're talking about more subjective things, therefore whether a person achieves a goal is determined by its meaning to that particular individual. The goal might be described with a word that has a number of different meanings. If it's a word like "happy", I'm going to ask a lot of questions about what that means.

There are different ways to assess these things. On one end of the spectrum, you can leave it up to the person's assessment and description. Or, you can always use a scale. With happiness, for example, a person might say either

"I'm happy" or "I'm not very happy". That's not very useful. It's better to use a scale, where "ten" means you are delightfully happy, and "zero" means you're not. Then you can ask, "Where are you at the moment"?

Q: Yes, I've seen video of you coaching, where you are constantly helping people check in with themselves using a one to ten scale. This can increase self-awareness and self-responsibility, which is different from an external evaluation. Is this the intent?

Yes, and it gives a more accurate description of the person's state. It's more information than just having them say "yes" or "no". It's an important technique, to find ways to create gradations between the two.

Goals Across the Lifespan

Q: You mentioned earlier that your own goals are in a hierarchy. How do you see people setting and managing goals over the lifespan?

This is an important question because I think goals change according to certain things in our lives. In our early days, we often have personal goals of achieving something, to develop belief in ourselves. A lot of people go into sports relatively early in life, probably because they love the game itself, but also because they want to feel successful within themselves, and that they can achieve something. A lot of motivation is about gaining that self-belief, rather than winning this game.

Often as people marry, have children and the like, the goal might be to buy a house, or to prepare for the cost of bringing up children and sending them to school. Goals at this stage can be quite materially oriented.

This may eventually change, as the person begins to have a broader vision of goals, and to have what I call more mature goals. There is nothing wrong with the goals before that, but I think when you are a mature person your goals are going to be for the good of humanity, so it can perpetuate itself. There is a sequence, and in most people changes occur according to age. I think a number of people get stuck at one point or another. There are goals that are relevant to your age and therefore perfectly reasonable, and then there are levels at which immaturity gets set in.

Q: So we're talking about levels of consciousness?

It's levels of consciousness, and there are plenty of older people running large companies, who may be adolescents in terms of consciousness. The two don't necessarily go together. There are some activities in life that absolutely demand psychological or psycho-spiritual maturity. There are other activities, like certain types of business, for example, that don't require much personal maturity to get to the top. I'm quite shocked that some of those people are in leadership roles.

Q: We've certainly seen some of the catastrophic results of that on Wall Street. You spoke earlier about maturity and personal development. Can you say more about this as it relates to goals?

I feel that humanity is evolving at this moment, and I think it's evolving faster than it has historically. People have been coming out of the autocracy that dominated the world. For most of history, the majority of people, over 90 percent, were told what to do by somebody else—by a king, a general, a prince, or a boss.

As people evolve collectively, on a large scale, we are moving out of the autocracy or hierarchy, into a more mature state of self-choice and self-responsibility. We're able to make our own choices about how to do things. This is emerging in our society. If you look at the Middle East, Egypt and Libya both had autocratic leaders for over 30 years. The revolutions they've had were not political. They were social. Younger people were concerned about their lack of choice, and their lack of access to resources for survival. It was not political; it was that these dictators were behind the times in the evolution of humanity.

Unfortunately we tend to think in silos. You may be in a business, or a country where you don't tend to have whole system thinking. When the world is changing as fast as it is at the moment, we have to have more of it. That is global maturity. It's a challenge to the world out there.

Q: It's a completely new thought for me, in terms of goal maturity. You're talking about how humanity is evolving so that we actually have an ever-expanding range of choices. If there are many more potential goals to pick from, how do you bring maturity to that? You were talking about it in terms of cultural evolution, and it makes me think about Bob Kegan's work on levels of consciousness. The goals you pick are very much determined by political and cultural evolution, and also individual development.

Absolutely, and there is a relationship between the two. The sequence of stages that an individual goes through in their personal development is replicable in the collective sequence. There are many models of the stages that people go through, and great similarities between them.

What shocks me is that education does not teach children that life is a journey of self-development. We say, "You must get a qualification to get a job." What a depressing thing to tell children. We should be telling them, "We want to prepare you to go forth in the world. You'll have successes and failures, excitements and disappointments, and everything will happen to you out there. We want to prepare you in the best possible way to cope with that." If schools were to tell children that, I think a lot of children would be a great deal happier than they are.

Q: You're looking at goals in terms of the range of what is possible, what influences that range, and how we can prepare children to think about goals. This is really a different context for goals, isn't it?

Yes. Can I take that a step further to say that right now the situation in the world is extremely serious in terms of the environment? It is much more serious than the experts are able to tell ordinary people. People don't want to know, and it seems politicians can't think about it. I would say that right now, the greatest goal that we have is the survival of human existence. We've got to do something about it.

Q: What goals do you have now, as you look forward?

My goal is, and it sounds ridiculous when I say so, but my goal is to make the world a better place than it is right now. I would like people to be happier than they are. I would like the world to be a fairer place. The difference between the rich and the poor is absolutely absurd, to the extent that there are a large number of people dying from starvation and shortage of water, and there are a large number of people who have more money than they know what to do with. That is the way society is, unfortunately, and I'm trying to spend the rest of my life trying to change that and improve that in any way I can.

A nice challenging goal, for example, is to shift how we see the building of energy. I am involved in a project that eliminates the use of fossil fuel, replacing it entirely with renewable natural fuel. It might take fifty years to get there. My goal right now is to get the right people involved in this project, so that I can reach the end of my life with confidence that it can actually happen. It is doable. It is possible. It is not ridiculously expensive to solve the energy problem on planet Earth. It's quite interesting because there is a series of steps on the way to get there. Mainly it is getting the people in power to wake up, and understand what is possible. It is a big challenge to get society to work the way it could.

Q: Talk about wonderful, inspiring long-term goals. So you are focused on goals that extend beyond your lifetime?

Yes; I think we need to think beyond our personal lives. At this point my goals are long-term, and I'm thinking of humanity rather than individuals. People do tend to think that way as they get older. In a spiritual sense, I think the way you are developing yourself affects how you see the future.

Q: I would like to thank you for your generosity, time, and wisdom. I know I have a lot of new things to think about, and I think this will be helpful to coaches. Thank you very much.

Let me thank you for asking me questions. It was like you were coaching me— you made me think.

References

Kauffman, C. & Coutu, D. (2009). *The Realities of Executive Coaching*. Cambridge, MA: Harvard Business Review Research Report.

Whitmore, J. (1992). *Coaching for Performance: GROWing People, Performance, and Purpose*. London: Nicholas Brealey.

Whitmore, J. & Einzig, H. (2006). Transpersonal coaching. In J. Passmore (Ed.), *Excellence in Coaching: The Industry Guide*, 134–46. London: Kogan Page.

13

Goals in Mentoring Relationships and Developmental Networks

Kathy E. Kram, Susan A. David, and Christina Congleton

Kathy Kram, PhD, is the Shipley Professor in Management at the Boston University School of Management, and the author of numerous books and articles on mentoring, adult development, and leadership. As a result of her research, Dr Kram has re-conceptualized mentoring as a "developmental network", rather than a strictly dyadic relationship. In this interview by Susan David, co-director of the Institute for Coaching (McLean Hospital/Harvard Medical School), Dr Kram reflects on the origins and evolution of her research on mentoring, and its relationship to goals.

Goals in Informal and Formal Mentoring

Q: In your original study on informal mentoring, you explored relationship dynamics, including how mentor and protégé established career and other objectives for the protégé. Would you like to describe that research, and its relationship to goal setting and goal management?

In this original study of mentoring pairs, I started by identifying a group of young managers, ages 25 to 35, who were perceived by the organization's HR staff as having mentors. My idea was to interview these 28 individuals about their career histories, and specifically about these supportive relationships.

I never used the word "mentor" in the original research because I knew that word had a lot of different meanings. Instead I asked, "Who stands out as having taken special interest in your development?" During the first interview they usually identified one or two individuals, and by the end we made a decision to focus on one of those relationships. Then I had a second interview in which we explored the relationship in further detail. I also had the opportunity and permission to interview that significant other.

My idea was to get two perspectives on each relationship. Up to that time the only research that had been done on mentoring was outcome research. It showed that if you had a mentor you ended up more satisfied, or were promoted more quickly than those without mentors. But we knew nothing about what actually went on between the two individuals. Mine was a process-oriented study and it basically consisted of questions like, "How did the relationship get started?", "What did you want from the relationship?", "What do you remember happening in the first six months to first year?", "How has it changed over time?", and "What benefits have you derived from the relationship?" I asked both parties the same questions, and out of that I developed my own theory of mentoring relationships.

Table 13.1   Functions of the mentoring relationship

Career functions[1]	Psychosocial functions[2]
• Sponsorship • Exposure-and-visibility • Coaching • Protection • Challenging assignments	• Role modeling • Acceptance-and-confirmation • Counseling • Friendship

Table 13.2   Phases of the mentoring relationship

Phase	Definition	Turning points[3]
Initiation	A period of six months to a year during which time the relationship gets started and begins to have importance for both managers.	Fantasies become concrete expectations. Expectations are met; senior manager provides coaching, challenging work, visibility; junior manager provides technical assistance, respect, and desire to be coached.
Cultivation	A period of two to five years during which time the range of career and psychosocial functions provided expand to a maximum.	Both individuals continue to benefit from the relationship. Opportunities for meaningful and more frequent interaction increase. Emotional bond deepens and intimacy increases.

---

1   Career functions are those aspects of the relationship that primarily enhance career advancement.
2   Psychosocial functions are those aspects of the relationship that primarily enhance a sense of competence, clarity of identity, and effectiveness in the managerial role.
3   Examples of the most frequently observed psychological and organizational factors that cause movement into the current relationship phase.

Phase	Definition	Turning points
Separation	A period of six months to two years after a significant change in the structural role relationship and/or in the emotional experience of the relationship.	Junior manager no longer wants guidance but rather the opportunity to work more autonomously. Senior manager faces midlife crisis and is less available to provide mentoring functions. Job rotation or promotion limits opportunities for continued interaction; career and psychosocial functions can no longer be provided. Blocked opportunity creates resentment and hostility that disrupts positive interaction.
Redefinition	An indefinite period after the separation phase, during which time the relationship is ended or takes on significantly different characteristics, making it a more peerlike friendship.	Stresses of separation diminish, and new relationships are formed. The mentor relationship is no longer needed in its previous form. Resentment and anger diminish; gratitude and appreciation increase. Peer status is achieved.

Source: Kram, 1983.

It's noteworthy that I did not ask anything about goal setting in that original study. But I would say that among the 28 pairs, there was a subset that talked very explicitly about goals. They said things like, "My goal is to get promoted within the next number of years, and that's why this relationship became important to me." There were people who thought and expressed themselves in those instrumental terms, but they were not the majority. Goals were usually implied or implicit, or not mentioned at all.

Q: One idea we are exploring in this book is the difference between pre-determined goals—goals that one enters a coaching conversation with, and emergent goals—those that emerge out of the conversation. Do you have a sense from your research whether individuals came into mentoring relationships with goals like "I want be promoted", or whether they evolved through conversation?

I definitely have a sense of what you're describing as emergent. That is, these relationships were important precisely because they enabled the junior person to clarify what they were aiming for and what would be meaningful to them. These were young adults with just a few years of work experience, and the relationship was important precisely because it helped them establish some sense of purpose and meaning.

This contrasts with the formal mentoring programs that I've observed or helped design in US settings over the last 20 years or so. These programs often have goal setting as a principle part of the relationship, so it is a different approach.

That is interesting in itself—that in informal relationships, goal setting is often emergent, as you defined it. In formal mentoring relationships, the goals that individuals bring often help structure the relationship. It's actually used as a criterion for matching people in a formal program.

Q: When protégés do establish goals to bring to mentoring conversations what do you think the role of the mentor might be in helping them to validate and explore these?

You find a much wider variation in this in informal relationships, as compared to formal mentoring relationships. Again, in the formal relationships, goals are often the driver for matching the pair in the first place. Therefore the agenda for the initial meeting is usually based on the goals of the protégé. In informal relationships, the initiation of talking about goals depends on the style and approach of each party to the relationship.

Balancing Career-focused and Psychosocial Mentoring

Q: When you've been involved in implementing formal mentoring programs in organizations, have you witnessed missteps related to goal setting?

I think there are several. One is when mentors have a very narrow focus for goal setting. For example, is the goal "to achieve that next promotion" or "to achieve both a promotion and balance in my life" or is it "to build more self-confidence"? I think goal setting has more complexity than mentors often are comfortable acknowledging. Another is the assumption that the mentor knows better than the protégé what the goals should be; when the mentor conveys either explicitly or implicitly, "From my experience this is what you should be doing."

Q: In many organizations, goal setting and S.M.A.R.T. goals[4] have become so ingrained that people no longer discuss them; it's assumed that people have goals. There's been a recent backlash in the management literature suggesting that goals have "gone wild"[5] in organizations; that this strong focus on goals doesn't necessarily support effectiveness.

My interest in this debate has been from the emotions perspective. What is important in emotional effectiveness is being able to "go to"

---

4   See Doran, 1981.
5   See Ordóñez et al., 2009.

emotions and explore them with a person and only then to move to a goal-oriented "go through" phase that focuses on how to navigate the situation or issue. If the coaching is overly focused on goals one may not attend to what is going on with the person emotionally and inadvertently suppress emotions. In so doing, emotional effectiveness is undermined. How do you see the role of emotions in the mentoring process?

That's very interesting. This idea seems to parallel my original distinction between career-focused mentoring and psychosocial mentoring. In my original research, the career-oriented mentoring was instrumental: that's where the goals would be detected, discussed, and so on.

Psychosocial mentoring was more about the emotional connection and the sense of well-being that came from the relationship, as well as the self-awareness that grew within the relationship. It's interesting to ask the question, "What balance do people have?" In my research over the years, I have seen that balance shifting all the time. And, as I reconsider the connection between these two aspects of developmental relationships (such as mentoring), it seems that with greater self-awareness and self-confidence, comes greater ability to articulate meaningful goals. If goal setting dominates the conversation too early, the individual may articulate goals that are not aligned with personal values, talents and interests.

Q: That's fascinating. Exploring these kinds of ideas is important for a discipline like coaching. In very novice coaching there can be a strong focus on asking, "What's your goal? Have we achieved your goal?" There can be a certain security in having a specific goal to focus on. As the coach becomes more experienced—and this would likely depend on the coach's own emotional skills—there is an increasing tolerance of the ambiguity that comes with a more emergent process.

My observation is that professional coaches really vary in how they situate these two kinds of work—the instrumental and psychosocial approaches. Some are exclusively focused on goals and goal accomplishment, whereas others take a more emergent approach.

Again, my knowledge is mostly US based, but I find that sponsorship is usually associated with the more career, instrumentally focused mentorship, both formally and informally. You see more goal setting there than in relationships where psychosocial development is more primary to the relationship. In corporate settings you see a lot more career-oriented mentoring going on, with the psychosocial mentoring taking place more frequently either with family members or peers. Often times, women receive this type of mentoring from other professional women, not necessarily those within the organization. The idea of the relationship between goal setting and emotional effectiveness is a very interesting one. It's interesting to consider whether they can be joined, or whether they compete for time in the relationship.

Supervisory Mentoring and Diversity in Organizations

Q: A number of organizations have programs that involve mentoring from an immediate boss. This is largely rejected in Europe as there is perceived to be a significant danger of contamination of the mentee's goals by those of their manager. What are your views on this?

It's likely important that one's boss could not be one's mentor. I know a lot of organizations in the United States that implement formal mentoring also build in a component of bringing together supervisors, mentors, and protégés for the purpose of clarifying those roles, and acknowledging that they are quite different. At the same time, I know that when they are trying to create a mentoring culture, some organizations will build an expectation and hold supervisors accountable for mentoring others. So, it's kind of a mixed message. In my view, supervisors can certainly coach their subordinates on job-related challenges, but taking on the deep mentoring role is in direct conflict with managerial responsibilities. Since scholars now argue that individuals benefit from multiple developmental relationships, there is little reason to locate and limit the mentoring role to an individual's direct supervisor.

Q: Do you have any more thoughts on contextual factors, such as power within the relationship, diversity, or organizational support? How might those influence goal setting, and the sense of anxiety related to whether the person has achieved a goal?

The word "diversity" pops out at me in this question because it seems that things have changed a lot since I did my original research. It's true that even back then, cross-gender mentoring was not very prevalent. It was challenging for both individuals who found themselves in such a relationship, because there was a lot of stereotyping, suspicion, and rumors about what might be going on between a male mentor and a female protégé. I think a lot of that has changed as the workforce has become more diversified.

Nonetheless, there are some basic differences between women and men, and there has been research to support this. Women tend to have more holistic goals that include life beyond work, whereas men tend to have more instrumental goals around work itself. Sometimes it's hard for male mentors to really appreciate the goals of the women they are mentoring. The women don't feel understood or supported, and they end up turning to other women for support and validation. David Thomas has shown the same thing in his work on interracial mentoring and race more generally.[6] Minority group executives benefit from contact with both white and minority mentors, deriving different types of support from each.

Adult Development and the Life Cycle of Mentoring Relationships

Q: Reflecting on your research, do you get a sense of the responsibilities of the mentor and protégé in terms of articulating, refining, and pursuing goals? Does it seem like a natural process, or one that is more structured?

Focusing on the informal relationships I've studied, I would answer that question differently today than I would have 30 years ago when I did the research. It's because I have Robert Kegan's developmental framework[7] in my repertoire now. I can see, as I look back on those pairs, that the developmental position of both parties really did shape who was in charge of setting the goals, articulating them, and so on.

For example, many young managers will look toward their mentors for help in articulating goals, while others will feel more comfortable asserting goals themselves. This depends on where they are in their own development. In the research, it seemed that the less experienced folks would often allow their mentors to help establish the goals. Perhaps "less experienced" is not the correct term—it has more to do with one's attitude towards authority, dependency, and independence. When I conducted my research I didn't have Kegan's theoretical framework in hand, but I did write about developmental stages.

---

6   See Thomas, 2001.
7   See Kegan, 1994; also Chapter 11.

Q: How does this relate to the way that mentor and protégé share goals in the relationship?

I know that sometimes in my original work, I found examples of relationships that were ending as one or both parties were moving on to something else. They were not necessarily physically or geographically moving, but rather feeling the need for something different at that particular stage of their development. I think that is a natural separation phase of the relationship and I've seen it when either the protégé is ready to move on, wants a less involved mentor, wants more autonomy, or the mentor has something come up that prevents him or her from attending to the mentoring relationship in the same way.

Q: It's like the life cycle of the relationship.

Yes—that's a good way to put it.

Q: Do you have a sense of how this relates to whether goals remain fixed over time? What is the extent to which the pair ends up being flexible or changeable around goals?

In today's context, which is characterized by a fast pace of change and uncertainty, I would guess that goals do shift. Not just according to what we know is typical adult development, but according to changes in the context that require adaptability. I wouldn't be surprised at all if goals do shift over time.

Q: I'm wondering whether these issues of development and change are related to your perspective on one of the core themes we're exploring, which is that emergent goals in mentoring and coaching might be the end point of a mentoring intervention. The idea is that once you've achieved goal clarity, you might not want to be as connected with mentors. You are able to set your own goal, and go off to do the thing that you've discovered in the context of the mentoring relationship.

I'll tell you my thinking is very much influenced by the lens that I currently hold around the reality that most individuals have developmental *networks*, not just one mentoring relationship. For example, I ask my students to identify not just one but up to six people who they think are interested in and care about their development. I ask them to consider bosses, peers, subordinates, and family members. They can then explore the kind of mentoring and coaching support each of those relationships provides. We do this in the classroom setting. I know of people who are doing research with this tool as well.

I don't think it makes sense anymore to think only in terms of one relationship. It makes much more sense to have the individual reflect on this small network and consider how it's enabling forward movement in the desired direction. Perhaps a mentor does originally help the individual establish goals, which are then facilitated by other members of the network.

Beyond Dyadic Mentoring Relationships: Developmental Networks

Q: How has your thinking changed over time and how have you arrived at your current thinking on mentoring relationships?

There have been several evolutions in my thinking. First of all, there's a distinction between formal and informal mentoring which we talked about earlier. Second is this idea that one's developmental position shapes what one is looking for in that relationship. Third is the discovery that even when an individual has a mentoring relationship, they also have a network of relationships. Perhaps they are not learning, developing, and sharpening their goals with only one mentor; there may be a relational process spread across the developmental network. This is what my current interests are. I don't think we get the whole story by examining only one relationship, as I once thought we did.

Q: How did the research on mentoring dyads evolve in your own mind such that you started thinking about networks?

I'm glad you asked me that because I'm now very clear about it. Shortly after I finished the first study I was very much aware that although I focused on this one relationship that each person told me about, they had mentioned other relationships. Often those other relationships were with peers. My second study involved the study of peer mentoring (Kram and Isabella, 1985), where I actually asked people to identify peers who had taken an interest in their development. I followed basically the same protocol and wrote a paper on peer mentoring, an alternative to traditional mentoring. That began to open the lens for me to consider that if a person can experience a developmental process with a mentor as well as one or more peers, then perhaps it makes sense to consider more than just one mentor relationship.

Together, Monica Higgins and I worked through this idea of a developmental network—it was really through the lens of social network theory that we got there. Without her, I probably wouldn't have been able to conceptualize it very well. It makes a lot of sense, and it's really taking off.

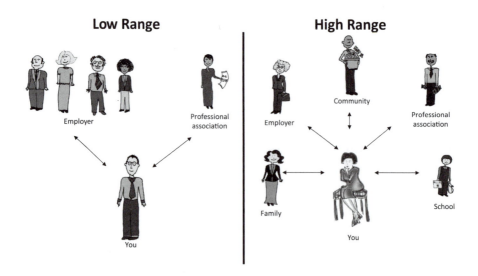

Figure 13.1   Structure of the network

© 1998, Monica C. Higgins, Harvard Business School

Table 13.3   Past and present conceptualizations of mentoring (Higgins and Kram, 2001)

Phenomenological boundaries	Traditional mentoring perspective	Developmental network perspective
Mentoring relationship(s)	Organizational	Intra- and extraorganizational (e.g. profession, community, family).
	Hierarchical	Multilevel.
	Single dyadic relationship	Multiple dyadic/networked relationships.
	Focus on protégé learning.	Mutuality and reciprocity.
	Provided in sequence of relationships throughout career.	Provided simultaneously by multiple relationships at any given time in career.
Functions served	Organization/job related	Career/person related
Levels of analysis	Dyad level	Network level and dyad level

Q: Are developmental networks conceptualized in relation to mentoring, or is it more about how individuals in your life support you in pursuing goals?

It's still being studied within the context of the mentoring phenomenon. I like that, because once it's taken as a separate support network, it becomes confused and diluted by the idea of a social network, and that's not what we are talking about. We are talking about a handful of relationships, identified by the focal person, that take an active interest in supporting an individual's development. I prefer for it to remain within the coaching and mentoring arena because it's very specifically focused on individual development.

Q: Do these networks encompass both formal and informal mentoring relationships?

Yes, they do. Monica Higgins has done a fair amount of empirical research on the extent to which developmental networks and their diversity shape career outcomes, such as job change, goal clarity and the like.[8] She has demonstrated that the more diverse a developmental network, the more progress individuals make on certain kinds of career goals. For example, individuals who want to change careers or change organizations are more likely to succeed at this goal if they have a developmental network comprised of individuals from several industries and a variety of organizations. Similarly, if advancement within a particular organization is the primary goal, then a more homogenous developmental network would make sense. It's interesting and very encouraging that we are actually seeing that play out. Intuitively it makes sense, but now she's providing empirical evidence.

Q: It strikes me that an organizationally-mandated mentoring process really opens the door for intentional goal setting, asking people what they want to achieve, and so on. How do you see developmental networks playing out in organizations in relation to intentional goals?

I have begun to see it in the context of leadership development programs, where leaders go through some assessment work and define developmental goals for themselves. Historically, they might have been assigned a formal mentor who they could work with as they pursued those goals. The developmental network perspective suggests that in doing their own assessment, they are also already assessing their existing developmental network. Sometimes people call

---

8   See Higgins, 2001; Higgins, Dobrow, and Roloff, 2010; Higgins and Thomas, 2001.

it a "personal board of directors": that small group of people who they go to for advice and counsel. By doing this assessment—recognizing that my boss can help in certain ways, my formally assigned mentor can help, as well as my peer who I have lunch with once a month, and a couple of my subordinates who know more about this than I do—they actually consciously lay out this developmental network as part of a plan to move forward on goals.

I'm teaching MBA leadership now, and toward the end of the semester I always have them do an assessment of their current developmental network. I ask them to consider, given what they've learned about their leadership and their development goals, how they might want to enrich this network going forward?

At the Center for Creative Leadership they use something like Peer Coaching or Partnering at the end of most of their leadership development programs. People are actually paired with another person in the group. They can stay in touch to help each other be accountable after the program. It's only one other person, but it's an addition to what they already have in their developmental network, such as a boss or mentor or other people at work who can help them.

I am working on a paper right now on developmental networks as holding environments for leader development. A holding environment provides challenge, consistency, and confirmation, and a developmental network can actually do that for an individual.

Q: How do you address goal setting and management with your MBA students—what kind of support around learning and skill-building do you find people need?

I've really been influenced by one of my doctoral students, Jeffrey Yip. He was with the Center for Creative Leadership before coming into our doctoral program. He recently worked with me on the MBA leadership course, and he said to me at the beginning of the semester, "Why don't we ask them to identify some learning goals for the course, and at the end, ask them how they feel they've progressed?"

We built that into the course, and I think it really had an impact. I can't tell you empirically, but anecdotally, articulating goals at the beginning and end seems important for ongoing leadership development. I think goals are very important in helping to focus attention and provide motivation for continuous learning.

Q: Is there an ideal research project related to these networks and goal setting that you think is important and ought to be done?

I'd love to see more research in organizations on developmental networks. It's not easy, but it can be done. In fact, I'm part of what is called a micro-community of researchers who are looking at positive relationships at work, and how they contribute to all kinds of important things like resiliency, personal growth, performance, and so on. The idea, at least for me, is that if you can experience high-quality connections with a coach or mentor, you can take what you have learned is valuable—mutuality, active listening, self-disclosure, etc.—into other relationships.

Q: Is there anything we haven't covered or spoken about in relation to goals and mentoring?

No. I'm really glad you encouraged me to talk about the evolution of the work on developmental networks. It's such an important idea for coaching and mentoring. One way to think about coaching, especially when it's external to an organizational setting, is that our primary purpose is to help individuals develop the skills they need to find their own support on an on-going basis. I think this is an essential lens to bring to the whole enterprise. And, if individuals enhance their self-awareness in the context of coaching, they will be able to establish meaningful goals that provide direction for the kind of support they will want to enlist.

References

Doran, G.T. (1981). There's a S.M.A.R.T. way to write management's goals and objectives. *Management Review, 70*(11), 35–6.

Higgins, M.C. (2001). Changing careers: The effect of social context. *Journal of Organizational Behavior, 22,* 595–618.

Higgins, M.C., Dobrow, S.R., & Roloff, K.S. (2010). Optimism and the boundaryless career: The role of developmental relationships. *Journal of Organizational Behavior, 31,* 749–69.

Higgins, M.C. & Kram, K.E. (2001). Reconceptualizing mentoring at work: A developmental network perspective. *The Academy of Management Review, 26*(2), 264–88.

Higgins, M.C. & Thomas, D.A. (2001). Constellations and careers: Toward understanding the effects of multiple developmental relationships. *Journal of Organizational Behavior, 22,* 223–47.

Kegan, R. (1994). *In Over Our Heads: The Mental Demands of Modern Life*. Cambridge: Harvard University Press.

Kram, K.E. (1983). Phases of the mentor relationship. *Academy of Management Journal, 26*(4), 608–25.

Kram K.E. & Isabella, L.A. (1985). Mentoring alternatives: The role of peer relationships in career development. *The Academy of Management Journal, 28*(1), 110–32.

Ordóñez, L.D., Schweitzer, M.E., Galinsky, A.D., & Bazerman, M.H. (2009). Goals gone wild: The systematic side effects of overprescribing goal setting. *Academy of Management Perspectives, 23*(1), 6–16.

Thomas, David A. (2001). The truth about mentoring minorities: Race matters. *Harvard Business Review, 79*(4), 98–112.

14

Emergent Goals in Mentoring and Coaching

Laura Gail Lunsford

Summary

Good mentors and coaches enable their mentees and clients to reflect, discover and learn. Goals are central to this process and provide the momentum for the development of the relationship. Researchers have made progress in understanding motivation and its connection to goal setting. This work has practical applications for mentors and coaches who wish to develop high-quality relationships.

This chapter reviews advances in understanding how goals emerge in mentoring and coaching relationships. First, the chapter analyzes how these relationships are distinguished by their focus on goals. The research on motivation and goal setting is reviewed next, including the origin of goals, how beliefs about learning influence goals, and the types of goals that characterize successful relationships. A system for charting goal progress is then presented. The chapter concludes with practical suggestions for mentors and coaches to use in their practice.

Relationships with Goals

The chapter begins by defining the unique functions of mentoring and coaching relationships and by reviewing the findings on goal emergence. This discussion sets the stage for consideration of the following questions. When do goals emerge in relationships? What motivates individuals to set goals? How can emerging goals be specific yet flexible enough to meet client needs?

How challenging should goals be to maximize individual performance? What are the elements of goal setting that are important in measuring progress? The chapter concludes with practical applications for mentors and coaches.

FUNCTIONS OF MENTOR AND COACHING RELATIONSHIPS

A relationship, perhaps even a close one, is what most individuals think about when seeking a mentor or coach. Some practitioners treat mentoring and coaching as comparable terms, although researchers report differences between coaching and mentoring relationships; refer to D'Abate, Eddy, and Tannenbaum, (2003) for a full discussion. However, these relationships are treated interchangeably in this chapter because goal emergence is similar in mentoring and coaching relationships.

Mentoring and coaching relationships provide three kinds of support. First, there is an appeal to having a trusted and knowledgeable 'other' to look out for you and to be your advocate. In fact, receiving encouragement and praise has been rated as one of the most important functions of mentoring relationships (Torrance, 1984). Second, mentoring and coaching relationships focus on professional development, also known as instrumental support. Therefore, it should not be surprising that goal-directed activities are important aspects of these relationships (Padilla, 2010). Mentoring and coaching relationships develop because of a desire of one or both individuals to develop a skill, usually in a vocation—although it might be in an avocation. This skill development is the shared purpose around which both individuals engage. More recently, a consideration of the relationship quality is reflected in a proposed third function of mentoring relationships known as the development of high-quality interactions (Stephens and Dutton, 2012). Therefore, mentoring and coaching relationships can be characterized as providing three kinds of support: psychosocial, instrumental, and positive interactions. Psychosocial support involves trust and listening; instrumental support involves sponsorship and learning professional skills; and the quality of that support relates to positive interactions. Providing instrumental support, which is goal-oriented by definition, is what differentiates a mentor or coach from a friend. Thus, while goals are rarely mentioned in the research or popular literature, it is in fact goals that move the relationship forward.

GOAL EMERGENCE THEORY

It is helpful to first understand how goals emerge more generally. There appear to be two systems of thinking in the brain (Kahneman, 2003), both of which regulate goals. Kahneman calls them system 1 and system 2. Most goal pursuits are unconsciously influenced by environmental and social cues. These goals are under control of system 1, our intuitive and automatic thinking. Aarts (2007) provides a good review of this work, with illustrative scenarios. For example, you may aim to drive to work (goal) and getting in the car (environmental cue) automatically triggers your knowing the route to drive (unconscious habit). Social contagion is an example of how goals are unconsciously influenced by social cues. It has been demonstrated that people are influenced by the goals of individuals in their social group. For example, individuals were found to select more competitive responses when they were exposed to short videos of competitive behavior (Loersch, Aarts, Payne, and Jefferis, 2008).

Despite the research above, most people think of goals as self-directed activities, which implies conscious control. Engaging in reflective thinking and self-direction is a feature of system 2. Mentors and coaches engage in reflection with mentees and clients to activate system 2 thinking. It could be argued that system 2 thinking is needed for goals to emerge in mentoring and coaching.

When do goals emerge in mentoring and coaching relationships? Mentoring doyen Kathy Kram was one of the early researchers to raise the importance of goals in mentoring relationships. Kram suggested that relationships unfold in four stages (Kram, 1985). Individuals learn about one another in the first stage, initiation. Goals emerge in the second stage, cultivation, when the main work of the relationship is completed. Termination and redefinition are the third and fourth stages, which refer to how the relationships end and are redefined into collegial or other types of relationships.

A motivated mentee or mentor may have a list of goals at the outset of the relationship. However, it is more often the case that individuals have a broad sense of their aims and aspirations but are not sure how to achieve them. An important function of mentors and coaches, during the initiation of the relationship, is to promote system 2 thinking through active listening and reflective inquiry. This work sets the expectations for goals to emerge naturally in the second stage of the relationship, cultivation. The value a mentor or coach brings to the relationship is to help clients achieve their goals more efficiently than they might on their own. For example, mentors might reduce the time individuals spend on nonproductive activities or ways of thinking. Coaches might help clients set more realistic goals to achieve. Thus, mentors and coaches help shape client goals as they become apparent at the outset of the cultivation stage of the relationship.

WHOSE GOALS?

Practitioners and researchers usually focus on the goals of the mentee or client. However, mentors and coaches have goals of their own that may influence the relationship. These goals may relate to the mentors' learning goals, which involve reflection and learning (system 2 thinking). Mentors and coaches also draw upon experience, which may unconsciously (system 1 thinking) influence goals they may inadvertently have about a mentees' skills and capabilities. The best relationships are those where the goals and beliefs of mentors and clients are explicit and align. Difficulty or dysfunction in the relationship often arises from a mismatch in goals. Therefore, it is important to understand both the motivations that lead to the goals individuals might have and how these goals relate to developing productive relationships.

Mentors and coaches in formal programs, who have input in the matching process, are more likely to have goals that align with the mentee's goals (Parise and Forret, 2008). A frank discussion of goals is important at the outset, or initiation stage, of the relationship. For example, the mentee or coach might ask the mentee or client how he or she will be different in 3, 6, or 12 months as a result of engaging in this relationship. Mentors and coaches might also consider their own learning goals as part of their reflective practice.

ORIGIN OF GOALS

Adult development theory provides a framework for understanding the motivations individuals might have for engaging in mentoring and coaching relationships (Lunsford, 2011a). Eric Erikson first recognized human development did not stop after childhood; adults continue to develop throughout their lifetime. Individuals face predictable crises, which must be successfully resolved at predictable stages for healthy psychological development (Erikson, 1963).

Three of these stages, identity, intimacy, and generativity, occur during adulthood when individuals engage in mentoring and coaching. These stages suggest what motivates individuals to engage in mentoring and coaching relationships. During early adulthood individuals are establishing their identity. Thus, their needs may revolve around selecting a career and a profession. In the last decade researchers have added a new stage to Erikson's theory called youthhood (Côte, 2000). Youthhood is characterized by a prolonged period during which young adults may lack career aspirations and delay establishing an identity and other personal and professional commitments. The next stage is intimacy versus isolation. During this period individuals seek life partners, start families, or otherwise seek close relationships outside of their family of origin. This stage may be most important for women (Josselson, 1988), who often establish their identity through their relationships with others. The last stage is generativity versus stagnation. During this stage individuals seek to leave a legacy or to give back to society and family.

It is possible for individuals to revisit the stages as they move through their lives when they experience major life changes. For example, a person may have successfully established a sense of identity. However, a job change may motivate a 35-year-old woman to revisit her professional identity to seek new opportunities in her new organization. A mentor or coach may be needed when an individual experiences such a transition because there may be a need for the person to establish a sense of professional identity in the new context. Transitional periods may provide a window when a mentor or coach may have the most influence.

Mentee/client goals

The age and related developmental stage of the mentee or client may provide insight into the kind of goals he or she may have. For example, young adults at the beginning of their professional career may be more likely to have goals related to establishing themselves in a career. Furthermore, young adults may not be completely committed to their profession and a mentor or coach may help clients make important decisions about their career. A mentee who has established a career may have professional needs around skill development. Psychosocial developmental theory also suggests that women may feel more isolated if they do not have a close network of support (Levinson and Levinson, 1996). Mentors and coaches may be able to assist women in establishing a network of support to achieve their goals.

Mentor/coach goals

Mentors and coaches have motivations for engaging in relationships and their life stage may reveal their motivations. Mentors, who are expected to develop others as a way to advance their own careers, might be establishing their professional identity. Mentors and coaches may want to leave a legacy (Cho, Ramanan, and Feldman, 2011). These individuals are motivated because they are in the stage of generativity (Erikson, 1963), with a desire to give back to a younger generation.

GOAL MINDSETS

Individuals may have a strong sense about the kinds of goals they hope to pursue or they may have vague notions of how to achieve ambiguous goals. Beliefs about learning influence how goals emerge. Researchers (Godshalk and Sosik, 2003) can reliably sort these beliefs into two categories that Dweck (2006a) refers to as a fixed mindset or growth mindset. People who like to do tasks in which they excel, feel good only if they 'win', or who focus exclusively on outcomes have a fixed mindset. Individuals who focus on effort, enjoy learning new skills, or feel good when doing a novel and difficult task have a growth mindset. Individuals with a growth mindset are interested in the outcome, but they measure their success or failure according to their effort. A mentee's or client's mindset will influence their ability to set goals and achieve them.

Dweck's (2006a) work has revealed interesting differences in how individuals view the world and relationships. People with a fixed mindset often blame others for their failure, which presents challenges in close relationships, like mentoring or coaching ones. A person with a fixed mindset focuses on success, and needs to explain failure. In contrast, individuals with a growth mindset experience failure as a learning opportunity.

Mentors and coaches can determine their client's mindset. Individuals who make comments such as, "I love a challenge" or, "You know I was hoping this would be informative" have a growth mindset (Dweck, 2006b). In contrast, individuals who make comments such as, "I might look foolish if I try this" have a fixed mindset.

Mentors and coaches can assess clients' beliefs by asking clients if they agree or not with the following statements, developed by Dweck (2006b). Individuals with a fixed mindset agree with these statements.

1. Your intelligence is something very basic about you that you can't change.

2. You can learn new things but you can't change how smart you are.

What does all of this have to do with mentoring and coaching relationships? These beliefs may place clients on two, diverging trajectories in the relationship. First, mentees with a growth mindset will be more likely to experience personal and professional growth in mentoring and coaching relationships than clients with a fixed mindset. A growth mindset helps a client focus on achieving realistic goals and enables him or her to develop a track record of success, despite setbacks. Imagine that an individual fails to earn a coveted promotion but notes his or her hard work will prepare him or her for the next round of promotions. This client has learned from failure and is prepared to keep trying to reach his or her goals.

Second, compared to individuals with a growth mindset, clients with a fixed mindset do well if their goals are met, but fare poorly when they encounter difficulty. Individuals with a fixed mindset struggle to overcome setbacks and seek to blame others. They believe that goals are 'all or nothing', which makes it difficult to identify small steps that lead to goal achievement. Furthermore, a fixed mindset may have unintended consequences that involve cheating or taking unethical shortcuts to achieve the goal. Individuals with a fixed mindset are more likely to overestimate their progress and lie about their achievements (Dweck, 2006a).

Researchers are just beginning to examine goal orientation in the context of mentoring and coaching relationships. Individuals with mentors are more likely to have a growth mindset (Lunsford, 2011b). Furthermore, there is evidence that mentors can change their mentee's goal orientation from a performance mindset to a growth mindset (Schultz et al., 2011). Thus, research suggests that mentors and coaches should focus on promoting a growth mindset in mentees and clients (Seijts, Latham, Tasa, and Latham, 2004), especially if the mentees and clients are novices in the area in which they have goals. Recent work indicates that mentees and clients perform better when both the client and the mentor or coach have a learning goal orientation, or growth mindset (Egan, 2005).

SELECTING CHALLENGING GOALS

The skill a mentor or coach brings to the relationship is in helping mentees or clients set appropriately challenging goals. Clients who pledge, "to do my best" are not likely to experience good performance. Hundreds of studies show that people who set specific goals perform better (Seijts, 2004) than individuals who have vague goals like "I will do my best." The research on goal difficulty and goal achievement shows the best goals have an appropriate level of challenge.

Avoid too easy or too difficult

Mentors and coaches can help clients avoid setting goals that are too easy or too difficult. Clients who have a tendency to set these kinds of goals may have a fixed mindset. Setting goals that are too easy may result in boredom on the part of the client, who then may fail to exert sufficient effort to achieve those goals. Individuals who set goals that are too difficult have an excuse for not achieving goals. When these individuals fail to reach their goals they make statements such as, "I always knew that goal was going to be too challenging; no one could realistically be expected to achieve that goal."

If a client develops a habit of setting goals that are too difficult, he or she may develop learned helplessness (Seligman, 2011). Learned helplessness is characterized by failure to exert effort because an individual has come to believe his or her effort will have no influence on the outcome. Goals that are too difficult may also result in stress. Clients with a history of setting difficult and stressful goals may experience chronic stress, which is associated with poor psychological and medical outcomes (Thoits, 2010).

Just right goals

Weick (1984) first identified a psychology of small wins, and this perspective has been connected to leading and mentoring (Friedman, 2008). Individuals should focus on moderate, versus big, outcomes when setting goals. The mentee or client will build confidence as he or she makes progress in achieving small, but important goals. Individuals who review a trajectory of success with a mentor or coach will be more successful in achieving future goals. Setting small goals also reduces stress, which increases performance.

The concept of flow is related to the psychology of small wins. Renowned psychologist Csikszentmihalyi conducted pioneering work to discover a 'flow' state (1990). A flow state is more likely to occur when individuals have a skill set that matches the challenge before them. An individual engages in optimal performance when experiencing flow. For example, employees may experience flow when they take on a new task that is somewhat different and a little more challenging than prior work. Flow states are associated with psychological health and optimal performance. Mentors and coaches can assist mentees and clients to set goals that will allow them to achieve flow.

CHARTING GOAL PROGRESS

Individuals are drawn to mentoring and coaching relationships because they wish to develop personal or professional skills. Goal emergence is a process rather than a product. That is, goals need to be reviewed and reassessed during the relationship. The first step, as described above, for mentors and coaches is to work with mentees and clients to set small goals that reflect a growth mindset. The next step involves describing goals using specific behaviors. A focus on behaviors sets up a feedback loop for mentees and clients to chart their progress.

Helping clients to focus on specific behaviors can be challenging. However, mentors and coaches can assist their clients in learning this skill. There are several successful strategies that can be used; only one such technique will be reviewed here. An effective technique is setting SMART goals (see Table 14.1). SMART stands for specific, measurable, actionable, realistic, and timely. There are different words that match up with SMART (Latham, 2004) but the words have a similar intent.

Using a system like SMART goals can help mentors and coaches improve client performance, even if the client has a fixed mindset, during the cultivation stage of the relationship. As noted above, individuals with a growth mindset are more likely to achieve their goals. However, individuals who have a fixed mindset will perform better if they set specific goals, rather than vague ones (Seijts, et al., 2004).

Table 14.1   SMART goals

Goal element	Description
Specific	Identifies the behavior
Measurable	Includes a metric—frequency, time
Attainable	Challenging but possible
Realistic	Builds on a baseline
Timely	Appropriate

Specific

Good goals are specific and refer to behaviors. For example, a client may describe a non-specific goal by stating she wishes to write more efficiently. However, it is not clear what she will write. The writing goal could be stated more specifically by stating, "I will write more efficiently by outlining my work first and then writing a draft, which I will edit the following day." Specificity enables the client to focus on the behavior related to goal achievement.

Measurable

Measurable goals involve a metric. How much effort will be involved or how often or long will a client engage in an activity? An individual may use time, e.g. an hour a day, or an amount, e.g. a pound a week, a page a day. Individuals focus on completing the behaviors that are measured. Therefore, establishing how progress on a goal will be measured is important. The caveat is to watch out for making the measurement too small; which becomes burdensome to track.

Attainable

A client might have a goal of being an astronaut, which is specific but may be unrealistic if the client does not meet eligibility requirements, e.g. age or vision. Attainable goals rely on a client having access to personal and professional resources needed to achieve the goal. For example, running a marathon might not be an attainable goal in three months if a client is not fit and has never run.

Realistic

A realistic goal refers to the difficulty or challenge of the goal, and if the goal is possible in the stated time frame. Realistic goals build on prior achievement. A goal to make 15 new sales contacts in the next week when the mentee has made no sales contacts in the last two months is not realistic. Establishing a baseline of a mentee's or client's current performance is an important element in setting realistic goals.

Timely

A timely goal refers to how appropriate the goal is in relation to the overarching aspirations of the mentee or client. A goal to earn a promotion in six months, when a client just started a new position, may not be timely if the organization promotes on a one or two year time frame. Timely goals align the client's aims with their developmental cycle in their personal and professional lives.

GOALS EVOLVE

Goals will and should change and evolve during a mentoring or coaching relationship. Mentors and coaches might set aside time at regular intervals to review and adjust mentees' and clients' goals and priorities. Mentee motivations might change, which will influence their goals and their need for continued mentoring or coaching. It is important to establish an end point where both parties can reflect on successful achievement and transition to redefining the relationship, Kram's (1985) fourth and last stage of mentoring relationships.

Contributions

Expert mentors and coaches recognize how goals emerge in relationships with mentees and clients. This chapter presents research that points to the importance of understanding developmental needs, motivations, and mindsets of clients. There are individual differences in individuals' proclivity to set goals or to even engage in mentoring and coaching relationships. However, mentoring and coaching relationships develop around setting and achieving goals. Goals are tightly integrated with mentee and client beliefs about learning. Mentors and coaches can use this information during the initiation stage of relationships to enable mentees and clients to describe their highest purpose and vision. The role of the mentor or coach is to help the mentee or client to set small, measurable goals, using a growth mindset. The relationship can then unfold around meeting goals and setting new ones.

This perspective makes three contributions to practice for mentors and coaches. First, understanding goal motivation suggests that mentors as well as clients may have goals. It is important to reflect on how mentor and mentee goals emerge and align with clients' developmental needs. Second, clients' beliefs about learning—their mindset—can dramatically influence the success of the relationship. Mentors and coaches have new tools to assess their clients' mindsets and help clients move to a growth mindset. Finally, setting goals is complex. Encouraging clients to focus on SMART goals, with an emphasis on behaviors, is more likely to improve performance.

In Practice

Mentors or coaches can use this research on goal emergence to maximize their relationships with their mentees or clients in three ways. First, the mentors or coaches should begin the relationship by discussing the motivations driving mentee or client goals. For example, mentors might assess the developmental needs of their mentees and discuss the mentee's goals in this context. Second, mentors or coaches might assess their mentees or clients' beliefs about their goals and cultivate a growth mindset. Third, mentors and coaches can enable clients to set 'flow' goals that are 'SMART'. This practice will enable mentees to experience feedback that will sustain their efforts to achieve their goals. Feedback loops enable mentors or coaches to support the client if he or she is not making the desired progress.

Reflection Questions

- How can mentors and coaches activate their mentees' or clients' system 2 (reflective) thinking during the initiation stage of the relationship?

- What kinds of goals would be appropriate for mentors and coaches to have for their own learning?

- How can mentors and coaches promote a growth mindset?

- When might SMART goals be problematic?

- What is the best way to initiate a conversation to invite goal sharing by both mentors/coaches and mentees/clients?

References

Aarts, H. (2007). On the emergence of human goal pursuit: The nonconscious regulation and motivation of goals. *Social and Personality Psychology Compass*, 1(1), 183–201. doi: 10.1111/j.1751-9004.2007.00014.x

Cho, C.S., Ramanan, R.A., & Feldman, M.D. (2011). Defining the ideal qualities of mentorship: A qualitative analysis of the characteristics of outstanding mentors. *The American Journal of Medicine, 124*, 453–8.

Csikszentmihalyi, M. (1990). *Flow: The Psychology of Optimal Experience*. New York: Harper & Row.

Côte, J.E. (2000). *Arrested Adulthood: the Changing Nature of Maturity and Identity*. New York: New York University Press.

D'Abate, C.P., Eddy, E.R., & Tannenbaum, S.I. (2003). What's in a name? A literature-based approach to understanding mentoring, coaching, and other constructs that describe developmental interactions. *Human Resource Development Review, 2*(3), 360. doi: 10.1177/1534484303255033

Dweck, C. (2006a). *Mindset: The New Psychology of Success*. New York: Ballantine Books.

Dweck, C. (2006b). Tech Nation Interview. Available at: http://itc. conversationsnetwork.org/shows/detail1011.html# [accessed May 1, 2012].

Egan, T.M. (2005). The impact of learning goal orientation similarity on formal mentoring relationship outcomes. *Advances in Developing Human Resources*, 7(4), 489–504.

Erikson, E. (1963). *Childhood and Society*. (2nd Ed., Rev. & Enl.). New York: Norton.

Friedman, S.D. (2008). Be a Better Leader, Have a Richer Life. *Harvard Business Review, 86*(4), 112–18.

Godshalk, V.M. & Sosik, J.J. (2003). Aiming for career success: The role of learning goal orientation in mentoring relationships. *Journal of Vocational Behavior, 63*, 417–37.

Josselson, R. (1988). *Finding Herself*. San Franciso: Jossey-Bass, Inc.

Kahneman, D. (2003). A perspective on judgment and choice: Mapping bounded rationality. *American Psychologist, 58*(9), 697–720. doi: 10.1037/0003-066X.58.9.697.

Kram, K.E. (1985). *Mentoring at Work: Developmental Relationships in Organizational Life*. Glenview, Il: Scott, Foresman and Company.

Latham, G. (2004). Motivate employee performance through goal-setting, in *The Blackwell Handbook of Principles of Organizational Behavior*, edited by E.A. Locke. 107–19. Malden, MA: Blackwell Publishing Ltd.

Loersch, C., Aarts, H., Payne, B.K., & Jefferis, V.E. (2008). The influence of social groups on goal contagion. *Journal of Experimental Psychology, 44*, 1555–58. doi: 10.1016/j.jesp.2008.07.009

Lunsford, L.G. (2011a). Psychology of mentoring: The case of talented college students. *Journal of Advanced Academics, 89*, 127–36.

Lunsford, L.G. (2011b). *Development of the Arizona Mentoring Inventory*, Mentoring Institute, University of New Mexico, Albuquerque, 26–28 October 2011.

Padilla, A., Mulvey, P.W., & Lunsford, L.G. (2010). Public leadership in *The Organizational Contexts of Public Leadership*, edited by J.A. Rameriz. 121–40. Hauppauge, NY: Nova Science Publishers.

Parise, M.R. & Forret, M.L. (2008). Formal mentoring programs: The relationship of program design and support to mentors' perceptions of benefits and costs. *Journal of Vocational Behavior, 72*, 225–40.

Schultz, P.W., Hernandez, P.R., Woodcock, A., Estrada, M., & Chance, R.C. (2011). Patching the pipeline: Reducing educational disparities in the sciences through minority training programs. *Educational Evaluation and Policy Analysis, 33*(1), 95–114.

Seijts, G.H., Latham, G.P., Tasa, K., & Latham, B.W. (2004). Goal setting and goal orientation: an integration of two different yet related literatures. *Academy of Management Journal, 47*(2), 227–39.

Seligman, M.E. (2011). *Learned Optimism: How to Change Your Mind and Your Life.* New York: Pocket Books.

Stephens, J.P., Heaphy, E., & Dutton, J.E. (2012). High-quality connections in *The Oxford Handbook of Positive Organizational Scholarship,* edited by K.S. Cameron & G.M. Spreitzer. 385–99. New York: Oxford Press.

Thoits, P.A. (2010). Stress and health: Major findings and policy implications. *Journal of Health and Social Behavior, 51*(1), S41–S53.

Torrance, E.P. (1984). *Mentor Relationships: How They Aid Creative Achievement, Endure, Change, and Die.* New York: Brealy Limited.

Weick, K.E. (1984). Small wins: Redefining the scale of social problems. *American Psychologist, 39*(1), 40–49.

15

Goal Setting in a Layered Relationship Mentoring Model

Maggie Clarke and Sarah Powell

Mentoring is not confined to one type or form of relationship and each type of mentoring can have its place in various contexts and different organizations (Haynes and Petrosko, 2009). This chapter seeks to provide some practical insight into a layered approach to informal mentoring by reflecting on the experiences of the authors—a Mentor and Protégé—in the context of a Layered Relationship Mentoring Model. It also considers the place and importance of setting and pursuing goals in the context of the mentoring relationship.

The research literature has primarily focused on formal mentoring programs within organizations. These programs are purposefully developed, monitored and evaluated by the management of the organization (Barrera, Braley, and Slate, 2010; Horvath, Wasko, and Bradley, 2008; Mullen and Hutinger, 2008), are generally designed for a predetermined length of time, and are of short duration (Parise and Forret, 2008). Within formal mentoring programs there are a number of approaches used in organizations to allocate the mentor. These approaches range from self-selection to appointment of the mentor by the organization. Organizational expectations of the protégé are developed through strategies such as formal goal setting and goal attainment. The goals are often set in relation to the organization's key performance areas and the protégé's success is then measured according to key performance indicators developed by the organization. Personal career goals may also be part of the formal mentoring program with the protégé mapping a career consistent with the organization's goals and strategic directions (Dobie, Smith, and Robins, 2010; Ewing, Freeman, Barrie, Bell, O'Connor, Waugh, and Sykes, 2008).

There is recognition that, in the context of the formal mentoring relationship, discrepancies between the goals of the protégé and those of the mentor can arise. Kim (2007) suggests that this comes as a result of the potentially "superficial" (p. 183) nature of the relationship, which can limit the freedom of communication between the mentor and protégé. A consequence of the inequality of status associated with a hierarchical relationship in a formal mentoring relationship is that communication between mentor and protégé can be one-way, however, in modern mentoring programs this is hardly ever the case. Early formal mentoring relationships saw the mentor direct and drive the communication downwards with little opportunity for the protégé to have input or respond to the communication from the mentor. The one-way communication in those formal mentoring relationships resulted in the protégé being unable to "connect" with the mentor (Searby, 2009; Parise and Forret, 2008; Barrera, Braley, and Slate 2010; Dobie, Smith, and Robins, 2010; Holmes, Land, and Hinton-Hudson, 2007). However, Rolfe (2012) and MacGregor (2000) would argue that modern organizations using formal mentoring utilize programs that are based on facilitated mentoring and building relationships.

To overcome this discrepancy of one-way communication, Sorrentino (2006) emphasizes the importance of co-constructing goals in a "collaborative process" (p. 242) even in the context of the traditional or formal mentoring style, and suggests that the success of the mentoring relationship is attributed to setting goals which are "specific, tailored, challenging, and attainable" (p. 242). Zachary and Fischler (2011) confirm the importance of the "goal-driven mentoring relationship" (p. 51). They describe a process of setting SMART goals based on the answers to specific questions related to personal and professional aspirations, development, direction and interest. By constructing goals together, both mentor and protégé assume responsibility for and commitment to pursuing these goals. The co-construction of goals is discussed further in the Layered Relationship Mentoring Model.

Unlike formal mentoring, informal mentoring relationships are spontaneously formed as a result of people getting to know each other in the work environment. The relationship is usually voluntary, based on mutual professional identity and respect (Singh, Ragins, and Tharenou, 2009), and is more personal in nature. Mentors in informal mentoring relationships provide direction, support and insight (Duncan and Stock, 2010). Essentially they provide "their protégés with a sense of what they are becoming" (Debolt, 1992: 30). Opportunities for recognition, encouragement, feedback, advice on balancing responsibilities, and knowledge of the informal rules of the organization have been cited in the literature as some of the benefits of informal mentoring (Kerka, 1998; Schwiebert, 2000). In their research Ragins and Cotton (1999) discuss personally-based strategies such as coaching, counseling, role modeling and providing friendship as being beneficial in informal mentoring.

Goal setting and goal attainment, although usually present in informal mentoring, is not conducted in any formal manner. It occurs through informal conversations and often serendipitously. Often informal professional relationships occur in organizations as people seek out others who may have similar goals to themselves. Murphy and Kram's research on mentor networks suggests that there is conscious or unconscious selection of a mentor by the protégé based on conscious or unconscious goal-focus (Murphy and Kram, 2010). The essence of informal mentoring is the establishment of beneficial interpersonal relationships based upon effective communication (Kerka, 1998; Trask, Marotz-Baden, Settle, Gentry, and Berke, 2009). Communication flows from the mentor to the protégé (and vice-versa) but the communication occurs in a more informal manner. The mentor's communication is usually in the form of support, guidance and advice (Haynes and Petrosko, 2009). Perna and Lerner (1995) concluded from their research that differences in effectiveness between formal and informal mentoring could be due to differences in the structure of the relationships. The pairing in an informal mentoring relationship is often the result of both the mentor and the protégé selecting personal qualities that mirror the qualities they would like to emulate. The informal mentoring relationship can offer both the mentor and the mentee the opportunity to select each other, an aspect not always present in formal mentoring programs. Kim (2007) supports this self-selection process and suggests that incompatibility in formal mentoring relationships which do not allow selection of mentors by the protégé can be detrimental to the mentoring relationship. This has further ramifications for the conceiving and setting of goals, and subsequently, for the pursuing and realizing of those goals, as the purpose of the relationship is not the same for both participants. Ragins and Cotton (1999) also indicate that formal mentoring programs often last less than a year whereas informal mentoring relationships can last for many years allowing for a personal connection to develop between the mentor and protégé.

Evidence from the literature indicates that there are fewer limitations in informal mentoring than formal mentoring. Ragins and Cotton (1999) found in their research that the benefits of informal mentoring were many. The two major areas of difference between formal and informal mentoring were in the levels of career guidance and psychosocial support. Informal mentors provided a higher level of coaching and increased the protégé's visibility in the organization. They also provided counseling, social interaction, role modeling and friendship. More recent research has challenged views of informal and formal mentoring and discusses the need to study the effects of both the negative and positive features of the mentoring relationship as experienced by mentors and protégés (Eby, Butts, Durley, and Ragins, 2010; Burk and Eby, 2010; Kim, 2007). Eby et al. (2010) studied the relative effect that positive and negative mentoring experiences had on mentor and protégé outcomes in the context of the workplace. The focus was on subjective aspects, such as perceptions regarding the quality of the relationship, and well-being. The critical factor in the success of both informal and formal mentoring was the quality of the relationship. It must however be noted that these models of mentoring studied were undertaken in specific cultural contexts. Kim (2007) suggests that the majority of research surrounding mentoring has focused on the benefits of the relationship for the protégé and therefore advocates the need for further research on the benefits to mentors. In addition, Kim (2007) advocates that a more deliberate approach to mentoring is required in order to capitalize on the mentoring opportunity. At present "few conceptual models" (p. 183) exist. The Layered Relationship Mentoring Model confronts these issues by providing a conceptual model based on a mutually beneficial relationship and friendship, a sense of equality and a natural 'matching' of mentor with protégé.

Mentors have been defined as guides (Bey and Holmes, 1992), counselors or coaches and role models (Crow and Mathews, 1998). These definitions describe mentoring as a one-way relationship. In their book *Women, mentors, and success,* Jeruchim and Shapiro (1992) presented a different view of mentoring, defining it as, "a complementary relationship, within an organizational or professional context, built on both the mentor's and the protégé's need" (Jeruchim and Shapiro, 1992, p. 23).

Following Jeruchim and Shapiro's work, the literature began to report this kind of relationship as co-mentoring (Jipson and Paley, 2000; Mullen, 2000; Kochan and Trimble, 2000). Mentoring was described as encompassing a mutual and beneficial relationship between the mentor and protégé (Megginson, Clutterbuck, Garvey, Stokes, and Garret-Harris, 2006; Clutterbuck, 2008; Megginson, 2000). Terms such as "mutual mentoring" (Fritzberg and Alemayehu, 2004), "synergistic mentoring" (Goodwin, 2004) and "reciprocal mentoring" (Gabriel and Kaufield, 2008) have been used interchangeably in the literature to describe the practice of co-mentoring. Co-mentoring recognizes the contribution that each person brings to the relationship and is based on reciprocal benefit (Holmes, Land, and Hinton-Hudson, 2007; Griffin and Beatty, 2010). In this relationship the status and role of each person is equal and the communication pathway is one of reciprocity, with each person mutually benefiting from the relationship. Mullen (2000) defined the co-mentoring relationship as synergistic. She viewed it as providing opportunities to be involved in each other's learning by sharing purpose and commitment in common projects. A number of other writers including Jipson and Paley (2000) and Kochan and Trimble (2000) documented their personal co-mentoring experiences. In their stories they discussed how these experiences were mutually beneficial. Their discussions were based on collaboration and shared decision-making. The ability to collaborate and share was seen as providing opportunities to strengthen personal and professional skills.

Rymer (2002) further discussed two essential components necessary for a successful co-mentoring relationship. The relationship should be a friendship of peers rather than a hierarchical relationship, and communication should be dialogue rather than the transmission of organizational information. The co-mentoring relationship serves the individual needs of each person involved. Within the relationship the individuals act as partners, often complementing each other's knowledge and skills. The co-mentors may be different ages and have different expertise, skills and knowledge, but what is important in this type of mentoring relationship is that it is of mutual benefit.

Table 15.1 provides examples of characteristics of each type of mentoring. Examples of characteristics of design, allocation, selection, goal setting and monitoring processes, communication, status, type of relationship, commitment and connection of mentors and protégés are drawn together in this table to illustrate the differences and similarities of each of the types of mentoring (Clarke, 2004).

Table 15.1   Examples of characteristics of types of mentoring relationships

Characteristic	Formal mentoring	Informal mentoring	Co-mentoring
Design structure	Pre-determined length of time in the relationship	Often relationships last for an extended period of time	Often relationships last for an extended period of time
Allocation of protégé to the mentor	Often allocated by the management of the organization	Usually emerges spontaneously	Based on each other's complementary knowledge and skills
Selection process	Little or no involvement of staff in the selection of mentor to protégé	Voluntary, often based on mutual professional identity and respect	Friendship of peers
Goal setting	Individual goals identified and pursued	Individual and co-constructed goals identified and pursued	Individual and co-constructed goals identified and pursued
Monitoring procedures	Monitored in terms of expectations and goal attainment	No formal monitoring although individual and co-constructed goals may be set	No formal monitoring although individual and co-constructed goals may be set
Communication	One-way communication from mentor to protégé	Communication takes place in an informal manner	Dialogue occurs
Status of each person in the relationship	Inequality of status	Still a hierarchical status but communication less formal	Equal status
Type of relationship	Non-reciprocal	Reciprocal benefit	Reciprocal benefit
Mentor connection with protégé	Sometimes lack of connection occurs	More personal connection of protégé to mentor through coaching, counseling and role modeling strategies	Individuals act as partners complementing each other's knowledge and skills
Commitment to the mentoring program	May not always be committed to each other or to the program	Self-selection based on personal and professional qualities	Mutual benefit gained from the relationship

As our experiences with mentoring develop and evolve in contemporary workplaces so too will the types of mentoring processes change and develop. One such evolutionary model of mentoring is described in the following case study. Within this model two forms of mentoring are apparent, these being informal mentoring and co-mentoring. The case study draws on a Layered Relationship Mentoring Model and discusses the characteristics that are part of the process and the outcomes that result from the mentoring relationship.

What is unique to this layered relationship model of mentoring is that it is conceptualized as a series of three overlapping layers and experiences (Clarke, 2004). These layers have been identified as:

- Collegial Friendship

- Informal Mentoring and

- Co-mentoring.

They are not separate layers but rather the mentoring relationship and its characteristics move between these overlapping layers as indicated in Figure 15.1. There is no distinct break between each layer but rather the process merges one layer into the other.

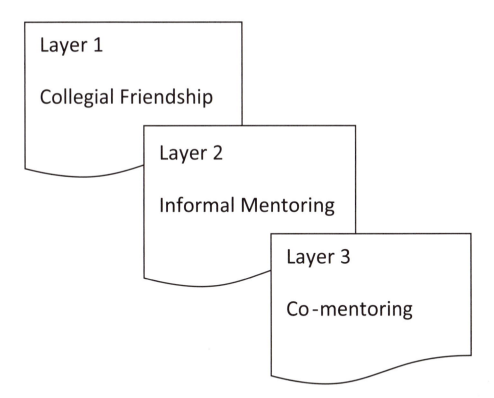

Figure 15.1   Layered Relationship Mentoring Model

In Layer 1, *Collegial Friendship* forms the basis of the professional relationship. The focus of this layer of the mentoring relationship is on the development of an interpersonal relationship with the mentor and the protégé. The characteristics of layer 1 in the initial study (Clarke, 2004) were identified as social meetings, protégé seeking advice, guidance and support of the mentor, project identification by the mentor and protégé involvement in project opportunities. The mentor and protégé operate in this layer as individuals. Long-term career goals may be discussed in this layer and can provide the direction and work of the protégé. Individual goals, short-term in nature, are identified and pursued in the collegial friendship layer.

The second layer, the *Informal Mentoring Layer*, has as its focus the relationship between the mentor and protégé's interaction regarding the protégé's professional learning and development. For the protégé the characteristics of layer 2 are developing a positive feeling about work, progressing and affirming work and seeking guidance and support from the mentor. It is in this layer that goal identification becomes more significant for the protégé. Short-term goals related to the protégé's long-term goals are identified and can be both individually constructed or co-constructed with the mentor in this layer. The short-term goals that are pursued by the protégé in this layer are usually related to their identified long-term goals and provide direction for the achievement of their long-term goals.

Layer 3, the *Co-mentoring Layer*, develops as a result of the interpersonal dynamics of the relationship. The relationship becomes equal, with support and guidance being offered by each of the participants in the relationship. The focus in this layer of the relationship is on an equal partnership and the quality of the interaction. The characteristics of layer 3 for both of the partners are the development of a positive feeling about their work, identification of and involvement in project opportunities, and seeking guidance and support (from each other). It is in this layer that goal setting becomes more co-constructed, with each of the partners taking responsibility for achieving the identified goals. Although goal setting in this layer may normally be co-constructed, individual goals are also pursued by both partners in the mentoring relationship. These individual goals may be discussed with the other partner who provides support and encouragement but they are pursued individually in addition to the co-constructed goals. In this way, individually constructing and co-constructing goals provides opportunities to pursue both individual and group interests. Co-constructed goals are more readily conceived and pursued in layers 2 and 3 of the Layered Relationship Mentoring Model as the relationship develops, moving from an individual focus to a more mutual focus or equal relationship.

Figure 15.2 depicts the relationship of the goal setting process to the Layered Relationship Mentoring Model. A long-term perceived goal encompasses the whole mentoring process whereby the protégé identifies a long-term goal to achieve and this goal provides the direction and purpose throughout the three layers of the mentoring process. The projection of goals is conceived as either short-term or long-term. Short-term goals are usually identified and pursued by the protégé in layers 1 and 2 while the long-term goals, although identified earlier in the mentoring process, are not achieved until layer 3. The responsibility for goal setting in this model is identified as being either individual goal setting or co-constructed goal setting. Individual goals are identified and pursued by the protégé in layers 1 and 2. As the mentoring relationship develops, co-constructed goals are identified and achieved together by both the protégé and the mentor.

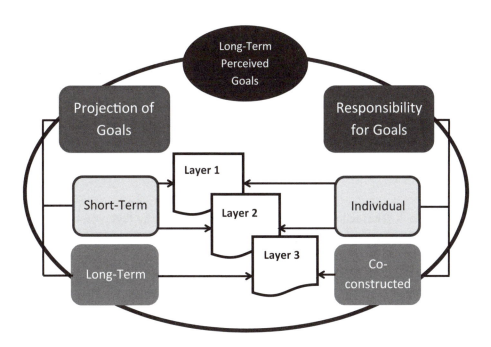

Figure 15.2   Goal setting and the Layered Relationship Mentoring Model

This case study is based on the mentoring process occurring between the authors, two academics at a metropolitan university in Sydney, Australia. One of the academics is a full-time academic and the other is a casual academic teaching in the same program at the university. In previous research (Clarke, 2004), the full-time academic was the protégé with another full-time colleague acting as mentor. In this research the former protégé is mentoring a casual academic. This supports the Layered Relationship Mentoring Model, providing the pathway for a protégé to develop into a mentor through their previous experience of being mentored. Both academics are female. One is newly appointed as a casual tutor and lecturer to Academia (Sarah, the protégé) and the other has been working in academia for fifteen years (Maggie, the mentor). The process began in February 2010.

The data for this case study was drawn from journal reflections by the academics. The two academics decided to keep journals on their professional relationship and these journals were written over a twelve month period. It was only after this twelve month period that the academics decided to analyze the journal reflections using the model developed by Clarke (2004) to test its applicability to a new mentoring relationship. The reflections are analyzed in terms of the identification of the characteristics of the Layered Relationship Mentoring Model using the examples of characteristics of types of mentoring relationships indicated in Table 15.1 and characteristics and outcomes of the layered model of mentoring indicated in Table 15.2.

Characteristics are apparent in each of the layers of the Layered Relationship Mentoring Model and specific outcomes are typical in each of the layers. These characteristics and outcomes in each of the layers are shown in Table 15.2.

Table 15.2   Characteristics and outcomes of each of the layers in the Layered Relationship Mentoring Model (Clarke, 2004)

CHARACTERISTICS	Collegial friendship layer	Informal mentoring layer	Co-mentoring layer
	Interpersonal relationship formed in the workplace	A safe haven is established for the protégé	Mutual guidance, support and encouragement is given
	Social meetings held	Guidance and support given by the mentor	An equal partnership is developed
	Conversations about work/research/life/ career self- management	Guidance is given by the mentor to assist with writing and research	Research and writing is undertaken collaboratively

CHARACTERISTICS	Collegial friendship layer	Informal mentoring layer	Co-mentoring layer
	Professional dialogues take place	Identification of work/ research opportunities for both partners (either separately or together)	Undertaking of collaborative writing and research
	Discussions about the "informal rules" of the organization	Affirmation of protégés work	Equal support provided to each other
	Encouragement given to the protégé	Encouragement given to the protégé	Encouragement given to each other
OUTCOMES	A network of friends is developed	Confidence building by the protégé	Own professional identity is developed by the protégé
	Common work/research interests discussed	Work progressed by the protégé	The mentor role is being phased out
	Friendship established	Trust developed by the protégé with the mentor	The protégé moves towards becoming a mentor for others

The Academic's (Mentor) Reflections

A collegial friendship was easily established with the protégé (as both Maggie and Sarah began teaching in the same unit at the University of Western Sydney). The relationship was "easy" with conversations focused on work and family. Social meetings were held off campus but usually had a work-related purpose.

Sarah's overarching long-term goal has been to establish herself in an academic career. With this communicated to Maggie in the early stage of their professional relationship Maggie has been quietly "shepherding" Sarah to develop the knowledge and skills required to achieve this goal. Some of Maggie's journal entries have identified short-term goals that Sarah needed to achieve in order to move her career forward in academia. In the early stages of the relationship Maggie identifies those tasks required to achieve Sarah's long-term goal. For example, Maggie writes:

> I will ask Sarah if she would like to co-ordinate a unit in the secondary program, this will provide her with a number of skills and experience required to apply for a full-time academic position. I am sure she will be more than capable of carrying out this responsibility. (Journal entry June 26, 2010)

Further journal entries from Maggie comment on the support given to Sarah. This has been in the form of conversations around teaching and pedagogy. Emotional support has been given providing advice on working with students and academics in the teaching team, and this has been given in both a formal and informal environment. In the workplace, support and advice is provided in a formal office environment, while at other times it is given "over coffee", either in the workplace or off-campus. Maggie writes:

> Sarah emailed me this morning and seemed concerned about a range of issues. I immediately rang her and asked her to meet me for coffee off-campus. Her email contained a long list of concerns ranging from not having resources to develop the lecture, student issues, staff issues ... She seemed like she just needed some guidance and a whole lot of support. (Journal entry September 1, 2010)

They were able to discuss her concerns away from the workplace in an environment where she felt comfortable talking. Sarah commented that she felt much better and that she had confidence to deal with the issues detailed in her email.

Maggie and Sarah's relationship merged into the informal mentoring layer over a period of time. Maggie provided professional learning and development opportunities for Sarah, a few of which included team teaching with Maggie, unit coordination of a newly developed unit and lecture responsibilities. Sarah's work was progressed, an outcome of layer 2 of the Layered Relationship Mentoring Model, by Maggie providing opportunities for Sarah to be involved in higher responsibilities than what is normally performed by a casual tutor.

Collaboration is also apparent in the journal entries providing evidence that the mentoring process is more than a one-way form of communication. Collaborative tasks were undertaken such as assessment tasks, development and rubrics for marking assessment. The journal entries discuss the guidance given by Maggie to Sarah in the early stage of the professional relationship.

Further analysis of Maggie's journal entries showed that her reflections revealed a number of supportive strategies used in the developing professional relationship. These strategies included nurturing collaboration and development of research and writing skills such as writing academic papers, characteristics of layer 2. Maggie writes:

Today, Sarah and I discussed the possibility of jointly preparing a conference paper that I would present at an international conference on our behalf. We began to develop the outline of the paper and the contribution each of us would make. Throughout our conversation I was able to provide Sarah with words of support regarding her ability to undertake this task. At the end of our discussion she said she felt comfortable to begin her writing. (Journal entry October 24, 2010)

These reflective statements identified the outcomes of the mentoring relationship and described the results of this relationship as providing trust and a critical friend to Sarah.

Sarah feels able to approach Maggie on both on a personal and work level. For Maggie, this is a sign that Sarah feels confident in asking for and receiving guidance and support. Maggie believes she has provided a "safe haven" for Sarah in her work life by providing opportunities to feel comfortable in her growth as an academic and in her collegial and professional relationship with Maggie.

These examples situate themselves in the informal mentoring layer. Providing a safe haven and affirmation of Sarah's work are indicative characteristics of this layer. Progressing work, uptake of new professional opportunities and development of confidence are typical outcomes achieved by the protégé in this layer.

As the relationship progressed, co-constructed goals were conceived and pursued. This occurred in layer 2. Collaborative writing for conferences and journal articles for publication are examples of co-constructed goals. At this stage of the relationship the protégé is moving toward a more equal partnership with the mentor. Both partners work together to achieve common and mutual goals.

To date, the relationship is in the first and second layer of the Layered Relationship Mentoring Model. Layer 1, the collegial friendship layer has been the initial phase in the relationship. In this phase, interpersonal interaction developed in a social environment in and outside the workplace. Maggie and Sarah met socially over coffee with conversations centered on their families, their work, their research and their teaching. Maggie's professional relationship with her colleague, Sarah, developed naturally because they taught in the same teaching unit. The mentoring relationship came together in an uncontrived way as Maggie was more experienced and guided Sarah in her first teaching position in a university. Sarah was enthusiastic and keen to learn. These characteristics and outcomes constitute the first layer of this mentoring relationship.

The Casual Academic's (Protégé) Reflections

When Sarah reflects on how the mentoring relationship between Maggie and herself began, it has been striking to see how naturally the elements of the model have manifested themselves. Maggie and Sarah began as work colleagues and effortlessly developed into friends. An important part of this process has been the setting of goals, and whilst these goals have been informally discussed, the focus has been the concrete end goal of Sarah establishing herself in an academic career. To pursue this end goal Maggie and Sarah's mentoring relationship has seen sub-goals develop. At present their mentoring relationship continues to develop through their ongoing professional collegiality, academic teaching commitments, and academic writing pursuits.

As a basis for structuring her reflections, Sarah has referred to a number of the key characteristics of the mentoring relationship, as outlined in Table 15.1.

Sarah's first contact with Maggie occurred a number of years ago when she was studying for a Master of Education degree. Maggie presented a session on leadership and mentoring, and as part of this subject, Sarah completed a small project in the school where she was teaching, focused on the mentoring model conceptualized by Maggie (Clarke, 2004).

It was not until another few years had elapsed that their paths crossed again, when it was suggested that Sarah contact Maggie to commence casual academic work. By this stage, Sarah's goal was to develop an academic career and so it seemed that this was a logical step to take. That first year of academic work formed the basis of what was to follow. By the beginning of the second year of working as a casual academic, the mentoring relationship between Maggie and Sarah was firmly established. It was at this point that Maggie asked Sarah if she saw herself pursuing a career in academia. This presented Sarah with the ideal opportunity to communicate and establish her goals in conversation with Maggie and subsequently led to many discussions on how this goal would be pursued and, ultimately, achieved.

Elements of an interpersonal relationship developed in that first year and match the characteristics and outcomes of the *Collegial Friendship Layer*, as described in Table 15.2 of the Layered Relationship Mentoring Model. This includes Sarah becoming established in the work environment, developing an understanding of workplace procedures and forming the foundations of a network of colleagues. Other relevant aspects are also described in Table 15.1

which emphasizes within *Design Structure* the longevity of such relationships. It also highlights two other characteristics: *Allocation of protégé to the mentor*. In this layered approach, the protégé is not formally assigned to a mentor but rather the mentoring relationship forms naturally according to the *complementary knowledge and skills* of the two individuals involved and is based on *Friendship of Peers* (Clarke, 2004, p. 5). All of this experience continued to serve the purpose of conceiving and pursuing Sarah's long-term goal of establishing and developing an academic career.

It was during this first year that Maggie recognized Sarah's enthusiasm for academic work and communicated her belief in Sarah's ability. As a result, Maggie worked with Sarah and together they set a number of week-by-week, work-related goals which were subsequently reached, and these continued to build Sarah's experience. Some examples of these include the planning and preparation of lectures and tutorials; communicating this material and liaising with tutors; marking of assignments; interacting with students on discussion boards; and numerous student related tasks associated with the role of unit coordinator. In addition to this, Maggie's knowledge and experience was invaluable in pointing the way forward in terms of achieving Sarah's long-term goal. For instance, the value of having research published in an academic journal, at this early stage of an academic career, is something Sarah would have struggled to accomplish without the support and expertise of an established and experienced academic such as Maggie (Diamond, 2010).

Sarah's main goal, whilst not yet fully realized, remains at the forefront of her academic pursuits. She has continued to work towards this end point through the completion and achievement of learning milestones. It is interesting to note how this relationship has fitted quite naturally into the layers described in Table 15.2. The experiences discussed above are consistent with the characteristics and outcomes of the *Informal Mentoring Layer*. It is important to observe that the *Collegial Friendship Layer* remains a significant aspect of this relationship, rather than being a particular stage that becomes obsolete. The research of Murphy and Kram (2010), whilst it focuses on a slightly different approach to the mentoring relationship, does, however, confirm the importance of a balance between the professional and personal life of participants. Searby (2009) discusses the way assumptions, brought to the relationship by both the mentor and protégé, influence the success or failure of the mentoring relationship. She suggests that in more formal mentoring relationships, each person brings a range of assumptions based on personal experiences and values. The mentor and protégé create "high expectations" (p. 12) of each other, creating increased pressure on the relationship. An example of such an assumption was Sarah's perception of her own ignorance or inexperience; however, because the Layered Relationship Mentoring Model is based on a relationship that is naturally formed, these issues or assumptions had little effect and ceased to be a concern. The equality and friendship experienced in this mentoring relationship facilitated two-way, collegial interactions, beneficial to both the mentor and the protégé.

One of the most significant aspects of this layered approach for Sarah has been the level and nature of communication. This has consisted mainly of emails, telephone calls, conversations over coffee—both in the workplace and socially; and impromptu visits to Maggie's office. Clarke (2004) identifies that the communication occurring within the co-mentoring relationship is particularly characterized by two-way dialogue, as opposed to a one sided line of communication where the more experienced person, or mentor, is passing on knowledge to the protégé (Diamond, 2010; Mullen, 2009). For example, Sarah has always felt comfortable emailing Maggie to ask for advice or resources, and to discuss her own teaching ideas or student issues. This may be as simple as asking: "What would you do in this situation?" or, "Can I have your feedback on these ideas?" On one occasion Sarah needed to write a lecture but had limited resources, which made her feel unequal to the task. The following excerpt from an email Sarah wrote to Maggie illustrates this:

> *I am preparing for next week's Pedagogies lecture and wondered if you would be happy to assist me with material to use—or base my lecture on.*
>
> *I am basically asking if you can direct me a bit. All I have is the text book and obviously the internet!!! I have an idea of what I could do but wondered if there were good examples of the Quality Teaching Model in terms of lesson sequences that you know of that I could use?*
>
> *I'll survive if you can't help me at this time, honestly! (Journal entry August 31, 2010)*

Despite obvious differences in experience and expertise, at no time has Sarah felt that her communications were an imposition. In fact, Maggie has readily engaged with her on every occasion, a situation that reflects a mutual respect and rapport. This also substantiates the characteristic of *Equal Status*, as identified by Clarke (2004) and is given further validation by Mullen (2009) who discusses the importance of mentoring relationships being devoid of power struggles. Mullen emphasizes that the success of a blended approach— an amalgamation of formal and informal mentoring elements—lies in the mutual benefit and equal status of those involved. *Equal Status* reflects an attitude of equality and simultaneously acknowledges that each person in the relationship has different experience and levels of expertise. At no point does this difference become hierarchical nor does it assign power to one individual over another. The wisdom of each is offered and reciprocated at different times in the ongoing relationship (Clarke, 2004).

Research suggests that the presence of friendship, sometimes described as attention to the personal or psychosocial aspect, between mentor and protégé is an imperative factor in the success of the mentoring relationship (Hargreaves, 2010; Mullen, 2009; Murphy and Kram, 2010; Freedman, 2008; Wanberg, Welsh, and Kammeyer-Mueller, 2007). Friendship (Gardiner, 1996; 1998) develops imprescriptibly and it is difficult to provide written evidence that it exists. The following extract however, reflects the supportive element that is integral to friendship.

> *Contacted Maggie today regarding classes tomorrow. Feeling really stressed about personal stuff and can't seem to focus on work. Maggie was very helpful and suggested rearranging a couple of classes. This has really taken the pressure off. Nice to know you have the support of someone in these situations, someone who would go through so much trouble to help. (Journal entry September 5, 2010)*

Clarke (2004) indicates *Reciprocal Benefit* and *Mutual Benefit* as characteristic of the co-mentoring layer and the fact that both participants gain from the relationship. This is supported by Sorcellini and Yun (2007) who describe "reciprocal partnerships" (p. 58) which benefit all of those involved. From Sarah's perspective, it seems that she is benefitting significantly more than Maggie, given the early stage of her academic career. Sarah sees what she has gained throughout this process, and how she will develop as it continues, particularly in relation to pursuing her overall goal. Because of the obvious differences in expertise and experience, initially Sarah found it difficult to appreciate the way in which Maggie may have benefitted. Upon further reflection, however, Sarah realizes that she has contributed something of value to the relationship. For example, Maggie has had the confidence to entrust her with some of her workload, including teaching responsibilities, unit coordination and collaboration. Additionally, in the course of fairly casual conversations, Sarah feels as though she may have provided some fresh ideas about relevant issues.

Table 15.2 outlines the characteristics and outcomes of a third layer, *The Co-mentoring Layer* and whilst the third layer of the Layered Relationship Mentoring Model is not yet fully realized, in Sarah's recent experience as unit coordinator, she had the opportunity to act, albeit in a small way, as *mentor* to new colleagues. This supports Clarke's (2004) view of *The Protégé Moving Towards Becoming a Mentor to Others* (Diamond, 2010).

Maggie and Sarah worked well together and it was some time into their professional relationship before Maggie realized that their collegial friendship was indeed the Layered Relationship Mentoring Model in action. More importantly, though, was how this relationship occurred. It began informally and developed naturally to include the essential elements of a successful mentoring partnership and in a very real sense it was not realized that this had occurred until well into the process. The research in progress is a specific example of how both academics have benefitted and will continue to benefit from the mentoring relationship as well as being directly connected to the attainment of Sarah's long-term goal. These reflections serve to examine and illustrate the Layered Relationship Mentoring Model in action. They also demonstrate how the model provides a forum for goals to be conceived and pursued by both mentor and protégé. The success of such a forum is directly related to the depth of relationship and partnership offered by the model as well as the equality and ease of the process.

Conclusion

This chapter aimed to provide insight into the practical workings of a partnership based on a Layered Relationship Mentoring Model by considering the reflections of Mentor and Protégé. The experience of the mentoring relationship for both participants confirms the findings from a previous study (Clarke, 2004) that the mentoring process can be a series of overlapping experiences which contribute to the development of the mentoring relationship. This case study draws on the conceptualization that mentoring can be a layered approach consisting of three overlapping and merging layers. Evident within each layer of the mentoring process are specific characteristics and outcomes that are typical of each of the layers of the mentoring relationship: *Collegial Friendship, Informal Mentoring, and Co-Mentoring*. In this case, the reflections of the Mentor and Protégé demonstrate the presence of these characteristics and outcomes indicative of the three layers. In essence, this approach to mentoring recognizes the significance of friendship, the contributions and equal status of each involved and the mutual benefit inherent in such a partnership. It emphasizes that personal, professional relationships form a vital part of mentoring. Effective mentoring relationships, in particular the layered model discussed, provide the opportunity for goals to be conceived, discussed and set; and as the mentoring relationship develops these goals continue to be pursued, altered and realized. It provides opportunities for both individual and co-constructed goals to be identified and achieved. Mentoring approaches vary and can have their place in different contexts. While many organizations use formal mentoring programs to achieve organizational and individual goals, it is evident from this, and a previous case study by Clarke (2004) that more informal mentoring practices can achieve extraordinary professional development, learning and growth.

References

Barrera, A., Braley, R.T., & Slate, J.R. (2010). Beginning teacher success: An investigation into the feedback from mentors of formal mentoring programs. *Mentoring & Tutoring: Partnership in Learning, 18*(1), 61–74.

Bey, T. & Holmes, C. (1992). *Mentoring: Contemporary Principles and Issues.* Reston, VA: Association of Teacher Educators.

Burk, H.G. & Eby, L.T. (2010). What keeps people in mentoring relationships when bad things happen? A field study from the protégé's perspective. *Journal of Vocational Behaviour, 77,* 437–46.

Clarke, M. (2004). Reconceptualising mentoring: Reflections by an early career researcher. *Issues in Educational Research, 14*(2), 121–43.

Clutterbuck, D. (2008). What's happening in coaching and mentoring? And what is the difference between them. *Development and Learning in Organisations, 23*(4) 8–10.

Crow, G. & Mathews, L. (1998). *Finding One's Way: How Mentoring Can Lead to Dynamic Leadership.* Thousand Oaks, CA: Corwin Press.

DeBolt, G.P. (1992). *Teacher Induction and Mentoring: School-Based Collaborative Programs.* Albany: State University of New York.

Diamond, C.T.P. (2010). A memoir of co-mentoring: The "we" that is "me"'. *Mentoring & Tutoring: Partnership in Learning, 18*(2), 199–209.

Dobie, S., Smith, S., & Robins, L. (2010). How Assigned Faculty Mentors View their Mentoring Relationships: An Interview Study of Mentors in Medical Education. *Mentoring & Tutoring: Partnership in Learning, 18*(4), 337–59.

Duncan, H.E. & Stock, M.J. (2010). Mentoring and Coaching Rural School Leaders: What Do They Need? *Mentoring & Tutoring: Partnership in Learning, 18*(3), 293–311.

Eby, L.T., Butts, M.M., Durley, J., & Ragins, B.R. (2010). Are bad experiences stronger than good ones in mentoring relationships? Evidence from the protégé and mentor perspective. *Journal of Vocational Behaviour, 77*(1), 81–92.

Ewing, R., Freeman, M., Barrie, S., Bell, A., O'Connor, D., Waugh, F., & Sykes, C. (2008). Building community in academic settings: The importance of flexibility in a structured mentoring program. *Mentoring & Tutoring: Partnership in Learning, 16*(3), 294–310.

Freedman, S. (2008). Effective mentoring. *IFLA Journal, 35*(2), 171–82.

Fritzberg, G.J. & Alemayehu, A. (2004). Mutual mentoring: Co-narrating an educative friendship between an education professor and an urban youth. *The Urban Review, 36*(4), 293–308.

Gabriel, M.A. & Kaufield, K.J. (2008). Reciprocal mentorship: an effective support for online instructors. *Mentoring and Tutoring: Partnerships in Learning, 16*(3), 311–27.

Gardiner, C. (1996). Mentoring: a study of the concept, theory and practice in the educational field. M.A. dissertation, University of Central England.

Gardiner, C. (1998). Mentoring: Towards a Professional Friendship. *Mentoring & Tutoring: Partnership in Learning, 6*(1–2), 77–84.

Goodwin, L. (2004). A synergistic approach to Faculty mentoring. *Journal of Faculty Development, 19*(3), 145–52.

Griffin, S.M. & Beatty, R.J. (2010). Storying the terroir of collaborative writing: Like wine and food, a unique pairing of mentoring minds. *Mentoring & Tutoring: Partnership in Learning, 18*(2), 177–97.

Hargreaves, E. (2010). Knowledge construction and personal relationship: Insights about a UK university mentoring and coaching service. *Mentoring & Tutoring: Partnership in Learning, 18*(2), 107–20.

Haynes, R.K. & Petrosko J.M. (2009). An investigation of mentoring and socialization among law faculty. *Mentoring & Tutoring: Partnership in Learning, 17*(1), 41–52.

Higgins, M.C. & Kram, C. (2001). Reconceptualising mentoring at work: A developmental network perspective. *Academy of Management Review, 26*(2), 264–88.

Holmes, S.L., Land, L.D., & Hinton-Hudson, V.D. (2007). Race still matters: considerations for mentoring black women in academe. *The Negro Educational Review, 58*(1–2), 105–29.

Horvath, M., Wasko, L.E., & Bradley, J.L. (2008). The effect of formal mentoring program characteristics on organizational attraction. *Human Resource Development Quarterly, 19*(4), 323–49.

Jeruchim, J. & Shapiro, P. (1992). *Women, Mentors, and Success.* New York: Ballantine Books.

Jipson, J. & Paley, N. (2000). Because no one gets there alone: Collaboration as co-mentoring. *Theory into Practice, 39*(1), 36–42.

Kerka, S. (1998). *New Perspectives on Mentoring.* ERIC Clearinghouse on Adult, Career and Vocational Education, Columbus, OH. ED 418 249. http://www.ericdigests.org/1998-3/mentoring.html [verified 6 Feb 2005]

Kim, S. (2007). Learning goal orientation, formal mentoring, and leadership competence in HRD: A conceptual model. *Journal of European Industrial Training, 31*(3), 181–94.

Kochan, F. & Trimble, S. (2000). From mentoring to co-mentoring: Establishing collaborative relationships. *Theory into Practice, 39*(1), 20–28.

MacGregor, L. (2000). "Mentoring: the Australian experience", *Career Development International, 5*(4/5), 244–9.

Megginson, D. (2000). Current issues in mentoring. *Career Development International, 5*(4), 256–60.

Megginson, D. Clutterbuck, D. Garvey, B. Stokes, P., & Garret-Harris, R. (2006). *Mentoring in Action: A Practical Guide.* London: Kogan Page.

Mullen, C. (2000). Constructing co-mentoring partnerships: Walkways we must travel. *Theory into Practice, 39*(1), 4–11.

Mullen, C.A. & Hutinger, J.L. (2008). At the tipping point? Role of formal faculty mentoring in changing university research cultures. *Journal of In-service Education, 34*(2), 181–204.

Mullen, C.A. (2009). Re-imagining the human dimension of mentoring: A framework for research administration and the academy. *The Journal of Research Administration, 40*(1), 10–31.

Murphy, W.M. & Kram, K.E. (2010). Understanding non-work relationships in developmental networks. *Career Development International, 15*(7), 637–63.

Parise, M.R. & Forret, M.L. (2008). Formal mentoring programs: The relationship of program design and support to mentors' perceptions of benefits and costs. *Journal of Vocational Behaviour, 72*(2), 225–40.

Perna, F. & Lerner, S. (1995). Mentoring and career development among university faculty. *Journal of Education, 177*(2), 31–45.

Ragins, B. & Cotton, J. (1999). Mentor functions and outcomes: A comparison of men and women in formal and informal mentoring relationships. *Journal of Applied Psychology, 84*(4) 29–550.

Rolfe, A. (2012). *Mentoring: Mindset, Skills and Tools. Mentoring Works.* Synergetic People Development.

Rymer, J. (2002). Only connect: Transforming ourselves and our discipline through co-mentoring. *The Journal of Business Communication, 39*(3), 342–63.

Schwiebert, V.L. (2000). *Mentoring: Creating Connected, Empowered Relationships.* Alexandria: American Counseling Association.

Searby, L. (2009). "But I thought …" An examination of assumptions in the mentoring relationship. *Adult Learning, 20*(1–2), 10–13.

Singh, R., Ragins, B.R., & Tharenou, P. (2009). Who gets a mentor? A longitudinal assessment of the rising star hypothesis. *Journal of Vocational Behaviour, 74*(1), 11–17.

Sorcinelli, M.D. & Yun, J. (2007). From mentor to mentoring networks: Mentoring in the new academy. *Change: The Magazine of Higher Learning, 39*(6), 58–61.

Sorrentino, D.M. (2006). The SEEK mentoring program: An application of the goal-setting theory. *Journal of College Student Retention: Research, Theory & Practice, 8*(2), 241–50.

Trask, B.S., Marotz-Baden, R., Settles, B., Gentry, D., & Berke, D. (2009). Enhancing graduate education: Promoting a scholarship of teaching and learning through mentoring. *International Journal of Teaching and Learning in Higher Education, 20*(3), 438–46.

Wanberg, C.R., Welsh, E.T., & Kammeyer-Mueller, J. (2007). Protégé and mentor self-disclosure: Levels and outcomes within formal mentoring dyads in a corporate context. *Journal of Vocational Behavior, 70*, 398–412.

Zachary, L.J. & Fischler, L.A. (2011). Begin with the end in mind: The goal-driven mentoring relationship. *T+D, 65*(1), 50–53.

16

Working With Emergent Goals: A Pragmatic Approach

David Clutterbuck

Being the iconoclast is relatively easy. It's clear from the preceding chapters that simplistic approaches to goal setting and goal pursuit can be limiting. They are seen by some authors as hindering a coach's ability to be truly mindful of the client and to maintain a largely non-directive orientation, as not recognizing coaching as an emergent process, and as resulting in coaching that focuses on objectives that may not be best matched to the client's motivations and needs.

In this chapter, we acknowledge that there is sometimes a place for beginning the coaching relationship with a specific goal, but we suggest ways in which coaches and mentors can take a more pragmatic and effective approach to establishing and working with goals across the range of situations that arise in the complex arenas of life and work. In our dialogues on this topic with coaches in several countries and continents, a number of issues have surfaced as they pertain to goals. These include:

- Managing client and sponsor expectations about goals.

- Goal feasibility—is the goal genuinely achievable?

- Negotiating goals with the sponsor/client's line manager.

- How to keep the focus sufficiently broad and flexible, where needed.

- How to feel comfortable in the coaching role, without specific goals to lean on.

If, as our conversations with coaches around the world indicate, goals in effective coaching and mentoring relationships are often emergent, rather than pre-set, this has significant implications for the coaching or mentoring conversation. For a start, it affects the assumptions that each party brings to the early conversations. Freed from the constraints of establishing and committing to a specific goal, both are able to relax into their roles and allow goals to develop out of a deeper understanding of the learner and his or her situation.

Instead of trying to pin the learner down immediately to a specific goal, to which he or she may or may not be committed, the effective coach/mentor in this scenario facilitates an exploration from a much wider horizon. Key areas of conversation may include:

IDENTITY

- Who are you? (Not what do you do?)

- Who do you want to become?

- How does what you do now align with who you aspire to be?

- What prevents you from being the person you aspire to be?

- Who/what supports you in being the person you aspire to be?

VALUES

- What do you care about?

- Why is this important to you?

- What difference do you want to make and why?

RESOURCES

- How well supported are you (at work and/or at home)?

- Who is in your developmental network? (See Chapter 13).

- How does this affect your sense of the possible?

- What resources would enable you to be more effective in your work and non-work roles?

PURPOSE

- What do you want to contribute? (other-directed).

- What do you want to achieve for yourself? (self-directed).

- What's the point of these?

- What achievements would give you great satisfaction to look back on in 10 or 20 years?

- What's wrong with the status quo?

Where the learner does come to the relationship with a pre-determined goal, it may be necessary to back-track and fill in the deeper level of understanding associated with the emergent process. In doing so, the learner may find that the goals he or she has enunciated are more complex than previously thought, and have implications of which he or she was not consciously aware. The learner may also come to question the importance that they have attached to the goal.

This re-examination is fundamental to the reflective process and will ideally continue throughout the relationship. Testing the learner's current action and issues against their goals helps to widen their attentiveness to factors, which help and hinder their goal achievement. At the same time, however, as learners acquire a greater understanding of themselves, their views on what they want to achieve and who they want to become, are likely to evolve. This evolution is especially likely if the coaching or mentoring process leads to a shift in the way they think i.e. if they take a further cognitive step in terms of personal maturity (Whitmore and Einzig, 2008).

Useful questions to apply when the learner articulates a pre-determined goal include:

- Why *this* goal? (What need does it address for you?)

- Why now?

- Is this truly your goal or is it partly or mainly someone else's?

- Is the goal a sub-set of a larger goal? Or is it really a number of connected goals?

- What will achieving this goal replace? (i.e. what will you have to stop doing to achieve it or once you have achieved it?)

A technique that can result in significant insights is to explore different perspectives of the same question. For example:

- Why do you care? (neutral tone).

- *Why* do you care? (confrontative).

- Why *do* you care? (rational explorative).

- Why *you* care? (personalizing).

- Why do you *care*? (emotional explorative).

Different Purposes; Different Approaches to Goals

It seems fairly obvious that not all coaching assignments and not all coaching conversations are the same. For example, coaches trained in one school or model of coaching might approach a client's issues in radically dissimilar ways. Equally, people come to coaching and mentoring for a wide variety of reasons. Some purposes might require a significant increase in self-awareness or self-insight before personal change can happen; others may simply require a shift of tactics.

In Table 16.1 below, we attempt to map out some of the main approaches to coaching and mentoring, along with their purpose, the kind of conversations that underlie them and some of the issues that arise. In general, the table shows a gradual shift from the immediate to the longer-term, and from relatively simple, linear purposes to more complex, adaptive purposes.

Table 16.1   Goals in different coaching and mentoring contexts

Approach	Purpose	Goal conversations	Issues
Task learning	"Sitting by Nellie" to learn skills	What do you need to know? What does good look like in this task? How will you know how well you are doing?	Who sets the standards?
Skills transfer or acquisition	Transition from incompetence to unconscious competence (develop skills as "second nature")	What skills do you need to learn? How will you apply them?	What does a coach provide that training doesn't?
Performance enhancement	Achieving specific targets	What do you need/want to do better than you do now? What does excellent look like? What coping strategies will help you manage your weaknesses?	Who decides what good looks like? How contextual is performance in this role?
Career development/ self-management	Achieving career progress	What is your ambition? What resources do you have (internally and externally) to help you achieve your career ambition?	Who is in control of your career?
Behavioral change	Developing specific competences or overcoming defined weaknesses	What needs to change in the way you think, to produce changes in the way you behave?	How do you sustain change? How do you ensure others see how you have changed?
Whole person development	Wider self-fulfillment	How can you grow as a person? Who do you want to become and why? How will you manage the conflicting demands on your time, energy and attention?	Why are you (here)?
Transformational/ transpersonal change	Clarifying life purpose; acquiring greater maturity	What is the critical transition you need to make in the way you approach your work? What insights do you need to acquire to bring about personal change?	How do you align your personal and professional identities? How can you be at peace with yourself? What do you need to let go of, to fulfill your potential?

Task learning could be considered to be instruction. However, we include it as a separate construct, because there is a considerable literature that uses both coaching and mentoring in this way—a relatively directive, largely passive means of learning by copying a more skilled practitioner. One of the factors that aligns it with the wider mentoring literature is the additional element of pastoral care that is often involved. Tom Pedersen's (2012) excellent review of mentoring programs for disadvantaged youth in Denmark fits well into this genus. Based on work with 7,000 mentees over a period of years, he details activities to develop and measure progress towards social and literacy skills, using customized competency frameworks. The goals here are generally specific, measurable and typically time-based.

Much the same can be said of skills transfer. Although there may be a long-term goal (e.g. becoming a black belt, or making the national sports squad), skills coaching typically involves many lots of small, short-term goals along a predetermined path. With skills-related goals, there is usually a standard set by a third party and feedback in the moment is an essential part of the process.

If there is overlap between task learning and skills transfer, then the same also appears to be the case between skills transfer and performance enhancement.

The degree of overlap depends on whether the goal and the standard, by which achievement is judged, are extrinsically or intrinsically generated. The more intrinsically generated they are, the greater the level of self-determination and goal ownership on the part of the learner (Deci and Ryan, 1985, 2000; see also Chapter 5). Performance enhancement through coaching or mentoring also involves both extrinsic and intrinsic feedback—the role of the coach is both to give feedback (via observation or collecting data from third parties) and to assist the learner in developing their own capacity to experiment, self-observe (i.e. give feedback to themselves), and reflect and act. Goals in performance coaching are often complicated by distributed ownership (for example, by both an employee and his or her line manager), by unequal commitment from the goal owners, and the influence of positive or negative rewards.

In career development, the goals are by their nature mainly long-term. As Ibarra and Lineback (2005) have suggested, it's important here to get the right balance between goals that are too narrow and those that are too broad. There is a much greater requirement to link the learning dialogue to issues of raising mentee self-awareness about personal values, strengths, how they define success and so on. Indeed, success can more generally be defined as "achieving what you value". A difference between career mentoring and the approaches already described in this section is that, while the objective (e.g. make partner within two years) may be relatively specific, the paths towards it are much more flexible and ill-defined. Goal management becomes a process of vigilance in identifying and taking advantage of opportunities (career mindfulness), refining personal capabilities and developing a relevant track record.

Goals in behavioral coaching/mentoring tend to divide again into extrinsically and externally intrinsically motivated. A worrying trend revealed in recent research into behaviors by executives (Kaiser and Craig, 2011) is that some of the key leadership behaviors people acquire at middle management levels—including listening, caring and showing integrity—diminish substantially when they become senior executives. It appears that the motivation for acquiring these behaviors can be extrinsic and largely negative ("If I don't behave in this way, I won't get my next promotion"). A challenge for behavioral coaches is how to avoid colluding in this kind of coercion. Sustainability of behavior change may be related to how the behavior anchors in the client's values. Shallow, extrinsically absorbed values might in some circumstances be less likely to lead to sustainable change than deeply rooted values, derived from internally generated identity—for example, in the case of goals related to well-being (Kasser and Ryan, 1996).

Whole person development might be described as "goal-light". Here, the essence is not on *what* the person wants to become, and only partially on *who* they want to become. More important is the journey itself and the learning that the mentee acquires on the way. Goals and self-understanding evolve together and the mentor's role is to help the mentee manage the journey.

Transformational/transpersonal change has many of the same characteristics as whole person development, but it typically has much clearer intended outcomes. The notion of adult maturity as proposed by Kegan (1982), Rooke and Torbert (2005), Laske (2009), and others, describes the process, by which a person gradually acquires more complex ways of thinking and relating to the world around them. At its simplest, the aim is for the client to acquire greater wisdom. This could also be seen as the purpose of whole person development, but the difference is that transformational coaching/mentoring views this transition in a specific context—most commonly acquiring the breadth of understanding and mindfulness to become an effective enterprise leader. Transformational coaching/mentoring, then, is about assisting people to mature.

These categorizations inevitably reflect only generalities of approach in coaching and mentoring—a set of metaphors rather than a dictionary of definitions. Other observers, from a different perspective, might choose different ways to classify the breadth of coaching and mentoring approaches. Note that we have not labeled any of these approaches exclusively coaching or mentoring, as this would impose yet another layer of qualitative judgment. Nonetheless, it seems, then, that the nature and focus of goals differs radically amongst these approaches to coaching and mentoring—in specificity, time horizon, complexity and intent. A logical conclusion (and one borne out by watching hundreds of coaches and mentors as they carry out their role) is that there can be no one-size fits all methodology for goal setting and/or goal management.

Hidden Goals

Alongside the overt goals in each of these approaches to coaching and mentoring may be hidden goals. For example, a sponsor for executive coaching may actually just want to get rid of the employee; or the career mentor may consciously or unconsciously want the mentee to follow in his or her own path and/or become like them. These hidden goals can distort the learning relationship in subtle ways. Identifying them isn't easy. One of the techniques we use from time to time is to create the expectation for and to initiate short bursts of "painful goal honesty" (PGH) with each stakeholder. These are planned or ad hoc conversations in which each party, including the coach or mentor, is encouraged to reflect on their motivations for the relationship and to push the boundaries of their openness. The P in PGH is a key element! Part of the value of this process is that, in order to be honest with each other, each party also needs to be honest with themselves. The contracting process may also lead to acceptance and legitimization of each other's goals.

Being aware of and surfacing hidden goals is, I suggest, a critical skill of goal management—but not one that generally figures highly in coach and mentor training.

Managing Client and Sponsor Expectations about Goals

Both the client and the sponsor may perceive a need for measurable targets at the very start of a relationship. For the sponsor, in particular, this is often about wanting reassurance of being in control, so that they can prove that the time and financial investment has been worthwhile. Either or both may also be looking for a quick fix to a current problem.

From the experiences of coaches and mentors in workshops around the world, some of the practical steps one can take to manage these expectations include:

- Explain that goals come in different levels of simplicity/complexity, time to achieve, impact on the client and on the team. Where appropriate, attempt to shift attention from a single simplistic goal to a range of different, interlinked goals with varying levels of specificity and time-boundedness.

- Discuss how each of the stakeholders will recognize change in line with the goal(s).

- Make it clear that goals may change as the coaching conversation enlarges clients' awareness of themselves and their contexts. Foster "buy-in" for this possibility in the initial contracting.

- Help the client and the sponsor differentiate between goals that are primarily about internal change (within the client) and goals that are primarily or in large part about external change (within the systems of which they are a part).

- Gain agreement for a goals review after, say, three meetings. This is the opportunity to adjust or even replace the original goals.

- In general, the easier it is to measure performance against a goal, the simpler the coaching and the less coaching time needed. Experienced coaches often report that they spend less than a third of each coaching session on the presented goal and the rest of the time on other, usually more fundamental, issues. Bearing this ratio in mind may help a less experienced coach overcome their "goal fixation". If appropriate, share this expectation with the client, explaining that the unscripted conversation is what will provide the deeper understanding and personal change that will make achievement of the presented goal more sustainable.

Goal Feasibility: Is the Goal Genuinely Achievable?

Coaches and mentors, by and large, are expected to work with the goals the client brings, although these may often be set by someone else. But perspectives on what constitutes an achievable goal can vary considerably! It can be tough for a coach to tell a sponsor that a goal isn't achievable, but ethics demand a level of honesty that explores goal feasibility at least at the contracting stage and ideally at subsequent stages of the assignment.

A particular danger signal is the concept of "stretch goals", which are widely touted as highly beneficial (Kerr and Landauer, 2004). However, evidence from studies of stretch goals at the organizational level (Sitkin et al., 2011) indicate that they only work under special circumstances and that much of the time they result in demotivation and reduced performance. The preconditions for success with stretch goals are that a) they capitalize on an existing wave of achievement, where energy and enthusiasm from previous successes fuels future efforts, and b) they are adequately resourced. If stretch goals are remedial in origin, they are unlikely to have a positive effect. And if the client does not have access to the support they need from colleagues and the work system in general (for example, having time pressures relieved so they can concentrate on new things), then success is also unlikely.

Studies by Brian et al. (2011) suggest that frequent, small behavioral changes building on people's strengths are much more likely to produce continuous positive improvements; so coaches and mentors may sometimes need to curb their own ambitions for their clients with more sober assessments of the amount of change that can be achieved in a given period and within a given system.

Negotiating Goals with the Sponsor

In the work context, a high proportion of coaching is initiated by the client's immediate line manager, who (usually quite rightly) perceives himself or herself as a stakeholder in the investment and its outcomes. Some of the more directive, task-focused forms of mentoring may also have some influence by line managers. In both cases, the line manager's influence can be beneficial or a major hindrance. It is likely to constrain the scope and the depth of the learning conversations if it focuses too much at the level of extrinsic motivation and not enough at the intrinsic level. Both parties in the learning relationship may feel conflict between the agreed goals and more challenging goals that require deeper self-understanding and reflection. Goals agreed with the line manager may appear simplistic (often because they are based on measurements that do not take sufficient account of contextual complexity) and relatively short-term.

In the three-way conversation between coach, client and client's boss (HR may also sometimes be a fourth party at the table), it's important therefore to explore in depth what each expects in terms of goals. Some of the topics on which to reach agreement (or at least an understanding) are:

OWNERSHIP AND MOTIVATION

- Who owns the goal? If it's a shared goal, who does it matter to most?

- What kind of goal is it? Which elements of Table 16.1 apply?

- Is there an appropriate balance between short-term "doing" goals and longer-term "being" goals?

- For whose benefit is this coaching assignment intended? The client's? Their team's? The boss'? Other third parties? What's the balance between these?

- How does the goal link with the other priorities of the client, their team, their boss, the organization?

- How likely is this goal to be as important in six months' time?

INTENDED OUTCOMES

- What does success look like, for each of the stakeholders? (This might include the client, their boss, the client's team and key internal or external customers.)

- How does the client evaluate the effort/reward ratio? That is, is the client's motivation sufficient to give this goal the priority it deserves?

- What will coaching lead to? When the assignment is finished, is that it? Or should there be an expectation that the client will also have acquired a greater capacity to self-coach?

- What resources will be needed to achieve it, from the client, from the boss and from other stakeholders? Are they all willing and able to provide those resources when they are needed?

- Over what period are the outcomes of coaching expected to become apparent?

- How clear are the consequences? Is the intent to ease promotion or to avoid being fired?

- What are the hidden agendas?

SUPPORT

- What support is the boss prepared to give to help the client achieve the goal? Is this enough?

- How will the boss and other stakeholders recognize positive changes, when they occur?

- How much does achievement of this goal rely on contextual factors? Is success wholly in the hands of the client?

REVIEW

- Under what circumstances and when should the goal be reviewed?

Having some kind of goal to start with can be comforting for all parties. The sponsor has to justify the expenditure, and the client and the coach may find it a useful starting point to give the relationship some initial impetus.

How to Keep the Focus Sufficiently Broad and Flexible

While a very narrow focus may be helpful at the task mentoring or skills coaching levels, it can be highly dysfunctional when working with more complex change. Approaches coaches and mentors can use here include:

- Visioning, in which goals are positioned in a much wider context or purpose, often with a longer time horizon.

- Viewing each session as having at least four streams, of equal importance:

- *Goal progress.* What is happening to bring about desired outcomes?
- *Personal awareness.* What is the client learning about him or herself, which will support current and future change?
- *Contextual awareness.* What is the client learning about his or her world that will either help with working within or in changing the system?
- *Issues awareness.* Is the client able to reflect on current concerns and opportunities in the context of the other three streams?

- Helping the client to reassess goals against changes in their environment and in themselves. Particularly helpful here is to ask clients to assess their emotional attachment to the goal, for example by using simple scaling. If the level of emotional attachment diminishes, this should initiate a conversation exploring what has changed, either within the client or in their circumstances.

Feeling Comfortable as a Coach, Without Specific Goals to Lean on

From our observation of hundreds of coaches in coach assessment centers, it appears that the less experienced coaches are, the more they need a model to follow and a client goal to facilitate the coaching engagement. Having a goal provides a sense of security and direction for the conversation. However, it is important to remember that coaching and mentoring are *learning* conversations, not *goal* conversations (Harri-Augstein and Thomas, 1991). Having a goal is only part of the process of dialogue.

One proposed way of contextualizing goals is shown below (Figure 16.1). Based again on observing effective coaches, it appears that a first stage in planned change is to have some sense of purpose. This purpose may be quite broad and fuzzy to begin with. To create volition, a sense of purpose may need to solidify into a number of more specific intentions that lead generally towards fulfillment of the purpose. Out of these may emerge goals, which make intent more specific still. Implementing goals requires the development of pathways and scenarios, which in turn require strategies and finally tactics. So, in this metaphor, goals are in the middle of the process, not the beginning!

Practitioners in coaching and mentoring can expand their comfort zones, therefore, by accepting presented goals initially, but gently steering clients towards purpose and intent, in the knowledge that this may well lead to a radical recasting of those goals. It is misguided to work down the chain towards strategy and tactics until you are quite sure that you are dealing with the "right" goal.

The more experienced a coach or mentor becomes with emergent, mutable goals, the easier it becomes to focus the learning conversation on the purpose and context—if you like, on understanding the client's internal and external systems. The client *may* then need help in working downward along the goal chain; but equally, they may not. They *may* value the coach's company along the journey; or they may not. The effective coach knows instinctively when they are likely to become a wallflower and constrains their need to help accordingly.

Purpose > intent > goal > path(s)/scenarios > strategy > tactics

Figure 16.1   The goal chain: The position of goals in the process of change

References

Brian, B.J., Brim, E.D., & Liebnau, D. (2011). Does Setting Major Development Goals Work? *Gallup Management Journal*, 3 November.

Deci, E.L. & Ryan, R.M. (1985). *Intrinsic Motivation and Self-Determination in Human Behaviour*. New York: Plenum.

Deci, E.L. & Ryan, R.M. (2000). The "What" and "Why" of goal pursuits: Human needs and self-determination of behaviour. *Psychological Enquiry, 11*, 227–68.

Harri-Augstein, E.S. & Thomas, L.F. (1991). *Learning Conversations: The Self-organised Learning Way to Personal and Organisational Growth*. London: Routledge.

Ibarra, H. & Lineback, K. (2005) What's your story? *Harvard Business Review, 83*(1), 64–71.

Kaiser, R.B. & Craig, S.B. (2011). Do behaviors related to managerial effectiveness really change with organizational level? An empirical test. *Psychologist-Manager*, Journal 14, 92–119.

Kasser, T. & Ryan, R. (1996). Further examining the American dream: Differential correlates of intrinsic and extrinsic goals. *Personality and Social Psychology Bulletin, 22*(3), 280–87.

Kegan, R. (1982). *The Evolving Self*. Cambridge, MA: Harvard University Press.

Kerr, S. & Landauer, S. (2004). Using stretch goals to promote organizational effectiveness and personal growth: General Electric and Goldman Sachs. *Academy of Management Executive, 18*(4), 134–8.

Laske, O. (2009). *Measuring Hidden Dimensions of Human Systems*. (Vol. 2). Medford, MA: IDM Press.

Pedersen, T.T. (2012). *How to be a Mentor for Disadvantaged and Marginalized People*. Ulstup: MEN2R Publishing.

Rooke, D. & Torbert, W. (2005). Seven Transformations of Leadership. *Harvard Business Review*, April, 67–76.

Sitkin, B.S., See, K.E., Miller, C.C., Lawless, M.W., & Carton, A.M. (2011). The paradox of stretch goals: Organizations in pursuit of the seemingly impossible. *Academy of Management Review, 36*(3), 544–56.

Whitmore, J. & Einzig, H. (2008). *Transpersonal Coaching* DVD. London: Association for Coaching.

17

The Way Forward:
Perspectives from the Editors

*Susan A. David, David Clutterbuck, and
David Megginson*

In this chapter the three editing authors offer personal reflections on the journey of preparing this book and what we have learned from engaging with the other authors and contributors. It is not so much a mandate for the treatment of goals in the future, but rather about our intellectual journey—addressing what we thought we knew and what we newly found we were uncertain about. Our invitation to our readers is to make their own journey into the fascinating world of goals and coaching, rather than to follow our or the contributors' prescriptions.

David Megginson's Reflections

I started this exploration with a clear prejudice against goals in coaching. I had found that many of my clients actively avoided goals and found profitable things to do in coaching without putting on what I came to see as the straightjacket of goals. Close reading and editing of the drafts of our distinguished contributors has led me in three directions. Firstly, the process has reinforced my views of the limitations of goals; secondly my view of the use of goals has been nuanced and made richer through pondering on the findings and ideas of others; and thirdly I have gained some insights into the relationship between purpose and goals that were new and enlivening. I will quote examples from the many perspectives offered in this book, not necessarily because they are the most important insights but rather because they best illustrate these themes.

LIMITATIONS OF GOALS

Some of the authors who endorse the centrality of goals in coaching seem to me to also make a good case in what they say for the contrary argument— that goals have at best a limited role to play. Grant (Chapter 4) makes the case for a goals hierarchy that calls for attention to values in order to ensure that subordinate goals and action plans do not become dominant. At the same time, most of his examples are of subordinate goals and actions. I get the impression that, given his wisdom and experience, his practice as a coach includes many of those big wrenching conversations that lead people to change their lives, but his ideology as a coaching psychologist encourages him to focus upon the tangible and the explicable. He also makes a marvellous critique of SMART goals (leading to scruffy thinking), which is a useful caution against the over- or naïve use of goals in coaching. Both Greif (Chapter 7) and Bright and Pryor (Chapter 9) emphasize the uncertainty and fuzziness of goals, and Bright and Pryor cite Tubbs's (1986) meta-analysis which indicated that setting goals helped in laboratory settings, but in the more complex and indeterminate world that we call real-life, goals are much less useful. Lunsford (Chapter 14) is the most spirited defendant in this volume of the use of SMART goals. She makes good use of the distinction between fixed and growth mindsets. Coachees with fixed mindsets are likely to value SMART goals.

Kram (Chapter 13) makes the point that goals will be of use mainly for those operating at an instrumental level. This will not apply to most of the people who receive coaching or mentoring in organizations.

The weight of the arguments in this book (I must confess) is that goals have a place. I concede to this collective wisdom. Overall, however, there is a strong critique of SMART goals and a related concern about performance goals.

A NUANCED VIEW OF GOALS

Berkman, Donde, and Rock (Chapter 6) using a combination of neuroscience and social psychology argue that in setting goals, motivation (approach or avoidance), planning, social context and self-control all need to be taken into account. Grant (Chapter 4) also addresses approach and avoidance goals and makes some telling points about the disadvantages of avoidance goals. Both Grant, and Bright and Pryor (Chapter 9) emphasize the benefits of learning goals in contrast to performance goals, and this is another area where the advocates of goals seem to undermine the core certainties of performance coaching. Grant also advocates approach, rather than avoidance, goals.

Boyatzis and Howard (Chapter 10) similarly emphasize the value of learning goals as opposed to performance goals. They advocate rebalancing the attention paid to the Positive Emotional Attractor of the Ideal Self and the Negative Emotional Attractor of the Real Self. They suggest that deficit goals that are grounded in the Negative Emotional Attractor (what one should do to put things right) have fewer beneficial effects and are less long lasting than those built on the Positive Emotional Attractor of one's vision of how one wants to be. There is room for the negative, but it is best limited. Coaches need to be aware of their own position on this topic, as it will impact on the state of our clients. Boyatzis and Howard also emphasize the impact of individual differences, and assessing the planning strategies and learning styles of each client.

Both Grief (Chapter 7) and Whitmore (Chapter 12) advocate monitoring progress towards goal achievement. This provided a wake-up call for my own practice and I can see that I need to learn how to offer more support for my clients' goal pursuit without becoming a hectoring boss, who is calling my clients into account. Bright and Pryor (Chapter 9), with their background in complexity theory, differentiate closed system thinking from open system reality, and suggest that the simplification necessary to set goals can break down in the face of the non-linearity of the world. Cavanagh (Chapter 8) too takes a systemic perspective, and sees future goals not as ends in themselves, but rather as a 'container of possibilities'. He provides a useful reminder that accommodating new ways of thinking can lead to worse performance in the short-term. Nonetheless, he seems to be saying, this is what the complex world demands of our clients.

I am reminded by the interview with Kathy Kram (Chapter 13) that goals have different places in formal compared with informal mentoring relationships. Kram found that informal relationships did not focus on goals, addressing instead purpose and meaning. Formal schemes seemed to encourage a focus on goals. The widely reported emergence and shifting of goals seems in her experience to lead to mentors being overwhelmed by the complexity of their task. This in turn leads to mentors over-simplifying the goal setting process. Kram also makes the case for developmental networks. She reminds me that although team coaching (one coach to many clients) seems to privilege the organization's agenda above the goals or purpose of individuals, developmental networks (many mentors to one mentee) create a holding environment that provides challenge, consistency and confirmation.

I have adopted the approach outlined here—seeking a mix of types of goal for particular individuals taking into account their preferences and styles. I still retain the possibility of goal-free coaching for some of my clients who articulate their preference for this approach. Sometimes this leads to difficult conversations with sponsors, but these too represent learning opportunities— for the sponsors, for the client and for me.

COACHING ON PURPOSE

Many of the contributors to this volume use Robert Kegan's (Chapter 11) model of adult development and this long-term direction can help coach and client orient themselves to the coaching process. Kegan views people developing from the instrumental; to societal; to self-authoring; to self-transforming mind. The concern he identifies for coaches is that they may focus upon performance, rather than upon the meta-goal of broadening knowing systems. Goals can broaden once individuals see their own immune systems and recognize that their commitments have them rather than them having their commitments. After drafting this summary I broke off from my work on the book to see someone who was pursuing a spiritual path and wanted to take the next major step in his journey. Dan is a serial entrepreneur with a strong social conscience. In talking about his next step, he described it as a project that he had to manage. He also spoke of striving for this development. Using Kegan's language of self-authoring and immune system, he was able to recognize that the way he was going about his task was paradoxically what was standing in the way of the spiritual development that he craved.

Boyatzis and Howard (Chapter 10) adopt a similar position to Kegan concerning their central point about attending to the Positive Emotional Attractor. This involves helping the client to focus on the vision of their ideal self rather than the deficits identified in their real self.

Spence and Deci (Chapter 5) give an excellent account of the relationship between self-determination theory and coaching. Their analysis of basic psychological needs—focusing upon autonomy, relatedness and competence— provides a touchstone for coaching with purpose. They enable an exploration of how individuals can be helped to learn to choose responses to extrinsic goals.

Whitmore (Chapter 12) describes goals "beyond winning" and asks the crucial question, "What's most valuable for everyone?" These views accord with my perception that no one should coach until they have answered for themselves the questions:

- What is my view of a fully functioning person?

- What is my view of what makes an effective organization?

Lunsford (Chapter 14) suggests that, particularly in the early part of a coaching or mentoring relationship, the goal of goals is to promote a growth mindset. If this is done, powerful and developmental goals will emerge spontaneously.

I am still left with questions about how these value-based orientations can accommodate the call to honor the client's agenda. I find that as I get older, I am increasingly ready to offer challenge to clients who have not yet articulated the purpose or meaning of their life. This seems to be at the heart of the coaching and mentoring mission.

David Clutterbuck's Reflections

I came to the issue of goals and goal management from a positivist perspective. As a young journalist, I had taken the great Peter Drucker as a role model. Admiring mostly from afar, I learnt from him the importance of clarity, focus, curiosity and observation.

Drucker made a powerful case against what he saw as the dangers of having vague objectives and institutionalized purposelessness. In many cases, functions and activities seemed to be there for their own ends, rather than to fulfill a common business cause. The role of management, in his view, was in part to create islands of certainty in an uncertain world.

From this perspective, it was perhaps inevitable that I would be receptive to the notion, so strongly proposed in the general coaching and mentoring literature, that effective coaching and mentoring required a high level of goal clarity. Then I started to research the dynamics of mentoring relationships. I included in my research, questionnaire statements relating to goal clarity (specificity) and goal commitment at the beginning of a mentoring relationship, with the hypothesis that these would be strongly associated with positive mentoring behaviors, perceived relationship quality, and outcomes at least for the mentee. To my surprise, I found no statistically significant correlations.

At about the same time, my colleague and co-author David Megginson was voicing his own concerns that having a specific initial goal might not always be necessary, or beneficial. So, as I always do when I am stimulated to question an assumption, I opened up the issue for dialogue in workshops and seminars, some of them with David. The reflections of these coaches and mentors provided further evidence that the issue of goals and goal management in coaching and mentoring was not as simple as it had been portrayed. A general pattern emerged from these dialogues that has been repeated wherever I have traveled in the world—the more experienced a coach or mentor is, the more they tend to see goals as an emergent feature of the learning conversation. Kathy Kram (Chapter 13) reveals that she, too, has found that goals in mentoring tend to be emergent.

In the mid-1990s, Walter Goldsmith and I explored the concept of *simplexity*. With a focus on the behaviors of leaders of high-performing organizations, we described "breaking down complex issues to the point where they can be dealt with by a combination of simple [but not simplistic] solutions" (Goldsmith and Clutterbuck, 1997, p. 2). Inherent here is the need to understand complexity, before one can distinguish between simple and simplistic approaches. Our thinking was influenced by concepts, such as fuzzy logic (Kosko, 1994) and by developments in chaos theory (see Chapter 9). The more we explored the experiences of coaches in relation to working with client goals, the more it seemed that the approaches espoused in so much of the coaching literature were rooted in simplistic assumptions about both goals and the complexity of clients' lives.

In the past five years, I have explored the evidence for the efficacy of standard HR practice in talent management and succession planning. My conclusion is that most of the charts, grids and competency frameworks are of dubious value—because they start from assumptions about the relationship between employees and employer that are rooted in simple, linear systems, when those relationships are in fact complex, adaptive systems. It is increasingly clear to me that classic approaches to goal setting in coaching and mentoring are part of this simplistic pattern of thinking.

The chapter by Jim Bright and Robert Pryor (Chapter 9) develops this perspective in great detail and for me provides a useful and coherent backdrop to the arguments about the place of goal clarity and goal commitment. A goal is only useful as long as the environment, in which it is framed and rooted, remains constant. So, the longer the period for achieving a goal, the more likely it is to become irrelevant. Or, as the authors state from the opposite perspective: "Non-linearity implies that goal setting is likely to be most effective over short time periods".

Each of the other chapters adds different perspectives to the recurrent theme that goal setting and goal management are much more complex than they are typically perceived to be by coaches, clients or organizational sponsors—all of whom may be attracted to the false certainty that very specific or SMART goals bring when applied to complex circumstances. Boyzatis and Howard (Chapter 10) explore how the potential to achieve goals is mitigated by the nature and quality of the client's reflections and their emotional state. Given the potential of Positive Emotional Attractors to facilitate beneficial personal change, it is sobering to think how many coaching assignments begin instead with negative emotional attractors—focusing on the client's weaknesses and failures, on their "shoulds" rather than on their "would like tos". There is an argument here for much greater courage from professional coaches in how they contract with sponsors.

This need for coaches to sensitize themselves to the complexity of goal setting is emphasized in Robert Kegan's discussion (Chapter 11) of presented or explicit goals versus implicit goals, and his proposal to use the former as a Trojan Horse into the latter. He shows how people at different stages of adult development may have different approaches to goals and different understandings of the role of goals. His contrast between helping clients change their behavior and helping them change their minds is particularly relevant in the context of coach maturity; coaches can only help clients think systemically, if they themselves also think systemically.

Grant (Chapter 4) illustrates the complexity of goal setting by describing 20 different types of goal that might occur in coaching. He argues strongly for the role of coaching frameworks, such as GROW and Solution Focus, that emphasize goal specificity, but places them firmly within the context of self-determination, as do Spence and Deci, (Chapter 5). I found the combination of these chapters useful in shifting some of my own perceptions—in particular, from viewing such models as innately simplistic, to seeing them as either simple or simplistic depending on the context and degree of insightfulness with which they are used (or not used).

Berkman, Donde, and Rock (Chapter 6) add to the picture of complexity by exploring the neuroscience of goal setting and goal management, while Greif (Chapter 7) provides a powerful metaphor of crossing the Rubicon in his analysis of how people do or do not follow through on goal intentions.

Some of these authors take a strongly performance oriented approach; others a more person-centered, holistic view. Yet what strikes me above all in reading these highly varied and well-argued viewpoints on the nature of goals in coaching and mentoring is that, while acknowledging the complexity, all of the authors also identify the potential for using a deeper understanding of goal dynamics to benefit clients. The world of coaching professionals has, until now, not intersected greatly with the academic world of goal theorists. Certainly, coaches have a lot to learn from the goal theorists. However, in the future, I suspect there is a role for coaching professionals to become the front-line troops for testing goal theories and providing new insights into the role of goals in human change.

Susan David's Reflections

Each of us brings to goals a personal orientation: for example, seeing them as providing useful structure or as being constraining; being naturally drawn to them or adopting a naturalistic, emergent approach. Research suggests that this orientation is predicated on individual differences including personality and cognitive processing preferences (Barrick, Mount, and Strauss, 1993; Brown, Lent, Telander, and Tramayne, 2011) and, as coaches, we likely infuse our client engagements with these tendencies.

My personal orientation to goals is inherently positive. I am an avid goal setter, working them out yearly, quarterly, and monthly, and tracking progress against these targets. At the same time, as an emotions researcher and a coaching psychologist who works with senior executives, I have noticed how goals, the very structures that are intended to direct our attention and energy to what is truly important, can paradoxically turn us away from these objectives and take us down paths of avoidance, simplistic thinking, and dissatisfaction.

Consider these three, true scenarios. (1) The head of people for a global organization who, concerned with decreasing engagement and retention in what is a highly regulated and compliance-oriented industry, develops "SMART" goals to address the issue. Amongst other similar initiatives, these goals mandate that every leader has "one more authentic conversation with each team member per year", and that "the organization's induction manual be updated". In their next engagement survey, scores have decreased even further with employees decrying a perception of being over-managed and· disempowered; (2) The leader, trying to promote a large-scale organizational change program spends a disproportionate amount of time persuading his team of the logic of the change and engaging them in goal-oriented project plans, all the while ignoring their anxiety and apprehension. The team's lack of uptake is framed as "resistance" with the frustrated leader demanding that the members decide whether they are "On or off the bus? With the change or against it?" Ultimately, like 70 percent of change initiatives (Kotter, 2008) this one fails; (3) The coach, working to change specific, goal-directed behaviors that are believed important to a client's leadership role, focuses near-solely on these at the cost of a bigger conversation about whether and how these align with the client's values and leadership purpose. They don't, and the coaching engagement doesn't facilitate the hoped for outcomes.

Examples of these types will be familiar to many. In a complex world, goals can provide a comfortable antidote, making intransigent desires appear tangible and attainable. Yet an approach that simplistically over-relies on goals can perpetuate a mechanistic view of human behavior and organizational life, deny reality, and subvert our objectives. There are at least three cautions against this approach. First, goals can imply linearity and predictability, where none exists. Second, goals can narrow our focus and hinder successful change. Third, the stated goal is not always the goal. I will briefly elaborate on each of these cautions.

CAUTION ONE: GOALS CAN IMPLY LINEARITY AND PREDICTABILITY, WHERE NONE EXISTS

Changes in one variable in a system can impact on others, and many organizational outcomes therefore, can neither be linearly predicted (if predicted at all) nor specifically tied to any one individual or team. In this context, even default organizational practices like the six-monthly goal setting session and performance review are of questionable value. Leaders are increasingly lamenting that the need for organizations to be agile and the resulting frequently changing strategic priorities, can render compelling goals set in one review session near redundant in the next.

A number of the book's contributors cogently argue for an awareness of this caution. I was struck that without any design on our part as editors, a full third of the chapters we received from our contributors either mentioned or focused on complexity theory. Greif follows on to his presentation of the Rubicon model with a nod to chaos theory, encouraging us to "expect the unexpected" (Chapter 7), while Bright and Pryor (Chapter 9) show us how chaos theory can be used to understand and grasp—if not always fully predict—patterns in goal setting and striving. Bright and Pryor's description of attractors is echoed in Boyatzis and Howard's commentary on Intentional Change Theory (Chapter 10), which suggests that by activating the Positive Emotional Attractor, clients not only home-in on their purpose while standing at the "edge of chaos", they are supported in making lasting, meaningful life changes. In Chapter 8, Cavanagh walks us through his compelling vision of a new era in which "Our core challenge is to develop new paradigms that help us understand and work with the environmental, economic, and social challenges that are emerging in a hyper-connected world." His vision of coaching in this context calls us to look beyond simple cause and effect relationships, and to position ourselves and our coaching relationships within "more inclusive system boundaries" and "a broader temporal view". These contributors remind us that it is an exciting time to be a mentor or coaching professional, and our work can be part of important shifts in the culture at large.

CAUTION TWO: GOALS CAN NARROW OUR FOCUS AND HINDER SUCCESSFUL CHANGE

Second, the frequent articulation of goals as behavioral outcomes or organizational deliverables can lead to a narrow focus on these, and an ignoring of other factors that may play a comparatively greater role in successful change. Self-regulation towards effective change involves a complex interplay among the situation, beliefs, emotions, cognitions, behaviors and values (Baumeister and Heatherton, 1996; Carver, Sutton, and Scheier, 2000; Deci and Ryan, 2002; Taylor and Repetti, 1997). Regardless of the infallible logic of an organization's strategic initiative and its associated goal-oriented project plans, there are unlikely to be sustained outcomes without cognizance of the vested parties' values, motivations, anxieties, or concerns or harnessing of excitement and influence via emotion contagion (Barsade, 2002). Similarly, despite a client's goal being both important and soundly reasoned, ample evidence from the literature on change and health outcomes, demonstrates that we do not always act in concordance with our intentions and best interests (American Dietetics Association, 2002; David, 2000; Mathers, Vos, and Stevenson, 1999). As coaches, we enhance mastery in our profession by being well-versed in the self-regulation literature and in incorporating this knowledge in our coaching engagements.

A number of chapter contributors highlight the need to take a broad socio-ecological and intrapersonal perspective when considering goal setting and attainment. In recognition of support, Kathy Kram (Chapter 13) notes the importance both of individual peers and developmental networks in assisting the focal person's development. Spence and Deci (Chapter 5) in their exploration of self-determination theory suggest that all goals are not equal, and that by attending to the psychological needs of the client, the coach enables a movement towards optimal outcomes. Like other chapter authors, Greif (Chapter 7) notes the limits of traditional goal setting: even when all of the classic SMART goal criteria are met and when motivation is high, clients may still not achieve effective implementation. Both he—with the extended Rubicon model—and Boyatzis and Howard (Chapter 10) through the lens of Intentional Change Theory—describe how to better facilitate real change for the client.

CAUTION THREE: THE GOAL IS NOT ALWAYS THE GOAL

Setting a goal is relatively easy. But, setting the true goal is not as simple. As complex beings we may set goals that on deeper exploration are not what we are actually aspiring to. Earlier, my co-editor David Clutterbuck mentioned Kegan's (Chapter 11) description of the client's presenting goal as a type of Trojan Horse into the greater change project of adult development. I find this to be a rich metaphor for the work we do with our clients, and an acknowledgement of the way we must listen and seek to understand people on multiple levels. One of the lenses we can use to reach this understanding is self-determination theory (Spence and Deci, Chapter 5). I have found that in my own practice, the simple remembering of the universal needs for autonomy, competence, and relatedness is a powerful anchor. Regardless of the client's presenting issues, can we sense that one or more of these needs is yet unfulfilled? And in this regard, what support can we offer?

Conclusion

From an intellectual perspective, in editing this book, I have noted with interest the theory and research presented. I have agreed with some views, disagreed with others, and overall have been prompted to question some of the norms in my own work. From an emotional perspective, my involvement has been both exciting and heartening. It was not too long ago that goals and their associated frameworks were seen as a default and incontrovertible facilitator of effectiveness without which successful coaching could not be achieved. In contrast, the contributions presented here speak to how goals can serve, how they can hinder, and almost universally, how a more sophisticated approach to them is necessary. The willingness of the authors and you the reader to engage in this discussion, to challenge assumptions, and to drive thinking on the topic signify that the fields of coaching and mentoring are coming of age, and are in good hands. It is my hope, as well as that of my co-editors, that like us you have learned from and enjoyed the journey.

References

American Dietetics Association. (2002). Attitudes, knowledge, beliefs, behaviors: Findings of American Dietetic Association's public opinion survey Nutrition and You: Trends 2002. 1–6.

Barrick, M.R., Mount, M.K., & Strauss, J. P. (1993). Conscientiousness and performance of sales representatives: Test of the mediating effects of goal setting. *Journal of Applied Psychology, 78*(5), 715–22.

Barsade, S.G. (2002). The ripple effect: Emotional contagion and its influence on group behavior. *Administrative Science Quarterly, 47*(4), 644–75.

Baumeister, R.F. & Heatherton, T.F. (1996). Self-regulation failure: An overview. *Psychological Inquiry, 7*, 1–15.

Brown, S.D., Lent, R.W., Telander, K., & Tramayne, S. (2011). Social cognitive career theory, conscientiousness, and work performance: A meta-analytic path analysis. *Journal of Vocational Behavior, 79*(1), 81–90.

Carver C.S., Sutton S.K., & Scheier M.F. (2000). Action, emotion, and personality: Emerging conceptual integration. *Personality and Social Psychology Bulletin, 26*(6), 741–51.

David, S.A. (2000). *Independence and Well-being: A Disabled Population.* Masters Unpublished, University of Witwatersrand, South Africa.

Deci, E.L. & Ryan, R.M. (2002). *Handbook of Self-determination Research.* Rochester, NY: University of Rochester Press.

Goldsmith, W. & Clutterbuck, D. (1997). *The Winning Streak Mark II: How the World's Most Successful Companies Stay on Top Through Today's Turbulent Times.* London: Orion Business Books.

Kosko, B. (1994). *Fuzzy Thinking.* London: Flamingo.

Kotter, J.P. (2008). *A Sense of Urgency.* Boston: Harvard Business School Press.

Mathers, C., Vos, T., & Stevenson, C. (1999). Burden of Disease and Injury in Australia, The (full report). ISBN 1-74024-019-7; AIHW Cat. No. PHE-17. 11-16-1999. Canberra: Australian Institute of Health and Welfare.

Taylor S.E. & Repetti R.L. (1997). Health Psychology: What is an unhealthy environment and how does it get under the skin? *Annual Review of Psychology, 48*, 411–47.

Tubbs, M. (1986). Goal setting: A meta-analytic examination of the empirical evidence. *Journal of Applied Psychology, 71*(3), 474–83.

Index

accommodation, 166
Ach, N., 6
action planning, 61, 72–3
adaptive changes, 13, 90, 158,
    163, 167, 215, 232–3; *see also*
    technical vs. adaptive changes
adult mental development, xv, xvii,
    229–42, 262–86
age, of connectedness, 153–4,
    156, 168, 170, 172; *see also*
    Metasystematic age
agreement/certainty matrix, 140
alignment (goal), 14–16, 38, 39, 64–77,
approach goals, 24, 31–2, 40, 60, 62,
    70, 73, 75, 77, 110–18
assimilation, 166
attractors, 12, 158, 168, 178, 185–6,
    188, 190–98, 203–8, 211–25
autonomous motivation, xix, 90–108
avoidance goals, 24, 32, 36, 62, 70, 73,
    78, 110–13, 213, 328, 334
Aristotle, 1

Bandura, A., 10–12, 14, 73
basic needs theory, 95–102, 330
behavioral inhibition system, 110
basic psychological needs theory,
    88–98, 108
behavioral coaching/mentoring, 317
Berger, J., xxx, 166, 170, 172, 180
Berkman, E., xiii, xv, 109–12, 119–22,
    328, 333

bounded instability 151–2
Boyzatis, R., 333
Brennan, D., xxx
Bright, J., xiii, xiv, 185–210, 328–36
Bröms, A., 8

career, vi, iix, xiv, xvii, xxi, xxvii,
    xxxi, 16, 43, 49, 53, 86, 104, 138,
    185–210, 223, 261–73, 278–9,
    289, 292, 296, 298, 299, 302–9,
    315–18, 338
Carver & Scheier, 10, 12, 57, 59, 63, 67,
    73, 85, 112, 114, 156, 336
catastrophe theory, 24, 154
Cavanagh, M., vi, xiv, 75, 85, 86, 89,
    99, 140–41, 151–78, 329, 336
causality (causality orientations
    theory), 64–5, 70, 91, 96, 99
Center for Creative Leadership, xvii,
    xxix, 272
chance, 186, 189, 207
chaos theory, 140–41, 151, 154, 161–2
Chaos Theory of Careers, xii, xxvi,
    185–210, 332–5
CIGAR model, 155
Clarke, M., vi, xiv, 289–307
Clutterbuck, D., v, vi, xi, xii, xxvi,
    xxvii, xxix, 1, 21, 55, 135, 149,
    292, 311, 327, 331–2, 337
coach maturity, 333
complementary and competing goals,
    63

complex adaptive systems, 151, 154, 158, 159, 167–8, 332

complexity, xxvi, xxx, 7, 10, 24, 48, 52, 69, 70, 140, 141, 149, 170, 172–3, 175, 176, 178–208, 226, 236, 251, 264, 318, 319, 320, 329–35

Congleton, C., v, vi, xiv, xxvii, 1, 37, 149, 229, 261

Cognitive Evaluation Theory, 91, 94

Constructive Developmental Theory, 170, 176, 180

culture, xv, xix, 2, 25, 29, 91, 186, 198, 224, 235, 238, 250, 252, 266, 336

David, S., ii–iv, xi, xxvi, xxvii, xxix, 1, 21, 37, 149, 229, 245, 261, 327, 334

Deci, E., v, xv, 2, 28, 63, 67, 85–103, 113, 116, 337

Default Mode Network, 217

Deming, W., 8, 9

Depression Anxiety and Stress Scale, 75

developmental journey, 251, 255, 256, 259

developmental networks, vi, xxii, 88, 218, 220, 261–73, 291, 329, 336

diversity, xvii, 30, 163, 173, 176, 222, 224, 266, 271

Donde, R., vi, xv, 109, 328, 333

Downey, M., 25, 26, 39, 86

Drucker, P., 6–9, 16, 23, 42, 331

Dweck, C., 13, 61, 280–81

Eliot, T.S., 161

emergent goals (goal emergence), vi, xxv, 12, 24, 48, 50–51, 55, 154–68, 177, 178, 191, 199, 263, 263, 265, 268, 275–87, 311–24, 332, 334

Emotional Attractor (Positive and Negative), 212, 215, 216, 218, 221, 225

Error Related Negativity, 117

European Mentoring and Coaching Council (EMCC), ii, xi, xii, xxix, 58

fast shift, 187

feedback, 9, 10, 12, 14, 31, 33, 52, 56, 70, 71, 73, 74, 91, 95, 133–7, 143, 156, 164, 170, 172, 177, 178, 194–6, 199, 214–16, 283, 286, 290, 304, 316

Fishbein & Ajzen, 10, 11, 127

Franklin, B., 3–5

Functional magnetic resonance imaging, 218

Gallwey, T., 22

goal

achievement, see goal, attainment

attainment, xxix, 1, 12, 13, 30–33, 40, 41, 56, 62, 63, 68, 70–76, 87, 88, 97, 99, 120, 125, 129, 133, 134, 135, 138, 139, 143, 144, 159, 160, 171, 185, 204, 206, 213, 247, 250, 255, 256, 281–5, 289, 291, 294, 296, 303, 306, 313, 316, 319, 320, 322, 329, 336

choice, 10, 15, 30, 70, 73, 91–5, 101, 103, 161, 169, 174, 175, 190, 258

contents theory, 9, 65, 91, 97, 98

evolution, xxx, 31, 32

feasibility, 311, 319, 320

Goal-focused Coaching Skills Questionnaire, 41, 42, 45, 75, 331

hierarchy(ies), 65–7, 110–18, 253, 257, 328

intention, vvi, 6, 11, 14–16, 55, 68, 69, 71, 76, 110, 115, 117, 118, 126–45, 211, 212, 214–17, 221,

222, 225, 240, 271, 323, 333, 336, 337

maturity, 75, 93, 251, 257–8, 313, 315, 317

neglect, 51, 67, 68,

orientation, xii, xxii, 2, 3, 8, 13, 14, 39, 41, 42–7, 59, 73, 91, 95–7, 213, 220, 281, 334

progress, 7, 9, 30, 33, 72, 75, 110, 116, 117, 156, 220, 221, 224, 233, 271, 276, 281, 282–4, 286, 323, 329, 334

representation, 64, 69, 110, 115

satisfaction/dissatisfaction, 58, 68, 73, 74, 95–104, 236, 247

setting, v, xi, xxi, xxii, xxix, xxx, 1, 3, 6–16, 30, 34, 35, 37, 40, 42, 43, 45–51, 55–82, 85, 96, 103, 109–22, 125, 126, 151, 152, 154, 159, 165, 185–206, 211–25, 232, 254, 256, 257, 261, 263–7, 271–6, 281–5, 289–307, 311, 318, 328, 329, 333, 335–7

striving, 15, 16, 43, 49, 57, 60, 64, 70, 72, 73, 93, 103, 330, 336

theory, xxi, xxv, xxvi, 6, 9, 10, 12, 13, 14, 21, 25, 31, 40, 43, 56, 57, 60, 64, 65, 69, 72, 74, 225, 310

Gollwitzer, P., 14, 15, 57, 61, 73, 126–8, 133, 143–4,

Grant, A., v, xv, xxii, 22, 24, 37, 38, 56–78, 85, 86, 89, 99, 101, 102, 103, 104, 129, 155, 160, 167, 215, 328, 333

Greif, S., vi, xvi, 125–49, 328, 333, 335, 337

GROW, vi, ix, xxxi, 37, 41, 75, 104, 109, 245–59, 333

Harvard Business Review, xvii, 247, 248

hidden goals, 318

High Reliability Organizations, 24

holism, 38, 39

Howard, A., vi, xvi, 211–28, 329, 330, 333, 336, 337

Ibarra, H., xxiii, 316

identity, xvii, xxi, 33, 118, 190, 262, 278, 279, 290, 294, 299, 312, 317

immunity to change, 229, 230, 236, 239–43

implementation intention, 11, 14, 15, 69, 70, 110, 115, 117, 118, 126–45, 211, 212, 214, 215–17, 221, 225, 227, 240, 271, 323, 336, 337

INSEAD, xxix

Institute of Coaching, xi, xxvii, 245, 261

intention memory, 129, 130

Intentional Change Theory, 225

internalization, 92–5, 103

intrinsic and extrinsic motivation, xv, 2, 15, 28, 29, 33, 40, 63, 64, 91–5, 98, 99, 103, 198, 204, 214, 215, 222, 250, 316, 317, 320

intrinsic feedback, 14

Johnson, H., 8

Kauffman, C., vi, xvi, xxvii, 245, 247–8

Kegan, R., vi, xvii, xxii, xxvi, 166, 170 172, 229–42, 267, 317, 330, 333, 337

Kets de Vries, M., xxix, 43

Kline, N., xxx

Kram, K., vi, ix, xvii, xxii, xxvi, 43, 261–73, 291, 303, 305, 328, 329, 332, 336

Latham, G., 1, 2, 6, 9, 10, 12, 13, 14, 17, 23, 25, 28, 40, 43, 61, 62, 85,

125, 192, 199, 213, 214, 217, 222, 281, 283

Layered Relationship Mentoring Model, vi, 289–307

levels of consciousness, 258

Lewis. L., xxix

life goals, 90, 96–9, 193, 196, 225, 311, 315, 328

Locke, E., xxix, 1, 2, 6, 9, 10, 12, 13, 14, 17, 23, 25, 28, 40, 43, 57, 61, 85, 125, 159, 192, 199, 213

Lunsford, L., vi, xvii, 275–86, 328, 331

Management by Objectives (MBO), 6–9, 16

mastery goals, 13–16, 62, 87, 201, 214, 221, 336

Maslow, A., 10, 11

medial prefrontal cortex, 111, 115, 119

Megginson, D., v, vi, xii, xxvi, xxvii, xxix, 1, 37, 43, 50, 88, 135, 292, 327–31, 332

mentoring, v, vi, xi, xii, xvii, xviii, xxiii, xxv, xxvi, xxix, xxx, 6, 7, 12, 16, 21–35, 261–309, 328, 329, 331, 332, 334, 338
 career focused, 261–73, 287, 289, 292, 296, 298, 299, 302, 303, 305, 315
 co-mentoring, 292–307
 formal and informal, 261–73, 278, 289–307, 329
 life cycle, 267–8
 peer, 263, 269, 272, 274, 293, 294, 303
 phases, 262–8, 301
 psychosocial, 262–6, 276, 279, 292, 305
 supervisory, 266

Metasystematic age, 153, 156

metasystematic model of leadership, 168, 170, 172

mindfulness, xix, 25, 49, 70, 120, 168–71, 219, 223, 317

mindlessness, 24

mirror neuron system, 117

Neuroleadership Institute, xiii, xix

neuroscience, vi, xiii, v, xix, xxvii, 21, 109–21

non-linear(ity), xxx, 141, 142, 151, 152, 154–8, 186, 187–99, 206, 329, 333

Ordóñez, L., 2, 25, 26, 27, 28, 29, 38, 54, 55, 195–9, 264

organismic integration theory, 87, 91, 92, 94

ownership, 30, 31, 39, 93, 101, 103, 113, 115, 316, 321

Piaget, P., 166

prefrontal cortex, 111, 115, 119, 121

painful goal honesty, 318

Parasympathetic Nervous System, 218

Perceived Autonomy Support Scale, 75, 78

performance coaching, performance goals, xvi, xvii, xix, 1, 7–16, 22, 24, 26, 27, 28, 29, 40, 41, 52, 58–63, 77, 80, 86, 87, 88, 90, 97, 98, 99, 116, 117, 119, 127, 134, 135, 137, 155, 164, 166, 167, 172, 173, 188, 193, 194, 199–202, 213–15, 217, 220, 221, 222, 225, 281–5, 315, 316, 319, 320, 328, 329, 330, 334, 335

performance vs. learning/mastery goals, 13–14, 213–15

positivity/positive psychotherapy, 23, 30, 35, 40, 168, 173, 174

Powell, S., vi, xviii, 289–308

Pryor, R., vi, xviii, 141, 185–206, 328, 329, 332, 335, 336

readiness to change, 59, 70, 71

relatedness, 91, 98, 99, 101, 102, 330, 337

remedial coaching, 165, 320

Riddle, D., xxix

right ventrolateral prefrontal cortex, 199

Rock, D., vi, xix, 109–206, 328, 333

Rubicon phase model, 126–45

Ryan, R., xv, 9, 63, 64, 67, 75, 85, 87–104, 113, 116, 125, 212, 290, 316, 317

self-concordant goals, 64, 65, 102

self-determination theory, v, xv, xxxii, 56, 74, 85–104, 212, 316, 330, 333, 337

self-organization theory, *see* chaos theory

self-regulation, 12, 22, 59, 60, 67, 72, 73, 85, 86, 88, 91–4, 100, 103, 104, 106, 119, 129, 139, 336

shadowing, 133–45

slow shift, 187

SMART, xxii, 21–6, 30, 37, 49, 58, 61, 109, 111, 125, 166, 195, 200–202, 80, 283, 285, 290, 328, 330, 334, 337

solution-focus, 40, 54, 58, 102, 104, 105

Spence, G., 9, 57, 82, 85–104, 171, 330, 333, 337

sponsor expectations, 311, 318

stretch goals, 51, 56, 57

sympathetic nervous system, 6, 218, 219

Self-reflection and Insight Scale, 75

Taylor, F., 3

technical vs. adaptive changes, 232–4

transpersonal coaching, vi, 245–60, 315, 317

vision(ing), 30, 39, 72, 142, 167, 202, 204, 214–25, 246, 251, 257, 285, 322, 329, 330, 336

well-being, v, xix, 62, 63, 70, 75–8, 85–104, 120, 155, 265, 292, 317

Whitmore, J., vi, ix, xix, xxvi, 22, 23, 25, 26, 39, 40, 41, 75, 86, 101, 155, 245–60, 313, 329, 330

World Association of Business Coaches, 32

If you have found this book useful you may be interested in other titles from Gower

Making Sense of Organizational Learning
Putting Theory into Practice
Cyril Kirwan
Hardback: 978-1-4094-4186-1
Ebook: 978-1-4094-4187-8

Managing Value in Organisations
New Learning, Management, and Business Models
Donal Carroll
Hardback: 978-1-4094-2647-9
Ebook: 978-1-4094-2648-6

Co-operative Workplace Dispute Resolution
Organizational Structure, Ownership, and Ideology
Elizabeth A. Hoffmann
Hardback: 978-1-4094-2924-1
Ebook: 978-1-4094-2925-8

Managing the Psychological Contract
Using the Personal Deal to Increase
Business Performance
Michael Wellin
Hardback: 978-0-566-08726-4
Ebook: 978-0-7546-8189-2

GOWER

Human Resources or Human Capital?
Managing People as Assets
Andrew Mayo
Hardback: 978-1-4094-2285-3
Ebook: 978-1-4094-2286-0

Gower Handbook of Leadership and
Management Development
Edited by Jeff Gold, Richard Thorpe and Alan Mumford
Hardback: 978-0-566-08858-2
Ebook: 978-0-7546-9213-3

Action Learning in Practice
Edited by Mike Pedler
Hardback: 978-1-4094-1841-2
Ebook: 978-1-4094-1842-9

Visit **www.gowerpublishing.com** and

- search the entire catalogue of Gower books in print
- order titles online at 10% discount
- take advantage of special offers
- sign up for our monthly e-mail update service
- download free sample chapters from all recent titles
- download or order our catalogue